LaTeX for Linux

Springer
New York
Berlin
Heidelberg
Barcelona
Hong Kong
London
Milan
Paris
Singapore
Tokyo

Bernice Sacks Lipkin

LATEX for Linux

A Vade Mecum

Springer

GNU Emacs is copyright by the Free Software Foundation, Inc.
LaTeX is a trademark of the American Mathematical Society.
Linux is a trademark of Linus Torvalds.
METAFONT is a trademark of Addison Wesley Publishing Company.
PostScript is a trademark of Adobe Systems, Inc.
TeX is a trademark of the American Mathematical Society.
Unix is a trademark of AT&T Bell Laboratories.

Library of Congress Cataloging-in-Publication Data
Lipkin, Bernice Sacks.
   Latex for Linux : a vade mecum / Bernice Sacks Lipkin.
      p.   cm.
   Includes bibliographical references (p. 525-532) and index.
   ISBN 0-387-98708-8 (softcover : alk. paper)
     1. LaTeX (Computer file) 2. Computerized typesetting. 3. Linux. 4. Desktop
publishing. 5. Document markup languages. I. Title.
Z253.4.L38L56 1999
686.2´25445369—dc21   98-051994

Printed on acid-free paper.

Production managed by Lesley Poliner; manufacturing supervised by Joe Quatela.
Photocomposed copy prepared from L^AT_EX files supplied by the author.
Printed and bound by Hamilton Printing Co., Rensselaer, NY.
Printed in the United States of America.

9 8 7 6 5 4 3 2 (Corrected second printing, 1999)

ISBN 0-387-98708-8 Springer-Verlag New York Berlin Heidelberg   SPIN 10747476

This book is in memory of my sister Charlotte.

Contents

PART II. PREPARATORY TASKS.   37

4   CONSTRUCTING *practice.tex*, A PRACTICE FILE   39

5   SETTING EMACS KEYS FOR COMMON CONSTRUCTIONS   45

6   VIEWING AND PRINTING MARKED UP FILES   55

7   DEALING WITH ERRORS   59

PART IV. FORMATTING IN TEXT MODE.   111

11   FONTS   115

APPENDIX   505

PREFACE

With the advent of *Linux*[1] and its increasing popularity, people who have split their personalities, working a *Unix* machine during the day and a *Windows* machine at home at night, have been transforming their home computers into *Linux* boxes. Others, who run large programs on Unix with no problem, are tired of being told there is not enough memory to compile or run their programs in *DOS* and older *Windows*, especially when they have invested in extra memory, which, apparently, these operating systems ignore. And the need to revamp an entire software wardrobe in shifting from one buggy version of *Windows* to another may make Bill Gates happy, but does little for the rest of us. Linux is a particularly attractive alternative, in that it provides an integrated configuration and a wealth of interesting packages.

As it gets easier to install Linux, it becomes more popular, so there are more people out there to whom you can turn for advice. This means it gets easier and simpler to install. Witness the number of books on installing and running Linux,[2] even for people who have never used Unix. There is even a journal devoted exclusively to Linux. The *Linux Journal*[3] provides general coverage of hardware and software issues, with timely articles, some

---

[1]Linux is the Unix-type operating system, whose kernel was constructed by Linus Torvalds from scratch. It revived the camaraderie that produced the shared and integratable programs and the freely distributed source code that characterized the early Unix community. It almost immediately drew a warm response from programmers world-wide, who have since expanded the repertoire of programs that are distributed as part of Linux.

[2]See, for example, *Running Linux* by Matt Welsh and Lar Kaufman [Welsh96], *Linux in a Nutshell* by Jessica Hekman [Hekman96] and *Linux Unleashed* by Kamran Husain, Timothy Parker *et al* [Husain96].

[3]The *Linux Journal* is published by Specialized Systems Consultants, Inc. They can be reached by mail at

of them for first-time computer users. There is also the *Linux Gazette*, a member of the
Linux Documentation Project. It is published by the *Linux Journal* and is available directly
on the Net at *http://www.linuxgazette.com*. To quote from its cover page, "The Gazette
is a compilation of basic tips, tricks, suggestions, ideas and short articles about Linux
designed to make using Linux fun and easy." And there are a number of news groups devoted to Linux. These include *news://comp.os.linux.announce*, which lists upcoming meet-
ings and new products; *news://comp.os.linux.help*, which handles individual questions; and
news://comp.os.linux.questions, which supplies FAQs.

Additional support is available from the growing number of Linux Users Groups (LUG).
There's a large number of LUG's in the States[4], and, I understand, more overseas. There
are three in the DC area alone: DCLUG in DC (the group I belong to), LUGMAN in
Manassas, Virginia and UMLUG at the University of Maryland.

Folks immigrating to Linux—and you may be one of them—even if they previously have
utilized (relatively) user-friendly PC formatters, have sensibly begun to see advantages in
marking up their documents in TEX or LATEX[5], both of which have been popular with the
Unix crowd for years and both of which look to be with us into the forseeable future.
LATEX can, after all, handle text, pictures, tables and graphics, all in the same document. It
produces what is called a DVI file, *dvi* standing for device independent. *xdvi*[6] is a lovely
program that lets you screen the print version of your *.dvi* document whenever you wish.

Resources packaged with *Linux* can turn your DVI file painlessly into PostScript (PS).
This is an enormous advantage because PostScript has become the universal language for
print transactions. With it, you can, as example, send a print-ready PostScript version
directly to the publisher, as I could do with this book. The versatile and robust *dvips*
program[7] turns the DVI file into a ready-to-print PS file or prints it immediately. The large
number of options in *dvips* let you print specific pages or only the odd pages or pages in
reverse order, and so forth. You can also view the PS file in *ghostview*[8], which not only

---

P.O.Box 55549, Seattle WA 98155-0549 or on the Net at *http://www.ssc.com/lj*.

[4]There's a list of LUG's in *www.linux.org/users/groups/USA*. But you need to query by state and I simply
didn't have the *sitzfleish* to pursue it.

[5]TEX was written by Donald E. Knuth [Knuth86], a formidable computer scientist. LATEX, written by Leslie
Lamport [Lamport94a], modularized various TEX commands into a set of directives that combine TEX primitives
into 'higher level' printspeak. The current version of LATEX, the work of Frank Mittelbach *et al*, is called LATEX2ε
and LATEX3 is in development.

[6]*xdvi* was written by Eric Cooper. It was modified for X by Bob Schefler and for X11 by Mark Eichin.

[7]*dvips* was written by Tomas Rokicki. It was extended to virtual fonts by Donald Knuth.

[8]*ghostview* was written by Tim Theisan.

previews the PS document in color, but can print it in its entirety, for a range of pages or for scattered individual pages. If you don't have a PostScript printer, you can run your LaTeX-processed DVI file through *ghostscript*,[9] which has drivers for a large number of non-PostScript printers.

Moreover, you can write a file with LaTeX glosses and convert it to HTML with *LaTeX2HTML* to cast your bottle of print into the waters of the Internet, an enterprise as currently popular as transcending worlds with the aid of a ouiji board once was.

And the nicest thing is that all these goodies are free. And the updates are free.

The glow you get from making the sensible decision to shift to TeX or LaTeX may, however, quickly evaporate when you try to get through the basic guides, books that seem to have been written for those who were involved in developing the programs in the first place. I admit that all I got out of the first skim (which, as a practiced user of other markup languages, I thought would be sufficient) was that if the brace keys on my keyboard ever stuck, I was a dead duck.

So I made a copy of a paper I was working on. Then I made an outline of what I needed to know to print it out. And as I read, whenever I came across something that I needed, I added it to the appropriate section.

This book is the result. It is not meant for the mathematicians who need to know how to make LaTeX transcribe their skyscraper equations with grace and elegance. It is meant for the other 98% of us, who need to pretty up articles and theses and letters or who do what has become known as desktop publishing.

I urge you not to skip Chapter 2 on the basic instruction formats. Once you master the syntax and how to write the instruction formats, you will find that your portion of mistakes recorded in the error log is much reduced. And your hard copy will look more the way you wanted it to look.

---

[9] *ghostscript* was written by L. Peter Deutsch of Aladdin Enterprises.

The Structure Of This Book

This book is certainly not a text for setting complicated mathematical formulae in print. Nor is it a compendium of all the commands and their variants in the different packages that have been written on top of LaTeX. It is intended to teach the elements of LaTeX, each in sufficient detail, I hope, to satisfy the needs of users of markup languages who write books and articles for publication.

Part 1 presents basic LaTeX concepts—its grammatical elements, its instruction types and how to compose them—and the LaTeX document classes.

Part 2 has two objectives. First, it shows you how to assemble the resources and materials that you will need to read the rest of the book most effectively. It discusses how to set up a practice file. It shows some typical LaTeX commands and describes how to set up keystroke macros in *Emacs* to write these commands rapidly. Second, it steps through the procedures for turning a text file into a viewable or printed document. And it introduces the error log file and discusses in detail how to go about correcting mistakes you make in marking up your document. You'll be back to this chapter often.

Part 3 is a detailed presentation of LaTeX instructions—how to write them and how to write your own instructions.

The markup instructions for the three LaTeX modes—Paragraph (Text) mode, Math mode and LR (Box) mode—are the subject of Parts 4:6. Part 4 deals with Text mode commands. These chapters contain specifics for writing instructions that change fonts, manipulate space, create lists, do cross references, design figures and tables. These include variations and fairly complete examples. Occasionally, illustrations include notation and ideas that are only meagerly explained at the time. Other times, the same concept—the *hspace* and *vspace* commands, as examples—is shown in different contexts. Part 5 outlines Math mode commands. Part 6 explores Box mode commands.

Part 7 describes how to add pictures and graphics to your text document. Part 8 details the finishing touches to your document—how to add a bibliography, a table of contents, an index and a glossary. Part 9 summarizes counters, lengths and page layout as prologue to the construction of style sheets.

The Appendix demonstrates how to divide a large document into sections during composition, while retaining the ability to print it as a single composite. It also includes ways to write HTML from LaTeX files and visa versa.

Typographic Conventions In Writing Instructions

Name. The names of most freestanding objects—a file, a program, a command—are in italics.

Response/Quote. If a statement is a response or a quote, the statement is usually in bold, not quotes.

\Instruction{*Argument*}. If the format is: **Write (or Print or Use ...)** **\instruction{argument}**, the statement will be in bold. If the argument to a particular instruction is generic, it will be in italics and enclosed in triangular brackets.

`\newcommand{`<`\Alias`>`}{`<`definition`>`}.` The format of a particular command will be in typewriter; the generic arguments will be in italics and enclosed in triangular brackets.

`MarkUp.` A complete markup will be in typewriter font; i.e., the actual source text is printed verbatim.

Key. A control character or a non-text key on the keyboard is written in slant. A control character will be written as: *CTRL#*, where *#* is a letter; e.g., *CTRLd*. To write it, you push *CTRL* and *d*, simultaneously.

[NameYear] References are listed in square brackets by First author's last name, Last two digits of the year. If there's more than one paper with that reference, the final character is *a* for the first paper, *b* for the second paper, and so forth.

mini-FAQ

Q: Can this book be used with Unix?

A: Sure.

Q: With MS DOS or Windows?

A: Yes, if you must. There are versions of LaTeX for Windows.

Q: Where do I get a copy of Linux?

A. Here are some sources:

You can *ftp* them from a main repository or mirror.[10] You can for example contact **http://sunsite.unc.edu/pub/Linux** for the software and **http://sunsite.unc.edu/pub-/Linux/docs** for documentation. This is not recommended for a first-time user.

SLACKWARE. The Slackware distribution of Linux is deservedly popular. LaTeX runs immediately after installation. The installation script by Patrick J. Volkerding (who maintains Slackware) is straightforward and allows easy individual package selection. Its base directory is */usr/lib/teTeX/texmf*.

RED HAT. This may be the simplest to install and have the most commercial add-ons. It comes with a manual that has directions for unbuttoning packages. LaTeX runs immediately after installation. Its root directory is in */usr/lib/texmf/texmf*. Caldera sells a variant of Red Hat, with a different applications package.

DEBIAN. This is said to have the best and most carefully prepared set of packages. I haven't figured out how to run its distribution of LaTeX as yet.

LINUX UNIVERSE. This is a distribution recently introduced by S. Stobel, R. Maurer and S. Middendorf. It comes with an installation manual and is intended both for the beginning user and the systems administrator. It is published by Springer-Verlag.

These can all be ordered directly. The first three can be ordered from a single source such as Cheap*Bytes (at www.cheapbytes.com or by email at sales@cheapbytes.com[11]), SSC (http://www.ssc.com or by email at linux@ssc.com), Walnut Creek (1 800 786 9907 or by email at orders@cdrom.com) and InfoMagic (http://www.infomagic.com).

---

[10]Mirrors are host machines at different places around the world that maintain files that accurately reflect the information at the main repository.

[11]I have no affiliation with the company; I like their prices.

Q: Do all the sources carry the same packages?

A: All the distributions provide a recent, stable kernel (i.e., the core of the system). All must give you source code for the kernel. Each includes a standard group of Unix-style programs that run on Linux. They differ in how easy they make it to install Linux and how many extra programs they make available.

Q: Are there local users groups?

A: Pacific HiTech maintains a web page on Linux at *www.pht.com*. This next is their list of Linux users groups (LUG's) in the States as of May 12, 1997.

Group Name	Link
Salt Lake LUG	http://www.sllug.org
Linux Hawaii Users Group	http://204.208.4.1
Southern Illinois LUG	http://www.silug.org
Atlanta Linux Enthusiasts	http://www.ale.org
Chippewa Linux Users/Enthusiasts	http://sawdust.cvfn.org/clubs/clue
LUG of Manassas	http://www.tux.org/lugman
Portland LUG	http://www.northwest.com/~plug
North Colorado LUG	http://www.vis.colostate.edu/nclug
North Texas LUG	http://www.ntlug.org
Piedmont Linux LUG	http://www.netpath.net/linux
Piedmont LUG (of North Carolina)	http://www.geocities.com/SiliconValley/8823/plug.html
East Coast USA LUG Server	http://www.tux.org
Ottawa Carleton LUG	http://www.storm.ca/~linux

This is a huge underestimate. But not all LUG's have websites. As a rule of thumb, if there's a university in your area, inquire in the Computer Science department. Or try *www.linux.org/users/groups/USA* on the web.

Q: Where do I get a copy of LaTeX?

A: It comes as part of the Linux installation.

Q: How do I install LaTeX?

A: As you would any other package that comes with your Linux distribution. Actually, you install *teTeX*—TeX for Linux. The cluster of program developed around TeX includes LaTeX. *teTeX* was implemented by Thomas Esser [Esser96]; it is a remarkable job, being clean, fast, and uniform across distributions. The program comes ready to run and fonts are in formats that the program can use.

Q: Where are the LaTeX files in the Linux package?

A: Look in *~/texmf/tex/latex*[12] which contains styles and fonts. *~/texmf/doc/latex* has documentation. In fact, many of the subdirectories under ~/texmf may be useful. The TeX Directory Structure (TDS) standard developed by TUG (TeX Users Group) places specific TeX and LaTeX library files in specific directories relative to *texmf*, so you usually don't need to worry about specifying paths. You can get an overall view of the directories and what they are about from *~/texmf/doc/help/tds.dvi* [Berry95b]. See also *~/texmf/doc/helpindex.dvi* [Anon], which lists the documentation and help files throughout the *texmf* subdirectories.

Q: Can I contact TUG?

A: Yes, indeed. As part of your membership, you receive *TUGboat*, which discusses new packages and design techniques. You are welcome to contribute financially or computationally to the upcoming LaTeX3. They can be reached at:

TeX Users Group
PO Box 2311
Portland, OR 97208-2311

Tel: 1 503 223 9994
Fax: 1 503 223 3960
website: http://www.tug.org

administrative email: office@tug.org
technical support email: support@tug.org
website email: webmaster@tug.org

Q: Is LaTeX stable?

A: Yes, very. But as with any program that has a group of people involved in increasing its versatility, it is constantly being upgraded. Your LaTeX program will come with news about

---

[12]LaTeX directories are standardized in the major distributions in that *texmf* is the root directory and the subdirectories are pretty much the same. But *texmf* may be placed in whatever directory path is convenient for the user or facility.

the latest additions, enhancements and fixes. You will find it and the previous releases in files called *ltnews*.tex*, where the asterisk is some number from *01* on. A new release comes out every six months.

Q: Do I have to make modifications to run and customize LaTeX?

A: *texconfig* in *˜/texmf/dvips/config* is a customizer in that it finds out about your editor and printer, and configures *xdvi* and *dvips*, so printing LaTeX-processed files is straightforward. */var/texfonts/pk* will store print fonts for printing your document in PostScript on the Lexmark family of laser printers, the Hewlett Packard LaserJet 4 and on non-PostScript printers using *ghostscript*. The program will select the appropriate set depending on how you answer *texconfig*'s queries.

Q: How do I find out about additional packages and tools that extend LaTeX?

A: The file *˜/texmf/doc/help/Catalogue/catalogue.dvi* is maintained by Graham J. Williams. It can be read in place using *xdvi*. Or it can be changed to PostScript for printing by a PostScript printer by typing: **dvips catalogue.dvi**. *catalogue* lists the various packages and tools available for LaTeX through CTAN.[13] An index is available on the Net; see *http://www.tex.ac.uk/tex-archive/help/Catalogue/ctindex.html*.

http://tug2.cs.umb.edu/ctan is a CTAN site at the University of Massachusetts. Ftp from *ftp://ftp.shsu.edu* in the States. *ftp://ftp.tex.ac.uk* is in England; *ftp://ftp.dante.de* is in Germany.

The file called *˜/texmf/doc/help/unixtex.ftp* lists the addresses from which to download LaTeX material. It also describes some available device drivers. It also describes what needs to be compiled for different machines. Similarly, the file called *˜/texmf/doc/help/ctan-/CTAN.sites* lists CTAN sites.

Q: Is there a website for information on LaTeX?

A: A complete catalogue of terms and definitions and guides and news and programs and ... and ... and ... can be found at *http://www.tug.org* or *ftp://ftp.tug.org/tex*. They also list accessible mirrors.

---

[13]CTAN is an acronym for *Comprehensive TeX Archive Network*. It is a group of dedicated people who maintain the ever-growing body of material that constitutes TeX and its satellites.

CTAN sites include:

cis.utovrm.it (Italia)	/TeX
ctan.unsw.edu.au (NSW, Australia)	/tex-archive
dongpo.math.ncu.edu.tw (Taiwan)	/tex-archive
ftp.belnet.be (Belgium)	/packages/TeX
ftp.center.osaka-u.ac.jp (Japan)	/CTAN
ftp.ccu.edu.tw (Taiwan)	/pub/tex
ftp.cdrom.com (West coast, USA)	/pub/tex/ctan
ftp.comp.hkbu.edu.hk (Hong Kong)	/pub/TeX/CTAN
ftp.cs.rmit.edu.au (Australia)	/tex-archive
ftp.cs.ruu.nl (The Netherlands)	/pub/tex-archive
ftp.cstug.cz (The Czech Republic)	/pub/tex/CTAN
ftp.duke.edu (North Carolina, USA)	/tex-archive
ftp.ee.up.ac.za (South Africa)	/tex-archive
ftp.funet.fi (Finland)	/pub/TeX/CTAN
ftp.gwdg.de (Deutschland)	/pub/dante
ftp.jussieu.fr (France)	/pub4/TeX/CTAN
ftp.kreonet.re.kr (Korea)	/pub/CTAN
ftp.loria.fr (France)	/pub/unix/tex/ctan
ftp.mpi-sb.mpg.de (Deutschland)	/pub/tex/mirror/ftp.dante.de
ftp.nada.kth.se (Sweden)	/pub/tex/ctan-mirror
ftp.oleane.net (France)	/pub/mirrors/CTAN
ftp.rediris.es (España)	/mirror/tex-archive
ftp.rge.com (New York, USA)	/pub/tex
ftp.riken.go.jp (Japan)	/pub/tex-archive
ftp.tu-chemnitz.de (Deutschland)	/pub/tex
ftp.u-aizu.ac.jp (Japan)	/pub/tex/CTAN
ftp.uni-augsburg.de (Deutschland)	/tex-archive
ftp.uni-bielefeld.de (Deutschland)	/pub/tex
ftp.unina.it (Italia)	/pub/TeX
ftp.uni-stuttgart.de (Deutschland)	/tex-archive (/pub/tex)
ftp.univie.ac.at (Österreich)	/packages/tex
ftpserver.nus.sg (Singapore)	/pub/zi/TeX
ftp.ut.ee (Estonia)	/tex-archive
joshua.smcvt.edu (Vermont, USA)	/pub/tex
sunsite.auc.dk (Denmark)	/pub/tex/ctan
src.doc.ic.ac.uk (England)	/packages/tex/uk-tex
sunsite.cnlab-switch.ch (Switzerland)	/mirror/tex
sunsite.icm.edu.pl (Poland)	/pub/CTAN
sunsite.queensu.ca (Canada)	/pub/tex-archive
sunsite.unc.edu (North Carolina, USA)	/pub/packages/TeX
wuarchive.wustl.edu (Missouri, USA)	/packages/TeX

Q: Is there a comprehensive FAQ for TEX and LATEX?

A: The file called *~/texmf/doc/help/faq/Tex-FAQ* is comprehensive. The United Kingdom TUG FAQ is at http://www.cogs.susx.ac.uk/cgi-bin. There is also a usenet group, *comp.-tex.text*, where you can get information about specific problems. Or join a *Linux Users Group* in your area. If my experience is typical, members tend to be knowledgeable and helpful.

Acknowledgments

I would like to express my appreciation to Dr. Przemek Klosowski, president of the DC Linux Users Group, for reviewing some of the material on Linux; to Dr. Rosemary Morris for vetting an early version; to Samuel Englander for his help in checking the index; and, most particularly, to Professor Alan Hoenig of the City University of New York for sharing his extensive knowledge of typesetting and fonts, as well as for critically reading portions of the book. Dr. William Sanders, Senior Editor of Computer Science at Springer-Verlag, provided the verbal encouragement and enthusiasm that every author dreams of. I thank the production staff at Springer, especially Lesley Poliner, for a careful review of the manuscript. Most of all, I thank my husband for his unflagging support, both moral and technical. He was kind enough to engage with good humor in what must have seemed interminable and single-minded conversations on formatting and typesetting. I want him to know I appreciate the restraint it took not to upgrade the hardware and add new software to my Linux machine every other month, his usual practice. In consequence, I had the comfort of working on a familiar system as I explored the subtleties of LATEX.

Bernice Sacks Lipkin
Bethesda, Maryland
bslipkin@erols.com
September, 1998

Part I.

READING LaTeX.

Concepts, Grammar and Basic Document Formats

There is always the problem in structuring a book such as this one: do you explain the pieces and then put them together or show the big picture and fill in the details? This book does some of both, because it is both tutorial and crib. In dealing with one topic, quite often smatterings from other commands and concepts are introduced. You should know that figures are formatted as environments and how to number them long before figures and tables are systematically discussed.

In Part 1, where you are now, you will become familiar with instruction formats, some LaTeX conventions, some basic and usable LaTeX document styles and some basic concepts. Nuances are lacking but the material should be sufficient to give you a general idea of LaTeX's ground rules.

If you are familiar with formatting languages in general, move right along to Chapter 2.

2

Chapter 1

WHAT A LaTeX COMMAND DOES

All formatting languages provide you with the means to display and/or print a text file that you have written under the aegis of a word processor such as *WordPerfect* or a text editor such as *Emacs*. All formatting languages more or less provide you with a repertoire of commands that clothe the text in various fonts, differentiate one piece of text from an adjoining piece of text, and locate a unit of text where you want to see it on the page.

All formatting languages have the common problem of how to distinguish a typesetting activity from document text. Solutions vary. Early formatters mostly relied on a simple signal. This is a set of instructions from *RUNOFF*, a formatter in use in the early 1970's on the Digital Equipment Corporation's DEC10 computer:

```
.page
.nonumber
.spacing 1
.tab stops 13, 16, 24
.paper size 62,70
.f.j.lm 5
.ls
.le;BADGER.DOC (On Creating Text Templates).
.le;BIBLIO.DOC (On Substituting Citation Numbers in a Mss).
.le;OFFICE.DOC (Office procedures: budgets, scores, labels, etc).
.els
```

A period as the first character in the line meant that what followed was a command, chosen from the pool of commands defined in the language. Multiple commands on the same line—such as the `.f.j.lm 5` for *fill, justify* and *left margin 5 characters* above—were allowed. This is still the method used in formatters such as *groff*[1] for many basic commands. TEX and LATEX provide you with a very rich set of formatting commands as well as giving you the Olympian ability to create new commands, but, in a limited sense, they can be described as having substituted the backslash for the period and allowed commands to appear anywhere in the text, not just on a separate line.

In some formatters, the program reserves specific keys on the keyboard, some of them alphanumeric or punctuation characters, some of them metakeys such as *ALT* or the direction keys. By combining keys, you can implement a rich set of commands. And since the promotion of the use of icons and menus, choosing commands from listed items in a set of menus is popular. Most formatters use a combination of menu selection and reserved keys. TEX and LATEX rely on a signal character, the backslash, and a rich set of instructions that can be further elaborated as you write your document. There is no reason, however, that some of LATEX could not be *menuized*.

Markup languages differ radically in how many of the typesetting possibilities that are routine in 'real' printing they make available—from controlling the spacing of individual letters in different contexts to setting complex mathematical equations to adding graphics and pictures.

Word processors such as *Word* or *WordPerfect* have markup features that go well beyond what the typewriter was able to do; and they continue to expand with each upgrade. Some variations in font and size are easy to accomplish. Boxes and table constructions can be done. Headers and footers can be constructed. Numbering sections and other partitions are exercises in masochism.

---

[1] *groff* is popular on Linux systems mainly to prettify the printing of plain ASCII text. It is the GNU typesetting language that serves as a simulation of the Unix *troff* formatting program.

On a more general level, GNU encompasses not only the Emacs text editor but the C and C++ compiler and debugger as well as multiple system and applications enhancements and utilities. It was developed by Richard Stallman and his colleagues at the Free Software Foundation, 59 Temple Place Suite 330, Boston, MA 02111-1307, USA. By advocacy and by example, the Foundation has impressively argued the case for free software, where you are paid for your services in installing or enhancing existing software but you do not withhold source code from the programming community by licencing procedures.

Linux has followed the same general philosophy; i.e., its entire operating system code is included with the Linux distribution. A large number of TEX programs that run under Linux can be siphoned freely from CTAN sites.

In sophisticated markup languages such as *Ventura* or *PageMaker*, you can deal with the global features of a document; for example, with a few instructions, you can block out the appearance of all the right-side pages and left-side pages. By picking and choosing items from a set of menus, each dealing with a different print feature, you can assign values to a set of parameters—font shape, font style, font size, space between rows of text, box dimensions, and so forth—and give the lot a tag name. Whenever you tag a paragraph (in Ventura, you write @*<tagname>* = at the beginning of the paragraph), the font and space and line features you assigned that name hold for the paragraph, except for whatever local variations you introduce to emphasize a couple of the words here or there. You also select what is called *body text*, the default print features of the paragraph if no tag is prepended. The set of tags that satisfy the demands for printing a particular document or a set of documents of the same type is called a *style sheet*.

In addition to providing character, font, line, paragraph and page control, TeX provides amazing control over print features such as accented letters, kerning (modifying the ordinary spacing between letter pairs for esthetic or contextual reasons) and ligatures (creating one character from adjoining letters; e.g., Æ instead of *AE*) that are considerably beyond the skills of the non-professional. And it probably has no equal in composing and type-setting mathematical equations. It has a very large group of instructions to control print activities, each of which has a specific name and most of which can be given values and later reset with other values.

Moreover, you can, by trial and error, develop a modular instruction by giving a particular sequence of TeX commands a specific and unique name. You can then reuse this sequence at any time simply by calling the name, somewhat as you would use a tag in Ventura, but much more powerful. In TeX you probably could compose instructions to describe all the print, textual and mathematical features you would ever need; but startup time is long enough to make LaTeX an attractive alternative.

LaTeX has prepackaged many of the typesetting activities you might want for different sorts of documents. It has incorporated different sequences of TeX typesetting commands, each callable by a different LaTeX command name. Some of these do much the same as a tag. Others design the layout of a page. Other constellations of TeX primitives[2] compose such essential entities as lists, equations, figures and tables.

---

[2]By *primitive*, we mean a built-in basic command.

LATEX instructions differ from Ventura tags in that the scope of even a non-layout instruction is not necessarily restricted to a paragraph. The scope of an individual instruction may be set by the extent of the environmental directive in which it resides or by the brace-bracketed argument associated with the command.[3]

---

[3]Hang on. Help is coming.

Chapter 2

CONCEPTS: HOW LATEX OPERATES ON TEXT

The basic structure of a manuscript that you markup in LATEX is simple. After suitable commands in the *preamble*, you write the entire document—text and typesetting instructions—between two statements:

```
\begin{document} \end{document}
```

We will explore the niceties of how to set up the document file below. But first let us look at the syntax of the basic instructions that you will use to ready your manuscript for printing.

The LATEX markup language is designed to be a major step in transforming a text file that may include pictures and graphics into a print-ready publishable document. As earnest of its intense concern with the nuances of font and layout and line, it has three distinct modes of operation for dealing with text:

1. **paragraph mode.** This handles the bulk of the work, processing words, sentences, paragraphs, and pages. This mode will be called **text mode** in this book because instructions are not necessarily restricted to the paragraph. Most of your markups will be in text mode.

2. **math mode.** Math mode does the classy typesetting of often dizzifying equations. It has its own fonts, spacings and layout rules.

3. **left-to-right (LR) mode.** LR mode acts as a container where the contents are treated as a unit that can not be subdivided. The text string in a single-line box is not automatically cut into lines, no matter how long it is. The primitive for this mode is the *mbox* command; and there is a large set of commands that govern the creation and location of different sizes and types of boxes. Imported pictures and graphics are introduced into a document as modified boxes. This mode will be called **box mode** in this book.

Modes are entered when the appropriate commands are given, with text mode being the default. Modes can be nested, one within the other.

In addition to text, LATEX can handle pictures, tables, color and graphics.

2.1 Grammatical Elements

These are the control elements of LATEX's grammatical constructs for processing text:

The Backslash. (\\) Except for the single character commands, the backslash is the start of a command, declaration or environment.

Left and Right Braces. ('{' and '}') An unlabeled left and right brace pair is used to delimit a self-contained unit. The brace pair can contain declarations, commands, and ordinary text. The brace-bracketed unit is usually short in length and is usually used as the *argument* in a *command* format.

The Begin-End Pair. (\\begin{*<name>*} and \\end{*<name>*}) declare that the piece of the document that they enclose is a self-contained unit, one that can contain declarations, commands and ordinary text. The construction is called an environment.

These are the types of instructions:

Single Characters. The stand-alone single character instructions to the program are all punctuation marks. They do NOT begin with the backslash. As an example, & marks the end of a column in a tabular environment. A tilde (˜) between two characters creates an unbreakable space in the printout.

Single Words. A command or a declaration is a single word composed of alphabetical characters. These instructions are prepended by a backslash. An environment instruction is a single word that has metamorphosed into being the name of a *begin-end* pair, where both *begin* and *end* are prepended by backslashes. LATEX instructions let you manipulate the various characteristics of font and layout and line that determine the appearance of the printed document. The three types of instruction formats—*commands*, *declarations* and *environments*—are discussed below.

This is how instructions are created:

Some instructions are **built-in**, developed as part of the LATEX program and immediately available when the program is called.

Some are **add-ons**, written as part of a group of related commands that comprise a package. The package as a whole is called into play by means of a \usepackage{...} command. These are written, as is LATEX, by manipulating TEX primitives.

Some will be **written by you**, by modifying available LATEX commands.

Some are **original TEX commands**, compatible with the current version of LATEX.

2.2 Instructions To LATEX

Except for the reserved punctuation symbols, any and all defined instructions begin with backslashes.

> **If an instruction isn't defined in LATEX or based on a TEX-defined command, it won't be processed.**

The differentiation made in the next paragraphs between the command and declaration formats is unofficial in that I haven't been able to find a formal separation of command types in TEX or LATEX. The intent is: (1) to familiarize you with instruction formats and (2) to emphasize the extent to which a particular instruction format can influence text.

2.2.1   Commands

The classic **command** is directly bound to a particular strip of variable text—specifically, it is the text, segregated by left and right braces, that immediately follows the command word. The command starts immediately to operate on the text to change its appearance or location. The impact of a command is restricted to the text strip it controls. Typically, the argument text is short. At most, it's a paragraph.

This is a typical command; it instructs the program to typeset a piece of text in slant.

The MarkUp: \textsl{This will be printed in slanted font.}

The PrintOut: This will be printed in slanted font.

Command. The command is the word from the backslash to the left brace; i.e., \textsl in our example.

Brace Pair. The left and right braces ('{' and '}') contain the argument of the command. The left brace signals that an argument follows; the right brace signals that the argument is complete.

Argument. The material inside the braces is called the **argument** of the command. The argument is likely to contain ordinary text. It can also contain other commands. In fact, commands can be issued within command arguments within command arguments, to any depth.

> **A command operates on the text in its argument.**
>
> **A command can be countermanded temporarily or permanently by another instruction within the argument.**

So when you see LATEX material in this format: **\command**{<*text*>},
you would read it as: Do **this command** on the text within the braces.

2.2.2 Declarations

As a first approximation, a **declaration** is a stand-alone instruction: a backslash attached to a single word, with no attached argument; e.g., the *\bfseries* declaration will typeset text in bold. A declaration can change some print feature downstream—the font is declared to be bold or the font is declared to be default size. A *\nopagebreak* prevents the program from starting a new page where the command is written. If the declaration is meaningful to document text written after the declaration statement but within the territory in which the declaration lives, the appearance of the text or its location will change in accordance with the instruction implicit in the declaration.

If the declaration is inside a matched pair of braces, the limit of its influence is the right-side brace that matches the paired left-side brace. So a declaration residing in a command argument can influence text starting at the declaration and up to the right-side brace of the argument. Thus for example, \textup{Ordinary text. \bfseries Bold text.} would be printed as: Ordinary text. **Bold text.**

If the declaration is bracketed by paired *\begin \end* statements, the right-side limit of the declaration is the *\end* of the matched pair. Typically, a declaration within a matched *\begin \end* pair impacts a larger area of the document than a declaration confined to the argument of a command.

> **A declaration operates on text to the end of the territory in which it resides, unless another instruction within the same territory and addressing the same feature countermands its effect.**

In the next markup, the *\slshape* instruction is a declaration within a *\begin \end* pair. It tells the program to slant the text that follows. It operates on all the text that follows, until it reaches the right-side limit of its territory; i.e., it is in force until it reaches the *\end{document}* barrier. A single **\begin{document} \end{document}** brackets your entire manuscript. So if you write the slant declaration just after the *\begin{document}* statement, your entire document—no matter how large it is—will print in slant, unless, of course, you later invoke another font shape instruction.

The MarkUp:

```
\begin{document}
\slshape
\LaTeX\ ignores a    run of spaces in
ordinary text. Even a great     many
spaces between two words are printed
as a single               space.

A blank line signals the beginning
of a new paragraph. A dozen blank lines
signal the beginning of a new paragraph.
\end{document}
```

The PrintOut:

LATEX ignores a run of spaces in ordinary text. Even a great many spaces between two words are printed as a single space.

A blank line signals the beginning of a new paragraph. A dozen blank lines signal the beginning of a new paragraph.

2.2.3   Environments

In the markup in Subsection 2.2.2, notice the pair:

\begin{document}
....
\end{document}

A piece of text delimited by a named *\begin–\end* pair is called an **environment**. Declarations written inside the *begin–end* pair affect all the text within that environment beginning from where the declaration is made to the *\end{...}* statement of the environment.

In Chapter 1, the RUNOFF commands were written under the verbatim environment, which typesets the text exactly as you write it; i.e.:

The MarkUp:

```
\begin{verbatim}
.page
.nonumber
.spacing 1
.tab stops 13, 16, 24
......
\end{verbatim}
```

The Printout:

```
.page
.nonumber
.spacing 1
.tab stops 13, 16, 24
......
```

Begin End Pair. These are prepended by backslashes. An area of the document enclosed by **begin** and **end** becomes a self-limited LATEX grammatical unit. Like the right and left brace pair in a command statement, the *\begin ... \end* statements draw invisible boundary lines. The \begin \end delimiters usually act on a larger amount of text than do braces in a command format.

Brace Pair. These follow immediately after \begin and after \end. They enclose the name of the environment.

Environment Name. Each environment has a name enclosed in braces. The name is specific and unique, just as each command is specific and unique. Notice that the name does NOT have a prepended backslash.

The \begin{document} and \end{document} environment is a mandatory environment in each document. It tells the program where your document begins and ends.

Commands can be written within environments. A command can be written within a command within a command.... to any depth within an environment.

Declarations can be written within environments. A declaration can be written within a command.... to any depth within an environment.

You can have environments within environments within environments, just as you have cities within counties within a state. It is the method of choice for isolating a segment of the document that is more than a few lines long.

> **The environment operates on the text within its \begin and \end pair.**
>
> **An environment can be countermanded temporarily or permanently by another instruction within the environment.**

All of these formats instruct the program to create page and paragraph templates, cloth the text in particular font features or relocate the text to particular places on the output page. At their foundation are 'primitives', i.e., words reserved by TEX or LATEX for performing certain actions. You can construct and name elaborate markup activities based on these primitives.

2.3   Basic Principles In Reading And Writing LATEX Commands

There are some important principles involved in using and constructing instructions:

- Except for the reserved single characters, instruction always begins with a backslash. An instruction ends in specific punctuation: a single-character instruction or an End-Of-Line or a space or the backslash that begins another command. In writing an instruction, you can write the start of an instruction smack up against the previous text, but you must leave a space—or some other obvious separator—after the instruction. The program will pull the right-side text in. Thus, if \LT and \RT are defined as < and >, respectively, writing \LT Smith\RT will print as <Smith>.

- In LATEX, the difference in usage between a declaration and a command is often consequential: a global declaration may influence the entire document. On the other hand, the same manipulation of the visual appearance of the text can often be stated either as a declaration or as a command.

- You must use the **\begin**{<*name*>} **\end**{<*name*>} format when you create a new environment. You must use the **\command** format for instructions that you create or for specialized LATEX constructions such as **\label**{**...**} or **\ref**{**...**} or **\framebox**{**...**}. In many cases, particularly in instructions that deal with fonts, format is a matter of preference.

- Even when the different instruction formats achieve the same result, the names of the declaration and the command are different.[1]

  The command format for slant font is: \textsl{...}.
  The declaration format for slant font is: \slshape.
  The environment format for slant font is: \begin{slshape}...\end{slshape}

- A unit is formed wherever a pair of LATEX boundary markers is written within the text. A unit is a section of the document that is bounded by a pair of left-right braces or by a pair of begin-end statements. Except for the document class assertion (\documentclass{<*class*>}) and some preamble instructions, any and all

---

[1]In previous versions of LATEX, you could use two letter font commands/declarations. Do NOT do this. Use the right names; these can be found in Chapter 11.

instructions are always part of at least one unit, and, in practice, an instruction is usually part of many units, one within the other.

- No matter what the format—whether the instruction is a declaration, a command or an environment—the instruction can only affect document text that is within its own territorial boundaries.

2.4   The Scope Of An Instruction

If you are familiar with programming languages such as Lisp or C or Pascal, you can skip this section.

LaTeX allows nesting instructions within instructions to great depth. So a major skill in controlling the appearance of text under the influence of multiple commands is the ability to pair up brace partners, given a slew of braces. One way of visualizing which braces belong with which is to imagine an onion sliced in half longitudinally. Now match up the onion circlets, the innermost pair first, then the next outside one, out finally to the outermost circlet. In the next set of illustrations, there are three brace pairs and unmarked text is shown as dots. Text within the scope of a specified command is shown as x's.

{......{......{......}......}......}
3......2......1......1......2......3

The scope of an instruction refers to the piece of the document in which the instruction can have influence. The instruction has the potential to change the appearance and location of the text within that part of the document in the printout.

The scope of an instruction is contained within the territory in which the instruction resides.

The scope of a command is always from the left-side brace of its argument until the right-side brace of its argument. It ignores the right-side braces of other commands that lie

between it and the end of its argument. In this example, we use **\textsl**, the command
for slanting text. The scope of the command is over the brace 1 pair.

{......{......\textsl{xxxxxx}......}......}

In this next example, *\textsl* extends over brace pair 2. So it also extends over the
innermost brace pair, brace pair 1.

{......\textsl{xxxxxx{xxxxxx}xxxxxx}......}

The scope of a declaration is the area of the document from the assertion of the declaration up to the right-side edge of the unit within which the declaration resides. It
ignores the right-side braces of commands that lie between it and the end of its territory. Declarations reside in command arguments or within environments. In this
example, we use **\slshape**, the declaration for slanting text. The declaration has
scope beginning from where it is written inside brace pair 1 until the right brace of
brace pair 1.

{......{......{....\slshape xxxxx}......}......}

In this next example, beginning from where it is written, the scope of *\slshape* extends to the end of brace pair 2. So it also extends over the entire innermost brace
pair, brace pair 1.

{......{....\slshape xxxxxx{xxxxxx}xxxxxx}......}

The scope of an environment terminates at the closure of its own border; i.e., at its **\end{...}**
statement. It is not affected by end statements or braces of small units that reside in
its territory. Here it is written within brace pair 2, so it also can influence the text
within brace pair 1 territory.

{......{...\begin{slshape}xxx{xxxxxx}xxx\end{slshape}...}......}

The direction of influence is always downward, beginning from where the instruction is written.

Contradictory Instructions. If a strip of text is within the territories of several contradictory commands/declarations, the instruction unit prior to and closest to the text is in control.

> **The scope of an instruction is the most important element in determining what text can be affected by that instruction.**

2.5 LATEX Conventions

These are some conventions you should know when reading or writing in LATEX. They are explained in greater detail starting in Part 3.

- As does any formatter, LATEX reserves characters. Some of them, such as the brace pair and the hashmark, are taken as literals only if they are prepended by the backslash.

- Any text on a line written after a % will not be typeset. To force the program to read the percent sign as a literal, prepend a \.

  The MarkUp: `Use the percent sign (\%). %Ignore rest of the line.`
  The PrintOut: Use the percent sign (%).

- The space taken to write a LATEX instruction in your source code does not *necessarily* use any space in the printed document. Instructions are themselves invisible. Thus, `It has so\textit{me.}` prints as: It has so*me.*

  Alternatively, the typesetting activity induced by a simple command may take a great deal of space. For example, writing **\vspace{4in}** will leave a 4-inch vertical gap in the text.

- An instruction may be very long, if it has multiple components, with optional parameters and multiple mandatory parameters. This, for example, is the way we wrote the lined box that summarized instruction scope in Section 2.2. The instruction creates a new environment called EMPH, which, like Russian dolls, encloses another environment that encloses an innermost environment.[2]

```
\newcommand{\SEP}[1]{\setlength{\fboxsep}{#1pt}}

\newsavebox{\EMPHbox}
\newenvironment{EMPH}{\hspace*{.5in}%
\begin{lrbox}{\EMPHbox}%
\begin{minipage}[t]{4in}\bfseries\large\sffamily}%
{\end{minipage}%
\end{lrbox}\vspace{6pt}\SEP{6}%
\fbox{\usebox{\EMPHbox}}\vspace{6pt}\SEP{3}}

\begin{EMPH}
If an instruction isn't defined in \LaTeX\
or based on a \TeX -defined command, it won't be processed.
\end{EMPH}
```

- LATEX ignores a run of spaces in ordinary text. Even a great many spaces between two words are typeset as a single space—or as two spaces, if the first word ends a sentence.

- A blank line signals the beginning of a new paragraph. A dozen blank lines signal the beginning of a new paragraph. You can't make the program output blank lines by leaving lines blank.

- A \\ forces a line break. Otherwise, LATEX brings in the text in a paragraph as a continuous string, cutting it according to the current line length rule. It ignores the Carriage Returns-Line Feeds imposed by your text processor or editor. If it's a good place to start a new page, it will.

- The **\pagebreak** command forces the program to start a new page. Conversely a **\nopagebreak** will keep a page from ending *unless* some other command has issued a page break order.

---

[2]As shown, if you write an instruction with many components over two lines, add a % at the end of a component to prevent a gap between instruction components. Gaps may cause LATEX errors.

- The **\enlargethispage**{<*amount*>} command forces the program to add the amount of space requested. As an example, write **\enlargethispage**{**12pt**} to add a line to the current page to prevent the last line of a paragraph from appearing on the next page by itself.

- These are some of the idioms:

  - A backslash followed by a space forces a space in the printout; e.g., {\large I want some textit{exxxtra}\ \ \ space here.} prints as: I want some *exxxtra* space here.
  - The left-side single quote mark is octal 140 (`), the mark usually found under the tilde (˜) on the keyboard. Double it to produce a left-side double quote mark. The right-side single quote mark is the ordinary single quote on the keyboard. Its ASCII code is octal 47 ('). Double it to produce a right-side double quote mark.
  - A backslash followed by a hyphen leaves it up to the program to hyphenate or not to hyphenate; e.g., This is a made\-up\-word.
  - If there's a tilde between two words, they are printed as a single word with an included space; e.g., Don't˜break˜this˜phrase produces: Don't break this phrase. If one or more of the words can be hyphenated, then the line will break one of the words; e.g., Don't˜separate˜this˜phrase produces: Don't separate this phrase.

Chapter 3

DOCUMENT CLASSES

3.1 LaTeX's Style Of Styling Styles

LaTeX went a step beyond packaging print objects. In developing what are usually thought of as style sheets, it made some major decisions for you.

In general, LaTeX, or at least TeX, is the most extensible of formatters. It is attentive to details and it can handle an extraordinary number of print features. Consequently, you can develop very precise and wide-ranging typesetting activities based on them. But on the face of it, the commands you can *easily* manipulate seem limited. In a formatter like *Ventura*, for example, you have a menu list of all the available sizes, from 6 to 30 something points from which to pick a size font. If you want occasionally to use a font that is very large, you pick another size out of the same pool. Your choice. Your guess. Maybe the results are ugly, maybe not. LaTeX, on the other hand, coordinates particular features beautifully, but it is hard to break out of the mold.

This lack of immediate flexibility is characteristic of many of the LaTeX commands. The default[1] font for slides is, as you would expect, larger than the font normally used for books. But you can not pluck the large sans serif font from the slide and use it in a report. You can of course duplicate the font with other, more general, instructions, but they would have to be other instructions. You can not *easily* invent your own document layout style, into

---

[1]If you don't specify a value, the program does.

which you write your own tags, based on the commands made immediately available by
LaTeX.[2]

Rather than facilitating selection from the full range of values for the various commands
to compose different style sheets, LaTeX canonized particular document styles which, in
LaTeX2ε (the current version), are called document classes: slide, letter, article, report and
book. It customized some commands useful in **letters**, but these are not necessarily inter-
changeable among classes. It tailored other commands specifically for **slides**, others for
letters, others just for **books**.

This is not as limited as it sounds. Fortunately, LaTeX has a very large number of commands
that can be used in various intersections of the document classes. Moreover, most classes
have a number of specific options. You can declare, for example, that an article or report is
to be written in size 11 or 12 font as the basic font instead of the default font, which is size
10.

If you do so, however, you run into another peculiarity of LaTeX. It makes other major
decisions for you. In LaTeX, the program scales size of such font commands as **tiny** or
large to the base size chosen; so **huge** in size 10 is a different size than **huge** in size 12. In
other words, rather than having you chose an absolute value out of a large range of values
for each parameter, it selects a cohesive set of related parameters for the particular value
you select.[3]

The good news is that for some classes—letters, slides, and some articles—you can rely
almost entirely on the default features these specialized commands produce. Even in more
complicated documents, such as *book*, you can certainly start with the built-in defaults for
page size, font style and size, title and section styles. So you can focus on different ways
to display the different parts of the document. You can decide on typographic conventions:
how you wish to convey uniformly over the document such text idioms as: *FileName* or
[RETURN KEY] or ATTENTION: THIS REQUIRES ... And you can develop frames
and boxes and figure styles that suit your subject matter. Later, when you have a better idea
of the gestalt of your book or monograph or article(s), you can adjust page and line length
precisely and take care of widows and orphans.[4]

---

[2]Page manipulation instructions and ways to develop your own style sheets are discussed in Part 9.

[3]Note that we are talking about the simple-to-use commands. See Section 11.5.3 for how to designate size
numerically.

[4]A **widow** is the final line of a paragraph that is written by itself at the top of a page; the rest of the paragraph
is on the preceding page. An **orphan** is the first line of a paragraph that is written by itself at the bottom of a page;

3.2   Format Of A Very Simple LATEX File

Figure 3.1 shows the contents of a file called *minskel.tex*. It is the minimum frame within which you can write a document in LATEX, in this case, an article.

We will use it or one of its more elaborate cousins as our example document class for much of this book.

\documentclass{*article*}

\begin{*document*}

Type your stuff here.

\end{*document*}

Figure 3.1: minskel.tex. Absolute minimum formatting in LATEX.

The area between **\documentclass**{*<ClassType>*} and **\begin**{**document**} is called the **preamble**. Global variables that affect the whole document are placed in the preamble. You write the entire document inside the *document* environment.

You start typing the document with interspersed LATEX instructions on the line after the **\begin**{**document**} statement. The **\end**{**document**} statement ends your document.

> **You can have only one document class per document.**
>
> **Do NOT insert one document class within another.**

3.3   LATEX-defined Classes

The LATEX classes are slides, letters, reports, articles and books. LATEX has developed different print formats based on the writing and printing conventions of the identifiable parts of these different document styles. Each identifiable division and structural component has a default font size and automatic numbering.

---

the rest of the paragraph is on the next page. Good typesetting practice dictates that in an ordinary paragraph there be at least two lines of text starting or ending the page.

The slide has few parts; the letter class has a single style but multiple namable parts. The article, report and book classes by their nature have more elaborate divisions; articles are more complex than letters. Reports are more formal than articles, and include monographs, theses, formal reports. And a book has the most named parts. Books and reports have chapters, articles do not. These last three classes—articles, reports, books—all partition the document into sections and subsections.

3.4   Slides

The slide has the simplest structure. The example shown will produce black text on a transparency. Making colored slides and overlays is described in Section 32.5.

Because my document class for formatting this book is *book*, it would be an error for me to introduce another document class. Instead, the markup shown below in Part 1 was produced in a separate file, processed by LaTeX and converted to PostScript (PS). Part 2 shows how this PS file was introduced into the main document as a graphics object by using the *includegraphics* command. It was encased in a Figure environment. Figure 3.2 is the print version. Introducing pictures and graphics into your document is discussed in Chapter 25.

Part 1.

```
\documentclass{slides}
\begin{document}
. . . . . . . . . . . . . . . .
\begin{slide}
\begin{center}
\Large This is an example of the bold command:
\Huge\textbf{CAN YOU SEE THIS IN THE LAST ROW?}
\end{center}
\end{slide}
. . . . . . . . . . . . . . . .
\end{document}
```

Part 2.

```
\begin{document}
. . . . . . . . . . . . . . . .
\afterpage{\clearpage%
\begin{figure}
\includegraphics%
[bb=95 220 625 550,clip]%
{./exslide1.orig.ps}
\caption{A slide.}
\label{fig:slidepix}
\end{figure}}
. . . . . . . . . . . . . . . .
\end{document}
```

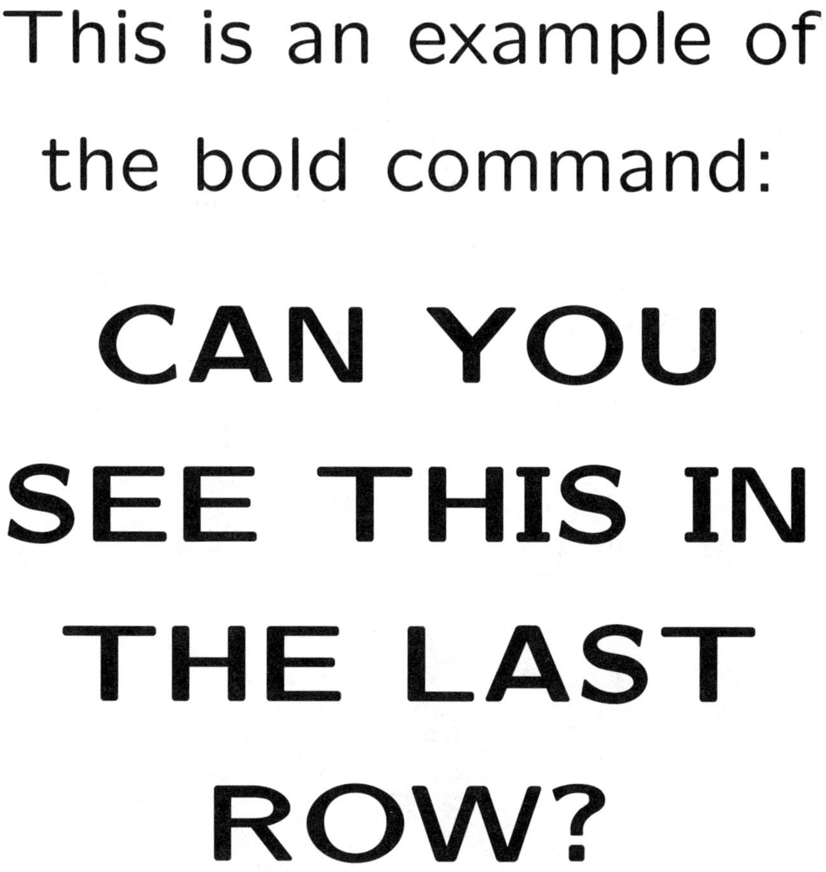

This is an example of the bold command:

CAN YOU SEE THIS IN THE LAST ROW?

Figure 3.2: A slide.

3.5   Letters

Letters are a separate document class. In a letter, the amount of text may not be much larger than in a slide, but we have a much larger vocabulary for naming the different parts of the letter. LaTeX has created a letter class and supplies commands for positioning familiar parts of the letter: the writer's address, the recipient's name and address, the signature, and so forth.

The date is added by the program automatically.

The program will add the preamble material—the writer's address and his signature—to all the letters.

By default there is a empty line between paragraphs.

The framed box below is a complete template for the LaTeX letter class. Notice that both the writer's address and signature are written in the preamble, not within the letter itself. This is because multiple letters can be written in the same document file, each delimited by a \begin{letter} and \end{letter} pair.

The Letter Document Class Format

```
\documentclass{letter}
\makelabels
\address{Your street address\\
City ST Zip\\
Tel: number\\}

\signature{Your Name \\
Your Title}
\begin{document}
\begin{letter}

{Recipient's Name \\
His Business/Title \\
Street Address \\
City ST Zip }

\opening{Dear Buddyname/Title-Name} %ex: Dear John, Dear Dr Jones

   BODY OF THE LETTER. WRITE THE ACTUAL TEXT HERE.

\closing{Yours truly,} %Respectfully yours,Thanking you in advance,...

\ps{Addendum added after the letter text}
\cc{1st copy\\
    2nd copy} %Who receives copies of the letter.

\encl{List of Participants/Form ABC23 for your signature.} %Enclosures
\end{letter}
\end{document}
```

The \makelabels command makes a label for each letter, using the material in braces just after the \begin{letter}. The labels are printed on the last page of the printout. If the label printout format suits you, use label paper for the last printing page.

The markup below is an example of how to write several letters in the same document. As in the markup skeleton above, the writer's name and signature are written in the preamble. They are reused in each of the several letters that are written in the document. In this illustration, they apply to two separate letters, each of which starts on a new page. (See Section 32.6 for other letter styles.)

As with the slides class, it is not possible to write an actual letters class document inside another class. So again we wrote the letters document in a separate file in LaTeX format, and converted it into PostScript in order to bring it in.

An Example Document Containing Multiple Letters

MarkUp:

```
\documentclass{letter}
\makelabels

\address{1234 Charles Street Annex, Boston MA 12345 \\
TEL: 617 555 2345}

\signature{John R Writer, Jr\\Manager, Subsystems Division
\\ Chips, Inc. }

\begin{document}
\begin{letter}
{Bob M Receiver \\CEO, Chips Inc\\ 234 Back Bay \\
Boston MA 12345 }

\opening{Dear Bob,}
I assume you have the email by now. Please sign the attached and
send it to Personnel.
\closing{Yours truly,}

\ps{By the way, Tom's figures arrived this morning.}
\cc{Mr. Big Boss\\ Tom Receiver }
\encl{Form ABC23 for your signature.}
\end{letter}

\begin{letter}
{Tom T Receiver \\ Treasurer, Chips, Inc. \\
```

234 Back Bay\\Boston MA 12345}

\opening{Dear Tom,}
I assume you have the email by now. Please sign the attached and
return it to Personnel.
\closing{Yours truly,}

\ps{Oh by the way, the figures for the next
quarter are impressive. }
\cc{Mr. Big Boss\\ Bob Receiver}
\encl{Form ABC23 for your signature.}
\end{letter}
\end{document}

The PrintOut:

                    1234 Charles Street Annex, Boston MA 12345
                    TEL: 617 555 2345

                    August 31, 1997

Bob M Receiver
CEO, Chips Inc
234 Back Bay
Boston MA 12345

Dear Bob,

I assume you have the email by now. Please sign the attached and send it to
Personnel.

                    Yours truly,

                    John R Writer, Jr
                    Manager, Subsystems Division
                    Chips, Inc.

By the way, Tom's figures arrived this morning.

cc: Mr. Big Boss
      Tom Receiver

encl: Form ABC23 for your signature.

1234 Charles Street Annex, Boston MA 12345
TEL: 617 555 2345

August 31, 1997

Tom T Receiver
Treasurer, Chips, Inc.
234 Back Bay
Boston MA 12345

Dear Tom,

I assume you have the email by now. Please sign the attached and return it to
Personnel.

Yours truly,

John R Writer, Jr
Manager, Subsystems Division
Chips, Inc.

Oh by the way, the figures for the next quarter are impressive.

cc: Mr. Big Boss
    Bob Receiver

encl: Form ABC23 for your signature.

3.6 Articles

The article class lends itself to countless variations. LaTeX also provides two classes based
on the article class: *proc*, which is used to format proceedings in two columns per page,
and the more limited *ltxdoc* class, used to document the LaTeX program for package writers.
You would create a proceedings document by writing **\documentclass**{**proc**} at the start
of the preamble.

Figure 3.3 is an enlarged version of Figure 3.1. It will serve as the basis of the starter file in which you can practice writing in LATEX. We used a verbatim environment to show the commands exactly as they would appear in your file.

To print your practice article in two columns, rewrite the document class instruction as: **\documentclass[twocolumn]{article}**. The size font defaults to 10 point, but you can change size to 11 or 12 in the bracket.

To print your article two columns per page in 12 point font, write: **\documentclass[twocolumn,12pt]{article}**.

3.7   Reports

A report is less complex than a book, but it has chapters and, by its nature, is more stylized and formal than an article. Document articulations such as *abstract* are typically used in reports. LATEX provides an abstract environment that writes the abstract on a separate page with a centered title. Footnotes and references are extensive. Specific reports—a thesis, the protocols for a clinical trial—have stylized formats dictated by the particular school or department, and these can be formatted by creating special style sheets, using LATEX modules.

3.8   Books

Books have much the same options as the article and report classes. In addition, they have more elaborate initial material and addenda. Formatting the three major divisions of a book is controlled in the definition of the book class (i.e., in *book.cls*) by three commands: *\frontmatter, \mainmatter* and *\backmatter*, respectively. Page numbering style, for example, is typically roman in the preface and arabic in the main section. The hierarchy of partitions in a book are shown in Figure 3.4.

With the exception of the front and back matter, the LATEX-defined divisions and subdivisions shown below apply to reports and, with the exception of chapters, to articles. The zero listed with **\part** indicates that **\part** is not incremented by LATEX, nor does it affect the other division levels. **\chapter**, the 1st level, is incremented by 1 each chapter. **\section**,

The MarkUp:

```
\documentclass{article}    % As a variation, you can write:
                           % \documentclass[twocolumn]{article}
                           % START OF PREAMBLE

\input{AnotherFile}        % If you have a group of commands that
                           % apply to several documents including
                           % this one, tuck them into a separate
                           % file. An input command will bring
                           % this other file in for processing.

% Write your own instructions, aliases, macros and
% abbreviations that are specific to this document here.

\title{NameOfDocument}
\author{Name(s)OfAuthor(s)}
\date{May 5 1997} % OR \date{\today}

\flushbottom            % Size all pages to the same length.
\parindent=0pc          % Do not indent the start of a paragraph.
\setlength{\parskip}{1pc}  %Put an empty line between paragraphs.

\begin{document}    % END OF PREAMBLE. START OF DOCUMENT.

\maketitle          % This produces the title.

% Just type the article or sections of the article here, using
% \LaTeX\ markup commands for tables, equations, figures, lists
% and local changes of font, as we come to them.
%
% Use \section{<text>} and \subsection{<text>} to partition article.
% Later you will partition the text and move sections to other files.
% You will list the files that contain the pieces of the article in
% this spot.

\end{document}
```

Figure 3.3: *skel.tex*: a format for a simple short article.

the 2nd level, is incremented from 1 on within each chapter; it begins a new cycle every new chapter. Similarly, subsection, the 3rd level, is incremented from 1 on within each section; at the start of a new section, it is reset. 4.5.6 indicates the 6th subsection of the 5th section of the 4th chapter.

3.9   Document Class Options

Even a single document class typically has a good deal of variation in the visual appearance of its members: there may be two rather than one column per page, printing may sometimes be sidewards to display large charts, and so forth. This is handled in LaTeX by a set of options, each with a limited set of values. To set these options, use the complete template for the document class: **\documentclass**[*<options>*]{*<class>*}.

Multiple options are included between the square brackets; separate them with commas and no spaces. If you use so many of the options that the line becomes overlong, split the command, but add a % at the end of any line that is split. For example,

```
\documentclass[twoside,twocolumn,landscape,%
11pt,draft,legalsize,notitlepage,leqno]{report}
```

If you are not sure whether a value is the default, it is usually safe to write it in. If you are not sure whether an option applies to the particular class, try it. If you're wrong, LaTeX may barf at you or just ignore the instruction. The slide class, for example, doesn't know what to make of such entities as *figure* or *caption* or *chapter*. It ignores a request to print in 10 point; instead, it uses a larger font.

Font Size.   This sets the font size in points for the whole document. Except for the Slide class, 10 point is the default, 11 point and 12 point the other options. Sizes that are set by direct command—from \tiny to \Huge—are relative to the base size chosen.

Print on One/Two Sides of the paper.   *twoside* is the default for a book; *oneside* is the default for reports and articles; and it is the only way slides and letters are printed. \documentclass[twocolumn,twoside,12pt]{article} prints the article as two columns in 12-point font. *twoside* does NOT mean that the program writes pages 1,3,5... then 2,4,6... That has to be done by the printer software. It does mean that you must make sure margins are adjusted properly for odd versus even pages.

\documentclass{book}
\begin{document}
\frontmatter
Credits
Trademarks and Copyrights
Library ID
Title Page
Thanks
Dedication
Table of Contents (\tableofcontents)
List of Figures (\listoffigures)
List of Tables (\listoftables)
Preface[a]
\mainmatter
0. \part{...} (optional)
1.   \chapter{...}
2.   \section{...} % of a chapter
3.   \subsection{...} % of a section of a chapter
4.   \subsubsection{...} % of a subsection of a section of a chapter
5.   \paragraph{...} % of a subsubsection of a subsection...
6.   \subparagraph{...}% of a paragraph of a
                                                       subsubsection...
\backmatter
\appendix
Bibliography or List of References
Glossary
Index
\end{document}

Figure 3.4: Defined Divisions of a Book

---

[a]If the chapter font and size is acceptable, you can use it for the Preface by writing **\chapter*{Preface}**. The asterisk ensures that the header **Preface** is not numbered.

One or Two Columns. Output on the page is one-column by default, but two column output is an option. Pick the one that will be used most often. You can shift between the options for a specific page or section; e.g., if you are printing the document with a double column, then in the document, the **\onecolumn** declaration will print the following pages in a single column. Only *onecolumn* can be printed in the letter and slide classes.

In using the *twocolumn* option, be careful about a block of text that is to be printed verbatim. If the width of the literal text is more than the column width, the text will encroach on the other column. In that verbatim text is 'set by hand', you can usually correct the width. Or reset the *columnsep* parameter.

It is not one of the options, but if you need more columns, the multicolumns package lets you print up to 10 columns across a page, portrait or landscape [Mittelbach96a]. Call it with a **\usepackage{multicol}** command in the preamble. Column splitting isn't restricted to a page; it will continue as long as there is text in the *multicols* environment.

Print Direction. The text can be printed in *portrait* or *landscape* mode, with portrait the default. In *landscape*, the printing is rotated 90° so that the virtual print page is wider than higher. It is used for spread sheets and for wide two-column printouts. If *landscape* doesn't work, use the **\includegraphics[angle=90]{...}** command in Chapter 25 to rotate single pages.

Paper Size. American measures are given in inches, width x length. European measurements are in mm, width x length. American sizes are *letterpaper* (8.5 x 11), *legalpaper* (8.5 x 14) and *executivepaper* (7.25 x 10.5). European sizes are *A4paper* (210 wide x 297 high), *A5paper* (148 x 210) and *B5paper* (176 x 250). *letterpaper* is the default. If you use, say, A4 paper, put it as an option in the documentclass statement; e.g., **\documentclass[10pt,twoside,A4paper,openright]{article}**.

Title Page. The options are *titlepage* and *notitlepage*. *titlepage* is the default for reports and it can be used in articles. It is usually insufficient for a book. The titlepage option:

1. causes the **\maketitle** command to create a separate title page.

2. causes the **abstract** environment to put the abstract on a separate page—if there is an abstract.

Abstract. An abstract is written inside the abstract environment in an article or report.

```
\begin{abstract}
 ... text...
\end{abstract}
```

The abstract is printed with a centered bold header **Abstract**, followed by the text. It appears on a separate page in a report as default. In an article, if the **\maketitle** command has been issued, the abstract appears on a separate page. Otherwise, it is written as a displayed paragraph. (See Section 15.6.) If required, an Abstract—sometimes called a Foreword—can be written in a book as a displayed quote or by using a centered bold heading and indenting the text somewhat inside a minipage. (See Section 15.8.)

Identifying Overlong Lines in Print. The options are *final* versus *draft*, with *final* the default. In *draft*, the program will mark lines it considers too long with black box icons.

Right-left Chapter Beginnings. Options are *openright* and *openany*. In book class, chapters usually start on a right-side page, so they are *openright* by default. Reports are *openany* by default. Articles don't have chapters.

Equation Placement. This applies to the *equation* and *eqnarray* environments. (See Part V.) Usually equation numbers are placed on the right; these options place them on the left. If you want numbering on the right, just ignore them. The options for left-side display are: *leqno* and *fleqn*. *leqno* places equation numbers at the left, not on the right; *fleqn* typesets the equations themselves on the left, not in the center.

Appendix. The appendix is the—or one of the—final segments of an article, report or book. The appendix consists of one or more individual chapters, where a chapter is a complete background report, a set of tables, some technical details. The *\appendix* declaration starts numbering chapters with letters. *\appendix* is equivalent to writing the first two lines of this layout of an appendix to a history:

\renewcommand{\thechapter}{\Alph{chapter}}
\setcounter{chapter}{0}

```
\chapter{Examples of 13th Century Chattel Laws}
\chapter{Chronology of Revisions}
\chapter{Genealogical Tables for Smith Family}
```

To print a report on both sides of the paper, two columns per page in size 11 point font, write the options inside square brackets and the class type in braces. Write the document class declaration this way:

\documentclass[twocolumn,11pt,twoside]{report}.

3.10   TOC Option

The text argument of a document division is used in the Table of Contents (TOC) and/or header. As an option, you can provide any and all of the defined document partitions with a short form that is used in the TOC and headers instead of the mandatory text. If for example, the text in a section is:

```
\section{The reconstruction of the four figures that were convolved
in the previous example}
```

You would write some short text phrase in square brackets for the TOC; e.g.

```
\section[Reconstructing the example figures]{The reconstruction of
the four figures that were convolved in the previous example}
```

Before we begin experimenting with the commands that modify the visual appearance of our text, we are going to take time to assemble some basic equipment and become familiar with important resources. These are discussed in the next Part.

Part II.

PREPARATORY TASKS.

Creating Practice Files and Other Resources

In Part 2, you will prepare a practice document and you will set up Emacs keys, to use when you begin learning LaTeX commands. Part 2 also takes you through the steps of correcting errors and printing a correctly formatted document. It's probably enough to just skim Chapters 6 and 7 for now.

When you finish Part 2, you should reread Part 1 before going on to Part 3.

Chapter 4

CONSTRUCTING *practice.tex*, A PRACTICE FILE

At first, it is a good idea to do all your formatting in a single file. Later, you will probably want to split your document up into segments that can be stored in several files. LATEX can process them one at a time as you develop the document. When you're done, LATEX can process the set of files as a unit. The procedures for separating a manuscript into multiple files with virtual unification are detailed in the Appendix, Chapter A.

An easy way to prepare a practice file is by making a copy of a few paragraphs of an existing paper. Remove formatting instructions introduced by previous text processors.[1] Initialize it as a LATEX document using Figure 3.3 in Section 3.6 as a model.

Or you can cut to Figure 4.1, shown below. This is a template for a practice file. Any time you need a fresh copy to practice in, make a new copy of *template.tex*.

A command name (also known as an alias or short form) is the text in the first argument following the *\newcommand* command. Note that the top of the template practice file contains 'homegrown' newcommand names, not official LATEX names. Feel free to substitute your own after reading Part 3.

---

[1]You usually do this by requesting the text processor to output a plain ASCII file. The output must NOT contain control characters and format instructions.

Or modify *template.tex* with your own material.

Or start from scratch, following the $S^{TE^{PS}}$ guide.

$S^{TE^{PS}}$ GUIDE

1. Open a file in *Emacs*. Name it *template.tex*.

2. Add this crib at the very top of the file. It will NOT appear in the printout.

```
%RESERVED CHARACTERS: \ # $ % & _ ^ { } ~
%
%NEWCOMMAND FORMAT: A simple substitute.
% \newcommand{<\NewCommandName>}{text}
%EX: \newcommand{\stamp}{\hspace{.5in}\textbf{Findings:}%
%                        \hspace{.5in}}
%
%NEWENVIRONMENT FORMAT: Involving a defined Environment Name.
% \newenvironment{<NewEnvironmentName>}%
%{\begin{<OldEnvironmentName>}<new stuff>}{\end{<OldEnvironmentName>}}
%EX: \newenvironment{smallcapit}%
%              {\begin{itemize} \scshape}{\end{itemize}}
%
%FORMAT OF MACRO WITH PLACEHOLDERS:
% \newcommand{<\CommandName>}[#]{A single argument: text and #.}
%EX:\newcommand{\phonebk}[3]{NAME: #1$|$ TEL: #2$|$ FAX: #3\\}
```

3. Write the document class command on a new line. The *article* class is versatile: **\documentclass{article}**. Or you may prefer *report* or *book* as argument. (TIP: Use the *draft* option during document polishing; the program will mark overlong lines by black rectangles: **\documentclass[draft]{article}**.)

4. Add this block of text starting on a new line. The first set of abbreviations come from Section 8.3. The print commands are discussed in Chapter 5.

```
%PUNCTUATION ABBREVIATIONS
\newcommand{\BS}{$\backslash$}    %backslash
\newcommand{\LB}{$\{$}            %left brace
\newcommand{\RB}{$\}$}            %right brace
\newcommand{\SP}{\ }              %space
```

```
\newcommand{\LSQ}{`}                          %left single quote
\newcommand{\LDQ}{``}                         %left double quote
\newcommand{\RSQ}{'}                          %right single quote
\newcommand{\RDQ}{''}                         %right double quote

%LIST COMMANDS
\newcommand{\bi}{\begin{itemize}}
\newcommand{\ei}{\end{itemize}}
\newcommand{\be}{\begin{enumerate}}
\newcommand{\ee}{\end{enumerate}}
\newcommand{\bd}{\begin{description}}
\newcommand{\ed}{\end{description}}

%PRINT COMMANDS
\newcommand{\prbf}[1]{\textbf{#1}}            %print in bold.
\newcommand{\prit}[1]{\textit{#1}}            %print in italic.
\newcommand{\prmd}[1]{\textmd{#1}}            %print in medium.
\newcommand{\prno}[1]{\textnormal{#1}}        %print in default font.
\newcommand{\prrm}[1]{\textrm{#1}}            %print in roman family.
\newcommand{\prsc}[1]{\textsc{#1}}            %print in small cap.
\newcommand{\prsf}[1]{\textsf{#1}}            %print in sans serif.
\newcommand{\prsl}[1]{\textsl{#1}}            %print in slant.
\newcommand{\prtt}[1]{\texttt{#1}}            %print in typewriter.
\newcommand{\prup}[1]{\textup{#1}}            %print in straight up.

%VERBATIM AND IGNORE
\newcommand{\bv}{\begin{verbatim}}
\newcommand{\V}{\verb} %Ex: \V=-d{#@~}= Expr must fit on a line.

\title{A \LaTeX\ Practice Document}
\author{<Your Name>}
\date{\today}
```

5. If you want paragraphs with starting indentations and no empty line between them, do NOT add the next 3 lines.

```
\flushbottom
\parindent=0pc
\setlength{\parskip}{1pc}
```

6. Next add:

   \begin{document} % End of preamble. Begin writing.

   \maketitle % Produces the title.

7. Next write a couple of paragraphs with section and subsection commands. (See *template.tex* below.)

8. At the very end of your prose, add this line:

   \end{document}

9. Your template for practice documents is complete. *template.tex* contains commands to convert your ordinary text file into a document that LaTeX can process. As you create macros that you find useful, add them to the preamble. As you have probably deduced, *\newcommand* is the command for creating an alias for a command or a set of associated commands.

10. Make a copy of *template.tex*. Name the copy, say, *practice.tex*.

11. Use *practice.tex* as your practice file. Practice the techniques as you read about them. When your practice file gets too cluttered, throw it away and make a fresh copy of *template.tex*.

Your template file might look something like this:

```
%RESERVED CHARS: \ # $ % & _ ^ { } ~
%
%NEWCOMMAND FORMAT: A simple substitute.
   % \newcommand{<\New CommandName>}{<text>}
   % EX: \newcommand{\stamp}{\hspace{.5in}\textbf{Findings:}\hspace{.5in}\\}
   %
%NEWENVIRONMENT FORMAT: Involving a defined Environment Name.
   % \newenvironment{<NewEnvironmentName>}%
   % {\begin{<OldEnvironmentName>}<new stuff>}{\end{<OldEnvironmentName>}}
   % EX: \newenvironment{smallcapit}{\begin{itemize}\scshape}{\end{itemize}}
   %
%FORMAT OF MACRO WITH PLACEHOLDERS:
   % \newcommand{<\CommandName>}[#]{A single argument: text and #.}
   % EX: \newcommand{\phonebk}[3]{NAME: #1$|$TEL: #2$|$FAX: #3 \\}


\documentclass{article}
```

```
%PUNCTUATION ABBREVIATIONS
\newcommand{\BS}{$\backslash$}          %backslash
\newcommand{\LB}{$\{$}                  %left brace
\newcommand{\RB}{$\}$}                  %right brace
\newcommand{\SP}{\ }                    %space
\newcommand{\LSQ}{'}                    %left single quote
\newcommand{\LDQ}{''}                   %left double quote
\newcommand{\RSQ}{'}                    %right single quote
\newcommand{\RDQ}{''}                   %right double quote


%LIST COMMANDS
\newcommand{\bi}{\begin{itemize}}
\newcommand{\ei}{\end{itemize}}
\newcommand{\be}{\begin{enumerate}}
\newcommand{\ee}{\end{enumerate}}
\newcommand{\bd}{\begin{description}}
\newcommand{\ed\}{\end{description}}


%PRINT COMMANDS
\newcommand{\prbf}[1]{\textbf{#1}}      %print in bold.
\newcommand{\prit}[1]{\textit{#1}}      %print in italic.
\newcommand{\prmd}[1]{\textmd{#1}}      %print in medium.
\newcommand{\prno}[1]{\textnormal{#1}}  %print in document default.
\newcommand{\prrm}[1]{\textrm{#1}}      %print in roman family.
\newcommand{\prsc}[1]{\textsc{#1}}      %print in small cap.
\newcommand{\prsf}[1]{\textsf{#1}}      %print in sans serif.
\newcommand{\prsl}[1]{\textsl{#1}}      %print in slant.
\newcommand{\prtt}[1]{\texttt{#1}}      %print in typewriter family.
\newcommand{\prup}[1]{\textup{#1}}      %print in straight up.

%VERBATIM AND IGNORE:
\newcommand{\bv}{\begin{verbatim}}
\newcommand{\V}{\verb}   % Ex. \V=-d{#@~}= The V expr must fit on a line.

% Write your own instructions, aliases, macros and abbreviations here.

\title{A \LaTeX\ Practice Document}
\author{Your Name}
\date{\today}

%FOR PRINTOUTS WITH EMPTY LINES BETWEEN PARAS AND NO INDENT AT START
\flushbottom
\parindent=0pc
```

```
\setlength{\parskip}{1pc}

\begin{document}
\maketitle

%HERE BE PROSE. SUBSTITUTE YOUR OWN.
\section{Programs}

\subsection{Alphabetize}
During alphabetization, a record is reduced to a struct containing as
members: the key, the position of the record in the original database; ....

\subsection{Squish sequential matching records}

If the files are 2-field indices, use squish to consolidate a series
of records that have identical text in field 2....

\section{Some More Text}
%Type the rest of the article here, using \LaTeX\ markup commands
%for tables, equations, figures, lists and local changes of font.
\end{document}
```

Figure 4.1. Constructing *template.tex*

Chapter 5

SETTING EMACS KEYS FOR COMMON CONSTRUCTIONS

5.1 Writing In Emacs

I am assuming *Emacs* is your text editor.[1] There's probably *AucTeX* code in your `~/.emacs` file, which came with the Linux distribution. *AucTeX* is written in Lisp, as are all Emacs *.emacs* macros. It adds useful editing and debugging commands. When Emacs is in LaTeX mode, *AucTeX* will run a region or the whole of the current file through LaTeX; it will locate the LaTeX commands in the file and lists them with line numbers; it can jump directly to view or print the document. This is some typical code.

```
(load "tex-mode")
(setq auto-mode-alist (mapcar 'purecopy
                       '(("\\.c$" . c-mode)
                         ("\\.h$" . c-mode)
                         ("\\.tex$" . tex-mode)
                         ("\\.txi$" . texinfo-mode)
                         ("\\.el$" . emacs-lisp-mode)
                         ("\\.a$" . c-mode) )))
```

---

[1]It makes no difference to LaTeX whether you write in Emacs or in some other plain-text processor. But the rest of this chapter on keying commands is Emacs-dependent.

```
(setq load-path (cons (expand-file-name \\
    "PATH_FOR_AUC-TEX") load-path))
(autoload 'tex-mode "auc-tex" "Automatic select TeX or LaTeX mode" t)
 (autoload 'plain-tex-mode "auc-tex" "Mode for Plain TeX" t)
 (autoload 'latex-mode "auc-tex" "Mode for LaTeX" t)
 (autoload 'LaTeX-math-mode "tex-math"  "Math mode for TeX." t)
 (defun Ctl-C-prefix ()
 (define-key Ctl-C-keymap "m" 'LaTeX-math-mode)
```

You can also download assignment keys for LaTeX so you can create templates for almost all LaTeX objects. Try *ftp://tsx-11.mit.edu/pub/linux/packages/TeX*.

You might wish to set some keys in your *~/.emacs* file to create some LaTeX object templates. When you push the key, the template will appear in your document. The rest of this chapter describes such templates. When you revise *~/.emacs*, restart Xwindows.

5.2   A Font Shape Template

This is a simple but useful template to use whenever you need to emphasize a text phrase.[2]

```
(defun empwrd ()
  (interactive)
  (setq str "\\emph{}")
  (insert str)
  (backward-char 1)
 )
```

Or you can create a template to use the actual LaTeX commands for changing fonts,[3] substituting, say, "\textit{}" for "\emph{}" in the third line of code, above. These are suitable for emphasis:

\textit{} italicizes the text inside the braces.

\textbf{} bolds the text inside the braces.

\textsl{} slants the text inside the braces.

---

[2]Italic is the default for emphasis. This can be changed to any other font shape.

[3]The complete list of font commands is in Chapter 11.

Alternatively, you can design a command specifically for printing, say, filenames or group names. In this way, you can continue to use \emph{} or \textit{} for general emphasis, but have additional control of a subset of the italicized words.

You can change the appearance of all the program names in the document—to slant or to small cap—with one modification, while leaving the \emph{} command for general emphasis. These are some possibilities.

```
%PRINT INSTRUCTIONS
\newcommand{\quotes}[1]{\textbf{#1}}        %print quotes in bold.
\newcommand{\programname}[1]{\textit{#1}}   %print program name in italic.
\newcommand{\GenericFName}[1]{\textsl{#1}}  %print filename placeholder in slant.
\newcommand{\GenericCmd}[1]{\textsc{#1}}    %print command placeholder in smallcap.
```

GenericFName and *GenericCmd* can, of course, be shortened to save typing. In fact, whichever way you choose to do it, it is useful to create a coordinated set of commands to print a text phrase in various ways. Once you know what command names you want for different typographic conventions, you can write them in the preamble of your document. And you can create a key that prints the command and its proper syntax directly in the document.

I prefer a shorter way to write the **text**xx font shape commands. In this next group, the *pr* prefix is short for **print**, and the two other letter represent a font shape. A shape command in the print group can easily be changed to one of the other shapes by changing two letters. You might wish to substitute *pit* for *textit* or *PIT* or any other abbreviation that is easy to remember.

We begin by storing these PRINT INSTRUCTIONS in the preamble of your document. (See Figure 4.1.)

```
%PRINT INSTRUCTIONS
\newcommand{\prbf}[1]{\textbf{#1}}        %print in bold.
\newcommand{\prit}[1]{\textit{#1}}        %print in italic.
\newcommand{\prmd}[1]{\textmd{#1}}        %print in medium.
\newcommand{\prno}[1]{\textnormal{#1}}    %print in document default.
\newcommand{\prrm}[1]{\textrm{#1}}        %print in roman family.
\newcommand{\prsc}[1]{\textsc{#1}}        %print in small cap.
\newcommand{\prsf}[1]{\textsf{#1}}        %print in sans serif.
\newcommand{\prsl}[1]{\textsl{#1}}        %print in slant.
\newcommand{\prtt}[1]{\texttt{#1}}        %print in typewriter family.
\newcommand{\prup}[1]{\textup{#1}}        %print in straight up.
```

To create a template for \prit, write this Lisp macro in your ˜/.emacs file:

```
(defun prit ()
  (interactive)
  (setq str "\\prit{}")
  (insert str)
  (backward-char 1)
 )
```

While you are still in ˜/.emacs, tie the code to a function key by writing a separate link instruction somewhere in the file. This code links the \prit command to F9.

global-set-key [f9] 'prit)

Later, when you are working on a document file in Emacs, hitting F9 will produce this:

\prit{}

The cursor will point to where you can start typing text inside the braces.

This format is useful, because it is easy to rewrite *Watch This* to **Watch This** to print the text in boldface or to WATCH THIS to print the same text in small cap.

5.3   A List Template

Next, we show how to create a template for writing items in a list. Note that the previously defined font shape command **\prit**{} is used as part of the skeleton list.

newlst, shown next, writes a string in ˜/.emacs that emulates an ordinary description list (discussed in Chapter 14), except that the initial text will be in italic rather than bold. Note that \bd and \ed—to be discussed below—are defined AKA's for \begin{description} and \end{description}, respectively.

This is the way to write newlst in ˜/.emacs:

```
(defun newlst ()
  (interactive)
```

```
 (setq str "
\\bd
\\item \\prit{.}

\\item \\prit{.}

\\item \\prit{.}

\\item \\prit{.}
\\ed
")
   (insert str)
   (backward-char 72)
 )
```

Link the macro to some function key, F10 for example, this way in ˜/.emacs:

global-set-key [f10] 'newlst)

Whenever you press F10, this appears in the document where your cursor is. The cursor automatically moves up to the first item.

```
\bd
\item \prit{.}

\item \prit{.}

\item \prit{.}

\item \prit{.}
\ed
```

It is ready for you to fill it. For example:

The MarkUp:

```
\bd
\item \prit{Style 1.} The article is single-columned and divided
into unlabeled sections. Divisions are marked by \texttt{\BS bigskip}.

\item \prit{Style 2.} The article is in two columns. Section starts
```

```
are in bold but are not numbered.

\item \prit{Style 3.} The article is single-columned. Sections are
numbered. Margin notes are scattered throughout.

\item \prit{Style 4.} The article is in 3 columns. Column 1
is a short description. Column 2 is a table. Column 3 is a
picture or a graph.
\ed
```

The PrintOut:

Style 1. The article is single-columned and divided into unlabeled sections. Divisions are marked by \bigskip.

Style 2. The article is in two columns. Section starts are in bold but are not numbered.

Style 3. The article is single-columned. Sections are numbered. Margin notes are scattered throughout.

Style 4. The article is in 3 columns. Column 1 is a short description. Column 2 is a table. Column 3 is a picture or a graph.

To add versatility to *newlst*, this next set of newcommands should be stored either in the preamble or in an **include** file. Actually, it is already installed in *template.tex*, the skeleton for your practice documents.

These are a set of aliases for the LaTeX list commands. They make the *newlst* template created above easy to revamp right in the document—change \bd to \be and \ed to \ee to change to an enumerate list. I hope it is clear that the aliases I chose are not part of LaTeX. You can create your own set of aliases. But it is a good idea to substitute short phrases for such commands as \begin{enumerate}. With a few keystrokes, you can modify the template to bold items in an enumerate list.

```
\newcommand{\bi}{\begin{itemize}}
\newcommand{\ei}{\end{itemize}}
\newcommand{\be}{\begin{enumerate}}
\newcommand{\ee}{\end{enumerate}}
\newcommand{\bd}{\begin{description}}
\newcommand{\ed}{\end{description}}
```

The MarkUp:

```
\be
\item \prbf{sort.} This sorts records by class names or by
numerical value or by alphabetical value.

\item \prbf{mergealp.}  This does a 'virtual' merge of two already
alphabetized files. The originals are read-only.

\item \prbf{squish.} In a 2-field record, if a sequence of records
has the same first field in common, this creates a record using a
single copy of the first field, and concatenates all the
second fields.

\item \prbf{genio.} This outputs a file of records in various
ways---in columns, prepended by accession numbers, same-size lines,
etc.
\ee
```

The PrintOut:

1. **sort.** This sorts records by class names or by numerical value or by alphabetical value.

2. **mergealp.** This does a 'virtual' merge of two already alphabetized files. The originals are read-only.

3. **squish.** In a 2-field record, if a sequence of records has the same first field in common, this creates a record using a single copy of the first field, and concatenates all the second fields.

4. **genio.** This outputs a file of records in various ways—in columns, prepended by accession numbers, same-size lines, etc.

5.4   A Verbatim Template

If you need to show the markup copy often or have computer code or some text that should be printed out exactly as it was input, you have a choice of several verbatim commands. The classic one is an environment named *verbatim*. To create a template for it, write this next lisp macro in ˜*.emacs*. Additional verbatim environments—*alltt* and *moreverb*—are discussed in Section 19.1.

```
(defun literal ()
(interactive)
```

```
(setq str " \\begin{verbatim}

\\end{verbatim} " )
(insert str)
(backward-char 16) )
```

and link it, say, to the F11 key, this way:

(global-set-key [f11] 'literal)

Whenever you push the F11 key, this will appear on the screen where your cursor is located.

\begin{verbatim}

\end{verbatim}

Actually, I find it more convenient to type a **\bv**[4] myself just before a chunk of code that I want to preserve as is. At the end of the chunk I use a key to write out: **\end{verbatim}**. You can not have an AKA for *\end{verbatim}*, because the program only responds to the literal phrase to terminate a verbatim output. It ignores aliases.

This is done by writing this in your home *.emacs* file:

```
 (defun literal ()
(interactive)
(setq str "
\\end{verbatim}
")
(insert str)
)
```

5.5   A Macro Template

This next code sets up a defined macro; just delete the place holders you don't need, or add more in your setup, if you use a lot of arguments. Write the macro name just after the backslash.

---

[4]\bv is defined in the preamble of your practice document as \begin{verbatim}.

```
(defun macro ()
  (interactive)
  (setq str "\\{}{}{}{}{}")
  (insert str)
  (backward-char 11)
 )
```

5.6   A Logo Template

If you run out of F keys, you can use the keys of the numeric pad on your keyboard. There are two things to remember:

1. The template is written as any other macro, but it is linked differently when defining it.

2. The template is written into the document by pushing *CTRL* and the numeric key simultaneously.

I found it convenient to prepare a macro for the LaTeX logo.

```
(defun logo ()
  (interactive)
  (setq str "\\LaTeX\\")
  (insert str) )
```

Link this to a numeric key. In this example, it is linked to key 8 on the numeric keypad:

global-set-key [C-kp-8] 'logo)   ;This is numeric keypad 8

Retrieve the template while writing in Emacs by pushing *CTRL8*.

Chapter 6

VIEWING AND PRINTING MARKED UP FILES

1. Make a copy of your template document. Name it *practice.tex* and bring it into an *Emacs* window. Let's do a few finishing touches.

2. First, fill in the title and your name. (It will encourage you during the long L^a Tre$_K$ ahead.) Add a couple of sentences. Try a couple of the font commands used above. Don't worry about ragged lines; the program will justify them. Don't worry about leaving more than a single space between words; the program turns a run of spaces into a single one. Start each paragraph or unit flush with the left margin. You can instruct the program later to indent the text and locate it where you wish on the page.

3. You should start getting used to giving a nickname to any LaTeX object that you will reference in the text. You don't want to give these objects absolute numbers, because such objects are likely to shift absolute or relative position as you write. To put a label—a nickname—next to a section or subsection command, for example, do this:

   `\section{RollerSkating the Net} \label{ss:roller}`

   `\subsection{Ping Pong over the Net} \label{ss:ping}`

   Randomly in the text write sentences using the labels. Do this by writing a ~**ref** followed by a defined label.[1]

---

[1] The tilde puts a space between the text on both sides of it, and keeps this text phrase together on the same line.

```
The methods are explained in Section~\ref{ss:roller}.
```

```
See Subsection~\ref{ss:ping} for additional information.
```

As you progress, label tables, figures, equations—any LaTeX object that:

(a) is one of a series that the program automatically numbers sequentially.

(b) you wish to reference anywhere in the text.

4. You have enough of a start to do a dry run on viewing the document. In Xwindows, you need to open several windows, so that you can go back and forth from document to viewer. A file that has been marked up is not easy to read. You have one *Emacs* window open for writing and modifying the source file. Now start two virtual terminals in Xwindows:[2] one for running LaTeX and viewing the resultant DVI file, the other for examining the error log file.

5. Go to the xterm that you have set aside for LaTeX processing. At the prompt, type: **latex practice**.[3] LaTeX provides a running account of problems that it finds. It continues processing as it rolls by overfull and underfull boxes. But it does stop at each mistake and asks what to do. For now, just do a Carriage Return (the **ENTER** key), to get past the problem if possible. Or write `\batchmode` in the preamble of your practice file. This forces LaTeX to examine the whole document without stopping, if the errors aren't serious enough to halt the program. It writes these errors into, in this case, *practice.log*. You can examine this file afterwards.

6. The most important LaTeX product is a file with a DVI extension; in this case, it will be called *practice.dvi*.

7. You can look at the file in an xterm[4] by typing: **\xdvi practice.dvi**. The print quality is outstanding. The many *xdvi* options are listed in the *man* page. Or type: **xdvi −help**. You can get a larger xdvi screen font by writing an alias such as this (assuming that the *xdvi* program is stored as shown):

```
alias xd='/usr/X11R6/bin/xdvi -S 15 -s 2 -margins 5
    -sidemargin 1 -topmargin 1 -mgs1 1200 $1'
```

---

[2]You type your manuscript in an Emacs window. You run LaTeX and any other program from a terminal. The virtual terminal in Xwindows is not only convenient, it is necessary for running *xdvi*. From now on, I will refer to writing in a virtual terminal in Xwindows as writing in an *xterm*, to make sure you don't assume it's another command to insert in your document.

[3]This assumes you are writing in a file called *practice.tex*. If a file has a TEX extension, you don't have to give the extension. Otherwise, you must write out the full name. If you are not in the same directory as the file, you have to provide the full path to the file (a real drag).

[4]This assumes that you are working in XWindows, as you most likely are. *xdvi* needs the dynamic X11 libraries in order to work.

On large screens the -s value might be 4 or 5 instead of 2. On one screen I routinely set s at 10 to see a whole page at a time. If the alias is *xd*, screen the document by typing: **\xd practice** or **\xd practice.dvi**.

8. Look at the log file. Go into the *Emacs* source file and correct an error. Run LATEX again. View the results in *xdvi*. Do this a few times.

9. If you haven't already done so, tell the program about your printer. *texconfig* in *˜/texmf/dvips/config* is a customizer in that it finds out what printer you use, how much memory it has, what dpi it prints at and paper size. The information is stored in a file in the ˜/texmf/dvips/config directory. It is *config.ps* for a PostScript printer.

10. Run *practice.dvi* through a program called *dvips*. Typing: **dvips -o practice.ps practice.dvi** in an xterm will result in a PostScript file; in this case, it would be called *practice.ps*. You can print it later on a PostScript printer by writing this in an xterm: **lpr practice.ps**. On some systems with some configurations, if you run **dvips practice.dvi** while the PostScript printer is on, it immediately prints the document. On others, write: **dvips practice.dvi | lpr** for immediate printout.

    dvips has a large number of command line parameters—for collating copies, printing only odd or only even pages, doing just a few pages, stating resolution, and so on. The list of options can be found by typing in an xterm: **dvips --help**. The *-A* option will print only odd pages; the *-B* option only even pages. To print a range of pages, use *-p #* and *-l #*; e.g., **lpr -p 4 -l 10 practice.ps**. Note that page numbers are as TEX labeled them.

11. If you wish to print only a few scattered pages, run the PS file through *ghostview*. In an xterm, type: ghostview ˜/practice.ps (where the tilde represents the path to get to where the file resides.) Pull down the file menu. You can mark some of the pages and then print just those pages. If you don't use Xwindows, you can also use *ghostview* to preview the *.ps* version of your document. It is somewhat slower than *xdvi* but has the advantage of showing colored boxes in color.

12. If you don't have a PostScript printer, run your PostScript file through a program called *ghostscript*; e.g., in an xterm, type: **gs practice.ps**. The results are printer-ready. Its documentation files are likely to be in the */usr/lib/ghostscript/doc* directory. Or you can find out about its available options by typing in an xterm: **gs -help**.

13. In Linux, printers take their orders from the /usr/etc/printcap file. With a PostScript printer such as Lexmark, I have found that a very simple print statement is sufficient; e.g., **lp:lp=/dev/lp1:sd=/usr/spool/lp1:mx#0:sh**.

14. As an aside, you will need a filter for printing ordinary non-PostScript text files in Linux or Unix. A major problem is converting the LineFeed (LF) that terminates lines in Unix or Linux to the CarriageReturn-LineFeed (CRLF) in DOS, Windows and Mac. If you don't correct it, you get what is known as the *staircase effect*, where the text prints zigzag for a bit and then stops. Depending on the printer, it requires a ˆ**[&k3G** or a ˆ**[&k2G** filter to change LF's to CRLF's. As an alternative, the switch from LF to CRLF can be put at the beginning of the text file. Or *cat* the text file with another file that contains the switch. For example, I have this alias in my *˜/.functions* file: **function rst { cat /home/rstairs $1 | lpr }**. It virtually prepends */home/rstairs* to any ASCII file that I print. It contains PCL code that switches the LF to CRLF and it prints the document with a 75 character right margin at 12 characters per inch. (TIPS: Change s12H to s16.6H for very small print. Change the *s0B* to *s3B* to print the text file in bold.) If the ASCII file is called *week.aug*, I'd type in an xterm: **rst week.aug**.

    ˆ[E
    ˆ[&k3G
    ˆ[(s12H
    ˆ[(s0B
    ˆ[&a75M
    ˆL

    If your printer isn't up and running, read about printing in Linux in *Linux Printing HOWTO guide* by Grant Taylor and Brian McCauley. It also has an excellent discussion on *ghostview*. It can be downloaded from *ftp://ftp.sunsite.unc.edu*. Or read the Printing Howto's ([Taylor96], [Komarinski96]) directly on the machine in the /usr/doc/faq/howto subdirectory.

15. If the file does not print, do the obvious—check that the printer is on, is connected to your machine and has paper. There is one condition that is a real bummer: the program finds no error and it produces a PostScript file that can be viewed. But the printer won't print it; that is, the instruction: **dvips practice.dvi | lpr** returns a message such as: **copy file is too large**. This has nothing to do with the printer as such, Adobe's PostScript or *dvips*. Instead it goes back to the days when printers were a lot slower, so a limit was put on the amount of blocks you were allowed to print. To stop the problem, go into */etc/printcap* and make sure that the *mx* parameter is set to zero, so that unlimited printing is allowed.

Chapter 7

DEALING WITH ERRORS RECORDED IN THE LOG

This chapter is to familiarize you with the error file. Refer back to it when you start doing markups. Get in the habit of doing a run through LaTeX whenever you finish a section or try some different type of markup. In an xterm, type: **latex** <*filename*>; e.g., **latex practice.tex**. Frequent runs help locate areas where mistakes lurk. Otherwise, if, for example, you start a list and don't terminate it, you may not find out about it until the **\end{document}** statement many pages downstream. The intermediate pages will be nicely formatted, including sections and chapters, which you might suppose would stop the runaway list.

I assume you are using LaTeX2ε, the latest version of LaTeX. Make sure there are no LaTeX files or packages from earlier versions that the program can access.

Initially, you can ignore statements about line length: overfull and underfull boxes. The program spouts comments on wrong length but it stops only at mistakes in syntax. You can get started on fixing the problem immediately by typing **x** a couple of times to get out of LaTeX. Or push the RETURN key to have the program continue processing for as long as it can. Or push **q** to make the program go into batch mode. In fact, you can get the program to write out as much as it can of the errors and comments without stopping for interactive chats if you write this in the preamble: **\batchmode**.

LaTeX will process the document and write the error into a log file—*practice.log* in our example.

7.1   Real Errors

1. If you run LaTeX and it stops with a **\stop**, the error is usually at the point where it stopped. If the error message is **runaway argument**, it is likely to be an earlier unpaired brace.

2. If the program ran through, examine the log file for errors. If you constructed a file in the previous section called *practice.tex*, the error file is called *practice.log*. Search out the exclamation marks, LaTeX́s subtle way of telling you there's a problem. The comment includes some of the offending text and its line number. Sometimes, however, the error might be a page or two off.

3. Errors in the Table of Contents (toc), List of Figures (lof) and List of Tables (lot) files and in captions will persist a run or two. If they have been corrected, run LaTeX a couple of times before bothering to examine the source file.

4. If you get a **TeX capacity exceeded, sorry [input stack size=300].** just after you did something very different, go back to that spot. Here are some possibilities:

   It it most likely that TeX didn't run out of space; you just had a runon that LaTeX terminated with this very scary statement. Make sure you have *all* your left delimiters properly paired, using the technique in #23, if need be.

   You can run out of space by writing a recursive definition such as this:

   ```
   \newcommand{\sweep}{\sweep{\sweep}}
   \sweep
   ```

   This will expand each sweep into the new definition that will expand into other sweeps— until the program runs out of space very quickly.

   You can make a particular page so complicated that you can't process it. You may not be able to print it either. Simplify.

   You really don't have enough memory for lavish processing. Before dumping cargo, make sure it is memory and not an ordinary error. Put a command like \clearpage in the text just before the point where the error message was issued. If the error goes away, you really don't have memory. So start dumping. These are things to try:

   Do sections in separate runs and put them into separate printouts; don't forget to establish the right page number at the beginning of each new segment. Copy your macro file that you use from one document to the next and store it. Trim the copy file to macros that you are currently using. If you defined some fancy frames and boxes, dump them when you are through using them; don't let them continue to take up memory. You may have used too many cross-references, so cut some of them out; insert the right numbers by hand the final run. Cut out the index and glossary for now. You can write a Table of Contents separately. Ignore pictures and graphs for now—they do soak up memory. Or photograph them and paste them in. (Many departments prefer this, anyways.) If the photograph is full-paged, print it separately and insert it—be sure to check page numbers. Shorten captions and (sub)section header text. (Probably a good idea, anyways.) Use fewer hyphenation commands and use a \\- in the source document as you need one. If all else fails, borrow a megacup of memory from a friend—run the full program on his machine. TEX and LATEX are available on all Unix and Linux machines and on many Mac's and PC's.

5. For each error message, go to the line number in the source document, and look at it carefully. By the way, it is useful to have a ˜/.emacs key to get to the line number in one stroke. You could, for example, write this in your home .emacs file:

(global-set-key [f19] 'goto-line) ;This is actually function key 2

Whenever you push F2, Emacs will ask what line number to go to and will get you there immediately.

6. If you are lucky (or a poor typist), the problem is a simple typing error. The instruction is spelled wrong. Or you added a colon to an \\item command in a list. Or there is an extra *s* on a newcommand alias. Or it should be plural, not singular. Or it should be lower case and you used an upper case letter. Run through the items, ridding them, where possible, of obvious typos.

7. **Extra alignment tab has been changed to \\cr** means you have a different number of text items on a line than the number of columns you have allotted.

8. Check that each \\verb has encapsulated just the text you want to show as a literal; check that it doesn't extend beyond a single line. (This is discussed in Section 19.1.) Check that you have paired each environment statement. A **\\begin{verbatim}** not properly terminated by a **\\end{verbatim}** will give problems until it is finally blocked (incorrectly) by another end statement. Remember that there can be no space between \\end and {verbatim}. Remember there can be no space between the brackets enclosing the components of a command; e.g., between the end of the optional bracket and the beginning of the brace argument. If you must split the command, use a % as the last character on the line that is split.

9. You wrote a \\ in between paragraphs to obtain an empty line between the paragraphs. This is a very common error. Substitute a **\par** or **\vspace**{<*amount*>}.

10. LaTeX-reserved characters need special treatment to write them as literal text. The program also will complain if the reserved character is written as a command but in the wrong context—in text mode, say, when it should be bracketed in math mode. (See Chapter 8.)

11. You tried to define an already defined command or environment with a *new* .. statement instead of a *renew* .. statement. Or you tried to use an environment that doesn't exist (probably a spelling error). Or you have written more (or less) arguments in a macro than you stated you would have.

12. **Missing number, treated as zero** means you didn't provide a number for a length measure. You may have left out a necessary argument. Also check you used the number zero, not uppercase o.

13. **Illegal unit of measure (pt inserted).** means you didn't provide a dimension for a length measure in the argument; e.g., you wrote **\hspace**{**4**} instead of **\hspace**{**4pc**}.

14. There are two math starting delimiters in a row without an intervening end delimiter. Or you didn't use an **\ensuremath** in a new command and the program toggled to the wrong mode.

15. Some instructions can only be used in the preamble: **\usepackage, \nofiles, \makeindex, \makeglossary, \includeonly**.

16. An *includegraphics* command without options took in a file that didn't have information on the size of the BoundingBox. Clear this up by adding BoundingBox information as an option.

17. Rerun LaTeX and look again at the shrunken error list. This time, make sure units match. You forgot one or the other of a brace pair. Or you forgot to terminate a list. Or you started a list with a **\begin**{**enumerate**} and ended it, many paragraphs later, with an **\end**{**itemize**}. Matching units is laborious, particularly when you have an enumeration inside a itemization list tucked inside a description list. The program will help you out, by pointing out inconsistencies.

18. You have a runaway argument error because you didn't complete a command argument. My most common mistake is forgetting the right brace that ends the footnote argument, if the last word in the argument requires a right brace. This is an example of the way it should read: \footnote{The complete list of font commands is in Chapter~\ref{ss:fonts}.}

19. Occasionally, you will study an error and see nothing wrong with the line. If you stop processing with an **x** and then view the printout, you may find processing actually stopped a page or two earlier. At the point of error, if you are lucky.

20. Any command with an optional argument in square brackets can be ambiguous in some context and prompt the program to declare it an error. For example, a \\[*length*] command expects a vertical length measure in the square brackets. It can be a source of confusion if a \\ without the optional length is followed by ordinary text; e.g., **...** \\ **[First:] The .....** Resolve this by bracing the actual text; e.g., **...** \\ **{[First:]} The ....**

    As another example, in a description list, initial text inside the optional bracket immediately after \item is printed in bold. It is not an error, but you won't get what you expect if there is no bolding instruction in brackets and the first word of the text is supposed to be in square brackets. **\item [First] Take...**, for example, can be mistaken for **\item** [*optional bolding*]. Again, surround ordinary text that immediately follows \item with braces; e.g., **\item {[First]} Take...**

21. Check that you did not write verbatim text (see Chapter 19) or a label (see Chapter 18) inside a command argument.

22. Incorrectly formatted labels are shown this way. **{}{{15.1}{98}}** below indicates Chapter 15, Section 1 on page 98. In an article, it would point to Section 15, Subsection 1 on page 98.

```
(med.aux (preface.aux) (part1.aux) (part2.aux)
! Missing \endcsname inserted.
<to be read again>
                    \protect
l.82 \newlabel{\nobreakspace  {}}{{15.1}{98}}
```

23. Eventually, there is an irreducable clump of 'weird errors'. Ignore them for the present, if LaTeX will let you. You may get lucky and they go away by themselves, as you rewrite. Or maybe small localized revisions will remove the problems. In the worst case, comment them out until you can resolve the errors. Eventually, you need to track them. Do this with binary splits. Write a **\end{document}** half way through the file.

    If the error persists, it means the error is closer to the top of the file. Put another **\end{document}** statement half way between the top and the last \end{document}.

    If the error goes away, it means the error is beyond the \end{document}. Put another **\end{document}** between the current end statement and the actual end of the document (or the previous end statement). Of course, you erase \end{document} statements that you have determined aren't involved.

    When you find the error, be sure to delete all the \end{document} statements, except the one at the end of the document.

7.2   Overfull And Underfull Lines And Pages

At some point—probably long after you have mastered most of the LaTeX commands—you'll decide it's time to attend to the too full and under full errors. Note that error commands begin with **h** for lines or horizontal space and **v** for pages or vertical space.

7.2.1   The overfull line

If you make *draft* an option in the document class assertion at the top of your manuscript, the program will print a black rectangle next to lines that bulge, making it easy for you to find overwide lines.

This next is an example of a LaTeX comment. Notice that LaTeX indicates hyphenation possibilities. To gauge the overage, recall that there are 72 points in an inch; so the text that annoyed the program, *rubber....measure*, is some .167 inches over.

```
Overfull \hbox (12.54883pt too wide) in paragraph at lines 3281--3292
\OT1/cmr/m/n/10 rub-ber. An ex-act met-ric is of course rigid, ab-so-lute.
But a mul-ti-ple of a flex-i-ble mea-sure|
 []
```

To deal with overwide lines, you need to understand the interaction between the *hyphenation rules* and *tolerance*.

Tolerance. The command is written as **\tolerance=#**, where # is the amount of right-side margin you allow TeX for widening the text line or loosening spacing between words without bringing ill-fitting text to your attention. Tolerance is maintained at 200 for most of this book. In Section 11.2.2, initially the log indicated that the *\large* example was 3 points over. So tolerance was changed to 600. This tolerance was continued until after the *\Huge* example, when it was reset to **\tolerance=200**.

Hyphenation Rule. LaTeX does normal hyphenating on the first pass. On the second pass, LaTeX doesn't hyphenate words followed by a large dash (e.g., *word—aside...*) or words that have already been hyphenated by LaTeX.

If, for the given tolerance, none of the hyphenation possibilities will produce a line within the currently set line limit, LaTeX declares it an overfull line.

An overfull line is corrected by finding some other hyphenation possibility or by increasing tolerance a little. Bear in mind that correcting the overfull box may result in a underfull box on the next line.[1]

These are several ways to try to correct the overfull box.

1. Hyphenate the last words on the line if it isn't split already. \- suggests a place to break the line. Thus:

   The MarkUp: ``XXXXXXXX....XXXXXX\-end\-of\-the\-long\-est\-word\-ever''

   The PrintOut: "XXXXXXXXXXXXXXXXXXXXXXXXXXXXXXXXXXXXXXXXXXXendofthe-longestwordever"

2. Line breaks are not used in math or box modes, only in text mode. The **\linebreak** command can be done as a demand or as a request.

   Demand \linebreak forces the program to justify the line and do an immediate line break.

   Request \linebreak[0] to \linebreak[4] are increasingly strong requests to break the line even inside a word, with [4] the equal of a demand.

   The MarkUp: ``XXXXXX....XXXXXX\linebreak[3]endofthelongestwordever''

   The PrintOut: "XXXXXXXXXXXXXXXXXXXXXXXXXXXXXXXXXXXXXXXXXXXXXXXXXX endofthelongestwordever"

3. If it is the last draft and you don't plan more rewriting, add your own hyphen and force an earlier line break in text mode with **\newline**. A newline command differs from the linebreak command in that it ends a line without justifying it. The \newline command has a shorter, more popular form—\\.

   The MarkUp: ``XXXX....XXXXXXXXXXXXXXXXendofthelongest\\wordever''

   The PrintOut: "XXXXXXXXXXXXXXXXXXXXXXXXXXXXXXXXXXXXXendofthelongest wordever"

4. Do a **\sloppy** declaration. **\fussy** restores the quest for interword perfection. This is used for a single paragraph or a single item at a time. A single paragraph can include an equation bracketed for running text. (See Section 21.1.) But it can't encompass a displayed equation. (See Section 21.2.)

---

[1] As you read this section, bear in mind the ancient truth I've just concocted: *The way to screw up something is to fix something else that's connected to it.*

The MarkUp:

```
{\sloppy The sloppy command will
break lines at the right margin
within its scope, but interwords on
the next line outside its scope may
be too loose. So use a blank line
at the end of the paragraph and
within the \textit{sloppy} scope.


}
\fussy
This is a new paragraph and it is
back to fussy.
```

The PrintOut:

The sloppy command will break lines at the right margin within its scope, but interwords on the next line outside its scope may be too loose. So use a blank line at the end of the paragraph and within the *sloppy* scope.

This is a new paragraph and it is back to fussy.

5. Write the entire paragraph in a sloppypar environment. It does the same as the \sloppy declaration.

The MarkUp:

```
\begin{sloppypar}
Write the paragraph text here. The
sloppypar environment provides the
equivalent of a blank line before
and after the text of the paragraph.
\end{sloppypar}

This new paragraph is no longer set
with sloppy interword spacing.
```

The PrintOut:

Write the paragraph text here. The sloppypar environment provides the equivalent of a blank line before and after the text of the paragraph.

This new paragraph is no longer set with sloppy interword spacing.

6. Change the tolerance of the interword spacing. Each font has its own ideal spacing as determined by the designer; e.g., it's 3.33 pts for Computer Modern Roman. Tolerance is zero if the line is at its ideal spacing. To give the program some latitude, you can increase the tolerance value to, say, 500, or even to 1000. Tolerance plateaus at 10000; i.e., values above that allow very bad lines to be printed without protest by the program. To set tolerance at 1000, type: **\tolerance=1000**. (*tolerance* is a TeX command and not a LaTeX command; which is why there is an equal sign and a value that is not braced.)

7. Increase the amount of text that is allowed to stick out horizontally beyond the set margin by increasing the horizontal fuzzy margin tolerance, which is initially around a point (1/723 inch). For example, to increase tolerance to around 1/64th of an inch, type: **\hfuzz=0.016in**. (This is also a TeX command, not a LaTeX command.)

8. Occasionally, lines in almost an entire paragraph appear to have escaped justification. First, check that words are not mispelled. If the log file shows the program has proper hyphenation for the paragraph, the likely culprit is a low tolerance level, which was somehow introduced. A level of zero or close to zero tolerance allows no margin for expansion.

7.2.2 The underfull line

Given a linebreak request or demand, the program will justify the line up to the break, even though, on the next line, this may mean an ugly stretching of the few remaining words on the next line. When there is too much space between words on a line, LaTeX alerts you. This is an example of a typical underfull line statement.

```
Underfull \hbox (badness 10000) in paragraph at lines 337--348
[]\OT1/cmtt/m/n/10 ordinary text. Even a great    many
```

These are ways to prevent gaps between the words:

A tilde This will keep two words together with a single space between them.

\mbox{} This keeps the text that is the argument of the \mbox command intact.

\nolinebreak This prevents a linebreak. Like the \linebreak command, it has both request and command formats. If you use it, the next few lines may need modifying as well.

7.2.3 The overfull page

Figures and tables are not broken across pages and you may have an figure or table too long even for a full page. The program alerts you that there's a problem; e.g., *Float too large for page by 121.8055pt on input line 250* . It may help to print the particular figure or table in landscape mode. Or try splitting the figure into two figures. Or fake the figure format as we did with Figure 4.1 by writing ordinary text and adding your own caption number. If there are several figures in the same chapter, you will, however, also need to readjust the figure number counter (see Section 30.1.) Or use the *longtable* package, shown in Table 16.9 in Section 16.3.2, for overlong tables.

The program chops the page, pushing the final line of the paragraph to the next page. Or it finishes the page with a Section header, with the text of the section placed on the next page.

Examine the page. See if you can shave some vertical space. For example, writing **\vspace{-1pc}** just before a \section command will shave off enough space for an additional line.

Play with the **\pagebreak** and **\nopagebreak** commands. These do for pages what the linebreak and nolinebreak commands (see above) do for lines, with the same demand and request formats.

See Section 31.4 for ways of breaking the page gracefully. As example, **\enlargethispage** will forceably extend a page. This will make room for another line:

```
......text.....
\enlargethispage*{12pt}
......text.........
```

If the program simply couldn't find a place to break ordinary text, use a **\newpage** command to force a break. If you need to move floats (figures and tables) at the bottom of the page, try a **\clearpage**, which will break the page at that spot and put the floats on the next page(s).

7.2.4   The underfull page

Commands forcing a figure in a particular place may create underfull pages. This can often be corrected by using the *afterpage* command with the figure. This and other techniques for handling figures can be found in Section 16.1.1.

A **\raggedbottom** may produce short text. But the program does not alert you; you need to examine the document pages yourself. Try adding a **\nopagebreak** before the point that the page was cut. And then do a **\pagebreak** a little further on.

Or try a **\flushbottom** command somewhere on the page previous to the sliced area. Downstream, in the text that will be on the next printed page, revert to the regular format with a **\raggedbottom** command.

7.2.5   Other alerts

The error file will tell you if you set an option in the document class in the preamble and then didn't use it in the document.

It will warn you if you defined a label more than once.

It will warn you if you reference a label that you didn't define.

'h' float specifier changed to 'ht'. [39] [40]) [41] (part2.tex [42 warns that a floating object such as a figure or table was moved to the next page.

If the style and size of the font you specify isn't available, TEX automatically substitutes another font and records the transaction in the log. This is usually quite acceptable. This next alert notes a font substitution that took place on page 60, line 398.

```
LaTeX Font Info:   Font shape 'OMS/cmr/m/n' in size <7> not available
(Font)             Font shape 'OMS/cmsy/m/n' tried instead on input line 398.
[60]
```

Part III.

WRITING LATEX.

Understanding Markup Instructions

Open your practice file: *practice.tex*.

The first significant line (**documentclass**{**article**}) marks the beginning of the preamble. The preamble is the region between that line and the line that reads: **begin**{**document**}. Store new commands in the preamble. You call necessary support files and convenience packages from the preamble. You make global changes in the appearance of your document by writing the appropriate commands in the preamble.

You write and format your text between the **begin**{**document**} and **end**{**document**}. No matter what the document class, you always use this environment pair.

The program disregards any text beyond the **end**{**document**} command, so at the beginning, place such a statement after only a few sections, and concentrate on fixing errors.

As you mark up *practice.tex*, practice labeling captions, figures, tables and other numbered objects that you refer to in the text. Use a different nickname for each label. Recall that you label an object this way: **label**{<*nickname*>}; for example, **section**{**Development from 1910-1930**} **label**{**teendev**}.

You reference the labeled object by writing: **ref**{<*nickname*>}. In our example, you might write: **Refer to Section~\ref{teendev}**.

Chapter 8, the first chapter in this Part, begins with a discussion of the single characters that play specific roles in LATEX markups. It also shows you how to write AKA's for them and how to use them as ordinary characters. Chapter 9 concentrates on the syntax of the generic instruction formats—commands, declarations and environments—that were first defined in Chapter 2. Chapter 10 provides examples of how to write your own instructions.

Chapter 8

LATEX-RESERVED SINGLE-CHARACTER COMMANDS

8.1 Single-Character Command Symbols

LATEX reserves ten punctuation characters as LATEX instructions. To say that LATEX *reserves* certain punctuation marks means that LATEX automatically reads these punctuation marks as markup symbols. This section discusses how these punctuation marks function in LATEX. Section 8.2 shows you what you must do if you want to use them as ordinary punctuation.

The symbols are:

```
# $ % & _ { } ~ ^ \
```

Unlike the single-word instructions, single-character commands do not begin with a backslash. They are commands in their unadorned state. In fact, in a few cases, you need to do some hefty typing to use them as literal punctuation. Forgetting to prepend a backslash is a common error in writing characters such as # and $ as literals. They are used in these ways:

| # | The *hashmark*, teamed with a number, acts as a placeholder in macro definitions. In this example, each hashmark-number combination indicates where variable text will be entered. If the definition is:

`\newcommand{\email}[3]{NickName: #1. FullName: #2. Email: #3.}.`

and in the text, we write: **\email{Lew}{L.E.Lewis}{lel@erols.com}**

The PrintOut reads: NickName: Lew. Full Name: L.E.Lewis. Email: lel@erols.com.

| $ | The *dollar sign* acts as both left and right bracket in math mode.

| % | The *percent sign* acts as a comment signal. Any text on the line after the % is ignored. Moreover, if it's the last character on the line, the End-Of-Line symbol is ignored, so the last word on one line and the first word on the next line run together.[1] This is often important in writing commands and macros whose components are not supposed to have spaces between them. Ending lines with a %'s allows us to chop a long command into convenient line segments. Yet the end of one line continues without a seam into the next.

Using the % can be a source of error if it erases a symbol needed for correct syntax. In this example, the right brace that ends the argument to the *\textbf* command will be ignored by the program because it follows the % on the line. This next causes a runon error.

\textbf{Use the box command. % Give fbox example.}

| & | The *ampersand* acts as a column tab in arrays and in tables made in the tabular environment.

| _ | The *underline* creates a subscript in math mode; e.g., `$x_{2}$` would be printed as x_2.

| {} | The *left and right braces* enclose command arguments.

| ~ | The *tilde* creates an unbreakable space in a text phrase. The word before the tilde and the word after the tilde together with the intervening space are treated as a single word. In this example, because the program can not break at the space, which it would ordinarily do, it crowds some of the line text and hyphenates. (We use some X padding to force the text toward the end of the line.) Notice the sentence contains

---

[1]Recall that extra spaces between words are ignored. In this case, it means deleting all spaces after the % on one line *up to* the first significant character on the next line.

two tildes that will keep the 'No. 10 Downing' together as a unit. 'Street' is not part of the unit.

XXXXXX XXX XXX XXX XXX XXX XXX XXX XXXX xxxNo. 10 Downing Street is typed as **XXX...xxxNo.˜10˜Downing Street**.

| ˆ | The *circumflex* creates a superscript in math mode. To produce x^2, type: x^{2}.

| \ | The *backslash* signals the start of any and all instructions, aside from the single-character commands. A double backslash (\\) is used at the end of a source line to force the program to start a new line in the printout. A double backslash followed by an asterisk (*) forces the program to start a new line but NOT to start a new page in the printout, even if it's an appropriate place to do so.

8.2 Writing Special Symbols As Ordinary Text

Most special symbols print as ordinary text if prepended by a backslash.

| \\# | \\$ | \\% | \\& | \\˜ | _ | \\ˆ | \\{ | \\} |

| {} | To use the left and right braces as visible characters in math modes, enclose them in $ brackets and prepend the backslash; Thus, to print: m = $\{xy\}$, type: **m = $\{xy\}$**.

| ˜ | A literal tilde is \symbol{'176} in octal, \symbol{126} in decimal and \symbol{"7E} in hex. The Double Quote Key is ordinarily *SHIFT* '. But if Emacs is in TeX mode, write a keyboard Double Quote as: *CTRLq SHIFT DoubleQuoteKey*. Prepending a tilde with a backslash places it over the next character.

| ˆ | The ˆ is part of a control character in program code and a circumflex in ordinary text. To markup a literal circumflex in octal, type \symbol{'136}. It is \symbol{94} in decimal and \symbol{"5E} in hexadecimal. You would write crême[2] as:

---

[2]The \hspace command shifts its argument 4 points to the left. As a result, with the current font and size, the circumflex appears over the **e**, as it should. You could also use the alias for the circumflex taken from the next section and write: **cre\hspace{-4pt}\UA me**.

cre\hspace{-4pt}\symbol{94}me in decimal

cre\hspace{-4pt}\symbol{'136}me in octal

cre\hspace{-4pt}\symbol{"5E}me in hex.

$\boxed{\backslash}$ For a literal backslash, type: $\backslash$. For printing, where you want it to look like a backslash without it being the start of an actual command,[3] this looks better: \texttt{\symbol{'134}}.

Several symbols are not reserved, but participate in LATEX commands and hence, they can be caught in unexpected interactions.

$\boxed{[\,]}$ The square brackets are not reserved characters but they are used in LATEX commands to denote optional arguments, such as the bolded text in a description list. For example: **\item [Method I.]** *<text>*...

It is an error to use a left bracket as an ordinary character immediately after \item in a description list. (See Section 7.1, Item 20 for the explanation.)

$\boxed{<>|}$ the angle brackets ($<$ and $>$) and the cut line ($|$) are not reserved but they must be written in math mode. For example: "If $x < y$ and $y < z$ then $x < z$.". This is typed as:

```
``If $x < y$ and $y < z$ then $x < z$.''
```

If you need to use the cut line or the angle brackets as ordinary text, treat them as if they were in math mode: delimit each individual bracket with $$; for example: `$<$Smith et al$>$`, which prints out as: $<$Smith et al$>$. The next section presents simple aliases for these symbols.

You can sandwich code and other large blocks of text in a verbatim environment. This will typeset exactly what you typed, so you do not have the extra work of rewriting each special character so that the program will know the symbol is ordinary text. The disadvantage (not a major one) is that the printout font is typewriter; you have no selection. (See Section 19.1 for additional verbatim environments that are less restrictive.)

You can create aliases for characters such as the tilde, the backslash and the braces. Substitutions for these characters are shown in the next section.

---

[3]See Section 8.4 on using the literal backslash to mimic a command backslash.

8.3 Writing Aliases For Single Character Commands

This 4-column table shows how to create and use abbreviations and/or aliases for symbols that are grammatically difficult to write in LaTeX. The *newcommand* command creates an alias—another command name—for a defined command, or a group of associated commands plus text. As used here, the format is:

\newcommand{$<$\alias$>$}{$<$defined command$>$}.

Column 1. A common name for the symbol.

Column 2. The symbol and its alias. For example, the complex way of writing a literal tilde is replaced by the \TLD command. You can of course rename it as you wish.

Column 3. The Markup of an example of the symbol's usage.

Column 4. The Printout of the example in column 3.

NAME	NEW COMMAND!	THE MARKUP	THE PRINTOUT
BackSlash	\NC{\BS}{$\backslash$}	Commands start with \BS	Commands start with \
Left Brace	\NC{\LB}{$\{$}	Args start with \LB.	Args start with {
Right Brace	\NC{\RB}{$\}$}	Args end with \RB.	Args end with }
Tilde	\NC{\TLD}{\symbol{'176}}	\TLD 5, \TLD A.	˜5, ˜A.
Cut Line	\NC{\CL}{$|$}	Use \CL\ as a boundary line	Use | as a boundary line
Left Angle	\NC{\LT}{$<$$}‡	\LT brackets text on the left.	<brackets text on the left.
Right Angle	\NC{\RT}{$>$}	\RT brackets text on the right.	>brackets text on the right.
Circumflex	\NC{\UA}{\symbol{'136}}	\UA D stops the flow	^D stops the flow.
A Space	\NC{\SP}{\ }	Force a space after the \RB\SP.	Force a space after the } .
en dash	--	Between numbers: 1--10	Between numbers:1–10
em dash	---	As an aside---such as this	As an aside—such as this
Lft SingleQuote	\NC{\LSQ}{'}	She said, \LSQ So?	She said, 'So?
Lft DbleQuote	\NC{\LDQ}{''}	\LDQ She said, So?	"She said, So?
Rt SingleQuote	\NC{\RSQ}{'}	She said, So?\RSQ \BS	She said, So?'
Rt DbleQuote	\NC{\RDQ}{''}	She said, So?\RDQ	She said, So?"
All 4 above:		\LDQ She said, \RSQ So?\RSQ\,\RDQ*	"She said, 'So?' "

! To save column space, we wrote an abbreviated substitute (*NC*) for the \newcommand command itself. The command is: **\newcommand{\NC}{\newcommand}**

‡ Commands end in spaces or the backslash of the next command. To print the angle brackets, you would write: **\LT text\RT**. You need a space after *LT*, otherwise the program will interpret it as **\LTtext**, an unknown command. *LT* and *text* will be joined in the printout: *<text>*.

* The \, (the backslash comma combination) is used to force a small space between the single and double quotes.

8.4   Meta Level Mimicking Of Text Commands

There is no set of characters universally reserved for commands. So every computer language and every computer program, and LATEX is no exception, is forced to reserve some ordinary text symbols for special use. What is ordinary in one program is special in another. For example, writing an ordinary *DOS* or *Windows* address in a document—\home\letters\Sam, say—can be confused with a LATEX command.

An extreme example of the overload of some ordinary characters occurs when you are writing about actual LATEX commands in LATEX. A backslash followed immediately by text triggers a program action if it is a defined command or an error message if it isn't defined. When writing markups to illustrate LATEX syntax, I needed a way of writing the backslash as an ordinary character so the program would treat it like ordinary text. At the same time, the text had to look like a command, but, of course, not be one. Enter the \BS command, which is defined in Section 8.2 as the backslash. It tells the program to write a non-command backslash.[4] The other essential characters are the brace pair. To make them visible as ordinary characters, they need to be prepended by a \. When the text is printed, the backslash and braces appear to be actual commands.

This next markup uses an excerpt from Figure 3.3 to illustrate commands that show commands. The backslash makes a literal of the percent sign.

The MarkUp:

```
\textbf{\BS begin\{document\}}   \% END OF PREAMBLE. \\
\textbf{\BS maketitle}           \% This produces the title.
```

The PrintOut:
\begin{document} % END OF PREAMBLE.
\maketitle % This produces the title.

---

[4]Other ways of forcing the program to ignore what looks like a command are to be found in Chapter 19.2. The advantage of the literal backslash is that it allows a variety of font shapes.

Mock commands can become very complex. The next markup highlights how a command can be articulated into components, to clarify command grammar. Assuming that the reader is given a key to the typographic conventions, different fonts can convey different messages. We use LaTeX syntax, but the principle can be applied to parsing any grammatical construct.

The command itself is shown in bold. Various ways to write placeholders are shown: the slant font of the environment name placeholder; the small caps of the *title* command argument; the angle brackets and italics after the *chapter* command; and the upright caps of the options in the *documentclass* command. Italics or slants are used to indicate exact names or generic names.

The MarkUp:

```
\textbf{\BS textbf\{\BS maketitle\}}
\textbf{\BS begin}\{\prsl{NameHere}\}
\textbf{\BS begin}\{\prit{document}\}
\textbf{\BS title}\{\prsc{TitleName}\}
\textbf{\BS title}\{\prit{Writing
   in \LaTeX}\}
\textbf{\BS chapter}\{\textit{\LT
   text\RT}\}
\textbf{\BS chapter}\{\textit{New
   Titles}\}
\textbf{\BS documentclass}[\LT\prsc{options}\RT]\{\textit{article}\}
\textbf{\BS documentclass}[\prsl{draft,11pt}]\{\textit{article}\}
```

The PrintOut:

\textbf{\maketitle}
\begin{*NameHere*}
\begin{*document*}
\title{TITLENAME}
\title{*Writing in LaTeX*}
\chapter{<*text*>}
\chapter{*New Titles*}
\documentclass[<OPTIONS>]{*article*}
\documentclass[*draft,11pt*]{*article*}

Chapter 9

SINGLE-WORD INSTRUCTIONS

Instructions preinstalled in LaTeX are single words prepended by a backslash. The general classes are: commands, declarations and environments. These were defined in Section 2.2. This chapter will explore the three formats, using font instructions to illustrate syntax. We begin with some basic information about fonts.

9.1   Font Features

serif font, such as the font used in the body of this book, has feet; i.e., short horizontal lines at the edges of many of the letters. It is also known as *roman*, hence the command: *\textrm{...}*. It is classic and is almost always the one chosen for textbooks and reports. Any font having *times*, *roman* or *dutch* in its name is likely to be footed. *sans serif* font has no feet and is commonly used in advertising copy and more 'modern' printing. It also creates attractive headlines and headers, even when the body text is footed. Any font labeled *swiss* or *helvetia* is probably non-footed. Within these two broad categories, there is a multitude of font designs, some proprietry, others freely available from the Net. Basic LaTeX provides footed, non-footed and typewriter fonts that blend well. They have a large range of size and shape and line thickness variations. Even if you use LaTeX with no font modification, they are probably sufficient for most of your documents.

Before we examine LaTeX command types, add this next block to the top of your *template.tex* and *practice.tex* files. By default, LaTeX documents utilize the three font families subsumed under the rubric *Computer Modern*, the font style designed by Donald Knuth and supplied with TeX. Each family contains a medium and a thick line version for each character. And each character comes in various shapes. The default font is *serif*, *upright* and *medium*.

These next instructions provide the means to manipulate the appearance of the printout. Later, you may wish to replace the default Computer Modern fonts with other fonts that also come with the program. These same instructions will manipulate text with any of these replacement fonts. (See Chapter 11.) Note that these instructions apply to fonts in both text and box modes. Math mode has its own set of default fonts.

```
%[Font Families]
%serif (default):     Command: \textrm{...}. Declaration: \rmfamily
%sans serif:          Command: \textsf{...}. Declaration: \sffamily
%typewriter:          Command: \texttt{...}. Declaration: \ttfamily

%[Font Series] (Line Thickness)
%bold:                Command: \textbf{...}. Declaration: \bfseries
%medium (default):    Command: \textmd{...}. Declaration: \mdseries

%[Font Shapes]
%upright (default): Command: \textup{...}. Declaration: \upshape
%italic:            Command: \textit{...}. Declaration: \itshape
%slant:             Command: \textsl{...}. Declaration: \slshape
%small cap:         Command: \textsc{...}. Declaration: \scshape
%emphasis:          Command: \emph{...}.   Declaration: \em
```

When a command argument terminates, the text is again under the influence of the most recent command that *still has control*. In these next examples, the defaults apply; that is, if no specific command holds sway, the text will be printed in serif, upright in shape and with medium line thickness. Notice that italic and slant are shapes, but bolding is not. A bold line is thicker than a medium series line.

For this next example, I typed some unadorned text inside the **\begin{document}** and **\end{document}**, then added some ordinary font commands. Practice some of these commands on some familiar text of your own.

The MarkUp:

```
\textbf{SHOW SHAPES:}
The comparison \textit{algorithm} places
\textup{the key-struct} alphabetically \textsl{in its proper place
among the} list of \textsc{structs, using the
stru}\textit{ct's}\footnote{Notice that we changed font in the
middle of a word. } \textit{pprev} \textsc{and pnext pointers},
\emph{which contain the addresses}

\textbf{SHOW FAMILIES:}
\textsf{of the previous and
\textrm{next structs in the list,}
\texttt{respectively. So the keys are always in alphabetic order}

\textbf{SHOW SERIES:}
\textmd{traversing the list} \textbf{of structs from
pA--$>$pnext--\RT pnext--\RT pnext\ldots pZ.}
```

The PrintOut:

SHOW SHAPES: The comparison *algorithm* places the key-struct alphabetically *in its proper place among the* list of STRUCTS, USING THE STRU*ct's*[1]*pprev* AND PNEXT POINTERS, *which contain the addresses*

SHOW FAMILIES: of the previous and next structs in the list, respectively.   So the keys are always in alphabetic order

SHOW SERIES: traversing the list **of structs from pA–>pnext–>pnext–>pnext...pZ.**

The next section continues the discussion of LaTeX instructions—commands, declarations and environments—begun in Section 2.2.

9.2   Commands

Commands begin with a backslash. A command is composed of alphabetic letters only.[2] The same command word is a different command in upper case than in lower case.

---

[1]Notice that we changed font in the middle of a word.

[2]The @ is frequently used in internal commands in **.sty* and **.cls* files, to prevent collision with your commands.

9.2.1   The LaTeX repertoire of commands

A classic LaTeX command is always bound to the braced argument to its right. The argument is the territory in which the command can operate; that is to say, any LaTeX-defined
command is capable of changing the appearance of the text inside its adjoining argument.
The argument area is usually fairly small, but it can be as much a paragraph in length.[3]

A simple example of this format is: \textit{this is a string.}

This tells the program that the text in the braced area is to be written in italic until or unless
some other instruction on font shape intervenes. Otherwise the text will be written in italics
up to the right brace.

Several commands may act on the same piece of text. In a complex command, with multiple
commands and complicated instructions in its argument, it may, in fact, be difficult to
identify the end of a command. Nevertheless, the rule is the same as with a single simple
command.

**The impact of a command is restricted to the braced
domain that constitutes its argument.**

**If a piece of text is within the domain of several com-
mands, the innermost command overrides the outer
command(s) during the time it holds reign.**

In the next three examples, the source text in written in outline format, to make clear what
commands are within what commands.

For comparison, the markup for case *a* below would usually be written this way:

```
\textsc{Here's smallcapped stuff. \textit{this
text is italicized.} This is smallcapped.} This is outside the
domain of the smallcap argument.
```

---

[3]Of course the markup paragraph when printed can look like several paragraphs if blank lines are introduced
by adding, for example, \\[**1pc**] at the end of some of the words.

In case *a* the *\textsc* command extends over the entire argument that follows. However, while it is in force, the *\textit* argument within the borders of small cap's argument override *\textsc*. In case *b*, a hierarchy of arguments override the smallcap effect for a time, but smallcap does not stop operating until it reaches the end of its own territory.

In both *a* and *b*, the text is smallcapped to the right-side edge of the smallcap argument. In both cases, other commands within the smallcap argument temporarily dominate.

In both cases *b* and *c*, the scope of the command appears to be partially violated. In case *b*, when the italic command is interrupted by the bold command, the text is both bolded and italicized. In case *c*, when the bold command is interrupted by the italic command, the text is both italicized and bolded. There is no contradiction; bold is not a font shape; it is in a different category—it is a font series. The bold series can only be countermanded within its domain by a medium series command. Any of the shape types can be mixed with bold—bold-slant, bold-italic, and so forth.

case a. *Markup:*

```
\textsc
   {
   Here's smallcapped stuff.
   \textit
      {
      this text is italicized.
      }
   This is smallcapped.
   }
This is outside the domain of the smallcap argument.
```

The PrintOut: HERE'S SMALLCAPPED STUFF. *this text is italicized.* THIS IS SMALLCAPPED. This is outside the domain of the smallcap argument.

case b. *Markup:*

```
\textsc
   {
   Here's smallcapped stuff.
   \textit
```

```
        {
        A little italic
        \textbf
           {
           interrupted by bold
           }
        and back to italic.
        }
     This is smallcapped.
     }
This is outside the domain of the smallcap argument.
```

The PrintOut: HERE'S SMALLCAPPED STUFF. *A little italic **interrupted by bold** and back to italic.* THIS IS SMALLCAPPED. This is outside the domain of the smallcap argument.

case c. *Markup:*

```
\textsc
     {
     Here's smallcapped stuff.
     \textbf
        {
        A little bold
        \textit
           {
           interrupted by italic
           }
        and back to bold.
        }
     This is smallcapped.
     }
This is outside the domain of the smallcap argument.
```

The PrintOut: HERE'S SMALLCAPPED STUFF. **A LITTLE BOLD** *interrupted by italic* **AND BACK TO BOLD.** THIS IS SMALLCAPPED. This is outside the domain of the smallcap argument.

To sum up, even a simple LaTeX command argument may itself contain declarations and other commands. As case *a* shows, the command may be overridden by instructions within the argument; in this case, the text is within the territory of both the small cap and the italics. The rule is: if two contradictory instructions both have command of the text, the program obeys the innermost instruction—the one nearest the text and to the left of it. In this case the text is italicized.

As you might suspect, a piece of text might become complexly crisscrossed with brace demarcators and markup instructions. Probably the most egregious error is not pairing one of the sets of braces. Be prepared to spend some of your editing time in counting and matching up left and right brace partners, an activity that makes keeping track of a slew of kindergardeners on a day trip seem a picnic.

9.2.2 User-created new commands

A powerful LaTeX feature is the *newcommand* facility, which gives you the ability to create new commands. Basically, these commands are constructed from previously defined LaTeX instructions and/or your own new commands like a large shape from small lego pieces. For example, this is a legitimate new command that makes use of *\textbf{...}* plus *\hspace{...}*, a command that forces space in the printed text, and *\today*, a command that writes today's date *in situ*. It is called *STAMP*. The name of the new command is the first argument of *\newcommand*. The sequence of commands that compose **STAMP** make up *newcommand*'s second argument and are written within a pair of encasing braces. The terminal % in the second argument keeps the components in the definition together without spaces intervening.

The MarkUp:

```
\newcommand{\STAMP}{\hspace{.5in}%
\textbf{\today\hspace{.5in}Findings:}\hspace{.5in}}
```

```
\STAMP
```

The PrintOut: **July 11, 1998**   **Findings:**

Note that once written and ready for use, the STAMP command does not have the look of the classic LaTeX command. In fact the STAMP command looks like a declaration, even though it is limited in its scope as is the typical LaTeX command.

The definition of a more general user-generated command can contain actual declarations and be wedded to specific environments, so writing a new command presupposes the ability to handle the basic instruction types. We will spend the rest of this chapter talking about declarations and environments, deferring discussion of the structure of a general new command. In the next chapter, we will show how to define a new command and how to write a reusable integrated instruction—the *macro*.

9.3   Declarations

A simple declaration begins with a backslash and may appear in the preamble or anywhere within an unlabeled pair of braces or within the argument of a command or within the domain of an environment. It is composed of upper or lower case alphabetic letters and is terminated by an End-Of-Line, a space, other punctuation or the backslash of the next command.

The declaration is limited by the right-side boundary of the unit in which it lives. So a declaration asserted close to the beginning of the file just after the **\begin{document}** statement may be viable until the end of the document. Or, at the least, until it is superceded by another declaration that affects the same print feature.

An instruction about font size can be neutralized by another instruction on font size but is not affected by a command or declaration that operates on font shape. A font size command can override a font size declaration of the same type; the reverse is also true. In short, size instructions work on size; shape instructions work on shape.

If the declaration is part of a hierarchy of commands within an environment, it can be temporarily neutralized by a declaration or a command that: (a) affects the same text feature as it does and (b) has the pertinent text in its scope and is closer to that text. Downstream, at the end of the countervailing instruction, the declaration is again in force until the end of its own territory. When you use an instruction involving a declaration, the implications for a specific piece of text may not always be immediately obvious.

Declarations can be scattered throughout the document.

Declaration without a value. These are ordinary LaTeX declarations. In this example, \upshape instructs the program to use ordinary upright characters in the text that follows, until instructed otherwise. This is temporarily ignored as the program enters an unlabeled unit that forces it to use a different font shape. But when it exits, the *\upshape* instruction is again in force. It is not a toggle. The upright font declaration is, in the example, first superceded by the italicized declaration, **\itshape**, and then by **\scshape**, which is in force until it in turn is overturned by the later **\upshape** declaration.

The MarkUp:

```
\upshape
Here's some ordinary text.
{\itshape Italicize this text.}
This text is outside the previous unit.
\scshape
SmallCaps supercedes the upright shape.
\upshape
```

The PrintOut:

Here's some ordinary text. *Italicize this text.* This text is outside the previous unit. SMALLCAPS SUPERCEDES THE UPRIGHT SHAPE.

Declaration with a value. These are TeX declarations that can be directly used in LaTeX, As an example, **\tolerance=500** instructs the program to stretch spaces between words on a line. *tolerance* values are not expressed in any unit. However, ordinarily, when referencing a font feature or a location, values must be labeled. They may be in points (pt), picas (pc), inches (in), ems (em), and so forth. For example, **\parindent=0pc**.

9.4 Environments

An environment is a unit delimited by a pair of begin and end commands, rather than by braces. The begin-end pair are named, thus:

\begin{*<EnvironmentName>*}...\end{*<EnvironmentName>*}

Each environment has a unique name, just as each defined command has a unique name, one defined by you or by LaTeX. You can write a large number of declarations and commands between the \begin and the \end statements.

In point of fact, you can create an unnamed unit by enclosing a set of declarations and commands together with text inside a pair of left-right braces. The advantage of the named environment construction is that you can use it over and over again.

The environment construction is unrestricted in size. An environment unit may contain environment units, which themselves contain multiple units, to considerable depth. Indeed, this entire document, except for its preamble, is written within a single overall unit:

\begin{document}

WRITE THE MSS HERE

\end{document}

9.4.1   Using an environment whose name is a defined declaration

We can often put together an environment from a defined declaration; no additional work is necessary.[4] If, say, we wanted a section of text written in slant, we write the appropriate environment just by giving it the name *slshape*, as in this example:

The MarkUp:

```
\begin{slshape}
The information can be supplied on the command line. If the name of
the MEDLINE database and the field types to be indexed are not
included on the command line, they will be requested interactively.
\end{slshape}
```

The PrintOut: The information can be supplied on the command line. If the name of the MEDLINE database and the field types to be indexed are not included on the command line, they will be requested interactively.

---

[4]Any of the font shape declarations can be used as an environment name. On the other hand, the **\centering** command becomes **\begin{center}...\end{center}**.

These are the elements of the environment.

\begin   The beginning of the environment.

\end   The end of the environment.

slshape   The name of the environment.

The advantage of writing a section of text in the environment format is that the section is self-contained; in this example, if we move it, it will still print in slant. Of course we can achieve the same effect by prefacing a section of text with a \slshape declaration. But if we move the section elsewhere and forget to bring along the slant declaration, the text will be printed in whatever style controls the new area. And we might unintentionally print the text left behind in slant. By incorporating the text in the environment format, we can control how a section of the document will be printed, no matter where we relocate it.

9.4.2   Constructing an environment from an existing environment

Environments are often created by coat-tailing onto an existing environment. For example, the **\begin{enumerate} \end{enumerate}** environment lists and numbers items.[5] Suppose we wanted to list and number a group of programs in scriptsize font. We would create a new environment by means of the *newenvironment* command, whose format is:

```
\newenvironment{<NewEnvironmentName>}%
{\begin{<OldEnvironmentName>}<Added Commands>}%
{\end{<OldEnvironmentName>}}⁶
```

In this case, we are calling the new environment *ProgramNames*. As in all LATEX commands, case is important. ProgramNames can not be written as programnames or PROGRAMNAMES.

The MarkUp:

```
\newenvironment{ProgramNames}%
```

---

[5]Lists are discussed in Chapter 14. For now, it is sufficient to know that the three named LATEX lists are: enumerate, itemize and description. Each item in the list begins with the \item command.

[6]You can redefine the newenvironment name by means of the **\renewenvironment** command, which has the same structure as the **\newenvironment** command.

```
{\begin{enumerate}\scriptsize}
{\end{enumerate}}
```

This is an example of ProgramNames usage:

The MarkUp:

```
\begin{ProgramNames}
\item alp sorts any size file, any size record.
\item alp.obs sorts any \# records; record size to 7K chars.
\item alp.exe sorts files with up to 50,000 records.
\end{ProgramNames}
```

The PrintOut:

1. alp sorts any size file, any size record.

2. alp.obs sorts any # records; record size to 7K chars.

3. alp.exe sorts files with up to 50,000 records.

9.4.3   Creating environments from scratch

Actually, new environments can't be created *ex nihilo.* You can't say:

WRONG: \newenvironment{newname}{\begin{newname}}{\end{newname}}

You can, however, define a very simple new command—*tr* in the example—and immediately write an actual **\begin{tr}**..**\end{tr}** environment. What's more interesting, you can base a *\newenvironment* command on it. As in this example:

Step 1. Invent a new command; e.g. \newcommand{\tr}{}

Step 2. The *tr* environment is immediately usable as is. Fill it with variable (changeable) text each time you use it; e.g.,

> \begin{tr}
> *This is some text in italics.*
> \end{tr}

Step 3. A new environment can be based on the newly created command (Step 1) and the environment constructed from it (Step 2). The new environment may contain fixed text, as in this example. By fixed text, we mean that the text will be printed every time the *ttr* environment is used.

```
\newenvironment{ttr}{\begin{tr}
\textit{This is enough.}\\
This stays as it is.\\
\textsf{This is written in sans serif.}\\[.5pc] }
{\end{tr}}
```

Usage. *The MarkUp:*

```
\begin{ttr}
\textbf{END OF EXAMPLE.}
\end{ttr}
```

The PrintOut: This is enough.
This stays as it is.
This is written in sans serif.

END OF EXAMPLE.

9.4.4 Trouble spots in creating a new environment

We use the *ProgramNames* environment in Section 9.4.2 above as example. In creating a new environment, take care in these places:

1. The NAME of the new environment does NOT begin with a backslash.

2. The new instruction on font size (*\scriptsize*) is added after **\begin{enumerate}** and the whole *begin* complex is wrapped in a pair of braces, making it a single entity.

3. The **\end{enumerate}** statement is also cocooned as a single entity. It can contain additional fixed text and font-changing instructions, but it's best not to tamper with the simple **\end{enumerate}** until you know what you're doing. Experiment.

A major advantage of this type of construction is its flexibility. You can write a simple new environment like *ProgramNames* and add different text and even other instructions within the new environment each time it is used. In our example, the text will always be in script size. But each time you use the construct, you could add other instructions on font shape or not. Internal instructions can be long and complicated or not, depending on what is needed.

Alternatively, you can construct an elaborate environment like *ttr* and reuse it as is. Or add text and other instructions.

To use a new environment to best advantage requires the writing of a 'macro', a procedure explained in the next chapter.

Chapter 10

NEWCOMMANDS AND MACROS

10.1 What A Macro Is

When we write a macro, we create a new markup instruction. The macro links a brand new command name—think of it as an alias, an AKA, a nickname—with a brace-enclosed unit, which can be looked upon as the new command name's *definition* or as its *long form* or as its *argument*. The definition will be substituted for the alias and acted upon whenever the alias—the command name—is used in the document. This name can be any sequence of letters, as long as it doesn't conflict with the name of an existing command. In this chapter we will restrict the discussion to creating new commands in text mode. The newcommand formats for math and box modes are similar, with some minor variations. We will discuss them in Section 20.3 and in Chapter 23, respectively.

10.2 Exact Substitution

At the very least, a macro can be an easier-to-write rephrase of an existing command; e.g., **\newcommand{\be}{\begin{enumerate}}**. Once the new command is defined, whenever we write **\be**, the program reads: **\begin{enumerate}**.

More generally, an exact-substitution macro aliases a word for a long text phrase. Or it creates an abbreviation for an oft-used LaTeX command. Or it represents the output of a set of commands operating on a specific piece of text. This formatted 'potboiler' text can be inserted just by writing the alias. On output, it is expanded *in situ*.

Example 1: `\newcommand{\homealp}{\textsl{/home/bern/bk/alphabetize.c}}`

The MarkUp: `The program is filed as \homealp.`

The PrintOut: The program is filed as */home/bern/bk/alphabetize.c.*

Example 2: Section 8.4 illustrated how to mimic a command. If used more than once, any one of these commands can be called up by a simple AKA; for example:

```
\newcommand{\GEN}%
{\textbf{\BS chapter}\{\textit{\LT text\RT}\}}
```

The MarkUp: \GEN

The PrintOut: **\chapter**{*<text>*}

In general, this type of macro is useful for reducing the typing and error correcting of a long phrase. And it imposes consistency; *database* is not spelled *database* one time, *data base* the next.

10.3   PlaceHolder Substitution

The real power of the macro lies in its ability to combine existing commands, declarations and environments. From this synthesis we fashion a new operator to do a specific task on significant portions of the text.

The macro can be defined anywhere in the document. It is usable and reusable anywhere thereafter.

The parts of the macro are:

1. The macro name.

2. The number of placeholders for variable text.

3. The macro argument, which can contain:

    (a) fixed text that will be printed as is.

    (b) commands, declarations and environments.

    (c) placeholders for text you will write, when you use the macro. Placeholders are numbers prepended by #.

10.3.1 Composing the macro

A macro is created using a newcommand instruction. It has this format.

```
\newcommand{<\MacroName>}[<number of placeholders>]{<argument>}
```

Suppose this example new command:

```
\newcommand{\fancyfont}[2]{\textsl{SMALLEST:\tiny\uppercase #1;
LARGER:\large\lowercase #2}}
```

This would parse as:

```
\newcommand
  {\fancyfont}
    [2]
      {
      \textsl{SMALLEST:\tiny\uppercase #1; LARGER:\large\lowercase #2}
      }
```

Macro name. *fancyfont* is the name of the macro. It is written with a prepended backslash. The name is a single word composed of letters.

Number of placeholders. The number of different patches of text you will add is written in square brackets, immediately after the macro name. In this example, there are two placeholders. You can have up to nine different placeholders in a macro definition.

Macro Argument. A single braced component, in which all the instructions and fixed text and placeholders that comprise the macro definition are stored. This includes:

- **Fixed text.** In this example, *SMALLEST:* and *LARGER:* will always be part of the printout. The size of *LARGER:* is controlled by the \tiny size declaration.

- **Commands/declarations/environments.** \textsl is a command. \tiny, \large, \lowercase[1] and \uppercase are declarations. There are no environments.

- **Placeholders for variable text.** #1 and #2. You will use the macro by writing text phrases to substitute for the placeholders. Placeholder numbering does not have to be in any particular order inside the macro argument.

10.3.2   Using the macro

To use the macro, write the macro command name, followed by the text for the placeholders, each placeholder text within a separate pair of braces. The text in the first brace will be the text for the #1 placeholder, wherever #1 is written in the new command. Similarly, the text in the second brace will substitute for placeholder #2. And so forth.

The form is:

\MacroName{<text for placeholder #1>}{<text for placeholder #2>}

Examples 1 and 2 show the macro used with different substitutes.

Example 2 text doesn't fit well with the semantics in the macro.

The MarkUp:

```
Example 1: \fancyfont{Write small.}{Write LaRGeR.}
Example 2: \fancyfont{This is much larger.}{Write tHis VerY sMalL.}
```

The PrintOut: Example 1: *SMALLEST:* WRITE SMALL.; LARGER: write larger.
Example 2: *SMALLEST:* THIS IS MUCH LARGER.; LARGER: write this very small.

---

[1] \uppercase and \lowercase are TEX commands. They are useful in forcing print consistency. They do NOT affect defined command words.

10.3.3   Revising a macro definition

There can be up to nine separate placeholders. But there can be an indefinite[2] number of copies of these placeholders. To show this, we revise the definition of *fancyfont* macro from the previous section, using the **renewcommand** command. The *renewcommand* format is exactly the same as the *newcommand* format.

Notice that placeholders in the definition can be in any order. When the macro is used, the substitute text inside the first set of braces is automatically labeled #1 text. The next set of braces encloses #2 text, and so forth.

The MarkUp:

```
\renewcommand{\fancyfont}[2]{#2 #2 #1 #1 \prsl{#2 #1 #2 #1 SMALLEST:%
#1 #2 \tiny #1 #1 #2 #1; LARGER: #1 #2 #2 #1 \large #2 #2 #2 #2}}

\fancyfont{Write small.}{Write Larger.}
```

The PrintOut: Write Larger. Write Larger. Write small. Write small. *Write Larger. Write small. Write Larger. Write small. SMALLEST: Write small. Write Larger.* Write small. Write small. Write Larger. Write small.; LARGER: Write small. Write Larger. Write Larger. Write small. Write Larger. Write Larger. Write Larger. Write Larger.

10.4   Using LATEX Instructions In The Macro

In this section, we will examine in more detail the effects of the different LATEX instructions in a macro.

10.4.1   Commands in the macro argument

LATEX commands behave inside a macro as you would expect. Their influence only extends to the right side border of their own argument. Notice that the text italicized is different in Example 1 below than in Example 2. Do you see why?

---

[2]Indefinite means I didn't try to incrementally bombard a piece of text to figure out the upper limit.

The MarkUp:

```
\newcommand{\ab}[1]{\textit{#1}. The politics of the wets.}
Example 1: \ab{RAIN FORESTS}
```

The PrintOut: Example 1: *RAIN FORESTS*. The politics of the wets.

The MarkUp:

```
\newcommand{\bb}[1]{\textit{#1. The politics of the wets.}}
Example 2: \bb{RAIN FORESTS}
```

The PrintOut: Example 2: *RAIN FORESTS. The politics of the wets.*

10.4.2   Declarations in the macro argument

Declarations, on the other hand, are NOT terminated by the right-side brace of the macro definition. This is because the program strips the *exterior* braces from the newcommand argument *before* text is inserted in the placeholder positions. In consequence, as we see in the paragraph after Example 3, there is no right-side brace left to contain the declaration's influence.

The MarkUp:

```
\newcommand{\bbb}[1]{\itshape\footnotesize#1 The politics of the wets.}
Example 3: \bbb{RAIN FORESTS}
```

The PrintOut: Example 3: RAIN FORESTS The politics of the wets.

As you can see by this paragraph, the scope of the declaration in Example 3 extends beyond the argument of the newcommand. You need to build a firewall yourself. One way to limit a declaration is to return the font to normal size with a \normalsize and return it to upright with an \upshape declaration before closing the argument. Let's do it now: \normalsize\upshape

The MarkUp:

```
\newcommand{\bbbb}[1]{\itshape\footnotesize #1 The politics of the wets.
\normalsize\upshape}
Example 4: \bbbb{RAIN FORESTS}
```

The PrintOut: Example 4: *RAIN FORESTS The politics of the wets.*

Another way to limit the scope of a declaration in a macro is to encase each declaration together with the text it should influence in a pair of unlabeled braces. This is done in Example 5.

The MarkUp:

```
\NC{\bbbbb}[1]{{\itshape\footnotesize#1 The politics of the wets.}}
Example 5: \bbbbb{RAIN FORESTS}
```

The PrintOut: Example 5: *RAIN FORESTS The politics of the wets.*

Or, as in Example 6, you can provide an italic environment, with *footnotesize* as an declaration encased in the environment.

The MarkUp:

```
\newcommand{\bbbbbb}[1]{\begin{itshape} \footnotesize #1%
The politics of the wets.\end{itshape}}
Example 6: \bbbbbb{RAIN FORESTS}
```

The PrintOut: Example 6: *RAIN FORESTS The politics of the wets.*

10.4.3 Environments and macros

This example is an extension of the use of the ProgramNames environment discussed in Section 9.4.2 in the previous chapter. The new command *LocateProg* is a macro that is reused within the *ProgramNames* environment. In *LocateProg*, different instructions are given scope over different chunks of text.

The MarkUp:

```
\newcommand{\LocateProg}[3]%
    {
    \bfseries
    Program Name: \textit{#1.}
    Location: \textup{#2.}
```

```
    System: \textsl{#3.}
    \mdseries
    }
```

```
\begin{ProgramNames}
\item Sorts any size file, any size record. \\
\LocateProg{alp}{/home/bern}{linux}
```

```
\item Sorts any \# record; record size to 7K chars. \\
\LocateProg{alp.obs}{/home/bern}{linux}
```

```
\item Sorts files with up to 50,000 records. \\
\LocateProg{alp.exe}{\dos\alpprog}{dos}
\end{ProgramNames}
```

The PrintOut:

1. Sorts any size file, any size record.
   Program Name: *alp.*
   Location: */home/bern.*
   System: *linux.*

2. Sorts any # records; record size to 7K chars.
   Program Name: *alp.obs.*
   Location: */home/bern.*
   System: *linux.*

3. Sorts files with up to 50,000 records.
   Program Name: *alp.exe.*
   Location: *\dos\alpprog.*
   System: *dos.*

An environment can be included within a macro, as in this next example. ProgramNames created an Enumerate List in scriptsize. In this example, the macro writes a single item and this is the complete list. So it can't be used in an Enumerate List. (Each use of Fussy would be labeled **1**.) But it can write single-itemed Description Lists and take advantage of the Description List indentation format.

The MarkUp:

```
\newenvironment{Fussy}{\begin{description}\scriptsize}{\end{description}}
```

```
\newcommand{\FUSSY}[4]%
{
\begin{Fussy}
  \item #1. \\
  {
```

```
  \bfseries
    Program Name: \textit{#2.} \\
    Location: \textup{#3.} \\
    System: \textsl{#4.}
  \mdseries
  }
\end{Fussy} }

\FUSSY{Sorts any size file, any size record}{alp}%
{/home/bern}{linux}
\FUSSY{Sorts any \# records; record size to 7K chars}%
{alp.obs}{/home/bern}{linux}
\FUSSY{Sorts files with up to 50,000 records}{alp.exe}%
{\dos\alpprog}{dos}
```

The PrintOut:

Sorts any size file, any size record.
  Program Name: *alp.*
  Location: */home/bern.*
  System: *linux.*

Sorts any # records; record size to 7K chars.
  Program Name: *alp.obs.*
  Location: */home/bern.*
  System: *linux.*

Sorts files with up to 50,000 records.
  Program Name: *alp.exe.*
  Location: *\dos\alpprog.*
  System: *dos.*

10.5   Incorporating One Macro In The Definition Of Another Macro

Using one or several macros as part of the definition of another is perfectly feasible. The larger macro can be written before or after the one(s) it incorporates, *but they must all be written before any one of the macros is used.*

In this next example, *locateit* is a macro that is incorporated as part of the definition of *proginfo*. Each use of *proginfo* produces another item in an ordinary enumerate list.

The MarkUp:

```
\newcommand{\locateit}[1]{\texttt{Location: }\textit{#1}}
```

```
\newcommand{\proginfo}[3]{\item {\bfseries Name: #1} \\
\locateit{#2}\\ \texttt{Notes:\ \ \ \ \ #3}  }

\begin{enumerate}
\proginfo{alp}{linux:\TLD/current}%
{Sorts any size record, any \# records.}
\proginfo{alp.obs}{linux:\TLD/obselete}%
{Sorts any \# records; record size to 7K.}
\proginfo{squish}{linux:\TLD/current}%
{Dumps duplicates of sorted records.}
\proginfo{squish.obs}{linux:\TLD/obselete}%
{Mostly interactive; limited commandline options.}
\end{enumerate}
```

The PrintOut:

1. **Name: alp**

   Location: *linux:~/current*

   Notes: Sorts any size record, any # records.

2. **Name: alp.obs**

   Location: *linux:~/obselete*

   Notes: Sorts any # records; record size to 7K.

3. **Name: squish**

   Location: *linux:~/current*

   Notes: Dumps duplicates of sorted records.

4. **Name: squish.obs**

   Location: *linux:~/obselete*

   Notes: Mostly interactive; limited commandline options.

10.6   The Complete Newcommand Format

The discussion to date has used this format for \newcommand:

\newcommand{$<$\alias$>$}[$<$# placeholders$>$]{$<$definition$>$}

This is sufficient for most uses. But the complete definition of the \newcommand (and \renewcommand)[3] command has two optional terms, both in square brackets:

\newcommand{$<$\alias$>$}[$<$# placeholders$>$][$<$value of 1st placeholder$>$]%
{$<$definition$>$}

\renewcommand{$<$\alias$>$}[$<$# placeholders$>$][$<$value of 1st placeholder$>$]%
{$<$definition$>$}

 # placeholders. The first optional term states the number of placeholders in the definition— if there are placeholders. You do not write an empty set of square brackets if there are no placeholders.

value of 1st placeholder. The second optional term—*if present*—states the default text for the first placeholder; i.e., you don't need to rewrite the first placeholder every time you call the macro. The intent, I think, was to save you some typing. You could, of course, save typing the same text over and over again by installing it as fixed text in the macro. But then you'd have to do a renew command every time you wanted to change the fixed text. This format allows you to have a *sticky* value, but one that you can modify easily. The default value will be used *ONLY* if you do not type in an argument for the first placeholder.

In this example, a new command called \history includes the default value of the first placeholder—NAME:. So you call the macro with only two arguments: replacement text for placeholder #2 and placeholder #3. The program writes out the *sticky* value for the first placeholder automatically.

The MarkUp:

\newcommand{\history}[3][NAME:]{#1 Write #2, then #3.}
\history{Your name}{Your address}

The PrintOut: NAME: Write Your name, then Your address.

You change the contents of the first placeholder by introducing new text in a square bracket. Otherwise, the default value for the first placeholder is output.

---

[3] Actually, there is still a third command \providecommand If the alias of a *providecommand* already exists, the program just ignores the new definition. This can be important for package writers. If you are an ordinary user, you are probably better off knowing that you attempted to reuse an existing command rather than wasting time wondering why the printout isn't what you expected.

The MarkUp:

```
\history[FAMILY:]{Parent's name}{Parent's address}\\
\history{Name of Sibling}{Address of Sibling}
```

The PrintOut: FAMILY: Write Parent's name, then Parent's address.
NAME: Write Name of Sibling, then Address of Sibling.

Presented in this fashion, the grammar seems reasonable, but it may be a tricky format to remember. In the ordinary way, replacement text for each placeholder is put inside separate brace arguments whenever the macro is called. So it becomes almost second nature to write placeholder text in braces. If you choose to use the complete macro form and want a non-default value for the first placeholder, be sure to bracket the text with square brackets (see above), not with braces.

Having a sticky first argument makes possible writing fixed-value simplified commands. As an example, *\hspace* is a LaTeX command that forces a horizontal space.

The MarkUp:
```
This size gap\hspace{.5in}between words is not acceptable.
```

The PrintOut: This size gap   between words is not acceptable.

Taking advantage of the complete definition of a newcommand, we can write:

\newcommand{\mgap}[1][.5in]{\hspace{#1}}

and rewrite the previous example using the simplified command, \mgap:

The MarkUp:
```
This size gap\mgap between words is not acceptable.
```

The PrintOut: This size gap   between words is not acceptable.

See Section 13.2 for creating a set of simplified commands for making space wedges of varying sizes.

10.7   Trouble Spots In Writing Macros

Macro Grammar. The complete format is: `\(re)newcommand{<`*`\Name`*`>}[<`*`Number of Placeholders`*`>][<`*`Default value for Placeholder #1`*`>]%` `{<`*`Definition`*`>}`

There must be no separation between grammatical modules. But the End-of-Line symbol is changed to a space automatically. So if you split a long macro definition just after a component terminator (} or]), the last character in the split line would put a space after the component. To prevent this gap between components: if the last character is a component delimiter, put a % sign after the delimiter on the chopped line.

renewcommand. Do not attempt to rewrite a command whose name ends in *end*.

Name. This can only be composed of letters.

- You can't use punctuation or numbers in the macro name. It makes LaTeX barf. So if you must have your macros numbered in sequence—*macro1* and *macro2*, say—write them as *Mone* and *Mtwo*.

- Lamport, the author of LaTeX, advises that you do not start a name with a capital L. It's a "weird mistake". I quote. I have no idea why.

- If you try to give a new command a name that already exists, the program will see this as an error. Don't fight it. Change the name.

Number of Placeholders. Up to 9 placeholders.

Options. There is a problem interpreting the square bracket when there is no optional argument but the actual argument contains a bracket. Wrap the text bracket within braces. Otherwise, this may result in the type of error message discussed in Section 7.1, item 20.

Definition. The definition contains fixed text, placeholders for variable text and local LaTeX instructions. The entire definition, no matter how complex, is enclosed in a pair of braces.

- **Placeholders.** If a # is not included inside the definition, the text you write as substitute for the placeholder won't be inserted; the program won't know where to write the text.

- **Fixed Text.** Imbedded text interspersed between placeholders is transcribed exactly as written inside the definition, including spaces. The only exception: the End of Line character is changed to a space.

- **Substitute text.** You can not insert new text except by writing it as one of the arguments.

10.8   The Complete Newenvironment Format

Environments can also behave as macros; i.e., you can use placeholders to be filled in by text arguments. Notice that the *Begin Definition* unit encloses all the placeholder location information. Do NOT put placeholders in *End Definition*.

The Most Often Used Newenvironment Format

```
\newenvironment{<NewName>}[<# placeholders>]%
{<Begin Definition>}{<End Definition>}
```

```
\renewenvironment{<NewName>}[<# placeholders>]%
{<Begin Definition>}{<End Definition>}
```

The MarkUp:

```
 \newcommand{\ff}{} %As a foundation to create the environment.
```

```
\newenvironment{fff}[2]{\begin{ff}
\small #1\\ \tiny #2 \\ \Huge #1 \\ \Large #2}%
{\end{ff}}
```

```
\begin{fff}{This is the beginning.}{This is the end.}
\end{fff}
```

The PrintOut:

This is the beginning.

This is the end.

This is the beginning.
This is the end.

The Complete Format For Defining A New Environment

`\newenvironment{`*<NewName>*`}%`
`[`*<# placeholders>*`][`*<default for first placeholder>*`]%`
`{`*<Begin Definition>*`}{`*<End Definition>*`}`

`\renewenvironment{`*<NewName>*`}%`
`[`*<# placeholders>*`][`*<default for first placeholder>*`]%`
`{`*<Begin Definition>*`}{`*<End Definition>*`}`

As with a *newcommand* command, a *newenvironment* command can have up to 9 place-holders. Similarly, if the default option is filled, it becomes the value of the first placeholder. Similarly, if the first option is one of placeholders, you write the placeholder text in square brackets, not ordinary braces.

In this example, the *fff* environment is redefined, so that it takes 3 arguments, the first of which has a default value.

The MarkUp:

```
\renewenvironment{fff}[3][\textbf{This is always first! }\\]%
{\begin{ff} #1\small #2\\ \tiny #3 \\ \Huge #2 \\ \Large #3}{\end{ff}}

\begin{fff}{This is the beginning.}{This is the end.}
\end{fff}
```

The PrintOut:

This is always first!
This is the beginning.
<small>This is the end.</small>
This is the beginning.
This is the end.

Part IV.

FORMATTING IN TEXT MODE.

Unless you are a mathematician who writes mostly in equations, most of your markups will involve what LaTeX calls Paragraph Mode instructions. They are also popularly known at *text mode instructions*, and that's what we will call them. In this part of the book, we take up these instructions systematically.

The emphasis is on the markup task, rather than on the markup instruction. We look at what instructions will help us to do the ordinary things we do in marking up a document. TeX is a rich language and there is often more than one way to do the same job.

We start with LaTeX default fonts, how to change typeset and how to insert special symbols.[4] This includes a discussion on how LaTeX classifies fonts operationally and how to parse the names of the font files that reside on disk. The differences between ASCII standard fonts and nonstandard fonts are illustrated. The emphasis is on flexibility, on how to develop the capability to bring any of the fonts resident on disk into the document, whether the members of the font are ordinary characters or special symbols.

We discuss the commands that let us control space between words, sentences, lines and paragraphs. Logically, the chapter on alignment and indenting should follow the chapter on using space. But because so much of the methodology depends on the use of lists, we first describe the classic LaTeX lists: *itemize, enumerate* and *description*, and some variations. Alignment, the next topic, includes outdenting, how to create an outline and ways to indent and/or center lines and paragraphs.

We go on to the float objects; i.e., the constructions that LaTeX must shift around on the page to fit them attractively within the text. Figures, tables, both tabbed and tabular, and marginal notes are discussed and illustrated. Footnotes are next. Finally, a systematic discussion of

---

[4]I suggest you read through Section 11.2 and then go to Chapter 13 on LaTeX spacing commands. Come back to fonts if and when you want to change the default fonts or add a font or need a special symbol.

112

cross-referencing, both by section and by page, is followed by demonstrations of how to write literal (verbatim) text and how to write notes to yourself.

Chapter 11

FONTS

In Section 9.1 we learned some basic LaTeX instructions for manipulating font shape, family and series; i.e., how to print in *italic* and/or **bold**, how to shift between serif and sans serif. Up until now we have ignored fonts; your documents have automatically been printed in one or another of the *Computer Modern* fonts. We now systematically examine font features and learn how to specify fonts to make use of the extensive collection that come with the Linux distribution.

Section 11.2 describes the basic instructions to change font size. It also examines how to change other features in whatever fonts are in control of the print appearance—TeX Computer Modern (CM) fonts by default. If the CM sizes and shapes satisfy your needs, you can skip the rest of this chapter, which deals with font classification and how to load new fonts from disk. You may later need these additional techniques for various reasons; e.g., you want the entire document printed in one or more specific fonts that are not automatically installed in memory when the program is called, you frequently need to change font style, your document requires 'quaint' or eye-catching special sections that use a wide spectrum of different fonts, you want a chunk of the document printed in a specific font that is not immediately callable, or you need special symbols that are not available in the default font styles.

11.1   Font Terminology

bitmapped versus outlined fonts. Computer Modern (see the table in Section 11.3.3) and many of the other fonts discussed in this chapter and the next are bitmapped. They are designed in specific sizes and can be scaled in a limited fashion. In contrast, PostScript fonts are outline fonts and can be scaled to any size.

font. A named or unnamed type. A font can have up to 128 or up to 256 symbols (alphanumeric characters, punctuation marks, control characters, special symbols) that all share the same style of design and the same values in certain features—footedness, stroke thickness, slant, size; e.g., *sans serif, bold, italic, 10-point* would describe a particular font in a particular family. The same description would fit another font in another family.

font family. The members of a font family all have a common style, the same design, but each font in the family will differ in size or shape or width/weight. It is rather like flatware. For a given family (read *pattern*), there are knives, forks, spoons of different weights, shape and size, but a common style. A major differentiation among families is whether the font is footed or not. The default family in LaTeX is footed; it is called *Computer Modern Roman (Serif)*. The other two families are: *Computer Modern Sans Serif* and *Computer Modern Typewriter*.

font series. A combination of width and weight. Medium width-medium weight is the default for TeX fonts.

font shape. This refers to the general appearance, irrespective of type: upright, slanted, italic or small cap. Upright is the default in TeX.

font size. Size is the measure of the average height of the characters in the font or the height of some normative character(s), so two fonts both rated at 10 points can seem (and be) different in size. With 10 point font, the program sets the baselineskip[1] to 12 points by default, producing some 6 lines of type per inch, with variation between fonts all sized at 10 points. As the baselineskip size increases, the number of lines per inch decreases. These next are some of the commonly-used measurement units.

---

[1]The distance from the bottom of one line of text to the bottom of the next line is called the baselineskip; it is NOT, as one might expect, the space between two lines of print.

1 pc^2 = 12 pt.

6 pc = 72.27 pt = 1 in = 2.54 cm = 25.4 mm.

1 em (M) = 10 pt roman. The width of the capital letter *M*.

1 ex (x) = 4.3 pt roman. The height of the small letter *x*.

Common point sizes in publishing are: 7–12, 14, 16, 18, 20, 24, 30. In the early days, many a computer facility that ran TEX tended to produce a size it didn't have by magnifying or shrinking all members of an available font. This practice is changing as it becomes easier to integrate new fonts.

font table. This is also called a *code page*. Both names refer to the 128- or 256-element matrix of characters and symbols that compose a single font. Depending on its position in the table, each element has a separate and unique code, where the code is some value from zero to 127 (or to 255). In the majority of ordinary font tables, letters, numbers and some punctuation retain their ASCII values. (See Section 12.2.) Table codes can be stated in decimal (base 10), octal (base 8) or hexadecimal (base 16).

font weight. Line thickness. This includes descriptors such as: light (thin strokes), medium (the normative weight), heavy (bold) and extremes such as extra light and ultra bold. Medium and bold are typical weights—*medium* and *bold extended* (bx) are used in Computer Modern.

font width. The amount of expansion or contraction available relative to the medium width of the particular font.

main font or normal font. The default font for the document. The text will be printed in this font, unless some other specific font is in command.

monospaced versus proportional spacing. Monospaced fonts, where each letter takes the same amount of horizontal space, are better for tables. Proportional fonts, where spacing is dependent on the specific letter and on context, are better for justified text.

typeface. As used by Berry [Berry96], a *typeface* is a 'collection of related fonts', where a popular style may have spawned several lines, i.e., specific suppliers. In LATEX, Computer Modern is a typeface that encompasses three specific text font families and can be described as a *clan*, by analogy to a Highland clan of related families with a comman ancestor. The common ancestor of a set of related font families is usually the designer (or the name bestowed by the designer).

---

^{2}Abbreviations: pc = pica. pt = point. in = inch. cm = centimeters. mm = millimeters.

type style. A set of text fonts have the same type style in LaTeX if they have the same shape, series and family values. A type style in a specific size is a font.

11.2 Commands/Declarations That Control Font Features

Computer Modern (CM), the default typeface in TeX, automatically makes available three distinct families, two weights and a variety of shapes and sizes. The same commands and declarations will manipulate the print appearance of any substitute font. This applies both to the other bitmapped fonts and to the PostScript outline fonts that comes with the Linux distribution. The main font in this book is PostScript Times Roman (ptm) and is 10 points in size. It is a proportional, footed (serif) font, as is Computer Modern Roman. The sans serif and typewriter fonts we use are Computer Modern Sans Serif and Computer Modern typewriter, respectively.

11.2.1 Manipulating font family, series and shapes

This next table reproduces the command and declaration forms for manipulating font family, font series and font shapes that were written in Section 9.1. They are repeated here to have all the information on font features in one place.

In examining the table, recall that you can create an environment from the declaration form. Thus, if the declaration form for the bold series is **\bfseries**, the environment would be: **\begin{bfseries} \end{bfseries}**.

Font Families

```
serif (default):        Command: \textrm{...}      Declaration: \rmfamily
sans serif:             Command: \textsf{...}      Declaration: \sffamily
typewriter:             Command: \texttt{...}      Declaration: \ttfamily
```

Font Series

```
bold:                   Command: \textbf{...}      Declaration: \bfseries
medium (default):       Command: \textmd{...}      Declaration: \mdseries
```

Font Shapes

```
upright (default):      Command: \textup{...}      Declaration: \upshape
```

```
italic:          Command: \textit{...}   Declaration: \itshape
slant:           Command: \textsl{...}   Declaration: \slshape
small cap:       Command: \textsc{...}   Declaration: \scshape
emphasis:        Command: \emph{...}     Declaration: \em
```

A font command is limited to its argument and a font declaration is usually intended to influence text within an environment. With either instruction, you can at any time reset the major font features (family, series, shape) with the 'return to normal font' directive shown next. The size directives will return the size to the main font size.

```
Normal Font:     Command: \textnormal{}  Declaration: \normalfont
Normal Size:     Command: \sizenormal{}  Declaration: \normalsize
```

Unless the shift to the main font is very short term, the declaration form is usually used.

The *normal* instructions work in the same way as any other command or declaration; i.e., they operate within the scope you allow them. In the last example below, without the *normalfont* statement, the document would continue in sans serif.

The MarkUp: *The PrintOut:*

```
\sffamily This is in sans serif.\\
\normalfont
\itshape This is in italic.\\
\normalfont
\Large This is in large. \\
\normalsize
\sffamily\textup{\textbf{This is in sans serif bold upright.}}
\normalfont
```

This is in sans serif.
This is in italic.
This is in large.
This is in sans serif bold upright.

Examples Of Font Family, Shape And Series At Size 10:

This next table lists a few examples using one possibility from each of these three: family, series, shape. Default features are in parentheses. You don't have to write commands for these unless the current text is in a non-default feature.

Not all the combinations are available. A font that doesn't exist is marked with an asterisk. If LaTeX doesn't find the requested font, it ignores some or all of the directive. It does what

it can. It substitutes the default shape; and, if need be, the default series. If it must, it
substitutes family. But it never changes the Encoding.

(serif medium upright): ABCDEFG HIJKLMN OPQRSTU VWXYZ abcdefg hijklmn
opqrstu vwxyz 0123456789

sans serif (medium upright): ABCDEFG HIJKLMN OPQRSTU VWXYZ abcdefg hijklmn opqrstu vwxyz 0123456789

typewriter (medium upright): ABCDEFG HIJKLMN OPQRSTU VWXYZ abcdefg hijklmn opqrstu vwxyz 0123456789

**serif bold (upright): ABCDEFG HIJKLMN OPQRSTU VWXYZ abcdefg hijklmn
opqrstu vwxyz 0123456789**

**sans serif bold (upright): ABCDEFG HIJKLMN OPQRSTU VWXYZ abcdefg
hijklmn opqrstu vwxyz 0123456789**

***typewriter bold (upright): ABCDEFG HIJKLMN OPQRSTU VWXYZ abcdefg hi-
jklmn opqrstu vwxyz 0123456789**

**(SERIF) BOLD SMALLCAP: ABCDEFG HIJKLMN OPQRSTU VWXYZ ABCD-
EFG HIJKLMNOPQ RSTU VWXYZ 0123456789**

***sans serif bold smallcap: ABCDEFG HIJKLMN OPQRSTU VWXYZ abcdefg
hijklmnopqrstu vwxyz 0123456789**

***typewriter bold smallcap: ABCDEFG HIJKLMN OPQRSTU VWXYZ abcdefg hi-
jklmnopqrstu vwxyz 0123456789**

*(serif medium) slant: ABCDEFG HIJKLMN OPQRSTU VWXYZ abcdefg hijklmn opqrstu
vwxyz 0123456789*

*sans serif (medium) slant: ABCDEFG HIJKLMN OPQRSTU VWXYZ abcdefg hijklmn
opqrstu vwxyz 0123456789*

**sans serif (medium) italics: ABCDEFG HIJKLMN OPQRSTU VWXYZ abcdefg hi-
jklmn opqrstu vwxyz 0123456789*

typewriter (medium) slant: *ABCDEFG HIJKLMN OPQRSTU VWXYZ abcdefg hijklmn opqrstu vwxyz 0123456789*

typewriter (medium) italics: *ABCDEFG HIJKLMN OPQRSTU VWXYZ abcdefg hijklmn opqrstu vwxyz 0123456789*

(serif) bold slant: ABCDEFG HIJKLMN OPQRSTU VWXYZ abcdefg hijklmn opqrstu vwxyz 0123456789

*sans serif bold slant: ABCDEFG HIJKLMN OPQRSTU VWXYZ abcdefg hijklmn opqrstu vwxyz 0123456789

*sans serif bold italics: ABCDEFG HIJKLMN OPQRSTU VWXYZ abcdefg hijklmn opqrstu vwxyz 0123456789

*typewriter bold slant: ABCDEFG HIJKLMN OPQRSTU VWXYZ abcdefg hijklmn opqrstu vwxyz 0123456789

(SERIF MEDIUM) SMALLCAP: ABCDEFG HIJKLMN OPQRSTU VWXYZ ABCDEFG HIJKLMN OPQRSTU VWXYZ 0123456789

SANS SERIF (MEDIUM) SMALLCAP: ABCDEFG HIJKLMN OPQRSTU VWXYZ ABCDEFG HIJKLMN OPQRSTU VWXYZ 0123456789

TYPEWRITER (MEDIUM) SMALLCAP: ABCDEFG HIJKLMN OPQRSTU VWXYZ ABCDEFG HIJKLMN OPQRSTU VWXYZ 0123456789

11.2.2 Font sizes

Size declarations are routinely by name rather than by number. The effect of a size declaration is relative to the size of the main font; i.e., *tiny* on 10 point produces a different print size than does *tiny* for 12 point. For a 10 point main font, the named declarations are equal to these sizes:

\tiny = 5 pt	\scriptsize = 7 pt	\footnotesize = 8 pt
\small = 9 pt	\normalsize = 10 pt	\large = 12 pt

\Large = 14.4 pt   \LARGE = 17.28 pt   \huge = 20.74 pt

\Huge = 24.88 pt

Changing The Size Of Normal (serif medium upright 10-point) Font:

\tiny: ABCDEFG HIJKLMN OPQ RST UVWXYZ abcdefg hijklmn opq rstu vwxyz 0123456789

\scriptsize: ABCDEFG HIJKLMN OPQ RSTU VWXYZ abcdefg hijklmn opq rstu vwxyz 0123456789

\footnotesize: ABCDEFG HIJKLMN OPQ RSTU VWXYZ abcdefg hijklmn opq rstu vwxyz 0123456789

\small: ABCDEFG HIJKLMN OPQ RSTU VWXYZ abcdefg hijklmn opq rstu vwxyz 0123456789

\normalsize: ABCDEFG HIJKLMN OPQ RSTU VWXYZ abcdefg hijklmn opq rstu vwxyz 0123456789

\large: ABCDEFG HIJKLMN OPQ RSTU VWXYZ abcdefghijklmn opq rstu vwxyz 0123456789

\Large: ABCDEFG HIJKLMN OPQ RSTU VWXYZ abcdefg hijklmn opq rstu vwxyz 0123456789

\LARGE: ABCDEFG HIJKLMN OPQ RSTU VWXYZ abcdefg hijklmn opq rstu vwxyz 0123456789

\huge: ABCDEFG HIJKLMN OPQ RSTU VWXYZ abcdefg hijklmn opq rstu vwxyz 0123456789

\Huge: ABCDEFG HIJKLMN OPQ RSTU VWXYZ abcdefg hijklmn opq rstu vwxyz 0123456789

11.2.3   Changing both font size and type style

The MarkUp:

```
This is a
   {\tiny \scshape tiny smallcap FONT}
paragraph following the last
   {\huge {\bfseries huge boldface list}}.
MEDLINE is a
   \textsc{\large smallcap large computer-based information system}
developed by the
   {\LARGE {\em Italicized LARGE National Library of Medicine}}
to furnish
   {\small \slshape small slanted investigators with abstracts}
of
   {\Large \texttt{Large typewriter journal articles in biology.}}
This should returns to the default font.
```

The PrintOut:

This is a ᴛɪɴʏ ꜱᴍᴀʟʟᴄᴀᴘ ꜰᴏɴᴛ paragraph following the last **huge boldface list**.
MEDLINE is a SMALLCAP LARGE COMPUTER-BASED INFORMATION SYS-
TEM developed by the *Italicized LARGE National Library of*
Medicine to furnish *small slanted investigators with abstracts* of Large typewriter
journal articles in biology. This should returns to the default font.

11.3   Naming Conventions For Fonts

11.3.1   Classic TEX fonts

When Donald Knuth created TEX, he also designed fonts to dress its printed products. TEX
began with 16 basic fonts, 8 for text, 1 to emulate typing and 7 for math. The number of
fonts could be handled with minimal classification. To decode the abbreviations, written in
current classification style: *cm* stands for Computer Modern. This is followed by one or
two letters such as *bx* for bold extended or *tt* for typewriter, and so forth. The number at
the end of the abbreviation indicates the size.

As you can see, some fonts were designed specifically for use in math mode. Computer modern math symbol font produces mathematical symbols rather than small letters and digits; i.e., they use codes ordinarily assigned to letters and digits. (See Section 12.2 for a listing of the ordinary codes.) Math font usage is discussed beginning in Chapter 20.

NAME	*DESCRIPTION*	*SIZE*	*TEXT*
text fonts			
cmr10	computer modern roman	10 point	ABCabc123
cmr7	computer modern roman	7 point	ABCabc123
cmr5	computer modern roman	5 point	ABCabc123
cmbx10	computer modern bold extended	10 point	**ABCabc123**
cmbx7	computer modern bold extended	7 point	**ABCabc123**
cmbx5	computer modern bold extended	5 point	**ABCabc123**
cmsl10	computer modern slanted roman	10 point	*ABCabc123*
cmti10	computer modern text italic	10 point	*ABCabc123*
typewriter type			
cmtt10	computer modern typewriter type	10 point	ABCabc123
math fonts			
cmmi10	computer modern math italic	10 point	*ABCabc123*
cmmi7	computer modern math italic	7 point	*ABCabc123*
cmmi5	computer modern math italic	5 point	*ABCabc123*
cmsy10	computer modern math symbols	10 point	$ABC\dashv\lfloor\rfloor\infty\in\ni$
cmsy7	computer modern math symbols	7 point	$ABC\dashv\lfloor\rfloor\infty\in\ni$
cmsy5	computer modern math symbols	5 point	$ABC\dashv\lfloor\rfloor\infty\in\ni$
cmex10	computer modern math extension	10 point	$\int^!\,'\amalg\quad\backslash\sqcap$

Early on, the command **\newfont** was used to switch among specific fonts. Like the new-command, it created an alias, (*\NDH* in this following example). It did not, however, allow shape changes, as you can see in the next printout; i.e., the font reverted to Computer Modern Roman when bold or italics or slant shapes were requested. (To show this, shapes other than upright are enclosed in square brackets.)

To rewrite text in Dunhill upright medium series size 10—a more recent addition—you'd write:

The MarkUp:

```
\newfont{\NDH}{cmdunh10}
```

```
\NDH
Should it be NECESSARY to pool \textbf{[the databases()]}, it
\textbf{\textit{[it well to know that]}} the \textsl{[original
database]} FILES are virtually \textsc{[concatenated.]}
```

The PrintOut: Should it be NECESSARY to pool **[the databases()]**, it *[is well to know that]* the *[original database]* FILES are virtually [CONCATENATED.]

Other fonts can be introduced, each requiring a different *newfont* alias. *\newfont* may still be useful for writing a complete document in a single font. For more general and up-to-date ways to change fonts and, in particular, font families, see Section 11.5.

11.3.2 Using NFSS to classify names

Over time, there has been a considerable increase in the number of fonts in the basic installation package. Hence the need for a systematic classification, a need that has been filled by the New Font Selection Scheme (NFSS).[3]

It is not unusual to treat classification schemes as stuff you don't need to know. Don't do it with NFSS. If a font is not a member of one of the Computer Modern families or part of a package that is immediately usable, you need the NFSS components as arguments for the commands that will print your text in the font you want. These commands—and the way to control font size(s)—are described in detail in Section 11.5.

NFSS has four components.

Component 1: `Font Encoding Scheme`
Component 2: `Typeface` plus `Font Family`
Component 3: `Font Series`
Component 4: `Font Shape`

---

[3]The original New Font Selection Scheme, (NFSS), was devised by Frank Mittelbach and Rainer Schöpf; it has since been amplified and refined by them and others. An essay on LaTeX2ε font selection was issued by the LaTeX2ε group in November, 1996 [Latex3PT96]. It discusses naming conventions and how to use *font definition* files. In addition, Chapter 7 in Goossens et al [Goossens94] provides a comprehensive discussion and summary of various fonts and how to make use of them.

In this template, using recognizable abbreviations, we can fill in most of the blanks for Computer Modern Serif Medium Normal that, at size 10, serves as default font in LaTeX.

Component 2: cmr   (computer modern and serif)
Component 3: m   (medium series)
Component 4: n   (normal upright shape)

Encoding Scheme

The missing first component above is the name of the encoding scheme. A font's encoding is simply a listing of each character and symbol available in that font *in a particular order*. The first character/symbol in the list has Position Zero, so its Code is Zero; the second character/symbol has Position 1, so its Code is 1, and so forth. All fonts in a family have the same encoding scheme. Many families may have the same encoding scheme—they are differentiated by the other font features—family, series, shape and size. A large number of fonts abide in whole or in part by the ASCII convention, where, for example, **A** is always coded as decimal 65, **1** is always coded as decimal 49. (See, Section 12.2 for a complete listing of the ASCII positions.)

For Computer Modern, the encoding is at present usually *OT1*.[4] The default CM font can be described in NFSS as *OT1/cmr/m/n*. (Components are separated by / for clarity.) The math encoding schemes in the table in Section 11.3.1 are: *OML* for Original Math Text Italics, *OMS* for Original Math Symbols and *OMX* for Original Math Extended Symbols. In addition, *U* is used when the encoding is unknown, *L* prepends local encodings and *OT2* is limited to Cyrillic. As we will see below, the specific Encoding for any font can be found in the FD file for the family that includes the font.

If you will be using several encodings—say Cork and Cyrillic, with Cork as the default—state it in the preamble, writing the default font as the last of the options for the *fontenc* package: **\usepackage[OT2,T1]{fontenc}**.

---

[4]*OT* stands for Original TeX encoding scheme. It is sometimes facetiously said to stand for the Obsolete TeX encoding scheme. Plans are afoot for the Cork encoding scheme to replace OT; it is labeled *T1*. Why Cork? Because the decision to replace the 7-bit OT1 with the 8-bit T1 as the encoding standard was made at the TeX Users Conference held in Cork. If it exists on your machine, you can force Cork encoding by writing **\usepackage{t1enc}** or **\usepackage[T1]{fontenc}** in the preamble.

Family

Family names that can be used in the second NFSS parameter include *cmr* for Computer Modern Roman, *cmss* for Computer Modern Sans Serif and *cmtt* for Computer Modern Typewriter. The PostScript (PS) fonts include *ptm* for Adobe Times (serif) and *phv* for Adobe Helvetica (sans serif). The full list of family names is to be found in *fontname.dvi* in the ~/texmf/doc/fonts/fontname directory [Berry96].

Series

Computer Modern uses *bx* for Bold Extended, whereas Adobe Times uses *b* for Bold. Both use *m* for the normal medium line thickness. Possibilities in other fonts range from Thin Hairline and Extralight through Ultra UltraBlack and ExtraBold ExtraBlack. The entire list of series possibilities can be found in *weight.map* in the fontname directory.

Shape

These include *n* for normal (upright), *it* for italic, *sl* for slant and *sc* for small cap. Less common are the outline and upright italic shapes.

Size

The NFSS components select a particular font family, whose FD file (see below) spells out the sizes available for the various NFSS combinations. When a specific size is desired (see Section 11.5.3), it is defined by two values: the font size and the baselineskip, which is the distance from the bottom of one line of text to the bottom of the next line of text. Sizes default to point measurements if no unit is stated, but they can be given in any of the accepted units. Normally for 10 point font, the program sets the baselineskip to 12 points. You can, however, reset the baseline. This book, for example, uses a 15 point baselineskip together with a 12 point spacing between paragraphs. Ordinarily, *parskip*—the separation between paragraphs—is the same size as the baselineskip. But it appeared excessive with a 15-point baseline skip. So I reset the paragraph spacing to 12 points this way: **\setlength{\parskip}{12pt}**

If there's only one nonstandard baseline skip, then it can be set by writing in the preamble a new size baselineskip or redefining *\normalsize*; write, for example, EITHER **\setlength{\baselineskip}{15pt}** OR **\renewcommand{\normalsize} {\fontsize{10}{15}-\selectfont}**.

A different approach is needed if you want nonstandard and different baseline skips for different fonts. As an example, I wanted a different baseline spacing for the Markup in typewriter font that in the default font. One way of achieving this is to write a couple of macros that redefine the Roman and Typewriter fonts:

```
\newcommand{\R}{\fontencoding{OT1}\fontfamily{ptm}\fontseries{m}%
\fontshape{n}\fontsize{10pt}{15pt}\selectfont}

\newcommand{\T}{\fontencoding{OT1}\fontfamily{cmtt}\fontseries{m}%
\fontshape{n} \fontsize{10pt}{12pt}\selectfont}
```

I used them by typing a **\T** before a markup and a **\R** after it. Note that they can be incorporated with the *\begin* and *\end* verbatim statements that surround the Markup; e.g.,

```
\newcommand{\T}{\fontencoding{OT1}\fontfamily{cmtt}\fontseries{m}%
\fontshape{n}\fontsize{10pt}{12pt}\selectfont} \begin{verbatim}
```

If you want to be able to experiment with sizing both baselineskip and paragraph skip, create Emacs hot keys (see Chapter 5) that type a **\BLTEN\PARTEN** before a Markup and **\BLSK\PAR** after it.

```
\newcommand{\BLSK}{\setlength{\baselineskip}{15pt}}
\newcommand{\PAR}{\setlength{\parskip}{12pt}}

\newcommand{\BLTEN}{\setlength{\baselineskip}{12pt}}
\newcommand{\PARTEN}{\setlength{\parskip}{11pt}}

\newcommand{\PARSET}[1]{\setlength{\parskip}{#1pt}}
```

The last macro, *\PARSET*, is useful for decreasing paragraph spacing for occasional local manipulations.

The Font Definition (FD) File

There is a single Font Definition (FD) file per family, and the root of the FD file name (the name up to the Dot and Extension) is composed of the family's encoding scheme and name. As an example, *OT1cmr.fd* is the font definition file for Computer Modern Roman. A FD file describes the series, shape and size combinations available for a particular font family. It has a single Font Family declaration and one or more Font Shape declarations. To illustrate, this is *Ursfs.fd*, a math calligraphy package (*mathrsfs.sty*) designed by Jörg Knappen. It creates fancy uppercase letters.

```
\ProvidesFile{Ursfs.fd}[1996/01/01 rsfs font definition file (jk)]
\DeclareFontFamily{U}{rsfs}{}
\DeclareFontShape{U}{rsfs}{m}{n}{%
   <5> <6>  rsfs5
   <7>  rsfs7
   <8> <9> <10> <10.95> <12> <14.4> <17.28> <20.74> <24.88> rsfs10
 }{}
\endinput
```

The *rsfs* family has only three font members. We learn that there are three basic sizes (5, 7 and 10), only one series (m) and one shape (n). Sizes 5 and 6 are produced from rsfs size 5. The rsfs10 font can be scaled to certain values from size 8 to size 24.

In this next statement taken from *OT1cmr.fd*, **gen** * is shorthand. In this context it means that there are actual bold extended (bx) fonts in sizes 5 through 9 in Computer Modern Roman. The size 10 cmbx font scales to 10.95 (11). Sizes 14.4, 17.28, 20.74 and 24.88 don't exist independently; they are produced by scaling from size 12. The FD file can be complex. There is a grammar for making size and shape substitutions explicit and there are various shortcut ways of writing long rules. For a discussion of the complete syntax, see Section 7.7 in [Goossens94].

```
\DeclareFontShape{OT1}{cmr}{bx}{n}
   {
      <5> <6> <7> <8> <9> gen * cmbx
      <10><10.95> cmbx10
      <12><14.4><17.28><20.74><24.88>cmbx12
      }{}
```

Running **locate .fd** is a simple way to determine what coding scheme is used for what family for bitmapped fonts such as CM and the fonts shown in the table in Section 11.3.3. Examination of a family's FD file will indicate the abbreviated names of all its member fonts. As seen above, the NFSS short name for the Computer Modern Roman Bold Extended size 12 font is *cmbx12*, not *cmrbx12*.

The abbreviated font names in the FD file *without the Encoding* can also be used to guess at the files that carry the shape and space information that characterize a particular font. Thus, *cmbx12* is also the straightforward root name of files that hold material for the cmbx12 font; e.g., *cmbx12.mf, cmbx12.tfm* and *cmbx12.2488pk*. A different set of informational files are associated with CM Bold Extended size 10; i.e., *cmbx10.mf, cmbx10.tfm* and *cmbx10.2488pk*. In most cases, however, the root name of files associated with a particular font may be somewhat different than a simple concatenation of NFSS factors may lead us to expect. Filenames are partly dictated by other considerations. This is discussed in the next chapter in Section 12.1.1.

The FD files for the PostScript fonts on disk have a somewhat different grammar. With PS fonts, all sizes, not just specific sizes, are obtainable by scaling. In consequence, the FD file lists the root name for each different shape and series available in the font; sizes are ignored. (See [Berry96] and Section 12.1.1.) Thus, the FD file for Adobe Times (T1ptm.fd) indicates that the specific root name for any file associated with Adobe Times Bold Italics is *ptmbi8t* and the specific root name for files for Adobe Times Medium Small Cap is *ptmrc8t*. (Note that the 8 in the name does not indicate size.)

```
\DeclareFontShape{T1}{ptm}{b}{it}{
   <-> ptmbi8t
}{}
```

```
\DeclareFontShape{T1}{ptm}{m}{sc}{
   <-> ptmrc8t
}{}
```

11.3.3 Fonts supplied with LaTeX

The next table lists some basic, non-PostScript fonts that typically come with the current LaTeX distributions for Linux. All these fonts are on disk, but only the default Computer Modern text fonts and math fonts are in memory and immediately accessible. We discuss how to utilize the large number of fonts packaged directly with LaTeX or with packages that accompany LaTeX below, starting in Section 11.5.

Computer Modern now includes the essential Sans Serif, *art deco* Dunhill and the backward slanting sort of Funny Roman. *bx* stands for bold extended; *bc* for bold condensed. The number of typewriter fonts has increased.

Concrete Roman, a variant of Computer Modern, was also designed by Donald Knuth. Its name comes from its role as the primary font for the textbook, *Concrete Mathematics: A Foundation for Computer Science* by Ronald L. Graham, Donald E. Knuth and Oren Patashnik.

The Pandora package can be called with a **\usepackage{pandora}** statement in the preamble. It was designed by Nazeen N. Billawala. It has both serif and sans serif, with upright and bold fonts in both families.

The Old German package by Yannis Haralambous [Mittelbach96e] supports printing three families, each of which is a type of gothic font; namely, gothfamily, frakfamily and swabfamily. If you want to print a document in Old German, call it with a **\usepackage{oldgerm}** statement in the preamble. See Section 11.5.3 on how to typeset a small amount of text without loading the package.

The Euler package [Jensen95b], designed by Hermann Zapf, provides math symbols and alphanumerics that blend nicely with various text fonts: beton—which provides the Concrete fonts with enhancements; for example, it enlarges the baseline skip—and PostScript, *inter alia*. The package automatically replaces Computer Modern Math Italic with Euler Roman. If you load the package with the mathcal and mathbf options (**\usepackage[mathcal,mathbf]{euler}**), the **\mathcal** command will use Euler script in place of the default math calligraphy alphabet, and **\mathbf** will produce bold Euler Roman alphanumerics in place of Computer Modern bold math. Euler Roman is also excellent for 'handwritten' comments in sketches—use the commands in Section 11.5.3 to print text without needing to load the package.

Other fonts available in the Linux LaTeX distribution—the DC emulation of Computer Modern for European and other non-English languages, Bitstream Charter, the Adobe PostScript fonts and the American Mathematical Society $\mathcal{AMS}$ fonts—are not shown in the next table. Many of them, however, are discussed or illustrated below in this part of the book or in Part V. Adobe Postscript Times Roman serves as default font throughout the book.

The NFSS values shown in the table are those for font encoding, font family, font series, font shape. Values are separated by /.

If a family and series comes in several shapes, the NFSS listed is for the text example shown.

Sizes listed are base sizes; other sizes are derived from them by scaling. All examples are at size 10 points. Not all the sizes listed for a family come with each of the other font features.

The table is modeled on tables in Chapter 7 in Goossens et al [Goossens94].

FAMILY	SERIES	SHAPES	NFSS	TEXT
COMPUTER MODERN (OT1)				
Roman: cmr (Sizes: 5,6,7,8,9,10,12,17)				
	m	n,it,sc,sl,u	OT1/cmr/m/n	ABCabc123
	bx	n,it,sl,u	OT1/cmr/bx/n	**ABCabc123**
	b	n	OT1cmr/b/n	**ABCabc123**
Sans Serif: cmss (Sizes: 8,9,10,12,17)				
	m	n,sl	OT1/cmss/m/n	ABCabc123
	bx	n	OT1/cmss/bx/n	**ABCabc123**
	sbc	n	OT1/cmss/sbc/n	ABCabc123
Typewriter: cmtt (Sizes: 9,10,12)				
	m	n,it,sc,sl	OT1/cmtt/m/n	ABCabc123
Fibonacci: cmfib (Size: 8)				
	m	n	OT1/cmfib/m/n	ABCabc123
Funny Roman: cmfr (Size: 10)				
	m	n,it	OT1/cmfr/m/n	ABCabc123
Dunhill: cmdh (Size: 10)				
	m	n	OT1/cmdh/m/n	ABCabc123
CONCRETE (OT1 for Roman; OML for Math)				
Roman: ccr (Sizes: 5,6,7,8,9,10)				
	m	n,sc,it,sl	OT1/ccr/m/n	ABCabc123
	c	sl	OT1/ccr/c/sl	*ABCabc123*
Math: ccm (Size: 10)				
	m	it	OML/ccm/m/it	*ABCabc123*
PANDORA (OT1)				
Roman: panr (Size: 10)				
	m	n,sl	OT1/panr/m/n	ABCabc123
	b	n	OT1/panr/b/n	**ABCabc123**

Sans: pss (Size: 10)				
	m	n,sl	OT1/pss/m/n	ABCabc123
	b	n	OT1/pss/b/n	**ABCabc123**

OLD GERMAN (U)

Gothic: ygoth (Size: ygoth)				
	m	n	U/ygoth/m/n	𝔄𝔅ℭabc123
Fraktur: yfrak (Size: yfrak)				
	m	n	U/yfrak/m/n	𝔄𝔅ℭabc123
Schwabacher: yswab (Size: yswab)				
	m	n	U/yswab/m/n	𝔄𝔅ℭabc123

EULER (U)

Roman: eur (Sizes: 5,6,7,8,9,10)				
	m	n	U/eur/m/n	ABCabc123
	b	n	U/eur/b/n	ABCabc123
Script: eus (Sizes: 5,6,7,8,9,10)				
	m	n	U/eus/m/n	𝒜ℬ𝒞
	b	n	U/eus/b/n	𝒜ℬ𝒞
Fraktur: euf (Sizes: 5,6,7,8,9,10)				
	m	n	U/euf/m/n	𝔄𝔅ℭabc123
	b	n	U/euf/b/n	𝔄𝔅ℭabc123

11.4   The Directory Structure For Storing Fonts

It is not necessary to state the path to any font file for any font distributed with TEX in Linux. The fonts shown in the table in Section 11.3.3 and in the tables in Chapter 12 come installed in specific directories.

The TEX Users Group (TUG) developed the TEX Directory Structure (TDS) to provide, as the name would suggest, a flexible but standardized directory tree to faciliate the management of TEX files by system administrators. The major branches are occupied in parallel by TEX and its associated programs: METAFONT, MetaPost, web2c, BIBTEX and the DVI drivers. LATEX is within the direct TEX line.

Within a branch, some names are reserved for specific types of files. Care is taken to name and locate font files: (1) by type (e.g., *afm* for Adobe font metrics, *pk* for packed bitmap files, *tfm* for TEX font metrics, *vf* for virtual fonts); (2) by supplier (e.g., *ams* for American Mathematical Society, *public* for public domain fonts, *jknappen* for the dc European fonts); and (3) by typeface (e.g., *cm* for Computer Modern, *concrete* for Concrete, *euler* for Euler).

The structure can be implemented using the Microsoft and Apple operating systems as well as in Unix and Linux. The root of the directory tree that comprises TEX *et al* may be located or relocated to any directory. The TUG working group recommends the root (sub)directory of the TDS be called *texmf*, an amalgam of TEX and METAFONT. In Slackware, texmf is under /usr/lib/teTeX; in Red Hat, it is under /usr/lib/texmf. *tds.dvi* in the ˜/texmf/doc/help directory contains information on TDS.

teTEX is a TEX distribution for Unix-like platforms; it is *the* distribution for Linux. The directory organization of the whole TEX conglomeration follows the TDS layout. Thomas Esser, the author of teTEX—te (his initials) plus TEX—implemented teTEX in such a way that, when you installed TEX and LATEX, fonts were automatically placed in directories accessible to TEX and to the programs that supply the view and print drivers with information on fonts.[5]

11.5   To Load A New Font

11.5.1   Why load yet another font?

Essentially, there are two major reasons for loading a font from disk to memory.

- **To change the main font family or default *clan*.** This involves changing defaults and is conveniently done using one or more of the available packages residing on disk. If you plan on using the new font(s) permanently in lieu of the default Computer Modern, introduce the package name(s) into the preamble of the document with a *\usepackage* command.

---

[5]Documentation on teTEX is called *The teTEX Guide—Installation and Maintenance* [Esser96]. It includes directions on where to put new fonts so that the TDS is maintained. It is filed as *TETEXDOC.dvi*. Look for it in the ˜/texmf/doc/teTeX directory. teTEX utilizes Karl Berry's *Kpathsea* path searching and library maintenance procedures [Berry95a, Berry95b]. Berry maintains the libraries now used by dvijk, dvips, xdvi, the GNU font utilities and Web2c; the *Kpathsea* was developed to keep track of things in the face of new releases of these programs.

- **To use a temporary additional font.** Load a resident font into memory from its NFSS description wherever it is required, using either the *\selectfont* or *\usefont* command. Actually, as Section 11.5.3 demonstrates, you can use this method for loading the default family and coordinated families; but it is simpler to load a package.

11.5.2   To change the main font family for the entire document

The default Computer Modern Roman family is not wired in. Any other accessible family may be substituted as the main family.

Swapping The Computer Modern Default Families

The Computer Modern Sans Serif family may be declared to be the main one in place of the customary serif family. When this occurs, the sizing commands—\large, \tiny, and so forth—work with the new font. As do \textsl{...} and the other shape commands. You can also substitute Computer Modern Roman for the Computer Modern Sans Serif family. You would effect this swap by writing at the top of your document in the preamble or after the *\begin{document}* statement:

\renewcommand{\familydefault}{cmss}
\renewcommand{\rmdefault}{cmss}
\renewcommand{\sfdefault}{cmr}
\normalfont\normalsize

Using A Package

The simplest way to change the main font family is to load one of the packages that come with the Linux distribution of TEX. Aside from providing the program with release date data, most font packages do little more than include a statement resetting the main default family and possibly the ancillary families. Obviously, you can write these statements yourself, but package names are usually easier to remember than abbreviated font names; e.g., *pandora.sty* rather than *panr*, *helvetic.sty* rather than *phv*. Note that the .sty exten-

sion is NOT used in the argument of the *usepackage* command. Consult ˜/texmf/tex/latex-
/mfnfss for several METAFONT bitmapped styles and ˜/texmf/tex/latex/psnfss for various
PostScript scalable font families that can be loaded with a *usepackage* command in the
preamble; the *psnfss* fonts were created using Alan Jeffrey's *fontinst* [Jeffrey94b] program.

Some packages redo the fonts for all three families—roman, sans serif and typewriter—as
well as redoing the fonts for the series, size and shape parameters. The Bookman package
(**\usepackage**{**bookman**}) uses Adobe PostScript Bookman (pbk) for serif, PostScript
AvantGarde (pag) for sans serif and PostScript Courier (pcr) for typewriter.

Other packages such as Pandora install serif and sans serif but not the typewriter family,
which defaults to Computer Modern Typewriter.

Other packages such as Bitstream Charter (bch), which we load with a **\usepackage-**
{**charter**} in the preamble, only install the main roman (serif) font. If we do nothing,
the Computer Modern Sans Serif and Typewriter families will continue to be summoned
by the \textsf{...} and \texttt{...} commands.

Alternatively, we can choose specific fonts for one or both of them. As example, we can
load Courier (pcr) with a **\usepackage**{**courier**} statement. The Courier package is unusual in that it sets the typewriter family, not the serif family. All the available size declarations (\small, \large, etc.) and shape directives (\itshape, etc.) will work.

Still other packages set their own declarations and commands. An example is the Old
German package, which is called with a **\usepackage**{**oldgerm**} statement. The package defines three new commands: *\textfrak{...}, \textswab{...}* and *\textgoth{...}*, each
of which calls one of the old german families to operate on the associated text argument.
The corresponding declarations are *\frakfamily, \swabfamily* and *\gothfamily*. Many of
the size commands will work.

The Knappen European fonts [Knappen96] emulate Computer Modern. In addition, they
provide the accents needed in European languages. To call all of them, it is sufficient to
write a **\usepackage[T1]**{**fontenc**} statement to substitute T1 encoding for OT1. Then
use the same series, shape and size commands you used with Computer Modern. (See
Section 12.3.3 for additional information.)

Redefining The NFSS Default Values

NFSS provides a separate default command for each of its four components: *\encodingdefault*, *\familydefault*, *\seriesdefault* and *\shapedefault*. The fonts that are loaded are the ones that have the values given these default commands. The number of different fonts in the set depend on how many basic sizes are available for that encoding-family-series-shape combination.

At the beginning of the run the program installed these values:

\newcommand{\encodingdefault}{OT1}
\newcommand{\familydefault}{cmr}
\newcommand{\seriesdefault}{m}
\newcommand{\shapedefault}{n}

The default fonts can certainly be reset through a package, but they can almost as easily be set 'by hand' inside the document itself. This is especially useful for fonts that are not part of a package.

Given that the font we want exists on disk and its NFSS features are known, we can force the program to use it in place of the current main font by resetting NFSS default values in one of several different locations.

- We can write a set of commands to reset the default font in a separate file that we introduce in the document with an *\input* command. If the file is called *changeit.tex*, we would write **\input{changeit}** in the preamble. If the extension is anything but *tex*, we'd write the full name.

- We can reset the values of any or all the four default components in the document itself, in the preamble or just after the *\begin{document}* statement. This is permanent unless we later substitute another font.

- We can reset font(s) within a limited environment for a temporary but significant change. Just before the end of the environment, we'd reset the default value(s) to the previous one(s).

These next renew commands would make the main font the distinctive Dunhill style. It is so unusual it is a good one to try for practice.

\renewcommand{\encodingdefault}{OT1}
\renewcommand{\familydefault}{cmdh}
\renewcommand{\seriesdefault}{m}
\renewcommand{\shapedefault}{n}
\normalfont\normalsize[6]

Often, as can be done in loading Dunhill, you need only change the \familydefault command, because the encoding, series and shape are the same as Computer Modern.

As another example, just placing these commands in the preamble or right after \begin{document} will make Adobe Bookman your main font for the whole document, unless, of course, you issue commands to replace it later in the document. It is not necessary to write a \usepackage{bookman} statement in the preamble, unless you also want to change the sans serif and typewriter fonts. Renewing \rmdefault ensures you return to pbk after issuing a \sffamily or \ttfamily command.

\renewcommand{\familydefault}{pbk}
\renewcommand{\rmdefault}{pbk}

By browsing font directories with knowledge of how font files are named, we can often guess at the values for the reset parameters for a particular font. If we guess wrong, the LaTeX log will tell us. Font file naming is discussed in Section 12.1.1.

Although you will seldom need to use them all, you should know that there's an extensive set of defaults that can be reset. Setting the family defaults—\rmdefault, \sfdefault and \ttdefault—was shown above. In similar fashion, the default fonts for the series members can be reset using the \bfdefault and \mddefault commands. For example, \renewcommand{\bfdefault}{b} would reset the series to b from the default bx. The shape parameters can be reset individually: \itdefault, \sldefault, \scdefault and \updefault. As an example, \renewcommand{\sldefault}{it} would be the way to select an available italic font in lieu of a non-available slant. Whatever sizes are listed in the FD file are usable. A specific size can be set by methods discussed in the next section.

After you've mastered some of the text commands starting in Chapter 13 in this part of the book, you might want to try some of the other styles: Bitstream Charter and the Adobe

---

[6]Be sure to postpend the normalfont and normalsize commands. Otherwise, the previous default font might occasionally retake control.

PostScript fonts that are distributed with Linux. They can be found in subdirectories under
~/texmf/fonts. Adobe font names begin with *p*—*pbk* is the family name for the Adobe
Bookman font; *pag* stands for AvantGarde; *pnc* for New Century Schoolbook; *pcr* for a
nostalgic recollection of typewriter Courier. A complete list of the PostScript names can be
found in *A LaTeX survival guide for Unix systems* [Rahtz94a] and in *Fontname* [Berry96].
Both documents are in the Linux distribution.

11.5.3   To load an additional font from NFSS descriptors

This section discusses how to bypass the default commands and work, instead, directly
with NFSS components. This is most useful for writing a short piece of text in a specific
font that is rarely used. This next is the procedure to use a specific single font from the
disk.

1. **Determine the family name of the font you want.** The full list of abbreviated
   family names and the associated actual name is to be found in [Berry96]; e.g., *cmr*
   for Computer Modern Roman; *panr* for Pandora Roman.

2. **Check that there's a Font Description (FD) file for the family.** The family FD
   filename will start with a code name followed by the abbreviated family name. For
   example, *OT1cmss.fd* contains the NFSS values for the shapes, series and sizes available with Computer Modern Sans Serif, *OT1panr.fd* for Pandora Roman.

3. **Determine the abbreviation of the font member you want.** As example, the FD
   file for Pandora contains this information:

   ```
   \DeclareFontShape{OT1}{panr}{m}{sl}{
       <5> <6> <7> <8> <9> <10> <10.95> <12>
       <14.4> <17.28> <20.74> <24.88> pnsl10 }{}
   ```

   This tells us that filenames associated with the slanted Pandora size 10 font will have
   pnsl10 as root.

4. **Preview the font.** If the font has a TFM file associated with it (e.g., pnsl10.tfm), you
   can produce a table showing each character in that font by running *latex nfssfont*.
   (See Section 12.1.3.)

5. **Load the font into memory.** Two ways to use the font to print delimited chunks of the text are discussed next. In both, commands are listed in NFSS order.

For either of the methods shown next, the program provides a set of command names for you to describe the features of the font you want. Using this 'order form', the program will then seek out the font on disk and load it into memory. If the font that satisfies the parameters does not exist, the program will substitute a font and announce the transaction in the log file.

Method 1: Using \selectfont

Use one or more of these font description commands to specify the new font(s) you wish to introduce. These commands are given values independently, but they must be written in this sequence and terminated by the *selectfont* command. This is the format.

```
\fontencoding{<enc>}\fontfamily{<family>}\fontseries{<series>}%
\fontshape{<shape>}\fontsize{<size>}{<baselineskip in points>⁷}%
\selectfont <text>
```

You do not have to revalue all five of the parameters. You can, say, change just the value of the encoding scheme, leaving the other parameters as they are, by writing: **\fontencoding{T1}\selectfont**.

Or you can request fonts that match a particular fontseries value as well as a particular fontshape value; e.g., **\fontseries{m}\fontshape{it}\selectfont** would locate the italic font for the non-bold series in the available sizes in whichever family is the main font at the time.

Were you to set values for all the five font commands at one time, you would be culling the available fonts for a particular one. This, for example, would describe the large italic Computer Modern Sans Serif font.

```
\fontencoding{OT1}\fontfamily{cmss}\fontseries{m}%
\fontshape{it}\fontsize{17}{21}\selectfont
```

---

[7]Note that size has two arguments. A rule of thumb is that the baselineskip should be 1.2 times the font size.

In all cases, you finish the font commands with a \selectfont command. The program will begin to process the one or the cluster of *font* commands when it sees the *selectfont* command. Text is inserted after the \selectfont. For example:

The MarkUp:

```
\fontencoding{OT1}\fontfamily{cmss}\fontseries{m}\fontshape{it}%
\fontsize{17pt}{21pt}\selectfont Headlines
\normalsize\normalfont
```

The PrintOut: Headlines

Note that the *normalfont* and *normalsize* commands terminate printing in Sans Serif and resume printing the output in Serif, the default font.

You don't want to have to rewrite the entire command each time you need the font. So create a new command to use this size permanently:

```
\newcommand{\HDLINE}[1]{\fontencoding{OT1}%
\fontfamily{cmss}\fontseries{m}\fontshape{it}%
\fontsize{17pt}{21pt}\selectfont #1 \normalfont\normalsize}
```

The MarkUp:

```
\HDLINE{Write Some Headlines}
```

The PrintOut: Write Some Headlines

This technique can be used to reset the Serif, Sans Serif and Typewriter family fonts. We use three highly distinctive styles that are unlikely print partners. *bbm* by Torsten Hilbrich and the Adobe PostScript symbol font (*psyr*) have small, 10-point and large sizes. *bbm* has no punctuation. The Adobe Zapfdingbat (*pzd*) font has a single size only and no punctuation. When one of these fonts takes over, if it has the requested size and shape forms, the ordinary size declarations (\footnotesize, etc.) and the shape directives (\itshape{...}, etc.) will work for sizes and shapes available in the font.

Figure 11.1 shows the command form. This is useful for printing a small amount (up to a paragraph) of text in a specific font. Figure 11.2 shows the declarative form, which is suitable for text that stretches over several paragraphs, even over full sections. The font for the subsection text in Figure 11.2 is NOT affected; it is controlled by the default main font and the subsection definitions built into the document class files; i.e., the *.cls* files.

Method 2: Using \usefont

The *\usefont* command is a shortcut for the complete *\selectfont* command, and, of course, it, too, is modeled on the NFSS sequence of features that describe a font. Its format is:

```
\usefont{<encoding>}{<family>}{<series>}{<shape>}
```

This has the same effect as calling and parameterizing \fontencoding, \fontfamily, \fontseries and \fontshape, followed by \selectfont in Method 1. The product is a group of fonts in various sizes that all meet the other criteria.

If you wish to restrict this limited set of fonts to a particular size, prepend the font size instruction; for example

The MarkUp:

```
\fontsize{17pt}{21pt}\usefont{OT1}{cmss}{m}{it} Headlines
\normalsize\normalfont
```

The PrintOut: **Headlines**

As in method 1, you can create a new command to avoid a long rewrite. In this version, the new command takes three arguments: the two size values and the text.

The MarkUp:

```
\newcommand{\UHDLINE}[3]{\fontsize{#1}{#2pt}\usefont{OT1}{cmss}{m}{it}%
#3 \normalfont\normalsize}
\UHDLINE{17}{21}{Write Some More Headlines}
```

The PrintOut: **Write Some More Headlines**

Incidently, the text examples in Section 11.3.1 were created using \SWF, a new command based on the *\usefont* command.

\newcommand{\SWF}[6]{\fontsize{#1}{#2pt}\usefont{#3}{#4}{#5}{#6} ABCabc123}

Command Format for small amounts of text.

The MarkUp:

```
\parindent=1pc
%Uses the psyr family in the Sans Serif slot.
\NC{\SANS}[1]{\fontencoding{U}\fontfamily%
{psy}\fontseries{m}\fontshape{n}\selectfont
#1 \normalfont\normalsize}

%Uses the pzd family in the Typewriter slot.
\NC{\TT}[1]{\fontencoding{U}\fontfamily%
{pzd}\fontseries{m}\fontshape{n}\selectfont
#1 \normalfont\normalsize}

%Uses the bbm family in the Serif slot.
\NC{\MAIN}[1]{\fontencoding{U}\fontfamily%
{bbm}\fontseries{m}\fontshape{n}\selectfont
#1 \normalfont\normalsize}

\MAIN{The program builds on a portion of the
alp program. \small When alp operates on a
large database, it can run out of heap space,
\large so it dumps the record keys it has
alphabetized into a temporary file.}

\SANS{The program builds on a portion of the
alp program. \small When alp operates on a
large database, it can run out of heap space,
\large so it dumps the record keys it has
alphabetized into a temporary file.}

\TT{The program builds on a portion of the
alp program. \small When alp operates on a
large database, it can run out of heap space,
\large so it dumps the record keys it has
alphabetized into a temporary file.}

\MAIN{The program builds on a portion of the
alp program.}\TT{\small When alp operates on a
large database, it can run out of heap space,
\SANS{\large so it dumps the record keys it
has alphabetized into a temporary file.}
```

The PrintOut:

The program builds on a portion of the alp pro gram When alp operates on a large database it can run out of heap space SO it dumps the record keys it has alphabet ized into a temporary file

Τηε προγραμ βυιλδσ ον α πορτιον οφ τηε αλπ προγραμ. Ωηεν αλπ οπερατεσ ον α λαργε δαταβασε, ιτ χαν ρυν ουτ οφ ηεαπ σπαχε, σο ιτ δυμπσ τηε ρεχορδ κεψσ ιτ ηασ αλπηαβετιζεδ ιντο α τεμποραρψ φιλε.

The program builds on a portion of the alp pro gram

The program builds on a portion of the alp pro gram σο ιτ δυμπσ τηε ρεχορδ κεψσ ιτ ηασ αλπηαβετ— ιζεδ ιντο α τεμποραρψ φιλε.

Figure 11.1: To print a small amount of text.

Declaration format for long stretches of text.

The MarkUp: *The PrintOut:*

```
%Uses the psyr family in the Sans Serif slot.
\NC{\SANSg}{\fontencoding{U}\fontfamily%
{psy}\fontseries{m}\fontshape{n}\selectfont}


%Uses the pzd family in the Typewriter slot.
\NC{\TTg}{\fontencoding{U}\fontfamily{pzd}%
\fontseries{m}\fontshape{n}\selectfont}


%Uses the  bbm family in the Serif slot.
\NC{\MAINg}{\fontencoding{U}\fontfamily%
{bbm}\fontseries{m}\fontshape{n}\selectfont}
```

```
\parindent=1pc
\subsection*{SERIF}\MAINg
```
The program builds on a portion of the alp
program. When alp operates on a large database, if it runs out of heap space, it dumps
the alphabetized keys into a temp file.

```
\small
```
The output file can be named on the command
line with the -o option.
```
\normalfont\normalsize
\subsection*{SANS SERIF} \SANSg
```
The program builds on a portion of the alp
program. When alp operates on a large database, if it runs out of heap space, it dumps
the alphabetized keys into a temp file.

```
\small The output file can be named on the
command line with the -o option.
\normalfont\normalsize
\subsection*{TYPEWRITER} \TTg
```
The program builds on a portion of the alp
program. When alp operates on a large database, if it runs out of heap space, it dumps
the alphabetized keys into a temp file.

```
\small The output file can be named on the
command line with the -o option.
\normalfont\normalsize
```

SERIF

The program builds on a
portion of the alp program
When alp operates on a
large database if it runs
out of heap space it dumps
the alphabetized keys into a
temp file

The output file can be
named on the command line
with the o option

SANS SERIF

Τηε προγραμ βυιλδσ ον α
πορτιον οφ τηε αλπ προγραμ.
Ωηεν αλπ οπερατεσ ον α λαργε
δαταβασε, ιφ ιτ ρυνσ ουτ οφ ηεαπ
σπαχε, ιτ δυμπσ τηε αλπηαβετιζεδ κεψσ ιντο α τεμπ φιλε.

Τηε ουτπυτ φιλε χαν βε ναμεδ ον
τηε χομμανδ λινε ωιτη τηε –ο οπτιον.

TYPEWRITER

Figure 11.2: To print a document

The arguments to SWF are:

$\text{\SWF}\{<size>\}\{<baselineskip>\}\{<encoding>\}\{<family>\}\{<series>\}\%$
$\{<shape>\}$

Similarly, the text examples in Section 11.3.3 were printed by an alias also based on the *\usefont* command:

\newcommand{\WF}[4]{\fontsize{10}{12pt}\usefont{#1}{#2}{#3}{#4} ABCabc123}

where:

#1 stands in for *encoding scheme*, *#2* for *family*, *#3* for *series* and *#4* for *shape*.

Using A Math Font As a Text Font

Section 11.3.3 mentioned that the Euler font produces a very good looking 'handwritten' effect. To use this math font as text, do not load the package; instead, use either the *\usefont* or *\selectfont* command. To ensure that commas and periods are printed, use their symbol notation as shown.

The MarkUp:

```
\newcommand{\EU}[1]{\fontsize{10}{12}\usefont{U}{eur}{m}{n}#1
\normalfont\normalsize}
\EU{This uses Euler\symbol{'073} to comment an illustration\symbol{'072}}
```

The PrintOut: This uses Euler, to comment an illustration.

11.5.4   The main font and the *selectfont* font

There are several points to be made about the relationship between the body font and a new font introduced by **\selectfont** or **\usefont**.

★   The *selectfont* (or *usefont*) command that shifts power to a new font behaves as any other directive; i.e., it stays active within the scope you give it. The new font will remain in power indefinitely unless it is: (1) restricted by braces, (2) inside an environment, (3) terminated by *\normalsize \normalfont* declarations or (4) countermanded when a different font is set.

⋆ The new font can serve to change the main font for the rest of the document but it has limitations—it can't affect the text in document divisions such as the (sub)section. These are under control of the default font and the definitions in the *.cls file.

⋆ You can load a new font by package or by resetting default values and, at the same time, segregate a portion or portions of the document with another new font using a **\selectfont** (or **\usefont**) command. The two essentially ignore each other; i.e., the segregated section(s) are printed in the selectfont font, the rest of the document in the package font(s).

11.5.5   Behind the scenes in loading and using a font

Loading The Default Fonts Into Memory

When you call LaTeX, the binary equivalents of *latex.ltx* bring several starter files into memory; the major ones are *fonttext.ltx, fontmath.ltx* and *preload.ltx. fonttext.ltx* loads the Font Description (FD) files for the basic Computer Modern text families—cmr, cmss and cmtt. It provides command names for calling in the 'built-in' text accents and symbols. It defines the default fonts; e.g., *\newcommand{ \sfdefault}{cmss}*. Similarly, the math alphabet and symbol codes, declarations, definitions of the default fonts and instructions to input the FD files for the basic math families—cmmi, cmsy and cmex—are written in *fontmath.ltx*. Some basic font sizes are declared in *preload.ltx*; and the CM fonts and TeX symbol fonts are loaded. These files are all in *~/texmf/tex/latex/base*. The FD file for each of the default families—and indeed the FD file for any family that reside on the machine—contains the series, shapes and sizes available for the family and applicable series, shape and size substitutes.

Loading Other Fonts From Disk Into Memory

A new font family can be loaded into memory permanently (i.e., for the entire program run) by changing the values of the defaults for the four components of NFSS. This can be done by way of the *usepackage* command or by changing the values inside the document. In contrast, you load a font to print a specific segment of the document by using the *selectfont* or *usefont* commands; these fonts inhabit memory only while they are in use.

The METAFONT System

The number of different types of files involved in printing is at first bewildering. But each is responsive to the logic of what is necessary at some particular place in the complicated process that brings text to paper dressed in its font finery.

In TₑX the puppet master that controls the different stages is the METAFONT system, developed by Donald Knuth. It oversees the creation of TₑX Font Metric (TFM) files (i.e., binary files with a *tfm* extension), where each file describes the box size of each character in that font. (Other systems call these *width tables*.) It holds the actual recipes for how to draw each of these characters in METAFONT (MF) shape descriptor files (i.e., files with a *mf* extension). It arranges for a substitute when a symbol is not available. Through a complex process, these shape directives are mapped onto a 'grid', the fineness of which depends on the resolution of the printer. It is the characters in this final PK file that are 'stamped' on the paper.

These are font filename extensions involved in printing CM and PostScript fonts:

.afm	Adobe font metric files.
.fd	Font definition files for font families in particular encodings.
.*gf	Generic font bitmap files.
.mf	METAFONT shape description files.
.pfa	PostScript shape description files in ASCII.
.pfb	PostScript shape description files in binary.
.*pk	Packed bitmap fonts.
.tfm	TₑX font metric files.
.vf	Virtual font files.

Getting a font template ready for an actual printer to do actual printing is complex. The discussion of files and procedures below is simplified; it highlights the major steps. The intent is to familiarize you with the general process, not its details.

Measuring The Size Of Print Characters

Recall the paper with double ruled lines teachers distributed in elementary school. We had the impossible task of tracing letters, using the double lines as guides, coping with the mysterious instruction that one letter must sit completely on the line while another letter must sit partially on the line, with the rest of it hanging down. I doubt that it would have made our task easier to know that, in printing terms, each letter has an specific (invisible) hook to attach it properly to the line.

The design of any letter, any symbol, in any font includes a specific point on its left-side called its *reference point*. Suppose we represent the reference point by a period. For some letters, like *a* or *b*, the reference point is exactly at the left bottom corner of the letter: **.a** and **.b**. For some letters, like *g* or *y*, the reference point is a distance up from the bottom of the letter: **.g** and **.y**. Draw a straight line perpendicular to the left and right sides of the paper and through the reference points of a sequence of characters on a line and you will have underlined the base of that line of print.

Each character has three independent measurements that state the amount of the space it will take in print.[8]

width. This is the amount of space the letter takes across the widest part of its horizontal extent.

height. This is a vertical extent, measuring from the reference point up to the top of the letter.

depth. This is a vertical extent, measuring from the reference point down to the bottom of the letter.

totalheight. Total height is height plus depth. It's a derivative measure.

TeX as typesetter regards a character only as a sized 'box'. It can, for reasons of space or aesthetics, snip some of the space between words or add some space. Kerning (squeezing or stretching space between a pair of letters) and making ligatures (merging certain sequences

---

[8] Actually, it's a bit more complicated. The extra space taken by an italic or slant character is also taken into account in sizing the box.

of letters such as **ff**) conspire to make typesetting still more complex.[9] Fortunately, we can rely on TEX doing the right thing for letter boxes. We need only concern ourselves with composing larger pieces of text within the environments available to us.

The TEX Font Metric (TFM) Files

The height, width and depth values of each of the up to 128 or up to 256 characters for a particular font are stored in a single, specific TEX font metric (TFM) file. Kerning and ligature information for character combinations is stored in the same file. Thus, *cmr10.tfm* stores measurements for Computer Modern Roman 10 point[10] upright.

When you use one of the loading methods shown above, it may be that the font you select is already loaded; i.e., its font metric file is already in memory. Otherwise, the program reads its internal list of file descriptors, matches a font name to the descriptors (if such a file exists), and brings the font's TFM file into memory because it needs the information stored in the file.

TEX, and consequently LATEX, is a typesetting program. In the many steps from submitting a document to TEX for processing to finally printing it, TEX's only job is to calculate how best to place characters on a page; and then to lay out the next page. To do so, it needs to know how much space each and every character in the text takes dressed in the current font; i.e., it needs box sizes and kerning information. LATEX cares nothing about specific shapes.

To position *Hello* in Computer Modern Roman upright size 12, the program looks up '110 (the octal code for *H*) in cmr12.tfm and use its size values: width, height, depth. It does the same to place the '145 character, (the octal code for *e*), and so forth. If it's not too fanciful, think of the end result on a line as a bunch of adjoining boxes of different sizes. On the outside of each box is a bar code indicating a code—the numerical position of that character in the particular font. TEX does this again for the next line. It stores all the box and code information in an output file with a *dvi* extension. The DVI file contains the equivalent of a set of marked boxes occupying all the lines of all the pages of the document.

---

[9]Box mode can also prevent ligatures. The ff in words such as *listoffigures* should not be tied. To prevent a ligation, write: **listof\mbox{}figures**.

[10]You can run Donald Knuth's *tftopl* program in an xterm to view any binary TFM file as text. Write **tftopl cmr10.tfm** to view the Computer Modern Roman size 10 font metrics. The program can also be used to view PostScript fonts; e.g., **tftopl pagko8t.tfm**.

No matter how the document will eventually be viewed or printed, the DVI file generated by TEX is the same—hence the name *DeVice Independent*.

The METAFONT (MF) Shape Descriptor Files

Programs such as *xdvi*, which shows the LATEX-formatted print-ready document on the display screen, and *dvips*, which translates the *.dvi* file into PostScript, need more than the TFM file data. They need to know:

1. The exact shape of each character, the thickness of each line—features that vary according to the font in which the character is printed. Shape information is held in MF files for bitmapped fonts. Lines, juts, arcs and fills are involved; and characters have 'body parts' such as *beaks, stems* and *notches* that can be sized.

2. The resolution of the printer that will output the document.

Using gsftopk And gftopk To Create Packed (PK) Files

METAFONT generates a generic font (GF) file from the shape information. *dvips* runs *gftopk*[11] on the GF file to obtain packed bitmaps of the symbols at the particular dots per inch (dpi) supported by the printer. Starting with the default font, *cmr10.300pk* would be produced for printing on a 300 dpi printer; *cmr10.600pk* would be for a 600 dpi printer; and *cmr10.1200pk* is the file for 1200 dpi printers. The GF files are erased as soon as the PK files are created. A PK binary file can be read in plain by running Rokicki's *pktype* program.

For non-PostScript printers, there is a similar program called *gsftopk*[12] for converting ghostscript fonts from the TFM file to a PK file to create packed bitmaps of the symbols at the particular dpi supported by the printer.[13]. As with *gftopk*, the results are packed into

---

[11]*gftopk* was written in the early 90's by Tomas Rokicki and soon ported to Unix by Paul Richards.

[12]*gsftopk* is a program written by Paul Vojta. It was, according to the author, inspired by *gsrenderfont*, which was written by Karl Berry. *gsftopk* uses ghostscript to create descriptions of print characters in TEX format.

[13]Actually you can run *gsftopk* yourself in an xterm, using this format: **gsftopk** *<fontname>* *<dpi>* For example, if the request is: **gsftopk phvbrn8r 1200**, the output file will be called *phvbrn8r.1200pk*.

a file whose name makes clear both the fontname abbreviation and the dpi. The resulting bitmapped file includes 'pk'[14] in the extension.

To understand *bitmapping*, imagine black letters in a particular font painted across an inch width of a mosquito screen. The screen mesh is modeling a dpi resolution grid. We say the pk file is bitmapped because each element of the resolution grid can only be one of two possible colors: white (zero) or black (one); i.e., its color can be represented by one bit of information. If the paint touches a mesh element, it's a one, even if only a little of the element is touched by the paint; it is as if the paint spread to cover the entire square element, making the outsides of some letters jagged. The bitmap for any letter is the pattern of zeros and ones in the space occupied by the letter. The finer this digital mesh, the closer the paint letters are to their ideal shapes—the less jagged they look. 300 dpi looks better than 150 dpi; 600 dpi looks better than 300 dpi.

PostScript Fonts: Real And Virtual

Adobe PostScript fonts differ from Computer Modern fonts in that they are not bitmapped. Instead, their shapes can be described by a set of vectors, so they are called *outline fonts*. They are readily expandable, because a zoom factor can be applied to the vector information. In their natural state, PostScript Type 1[15] font descriptions are kept in PostScript ASCII (PFA) files, which can be read (if not easily understood) and PostScript binary (PFB) files, which hold the same information in binary. The metric information for a particular font is in a AFM file; i.e., a file with a *afm* extension. Like a Computer Modern TFM file, an Adobe AFM file describes the size of each and every member of a particular font.

How TEX Uses Adobe Fonts.   TEX can not utilize Adobe PostScript AFM information; it is only equipped to understand TFM file data. So a program such as *afm2tfm* or *fontinst* takes the information from each AFM file and create a TFM file from it, which thereafter can be used by TEX just like a Computer Modern TFM file. PostScript TFM files prepared by the TUG group are available for these families: AvantGarde (pag), Bookman (pbk), Courier (pcr), Helvetica (phv), NewCentury Schoolbook (pnc), Palatino (ppl), Sym-

---

[14]If, when you run dvips or xdvi, the screen shows you that METAFONT is at work processing information about a never-before-used font to create a pk file, but no such file is actually made, you need to make the file world-writable. Or be *root* or *superuser*.

[15]Given the PostScript Classification scheme, this is the type that is germane to this discussion.

bol (psy), Times (ptm), Utopia (put), ZapfChancery (pzc), ZapfDingbats (pzd) and a couple of math fonts. Except for a few, each family has medium and bold series members, with normal and italics (or slant) fonts. Times-Roman, Helvetica and Courier go well together and can be used in place of the three Computer Modern families: Roman, Sans Serif and Typewriter, respectively. Fonts intended primarily for X11 are available in the fonts subdirectory under X11R6 and Ghostscript fonts are in the ghostscript subdirectory. In addition, various fonts can be downloaded from CTAN sites—the *freefont* file in the Linux/X11/fonts subdirectory, for example, has the PFB files for Agate, Baskerville, Bodoni and Capri, *inter alia.*

Loading a PostScript font to use on text is like loading ordinary bitmapped fonts—we call in a package to change default values or we use **\selectfont**. In either case, we specify an existing font, or the program substitutes an available font for the one we requested. Similarly, the TFM file information gets written into a PK file that, except for some header information, looks like a bitmapped PK file.

As part of its function, the *afm2tfm* program adds information about the font to *psfonts.map*: it relates the actual font name to its NFSS short name; it writes PostScript code to be inserted as is into the output; it names the encoding file for the font. *psfonts.map* lists the resident Adobe fonts that have the TFM tables that make them usable by LaTeX. *dvips* will search this file to determine PostScript font availability. Here are three examples taken at random:

```
phvbrn8r Helvetica-Bold " .82 ExtendFont TeXBase1Encoding
ReEncodeFont " <8r.enc

pncb8r NewCenturySchlbk-Bold " TeXBase1Encoding ReEncodeFont " <8r.enc

pplrre8r Palatino-Roman " 1.2 ExtendFont TeXBase1Encoding
ReEncodeFont " <8r.enc
```

phvbrn8r, for example, is the TeX name for Adobe's *Helvetica-Bold* font. Special instructions are bracketed by double quotes. *8r.enc* (in ˜*/texmf/dvips/base*) is called an encoding file; it lists the names of the characters of the *phvbrn8r* font in sequence from the first position on; and it describes relevant kerns and ligs. Unused positions are listed as */.notdef.*

Virtual Fonts. The previous section was incomplete in that it did not mention a difficulty in converting from Adobe PostScript to TEX. The same character in what seem to be similar fonts—Times Roman and Computer Modern Roman as example—may be in different positions in their font tables, hence have difference codes. So if code information for the characters is transferred in the same order as in the AFM file, some codes will produce the wrong character in the TFM file. (Because of similar positional code problems, you see funny punctuation like question marks instead of quotes frequently on the Web.) So a *raw* TFM file is not useful. Positions also need to be shifted. Moreover, some characters may not exist in the PostScript font. And kerns and ligatures are less precise. This complicates the task of creating a TFM file.

A solution is to create what are called *virtual fonts*.[16] PostScript fonts are easily adapted to serve as elements in this new way of creating fonts. The new font is created by assembling characters from one or several existing fonts—these actual fonts are called *base fonts*—and assigning these characters unique and specific code values in the newly-created virtual font.

What makes the new font *virtual* is that the characters do not need to be physically assembled. Instead, the new font consists of a set of pointers to different characters in the base fonts. A new character can be created in the new font from two characters in the base fonts (making an *ij* letter from an i and j), or even in other virtual fonts or even in itself. Either side of a composite character can be kerned. The order in which the pointers are listed determines the codes assigned to the members of the new font. Moreover, characters can be picked from any size real font and effortlessly set to the right size in the new font by linear scaling.

Starting with AFM files, a customized virtual font can be created and installed using *afm2tfm* or *fontinst*. *afm2tfm* was written by Tomas Rokicki and Donald E. Knuth; it comes with the Linux distribution. *fontinst* is a package written and maintained by Alan Jeffrey [Jeffrey94b].[17] Load it by writing a **\usepackage{fontinst}** statement in the preamble. *fontinst* is a set of TEX macros. It has the advantage over *afm2tfm* in that it can pull in characters from more than one font.

---

[16] An excellent discussion by Knuth can be found in [Knuth90].

[17] Get this off the Net from a CTAN archive; e.g., *http://www.sunsite.unc.edu/pub/packages/TeX/fonts/utilities-/fontinst/inputs/fontinst.sty*. Look in ftp://ftp.cdrom.com/pub/tex/ctan/fonts/utilities/fontinst/doc/ for documentation. Install it in the teTEX path; and run **texhash**. *texhash* rescans the entire teTEX directory tree to build an index of file locations, which it ships to a file called *ls-R* in the ~/texmf directory. Programs find files quickly because they search this index, not the actual directories. By running *texhash*, you make sure the new files are added to the index.

Beginning with the running of *afm2tfm* or *fontinst* on a AFM file, several different types of files are eventually produced: metric, shape and encoding. These are:

TFM files. Using *tftopl*, either program creates a Property List (PL) file for the AFM file. Knuth's *pltotf* program turns the PL file into a raw TFM file that holds the metric information TEX needs for typesetting. To be compatible with the TEX encoding scheme, some of the PostScript characters need to be moved from their AFM positions and other characters need to be borrowed from other font families to substitute for non-existent characters. This modified TFM file is created when *vptovf* is run.[18]

VF file. Either program produces a Virtual Property List (VPL) file that can be edited to add other characters or to shift positions. The VPL file is converted, using Donald Knuth's *vptovf* program, into a virtual font (VF) file[19] that contains the device-independent shape information for printing each character in the table. This is information that device drivers such as *dvips* need. As Jeffrey [Section 3, Jeffrey94b] puts it, 'Any device driver which understands VFs [virtual fonts] and can use Type 1 fonts can use the TEX Times-Roman VF as a drop-in replacement for Computer Modern.' This holds for the other PS fonts.

ENC file. Either program produces an encoding file, which lists the names of the characters in sequence. The character in position 60 has 60 as its code.

psfonts.map. The new resident font must be listed in **psfonts.map**, which *dvips* will read to see what PostScript fonts are available to it. The directions in the encoding file for a particular font (*8r.enc* in the previous example) will instruct the printer device to download whatever characters are needed by the virtual font mapping of the TEX encoding scheme.

FD file. This lists the available features for the members of a particular font family and its specific encoding. *afm2tfm* doesn't write an FD file, *fontinst* does.

Armed with encoding, metric and shape information about all the characters in the document, *dvips* produces a set of instructions in PostScript for the printer on how to print the DVI document. The PostScript interpreter is given a string of positions for the characters

---

[18]Of course, you can do more with virtual fonts than just copy a particular encoding. You can create your own particular font, encoded as you will, with symbols and kerns and combination letters that suit you.

[19]*vftovp*, also written by Knuth, performs the inverse conversion; it translates binary VF files into a readable VPL.

in the text, where each position is specific within its particular font. The interpreter determines the name of the character in each of these positions, using a code dictionary specific to the font. The character name might be */A* or */a* or */logicalnot* or */hyphen*, etc. It then looks up the name in another dictionary associated with the font. This dictionary provides the commands to write the vectors that describe a particular character.

A virtual font becomes real in a printer such as a Lexmark laser printer when the printer creates temporary bitmapped characters according to the virtual font's blueprints. The bitmapped characters are deleted after the print job is run.

After you have learned to manipulate LaTeX constructions such as lists and tables and after you have satisfied yourself that you can pretty much place text modules where you want them, more and more of your effort will go into finding just the right set of fonts to complement the meaning and nuances of the text. Which is to say that, eventually, you'll likely want fonts a little different than those that come 'off the shelf'. A partial solution is the *pslatex* package by David Carlisle [Carlisle96c], which makes the main fonts default to scaled versions of standard PostScript fonts: Times, Helvetica and Courier. (It requires adding *dvips/pcrr8rn.map* to *psfonts.map*.) A more satisfactory solution is to explore the possibilities of virtual fonts to create fonts appropriate to the specific document or set of documents. The recent book by Alan Hoenig [Hoenig98] provides a comprehensive discussion of how to create, install and modify virtual fonts, with clear examples of various constructions.

Chapter 12

ACCENTS, DINGBATS, STANDARD AND NONSTANDARD CODES

The previous chapter sketched some of the items in the large font wardrobe that is an integral part of the Linux distribution. For us to handle these various fonts successfully—to be able to mix them and match them to get a particular 'look' in the text—depends in large measure on (1) whether or not the fonts are currently in memory; (2) whether or not we are dealing with standard or nonstandard codes, or a mixture of the two; and (3) whether the fonts are being used in text mode or math mode.

First, and as a general principle, if we want a strip of text to be dressed in a font that is not currently in memory, we need to bring the font into memory and put it at least temporarily in control. In the previous chapter, we discussed ways of doing this either (1) by installing packages or writing specific commands that set default values; or (2) by writing macros that identified a specific font from information supplied about its NFSS components. Both methods presuppose we know the font we need.

Second, it matters how the font is coded. The keyboard is rigged so that the keys we push are translated to ASCII[1] codes. Each letter, number and punctuation mark is linked to a

---

[1] ASCII is an acronym for American Standard Code for Information Interchange. A font whose members have standard codes is using ASCII values.

different, specific, ASCII-coded 7-bit numeric value, some number between zero and 127. Alternatively, in many fonts, the font table contains 256 different characters, each with an 8-bit unique code value. This doubling of the number of values allows for the coding of many special and unique symbols in addition to the ordinary alphanumerics and punctuation. Then there are fonts—usually these are math fonts—that contain only symbols;[2] e.g., cmex10, in the table in Section 11.3.1 and below. As we saw in the previous chapter, it is the numeric value—the character's code—that serves as transmission coin between programs and devices and is eventually exchanged for the full character description.

Third, it matters whether the font is in text mode or in math mode. To anticipate the discussion below, a math symbol command name predefined by the program or some package must be enclosed in math brackets even when written in a *usefont-* or *selectfont*-based macro; e.g., $\star$ or $\Diamond$. All the elements in an equation—whether letters, numbers, punctuation or symbols—must be collectively bracketed with math delimiters. Using the *\selectfont* or *\usefont* commands, these same characters and symbols can be written as individual arguments to *\symbol* commands in text mode without math delimiters, although the printed spacings will likely be different than in math mode. (See, for example, the markup for using the Euler math alphabet font as text in Section 11.5.3.) Even a *pure* math font such as *cmex*, where symbols use the codes usually assigned to alphanumerics, can be written—if not understood—in text mode.

The MarkUp:

```
\newcommand{\MX}[1]{\fontsize{10}{12}\usefont{OMX}{cmex}{m}{n} #1
\normalfont\normalsize}
\MX{CM Math Extension is a math symbol font.}
```

The PrintOut:

---

[2]Is there a difference between a character and a symbol? If there is, it hasn't been standardized. The differences are vague enough so that symbols are often described as *special symbols*, not just as *symbols*. Characters are called *alphanumeric characters* or *ordinary characters* to make the meaning clear. These are some of the differentiations made. A character has an ASCII code; a symbol doesn't. A character is one where you push a single key on the keyboard; a symbol requires several keys. Some characters are alphanumeric; all other characters are symbols. (This seems to ignore ordinary punctuation.) A character is a symbol whose name we learned by the first grade. In point of fact, often all members of a font are lumped as characters. Or as symbols. To be really classy, or perhaps just neutral, you might call them all *glyphs*.

We begin by looking at ways to target appropriate fonts on disk. This means we need to know how they are named, where they might be and what they look like.

12.1   The Fonts On Disk

12.1.1   Naming font files

To make intelligent guesses about what files might contain characters and symbols we need in a particular context, it helps to know the grammar of font file names.

The file-naming scheme called *Fontname* was 'inspired' (to quote Karl Berry) by Frank Mittelbach and Rainer Schöpf and developed primarily by Berry and others [Berry96]. Most of the rest of this section derives from Berry's essay, entitled *Fontname, Filenames for TEX fonts*, which can be found in the ~/texmf/doc/fonts/fontname directory. It is an excellent introduction to font styles and other font features. It parses font filename abbreviations and shows how to decode a filename to obtain information about the features of the resident font. It also lists a large number of filenames; e.g., Appendix A defines *phvr* as an Adobe Standard PostScript font. PostScript files converted to TEX include: *phvro8tn.tfm, phvron8r.tfm, phvrrn.tfm, phvrrn8r.tfm* and so on and so on, all of which can be parsed using the *Fontname* scheme.

A filename is limited to eight characters, plus an extension, probably for compatibility with DOS-Windows. Fonts have many parameters, many of which branch. There is a lot of information to compress in such a small space. So the scheme is not cut and dried. That is why often 'normal' is ignored and only variants are especially identified. Each of the following parameters uses up one character in the filename, except *Typeface*, which is allocated two characters. Notice that some of these categories are familiar to us because they are also NFSS features, but some are not.

Supplier. The first character denotes the current supplier, not the original designer, if the two differ. Apple fonts begin with *e*, Bitstream with *b*, Adobe PostScript with *p*. A list of foundries can be found in *suppliers.map*.[3]

Typeface. *tm* represents, of course, the Times Roman (serif) style. *bk* is Bookman, *ch* is Charter, *g3* is Garamond Three, *g4* is Goudy Modern, *lc* is Lucida and *zd* is Zapf Dingbats. Several hundred more abbreviations can be found in *typeface.map*.

Weight. This indicates the amount of bolding. The thickness of a font line ranges from *a*, Thin Hairline, through *m*, Medium, and goes on to *x* for ExtraBold ExtraBlack.

---

[3] All the maps mentioned in this section are to be found in ~/texmf/fontname.

Variants. If the font and width are normal, this parameter is omitted. This is a complicated category, and includes typeface variants such as *c* for Small Cap and *e* for Engraved Copperplate Elite. A family may have multiple variants; i.e., Computer Modern Roman in classic TₑX and the same family in Cork 8-bit encoding. If the encoding scheme (the next grouping) is 7 for 7-bit encoding, 8 for 8-bit encoding or 9 for expert encoding, positions between the variant and the encoding category are reversed. Thus, TₑX Math Italic is *7m*, not *m7*. Similarly, TₑX Math Extension is *7v* and TₑX Math Symbol is *7y*. All three use 7-bit encoding. Using the same reversal rule, the Adobe Standard Encoding (*8a*), the Adobe TₑXBase1 Encoding (*8r*) and the Adobe Cork Encoding (*8t*) are all 8-bit fonts. Variants are listed in *variant.map*.

Encoding. If the encoding scheme is nonstandard, it is omitted here and surfaces in reversed position with the *Variants* category (see the previous item). The list is included in *variant.map*.

Width. Font compression to expansion ranges from *n* for Narrow to *w* for wide. At the one extreme are widths such as *o* for Ultra Condensed and *u* for Ultra Compressed; at the other, terms include *v* for Extra Expanded and *x* for Extended Elongated. PostScript scaling manipulates the width automatically. Virtual fonts should restrict width description to *n* for Narrow and *e* for Expanded. The list is in *width.map*. The character is omitted if it is *r*—Normal Medium Regular.

Design Size. This is an ordinary decimal digit(s), not octal, not hex. If it is omitted, the font is linearly scaled.

12.1.2   Directory names

With knowledge of how filenames are constructed, we can begin a search to locate the different fonts. Recall that Linux systems abide by teTeX rules (see Section 11.4). So the essential files for the different fonts will pretty much be in the same directories in the different distributions. (There is a rich collection of the DTX source files in the *tetex-texmf-src* subdirectory that are well-worth exploring.) The distributions differ in how they present the entire list of files that come with TₑX.

In Red Hat, use the *glint* package management system and the *Applications* subdirectory to locate the font files. You will find most of the 'working' files listed in the **tetex-latex** package. The subdirectories are alphabetically arranged, beginning with the *texmf-doc* documentation files. Just read down the list and, by now, you should recognize many of the fonts named. *˜/texmf/fonts/source/public* holds the MF files for such fonts as *bbm, concrete, pandora, stmary* and *wasy*. The $\mathcal{A}_{\mathcal{M}}\mathcal{S}$ *fonts* subdirectory is followed by the $\mathcal{A}_{\mathcal{M}}\mathcal{S}$-*LATEX* subdirectory, and it in turn is followed by the *base* subdirectory, which stores the Computer Modern fonts, and so forth.

Slackware compartmentalizes the same information in a set of files in the */var/log/packages* directory.

te-ams lists the locations of the $\mathcal{A}_{\mathcal{M}}\mathcal{S}$-LaTeX fonts, including *cyrillic, euler* and $\mathcal{A}_{\mathcal{M}}\mathcal{S}$ symbols.

te-base2 lists the basic files for Computer Modern. The TFM files are to be found in the `~/texmf/fonts/tfm/public/cm` directory.

tf-misc lists some of the text fonts shown in the table in Section 11.3.3; i.e., *concrete, gothic, pandora.* It also includes the *wasy* symbol family and several math fonts: *rsfs, stmary, bbm* and *bbold.*

tf-ps lists the Adobe and Bitstream fonts. The Adobe p text series includes such styles such as Avantgar (*pag*), Bookman (*pbk*), Helvetic (*phv*), Symbol (*psyr* is shown in Figure 12.11), Times (*ptm*). It also lists locations for the Adobe math fonts: mathppl and mathptm. The novelty Zapfchancery (slanted letters, many of which are with accents) and Zapfdingbats (see below) are also available. The files that hold the Bitstream Charter family are listed.

tf-sautr lists the files for the Sauter group. Their TFM files are not available. So you can't preview the various fonts in the family.

td-fonts lists various documentation files for the different fonts.

12.1.3 To view and use a font table

Find The Exact Filename. If you have no information at all on what font families are available or what they look like, run the system command *locate* in an xterm; i.e., run **locate .fd** to pick possible candidates. The FD filename for the family is composed of its coding scheme followed by the family name.

Or look at charts and examples of different fonts; e.g., [Rahtz94a]. As an example, were you to need some smallish bold mathematical symbols, the table in Section 11.3.1 would point to *OMScmsy.fd.*

Examine the FD file for the names of the different members. In this example, the *OMScmsy.fd* file indicates that bold fonts come in various sizes from 5 through 10 and have the root name *cmbsy.* Size 8 should be suitable. Filenames associated with the size 8 bold font will all be called *cmbsy8,* with some extension.

Any font listed in the FD file has an associated TFM file, so you need look no further. But you can, if you wish, double check. *locate* tells you that you will find *cmbsy8.tfm* in: `~/texmf/fonts/tfm/ams/cmextra.`

Run The *nfssfont* Program.   The *nfssfont* program lays out an entire font table so that you can scan for particular characters. The code values for all the characters in the table can be read off in octal or hexadecimal.

nfssfont.tex resides in *~/texmf/tex/latex/base*. It runs in whatever directories LATEX runs.[4] It will show the characters in any font that has a TFM file.

In an xterm, type: **latex nfssfont**

> The program will ask you the name of the font. (The example below shows how to request several font tables at one sitting, **cmbsy8** among them.) The extension is unnecessary.

> The program will notify you that you can obtain a list of commands by typing **help**. These include: *table*, which prints a table of fonts; *ALPHABET*, which prints all the upper case letters; *digits*, which prints the digits; *init*, which shifts interrogation to another font and *bye*, which ends the interview.

> The program prompts you with an asterisk and you type in one of the available commands. It then prompts for another command. A prompt followed by *[1]* means the chart will be split over two pages. If you need to erase a typing character, use the DELETE key. The Backarrow won't work properly.

> Visually, nothing happens until you terminate the program by typing: **bye** or **stop**. The table will be in *nfssfont.dvi* and can be viewed via *xdvi*. The nfssfont DVI files shown at the end of this chapter were converted to PostScript files and inserted into this document by way of the *includegraphics* command. (See Section 25.3.)

Figure 12.1 is a reproduction of a nfssfont session that requests tables for three different fonts. The program prompts with an asterisk; responses are in bold.

Determine Code Values From The *nfssfont* Chart.   Suppose, as example, you need the code for B in cmbsy8 font. To do this in octal, examine the output nfssfont.dvi file.

1. Find B in the table. View it as the intersection of the top row and leftmost column.

2. Read the first value in the row where the symbol resides. In this case it reads: '10x.

3. Go back to the symbol and read the first value in the column where the symbol resides. In this case it is 2.

---

[4]Recall from the previous chapter that the teTEX system follows the recommended TUG directory structure and lists all the texmf files in a database called *ls-R*. You can also input a file from a nonstandard directory, using the full path.

```
latex nfssfont

**********************************************
NFSS font test program version <v2.0d>

Follow the instructions
**********************************************
Name of the font to test = pzdr
*Now type a test command (\help for help):)
* \table
* \init
Name of the font to test = psyro
*Now type a test command (\help for help):)
* \table
* \init
Name of the font to test = cmbsy8
Now type a test command (\help for help):)
[1]\table
* \bye
Output written on nfssfont.dvi (2 page, 22212 bytes).
Transcript written on nfssfont.log.
```

Figure 12.1: A *nfssfont* Session

4. If *cmbsy8* is in control, typing \symbol{'102} will print B in your document. (You
   see an ordinary B here, because the *ptm* font is in control.)

If you prefer to express the code in hex, use the rightmost column.

1. Find the code for \symbol{"42} in the table by using the rightmost column. Note
   however that there are two rows associated with each right column element—call
   them rows *a* and *b*. If the symbol is in row *a*, use the top row of the table. If the
   symbol is in row *b*, use the bottom row of the table.

2. Read the last value in the row where the symbol resides. In this case it reads: "4x.

3. Go back to the symbol and read the value in the column where the symbol resides.
   In this case, it is 2, because the symbol is in the *a*th row.

4. If *cmbsy8* is in control, typing \symbol{"42} will print B in your document. (You
   see an ordinary B, because the *ptm* font is in control.)

You can find the corresponding decimal value by consulting the ASCII table in Section 12.2.

If, as is likely, some font other than cmbsy8 is in charge, you need to put the cmbsy8 font temporarily in charge. You can do this in several ways. One is to write a variation of the macro that empowers a new font. Recall that the \usefont command in Section 11.5 has this format: $\backslash fontsize\{<size>\}\{<baselineskip>\}$\usefont$\{<encoding>\}\{<family>\}\{<series>\}\{<shape>\}$. A macro we call CMB is based on \usefont; it will work with any symbol in the cmbsy8 table.

The MarkUp:

```
\newcommand{\CMB}[1]{\fontsize{8}{10pt}\usefont{OMS}%
{cmsy}{b}{n}\symbol{#1} \normalfont\normalsize }

Write \CMB{'102} here. And \CMB{"42} again.
```

The PrintOut: Write ℬ here. And ℬ again.

You can print any or many of the tables and then do a comparison of the symbols. **dvips nfssfont.dvi** will print the chart(s) on a PostScript printer. To save a chart, move it from *nfssfont.dvi* to some other file.

12.2   The Standard ASCII Codes

If the font currently in control of what is printed conforms to the ASCII standard—for example, CM and the other fonts in the table in Section 11.3.3 as well as Adobe and Bitstream all code in ASCII for the letters, numbers and punctuation of ordinary text—then we simply have to hit the right keys on the keyboard to print ordinary alphanumerics and punctuation. But even with these fonts, certain keys are reserved by LATEX. An easy way to properly print the character associated with a reserved key is to type its table value as argument to the **\symbol** command: \symbol{#} in decimal, \symbol{'#} in octal or \symbol{"#} in hex, where # is the code value. For example, a tilde is \symbol{176} in decimal, \symbol{'126} in octal and \symbol{"7E} in hex. In Emacs TEX mode, pushing the Double Quote key shows up as ' ' in the source document and prints as a right-side double quote ("). To obtain the " character, push the CONTROL key and **q** simultaneously; release; then push the CONTROL, SHIFT and Double Quote keys simultaneously.

This table lists all the 7-bit ASCII codes—for letters, numbers, ordinary punctuation and control characters. The code for each character is given in decimal, hexadecimal and octal.

Control characters use code values below decimal 32. Note that the lower case and upper case versions of the same letter have separate codes. For tables that are only partly ASCII, the punctuation and control characters will likely not be ASCII-coded, the letters and digits will.

A Complete Listing of 7-bit ASCII Codes.

DEC	HEX	OCTAL	CHAR		DEC	HEX	OCTAL	CHAR
0	0	0	nul	||	64	40	100	@
1	1	1	soh	||	65	41	101	A
2	2	2	stx	||	66	42	102	B
3	3	3	etx	||	67	43	103	C
4	4	4	eot	||	68	44	104	D
5	5	5	enq	||	69	45	105	E
6	6	6	ack	||	70	46	106	F
7	7	7	bel	||	71	47	107	G
8	8	10	bs	||	72	48	110	H
9	9	11	ht	||	73	49	111	I
10	A	12	lf	||	74	4A	112	J
11	B	13	vt	||	75	4B	113	K
12	C	14	ff	||	76	4C	114	L
13	D	15	cr	||	77	4D	115	M
14	E	16	so	||	78	4E	116	N
15	F	17	si	||	79	4F	117	O
16	10	20	dle	||	80	50	120	P
17	11	21	dc1	||	81	51	121	Q
18	12	22	dc2	||	82	52	122	R
19	13	23	dc3	||	83	53	123	S
20	14	24	dc4	||	84	54	124	T
21	15	25	nak	||	85	55	125	U
22	16	26	syn	||	86	56	126	V
23	17	27	etb	||	87	57	127	W
24	18	30	can	||	88	58	130	X
25	19	31	em	||	89	59	131	Y
26	1A	32	sub	||	90	5A	132	Z
27	1B	33	esc	||	91	5B	133	[
28	1C	34	fs	||	92	5C	134	\
29	1D	35	gs	||	93	5D	135	]
30	1E	36	rs	||	94	5E	136	^
31	1F	37	us	||	95	5F	137	_
32	20	40	space	||	96	60	140	`
33	21	41	!	||	97	61	141	a

34	22	42	"	‖	98	62	142	b
35	23	43	#	‖	99	63	143	c
36	24	44	$	‖	100	64	144	d
37	25	45	%	‖	101	65	145	e
38	26	46	&	‖	102	66	146	f
39	27	47	'	‖	103	67	147	g
40	28	50	(	‖	104	68	150	h
41	29	51	)	‖	105	69	151	i
42	2A	52	*	‖	106	6A	152	j
43	2B	53	+	‖	107	6B	153	k
44	2C	54	,	‖	108	6C	154	l
45	2D	55	-	‖	109	6D	155	m
46	2E	56	.	‖	110	6E	156	n
47	2F	57	/	‖	111	6F	157	o
48	30	60	0	‖	112	70	160	p
49	31	61	1	‖	113	71	161	q
50	32	62	2	‖	114	72	162	r
51	33	63	3	‖	115	73	163	s
52	34	64	4	‖	116	74	164	t
53	35	65	5	‖	117	75	165	u
54	36	66	6	‖	118	76	166	v
55	37	67	7	‖	119	77	167	w
56	38	70	8	‖	120	78	170	x
57	39	71	9	‖	121	79	171	y
58	3A	72	:	‖	122	7A	172	z
59	3B	73	;	‖	123	7B	173	{
60	3C	74	<	‖	124	7C	174		
61	3D	75	=	‖	125	7D	175	}
62	3E	76	>	‖	126	7E	176	~
63	3F	77	?	‖	127	7F	177	del

Characters that have key representation, the square brackets [and] for example, can be written as is or you can write their ASCII values. Write \symbol{91} and \symbol{93} in decimal. In octal, write the brackets as \symbol{'133} and \symbol{'135}. Write them in hex as \symbol{"5B} and \symbol{"5D}. These versions will all print as [and].

Computer Modern is ASCII-compliant for letters, numbers and ordinary punctuation. It uses the control character slots to hold Greek letters, math symbols and ligatures. Computer Modern Typewriter (cmtt) is otherwise fully ASCII. The other families are not. Some reserved symbols, < and >, must be $-bracketed and prepended with a backslash to be interpreted as a ordinary character by Computer Modern Roman; e.g., $\<$.

Incidently, the cryptic names of the control characters—the codes from 0 through decimal 31—go back before the 1960's. They refer to the original control signals for interacting with a communications device, e.g., the teletype. Original codes still in use in programming and printing are 7 (which will ring a bell) through decimal 13 (the carriage return) and 27 (the escape code).

00. nul	null	01. soh	start of heading	02. stx	start of text
03. etx	end of text	04. eot	end transmission	05. enq	enquiry
06. ack	acknowledge	07. bel	bell	08. bs	backspace
09. ht	horizontal tabs	10. lf	linefeed	11. vt	vertical tab
12. ff	formfeed	13. cr	carriage return	14. so	shift out
15. si	shift in	16. dle	data link escape	17. dc1	device control 1
18. dc2	device control 2	19. dc3	device control 3	20. dc4	device control 4
21. nak	neg. acknowledge	22. syn	synchronous idle	23. etb	end transm. block
24. can	cancel	25. em	end of medium	26. sub	substitute
27. esc	escape	28. fs	file separator	29. gs	group separator
30. rs	record separator	31. us	unit separator		

12.2.1 Built-In letter accents

For industrial strength jobs of printing in foreign languages, use the *babel* package.[5] It will mark up documents written in anyone of many languages—including Swedish, Danish, Turkish and Czech, *inter alia*. But you can use Table 12.1—adapted from the tables in Section 3.2 in Lamport [Lamport94a][6]—to add popular accents and ligatures to Computer Modern default families, with no need to bring in any special font or use the *symbol*{...} notation. They provide the appropriate accents when sprinkling foreign phrases on English text. Typically, imported phrases are written in italic, but these will work in all the fonts except typewriter. The accents are shown as they would appear on an **o**.

To accent an *i* or *j*, remove the dot with the \i or \j command, respectively. Write, for example, \'\i to print í.

The symbols in the table will all work in text or box mode. Some of the symbols in the table have been defined as command names; i.e., there is an alias for the symbol.

---

[5]To use it, add, for example, **usepackage[french]**{**babel**} to the preamble.

[6]Knuth provided several hundred named symbols—the Greek alphabet, binary operators, arrows, relational symbols, integers and filled circles—all of which can be used directly in Computer Modern. Most of these are intended for use in equations in math mode. To use them in ordinary text, bracket them with math delimiters.

Markup	Print	Markup	Print	Markup	Print	Markup	Print
\'{o}	ò	\~{o}	õ	\v{o}	ǒ	\c{o}	o̧
\'{o}	ó	\={o}	ō	\H{o}	ő	\d{o}	ọ
\^{o}	ô	\.{o}	ȯ	\t{oo}	o͡o	\b{o}	o̲
\"{o}	ö	\u{o}	ŏ	\r{o}	o̊		
\oe	œ	\OE	Œ	\ae	æ	\AE	Æ
\aa	å	\AA	Å	\o	ø	\O	Ø
\l	ł	\L	Ł	\ss	ß	?`	¿
!`	¡	\i	ı	\j	ȷ		
\dag	†	\ddag	‡	\S	§	\P	¶
\copyright	©	\pounds	£	$\pounds$	ℒ		

Table 12.1: Accents and Symbols for Foreign Languages

The top group (down to the first set of double lines) is never used in math mode, which has its own set of accents.

The symbols in the second third of the table (between the two sets of double lines) such as Œ or Å are used in ordinary text or in box mode. Protected inside a \mbox, they can be inserted into a math mode statement.

The last set of symbols will all work in math mode if bracketed with $. Write, for example, $\dag$ for †, $\ddag$ for ‡, $\S$ for §, $\P$ for ¶, and $\copyright$ for ©. Notice that *\pounds* is a different symbol in math mode than in text mode.

12.2.2 Trademarks and registries

Trademarks. The specific command name for trademark is **\texttrademark**. Or you can write your own using ordinary raised serif.

The MarkUp: `PostScript$^{\textrm{TM}}$`
The PrintOut: PostScript™

This can be abbreviated, for example, by writing a command such as this:
`\newcommand{\TM}{$^{\textrm{TM}}$}`

The MarkUp: `PostScript\TM`
The PrintOut: PostScript™

Copyright. Use the built-in: **\copyright**. For example:

The MarkUp: `MaText\copyright\/ is an integrated set of programs`
`to manipulate text.`

The PrintOut: MaText© is an integrated set of programs to manipulate text.

The copyright symbol can be abbreviated and raised; for example:

`\newcommand{\CP}{\raisebox{.75ex}{\copyright\/}}`

The MarkUp: `MaText\CP is an integrated set ...`

The PrintOut: MaText© is an integrated set ...

\textcircled will put a large, fixed size circle around a letter; e.g., **\textcircled{C}** will work.

GNU Copyleft. All of us who use Linux have benefitted from the philosophy of unhampered exchange of software, promulgated early-on by Richard Stallman and his associates at the Free Software Foundation. *copyleft* is the way the FSF promotes the unrestricted exchange of software. FSF urges GNU users to include source code when distributing programs. As noted in the GNU FAQ that accompanies Linux:

> The word "free" in the title of the Free Software Foundation refers to "freedom," not "zero dollars." Anyone can charge any price for GPL[a]-covered software that they want to. However, in practice, the freedom enforced by the GPL leads to low prices, because you can always get the software for less money from someone else, because everyone has the right to resell or give away GPL-covered software.
>
> ---
> [a]GNU General Public Licence

There is, however, no logo for *copyleft*. These would be some simple ways to write such a logo.

The MarkUp:

```
\prit{Style 1:} Emacs\raisebox{.75ex}{\prbf{CL}}\hspace{.15in}
Emacs\raisebox{.85ex}{\large\textcircled{\tiny%
\bfseries\sffamily\raisebox{.3ex}{CL}}}

\NC{\CpyLeft}{\raisebox{.75ex}{(GNU C\tiny opy\normalsize
L\tiny eft\normalsize )}}
\textit{Style 2:} Emacs\CpyLeft \hspace{.15in}
\newcommand{\CpyLft}{\raisebox{.85ex}[.8ex]%
{\bfseries\sffamily [GNU C\tiny opy\normalsize L\tiny eft
\normalsize]}}
Emacs\CpyLft \hspace{.15in}
\NC{\CpLft}{\fontfamily{cmfr}\fontseries{m}\fontshape{n}%
```

```
\fontsize{10}{12}\selectfont COPYLEFT}

\newcommand{\CLf}[1]{\raisebox{#1ex}{\CpLft}}
\textit{Style 3:} Emacs\CLf{1}\hspace{.15in}
\setlength{\fboxsep}{.6pt}
Emacs\/\shadowbox{\CLf{.5}}  \hspace{.15in}
Emacs\raisebox{1ex}{\Ovalbox{\CLf{.5}}}
\setlength{\fboxsep}{3pt}
```

The PrintOut:

Style 1: Emacs^{CL}   Emacs^(CL)

Style 2: Emacs^(GNU CopyLeft)   Emacs^[GNU CopyLeft]

Style 3: Emacs^{COPYLEFT}   Emacs^{COPYLEFT}   Emacs^{COPYLEFT}

If it seems ironic to have *copyleft*, when copy anything implies some restriction and ownership, recall what happened to Linux. The name was not copyrighted; so someone tried to claim it.

Registered. There is a special command name for registered: **\textregistered**. (See Table 12.1.) Again, you can write your own or raise it or create an abbreviated command.

12.3   Nonstandard Coding Tables

A font that has nonstandard characters creates a specific problem in how to print them; i.e., there are no corresponding keyboard keys for the symbols. These are some solutions. Those discussed in this chapter are variations on the two ways to introduce new fonts that were discussed in the previous chapter. If you use a variety of symbols from a large number of fonts, write macros based on NFSS components to cut down on the number of font packages you need to load. Part V discusses math symbols that participate in equations.

The font comes in a package that defines command names (aliases) for some or all of the symbols. Bring in the package with a **\usepackage** command. Thereafter you can use the built-in aliases.

Once these symbol names are brought into memory, they stay resident, no matter what changes are made in the serif, sans serif and typewriter default fonts both in family and size. A symbol package can equally well coexist with other packages that contain defined symbol names. Occasionally, there are specific exceptions. Euler, for example, a font that includes many named math symbols, specifically requests that *amsmath* rather than *amstex* be used.

The font package has no built-in names for the symbols. Bring in the package. Then create your own aliases with the **\newcommand** command. Or, if the font is in control of the print appearance, refer to the symbol by its code, using the **\symbol** command.

The font does not come in a package. Write a set of aliases for the different symbols based on their codes per font; the macros can be based on the **\selectfont** (or **\usefont**) commands for text symbols. For math symbols, if there's room for another math symbol font, use the *DeclareSymbolFont* command discussed in Section 20.2.5; command names for any and all symbols in the font can then be written without penalty.

The document is overburdened with math fonts. If the program announces it can't add another font, write equations that feature these symbols in another file and insert it into the document using *includegraphics*. To write a symbol or two in plain text, write aliases based on the character codes. Base the macro on the **\selectfont** or **\usefont** commands shown in Section 11.5.3.

The symbol command names (i.e., the predefined aliases) in math symbol packages can certainly be used in ordinary text but they must be encased in math delimiters. These packages provide math symbols whose size can usually be easily manipulated to match the current text font.

When a font—math or text—is in control, any character in the font table can be retrieved by using the *\symbol* command; e.g., writing **\symbol{5}** would print the character that occupies fifth place in the table. If you use the *\symbol* format, symbols from math fonts do NOT need to be encased in math brackets. In any table in which the letters and digits are ASCII-coded, each letter has the same code across tables: \symbol{'60} is the octal code for zero; \symbol{'101} is capital A, \symbol{'141} is small a. Punctuation tends to be more variable.

We begin the examples with Dingbat, a font primarily of novelty symbols, to show how to track information when a font is not part of a package. We use Saint Mary Road, the second font, to demonstrate the various ways that a nonstandard font can be utilized. We then look at the important text font: European Computer Modern and its text companion. A group of math mode fonts are discussed next, ending with *wasysym*, a font that contains both text and math symbols.

12.3.1   Dingbats

Dingbats are used as bullets, or icons, or alerters, or just generally to brighten up and lighten up text. Unfortunately, there is no package labeled *dingbat.sty* accompanied by a document that lists aliases for the symbols. So lets treat this as an example of what to do if we have no information about the font. Doing a **locate ding** in an xterm leads us to ~/texmf/fonts/tfm/adobe/zapfding. This has one listing: *pzdr.tfm*,[7] so we know we can view the complete table; it is obtained from *nfssfont* as *nfssfont.dvi*. Dingbats are shown in Figure 12.6.

But this doesn't actually give us the ability to print any of the symbols. So we do a **locate pzd**, which finds Upzd.fd (where the extension stands for *font definition*) in ~/texmf/tex-/latex/psnfss. This reassures us that there is a printable dingbat font accessible. So we write a new command, \DiF, that utilizes \usefont. Using a single large size, we try some of the values to see if they produce the symbols in the table. They do. Incidently, if this font—or any other—persists when you think you are quit of it, try writing the text that includes the special font in a separate new environment. Create a command and base the environment on it as shown in Section 9.4.3. Before you leave the environment, reset the body font default.

```
\newcommand{\dding}{}
\begin{dding}
WRITE THE DINGBATS HERE
\renewcommand{\encodingdefault}{OT1}
\renewcommand{\familydefault}{cmr}
\renewcommand{\rmdefault}{cmr}
\end{dding}
```

The MarkUp:

```
%The usefont args: {size}{baselineskip}{encoding}{family}{series}{shape}
```

---

[7]All Adobe's PostScript fonts begin with *p*. It's an easy guess that *zd* stands for zapfding.

```
\NC{\DiF}[1]{\fontsize{18}{22pt}\usefont{U}{pzd}{m}{n}\symbol{'#1}}
\normalfont\normalsize

\prbf{Some Dingbat Symbols:}
 \DiF{044} %scissors
 \DiF{070} % bold X
 \DiF{171} % filled rectangle
 \DiF{160} % shadowed square
 \DiF{054} % rabbit
 \DiF{376} % arrow
```

The PrintOut: **Some Dingbat Symbols:** ✂ ✗ ▮ ☐ ✌ ⇒

If you use these symbols constantly, create your own aliases. For the symbols above, you could write the long version shown or create a secondary macro:

The MarkUp:

```
\newcommand{\scissors}{\DiF{044}}
\newcommand{\boldX}{\DiF{070}}
\newcommand{\fillrct}{\DiF{171}}
\newcommand{\shsq}{\DiF{160}}
\newcommand{\rabbit}{\DiF{054}}
\newcommand{\arrow}{\DiF{376}}

Dingbats: \scissors\ \boldX\ \fillrct\ \shsq\ \rabbit\ \arrow\
```

The PrintOut: Dingbats: ✂ ✗ ▮ ☐ ✌ ⇒

If you don't want to write your own macros, use the *pifont* package, which you call with a **\usepackage{pifont}** statement in the preamble. Written by Sebastian Rahtz, it allows you to write individual symbols (e.g., \ding{'054} will print as ✌), a lineful of a single symbol, an itemize list with dingbat bullets or an enumerate list with dingbat numbers.

\dingline fills whatever size line on which it operates; in this case, the minipage is 2.4 inches wide. *\dingfill* fills the rest of an ordinary line, whatever its width.

The MarkUp: *The PrintOut:*

```
\dingline{'070}                            ✗ ✗ ✗ ✗ ✗ ✗
BoldX: \dingfill{'070}           BoldX:    ✗ ✗ ✗ ✗ ✗ ✗ ✗ ✗ ✗
```

The *dinglist* environment is a way of individualizing bullets in the equivalent of an itemize list.

The MarkUp:

```
\begin{dinglist}{'044}
\item Line item 30: 50\%.
\item Line item 17: 20\%.
\item Line item 24: 5\%.
\end{dinglist}
```

The PrintOut:

✂ Line item 30: 50%.

✂ Line item 17: 20%.

✂ Line item 24: 5%.

The *autodinglist* environment increments list items, starting with whatever style #1 symbol is used as argument. Moreover, if you provide labels for the list items, you can reference the individual items.

The MarkUp:

```
\begin{dingautolist}{'266}
\item This is the first item.
\label{item:dal1}
\item This is the second item.
\label{item:dal2}
\item This is the third item.
\label{item:dal3}
\end{dingautolist}
Refer to item~\ref{item:dal3}.
```

The PrintOut:

❶ This is the first item.

❷ This is the second item.

❸ This is the third item.

Refer to item ❸.

12.3.2 *Saint Mary Road* symbol fonts

This is a math symbol font. In addition to the wealth of boxes and circles with inserts, novel lines and arrows that it makes available, it has several points of interest. First, this font is an example of a virtual font, discussed in the previous chapter. It was developed by Jeremy Gibbons and Alan Jeffrey, author of *fontinst*, the program that helps you create virtual fonts. (See Section 11.5.5.) Saint Mary Road font is based in part on elements from the $\mathcal{AMS}$ *msam* and *msbm* designs and the Computer Modern *cmsy*. According to the authors, the font was "named after the palatial mansion (currently under investigation by the Environmental Health Officer) where we lived, and where many of the symbols were designed and discussed over a bottle of wine and some halva."

Second, it serves as an excellent example of the various ways you can customize the use of a particular font. Because of the slight variations in naming the components, finding the pieces is slightly tricky—not very, but just enough so you get to see some of the Linux countryside as you hunt and search.

These are ways to bring the font into memory and nickname the symbols.

Bring in the package. This is named *stmaryrd.sty* and is to be found in ~/texmf/tex/latex/misc. (The LATEX version of the *DeclareMathSymbol* method for naming math symbols is explained in Section 20.2.5.) The file contains an AKA for each of the symbols; these are two examples.

```
\stmry@if\DeclareMathSymbol\boxbar\mathbin{stmry}{"19}\fi}
\stmry@if\DeclareMathSymbol\leftrightarrowtriangle%
\mathbin{stmry}{"5D}\fi}
```

You can use these straight out of the box in equations or as individual symbols in running text; e.g., `Bracket the $\boxbar$ and $\leftrightarrowtriangle$ symbols.` The names are descriptive; you can rename them however you wish. Incorporate the math brackets as part of the definition. Two examples are:

The MarkUp:

```
\newcommand{\VBar}{$\boxbar$}
\newcommand{\PtLR}{$\leftrightarrowtriangle$}
Write \VBar\ and \PtLR.
```

The PrintOut: Write ⊟ and ⟷.

Run nfssfont The root of the filenames of the family members is stated in *Ustmry.fd* to be *stmary*. So you can preview the symbol tables by running *nfssfont* on *stmary5, stmary6...stmary10*. The table for size 9 is shown below in Figure 12.7.

Use the NFSS components. This is a way to avoid bringing in the package, which may count against the LATEX-imposed limit on the number of math fonts you can have simultaneously in memory. The FD file for the family is named *Ustmry.fd* [sic]. The several fonts in the family are integer-sized from 5 points to 10. Size 10 can be scaled in several sizes from 10.95 points to 24.88. The family name is *stmry*. Use this to write a couple of math symbols in text.

Designating A Symbol By Its Code. \MRY, a new command (see below), is used to write the symbol whose code value (in hex) is the third placeholder. We do NOT need to surround *symbol* and its argument with math brackets. The first two placeholders declare the size and baselineskip, leaving some latitude to change symbol size.

The MarkUp:

```
%NFSS args: #1,#2:size. #3:code. #4:family. #5:series. #6:shape:
%MRY args: #1,#2: size. #3: symbol code.
\newcommand{\MRY}[3]{\fontsize{#1}{#2}\usefont{U}{stmry}{m}{n}
  \symbol{"#3} \normalfont\normalsize}
Write a \MRY{8}{10}{5D} here.
```

The PrintOut: Write a ⇤ here.

Designating A Symbol by A Nickname in a Size-Variable Macro. Symbol names can be (re)defined in terms of defined symbol codes.

The MarkUp:

```
\renewcommand{\VBar}[2]{\MRY{#1}{#2}{19}}
\renewcommand{\PtLR}[2]{\MRY{#1}{#2}{5D}}

Write a Bar Box (\VBar{24}{28}) and a double pointed arrow
(\PtLR{24}{28}).
```

The PrintOut:

Write a Bar Box (▯) and a double pointed arrow (⟷).

Manipulating The Size Of The Surrounding Parentheses. Notice that ordinary parens are inappropriate. We solve this by writing a macro for varying parenthesis size.

The MarkUp:

```
\newcommand{\ASL}[2]{\fontsize{#1}{#2}\usefont{OT1}{cmr}{m}{n}
 \symbol{'50}\normalfont\normalsize}
```

```
\newcommand{\ASR}[2]{\fontsize{#1}{#2}\usefont{OT1}{cmr}{m}{n}
 \symbol{'51}\normalfont\normalsize}

Write a Bar Box \ASL{24}{28}\VBar{24}{28}%
\ASR{24}{28} and a double pointed arrow
\ASL{22}{26}\PtLR{24}{28}\ASR{22}{26}.
```

The PrintOut:

Write a Bar Box $\left(\boxed{} \right)$ and a double pointed arrow $\left(\longleftrightarrow \right)$.

12.3.3 European Computer Modern text fonts

Figure 12.8 is an example of the *dc* fonts, an extensive set of fonts developed by Jörg Knappen that provide the characters needed in different European languages in fonts that duplicate many of the Computer Modern styles. These fonts use ordinary ASCII codes for ordinary letters and digits. The other items in the font table are punctuation marks, single-character accented letters and ligatures. Documentation can be found in *The European Computer Modern Fonts* by Jörg Knappen [Knappen96]. Note that the *dc* fonts will eventually be known as *ec* fonts.

The fonts are named in NFSS style for family, series and shape. Size designation is unusual; it is indicated by a 4 digit number that is the size in points multiplied by 100. The example shown below is named *dcbi0900*; the characters are Cork-encoded (T1 instead of OT1), bold italic in 9 point size. The set of fonts is not packaged. and there is no FD file labeled T1dc... *whatever*.[8] Nevertheless you can use any dc font and its unusual symbols as the main font for the document.

1. Write either a **\usepackage{t1enc}** or a **\usepackage[T1]{fontenc}** statement in the preamble. This changes the codes for the document fonts to Cork encoding.

2. We need do nothing more to mimic Computer Modern, because cmr is the default in T1 encoding, just as cmr is the default in OT1 encoding.[9] It also means that we

---

[8]This is because the font definition filenames are the same as the Computer Modern fd filenames, with the difference that they begin in *T1* rather than *OT1*.

[9]There is a file called *T1cmr.fd* in */texmf/tex/latex/base*. This tells us that Computer Modern is defined in this encoding.

change shape and series exactly as we do when using Computer Modern.

3. To print a document in *dcbi900*, our example font, write this immediately after the \begin{document} statement: **\bfseries \small \itshape**. The document will look like any other document written in Computer Modern bold italics size 9, except that we also have a large range of accented letters at our command.

4. The file definition directory also contains *T1cmss.fd* and *T1cmtt.fd*; these mimic Computer Modern Sans Serif and Typewriter, respectively. You can make one of these the main font with ordinary family, series and shape declarations right after the \begin{document} statement. For example, writing **\sffamily \scshape \mdseries \normalsize** instead of **\bfseries \small \itshape** would write the document in ten point sans serif small cap ordinary line thickness.

5. If you use T1cmr as the main font, with frequent shifts to the Sans Serif and Type-writer families, it is a good idea to make the default font features specific. This next will do it for the dc substitute for Computer Modern Roman. It should be placed at the top of the document, in the preamble or just after the \begin{document} decla-ration.

```
\renewcommand{\encodingdefault}{T1}
\renewcommand{\familydefault}{cmr}
\renewcommand{\seriesdefault}{m}
\renewcommand{\shapedefault}{n}
```

Whenever you wish to return to Computer Modern Roman from one of the other two families, write: **\normalfont \normalsize**

Ordinary alphanumerics are typed as you would ordinarily type letters and numbers. Use \symbol{'#} to write any of the other items in the chart as an octal number.

12.3.4 *text companion* symbols

The *text companion* (tc) symbol package [Rahtz95] is the companion package to the dc fonts. Install the fonts package with a **\usepackage{textcomp}** in the preamble. The package has many simple, useful and hard-to-find symbols for currency, arithmetic and

\textdegree	°	\textcentigrade	°C	\textcenteredstar	*
\textdong	đ	\texttrademark	™	\textpertenthousand	‰₀
\textpilcrow	¶	\textbaht	฿	\textdollaroldstyle	$
\textcurrency	¤	\textsterling	£	\textcentoldstyle	¢
\textyen	¥	\textflorin	f	\textcolonmonetary	₡
\textcent	¢	\textpeso	P	\textthreequarters	¾
\textbrokenbar	¦	\textsection	§	\texthighdieresis	¨
\textcopyright	©	\textrecipe	℞	\textonequarter	¼
\textonehalf	½	\textlira	£	\textquotesinglbase	‚
\textbigcircle	○	\textsevenoldstyle	7	\textquotedblbase	„
\textacute	´	\textgrave	`	\textperiodcentered	·
\fraction	/	\textdivide	÷	\textregistered	®
\textborn	⋆	\textmarried	∞	\textdied	†

Table 12.2: Some Text Companion Symbols. Version 1.4.

genealogy. They work directly in text mode. Table 12.2 shows some of the symbols in Version 1.4; later versions have a modified set of symbol names. The complete set of symbols is described in *The European Computer Modern Fonts* by Jörg Knappen [Knappen96]. A list of aliases for writing the symbols is given in *The textcomp package for using Text Companion fonts* by Sebastian Rahtz [Rahtz95]. These are two examples of usage:

The MarkUp: It is 20\textdegree\ Centigrade outside.
The PrintOut: It is 20° Centigrade outside.

The MarkUp: \texttrademark\ is the trademark symbol.
The PrintOut: ™ is the trademark symbol.

12.3.5 Math symbol fonts

These are all math fonts. So you MUST enclose all aliases in $ math brackets even to serve as symbols in ordinary text. You don't, however, need math brackets if you represent a symbol by its code, where the code is the argument to the \symbol command in the current font.

$\mathcal{AMS}$ **mathematical symbols.** $\mathcal{AMS}$-$\LaTeX$ is a coming together of an earlier $\mathcal{AMS}$ package, $\mathcal{AMS}$-$\TeX$, and $\LaTeX$. Located in ~/tex/latex/amslatex, $\mathcal{AMS}$-$\LaTeX$ is a large source of defined mathematical symbols. Its multiple components are loaded separately as needed: e.g., *amsmath, amstext, amsfonts* and *amssymb*. *amsmath* contains additional features for displaying equations, *amstext* helps you introduce text phrases inside the display. The *amsfonts* font collection includes Euler, cyrillic and additional sizes in Computer Modern. Consult *amsfonts.sty*, *amssymb.sty* and *latexsym.sty* for their lists of defined symbols. Many of them are shown in [AMS95a]. See also [AMS95b] for a discussion on using the $\mathcal{AMS}$-LaTeX features.

The $\mathcal{AMS}$ symbols shown are part of the *amsfonts* package and are provided in sizes 5 to 10. Two separate tables are presented at the end of this chapter. The *a* set contains arrows, relational symbols and binary operators. A matrix in the *b* set contains a set of mathematical symbols including the negated binaries and a complete set of blackboard bold alphabetic letters. Figure 12.9 is the size 10 matrix for the msam set; Figure 12.10 is also in size 10.

PostScript symbols. This 256-element table, the *psyr* font, contains all the Greek characters, both upper and lower case. It contains a usable Hebrew block-style Aleph. (The other Hebrew letters commonly used in math formulae are in Figure 12.10.) Relational symbols, hooks and curves that can be seamed together are also available. The entire set is shown in Figure 12.11. The TFM file is in ˜/texmf/fonts/tfm/adobe/symbol.

There are also two Adobe math virtual font sets: *mathppl* and *mathptm*, both created by Alan Jeffrey's *fontinst* program. The *mathppl* tables contain 128 elements; e.g., *zpplcmr* has CM-style Greek letters and ligatures as well as alphanumerics while *zpplcmrv* has variously-sized brackets and circles with inserts. The *mathptm* tables are revised CM math fonts that are loaded using the *mathptm* package. They also emphasize Greek letters and alphanumerics. In addition, *zpzccmry* contains boolean, card and arrow symbols, while *zptmcmrm* has some musical note symbols.

***mathbbol* symbols.** The **mathbbol** package by Jörg Knappen contains interesting looking brackets and Greek alphabet letters.[10] It supplies command names for the members of the font. An alias needs to be encased in math brackets; e.g., $\bbtheta$.

***mathbbm* double strike letters.** The *bbm* package of double strike text characters (see Section 11.5.3) written by Torsten Hilbrich [Hilbrich96] is designed to be used in math

---

[10]I don't know if this is a random error or a concatenation of circumstances, but my copy of the package wouldn't work unless I commented out \ifbbgreekl on line 31 and the final \fi.

mode as additional math alphabets. The package defines the *\mathbbm* command for upright letters; *\mathbbmss* for sans serif; and *\mathbbmtt* for typewriter. A bbm math command and its argument must be inside math brackets; e.g., *$\mathbbmss{abc}$*. If a **\mathbold** declaration is prepended, the letters are printed in bold.

latexsym **math symbols.** This package contains only a few symbols, but they are popular ones. They include: $\Join$, $\Box$, $\Diamond$ and $\leadsto$. If you don't load the $\mathcal{AMS}$ fonts, which also includes them but is a much larger package, you can use this package to supply them.

12.3.6 *wasy* symbol fonts

Unlike dingbats, the *wasy* symbols (Waldis symbol fonts), developed by Roland Waldi [Waldi92] and copyright by Axel Kielhorn, are part of a package, with aliases for all the text and math symbols in the package. *wasysym* provide some novel small symbols, some of which are like dingbats. Evenhandedly, it includes a complete set of both astronomical and astrological symbols. It has symbols useful for complex mathematical displays and it has workaday icons such as a clock and phone.

The symbols have been given aliases, so, providing you have installed the package by means of the **\usepackage{wasysym}** command, you can print any of the symbols by using its command name (see *The Symbol Font wasy*, filed as *~/texmf/doc/latex/wasysym-/wasysym.dvi* for a list of symbol aliases.) The symbol table is shown in Figure 12.12. Sizes range from 5 points to 24 for symbols that work in text mode; both the medium and bold series are supported.

An alternative way to write a handful of the symbols without calling in the *wasysym* package is to use the nfssfont component values, determined from the *Uwasy.fd* file. For example, we picked a few symbols at random and wrote a new command as follows.

The MarkUp:

```
%The 7 WasiF args:
% {size}{baselineskip}{enc}{family}{series}{shape}{symbol}
\newcommand{\WasiF}[7]{\fontsize{#1}{#2pt}\usefont{#3}{#4}{#5}{#6}%
\symbol{'#7} \normalfont\normalsize}
```

```
These are some wasy symbols:
\WasiF{8}{10}{U}{wasy}{m}{n}{030} % hook
\WasiF{9}{11}{U}{wasy}{m}{n}{007} % phone
\WasiF{10}{12}{U}{wasy}{m}{n}{017} % music note.
\WasiF{11}{13}{U}{wasy}{b}{n}{100} % wave. Make this bold.
\WasiF{14}{17}{U}{wasy}{m}{n}{054} % face
\WasiF{16}{20}{U}{wasy}{b}{n}{142} % some kind M. bold.
```

The PrintOut: These are some wasy symbols: ⌐ ☎ ♫ ≈ ☺ ♏

12.4   Nonstandard Sizes: Banners, Posters And Spreads

PostScript fonts

The bitmapped fonts available in Linux are not suitable for banners and large-sized signs, but PS fonts are readily expandable. The example in Figure 12.2 makes use of the *usefont* command to write 150-point text. The *\ScaledPS* command takes three arguments, so size as well text can be reset.

The Markup For Figure 12.2

```
\NC{\ScaledPS}[3]{\fontsize{#1pt}{#2pt}\usefont{OT1}{ptm}{m}{n} #3
\normalfont\normalsize }

\ScaledPS{150}{180}{This\\is Big}
```

textfit

The *textfit* package, written by Sebastian Rahtz and Phil Taylor [Rahtz94b], is a welcome addition in that it expands size either vertically or horizontally. It provides large sizes by magnification steps or by points—you choose, but your choice holds for all the text in the document formatted by *textfit*. The package can be called with or without the magstep option.

```
\usepackage[magstep]{textfit}    %Expand by magnification steps
\usepackage{textfit}             %Expand by points
```

The PrintOut:

This is Big

Figure 12.2: Expanding A PostScript Font.

If you elect the magstep option, expansion is done exclusively by magnification. Otherwise, size is increased by points. In either case, you write two simple commands:

To increase height: use the **\scaletoheight** command.
>   Format: \scaletoheight{<*ToThisHeight*>}{<*text*>}

To increase width: use the **\scaletowidth** command.
>   Format: \scaletowidth{<*ToThisWidth*>}{<*text*>}

The results can be somewhat different, depending on whether the increase is by magstep or by points. If occasionally you want magstep increase and occasionally point increase, use the trick of writing another document and inserting it into your document as a PostScript file. You can use the magstep option or not for the small file.

There is a second option in the *textfit* package: *noisy*. If this is requested, the program reports its progress in working out the correct size.

These next examples were done by point increase. Note that *tiny* scaled to 2 picas in width prints slightly differently than *small* scaled to fit the same space.

The PrintOut:

tiny small large Huge

Figure 12.3: Scaling By Width. Point Scaling.

The Markup For Figure 12.3

```
\tiny\scaletowidth{2pc}{tiny}
\small\scaletowidth{2pc}{small}
\large\scaletowidth{100pt}{large}
\Huge\scaletowidth{2in}{Huge}
```

The Markup For Figure 12.4

```
\tiny\scaletoheight{2pc}{tiny}
\small\scaletoheight{2pc}{small}
\Huge\scaletoheight{1.8in}{BIG}
\normalsize
```

Several points need to be made.

1. The increase is relative to the size of the font in power. We conditioned our examples by starting them at a particular size: \tiny...\Huge.

2. You can NOT expand a small initial size as much as a larger one. Suppose, for example, you request a tiny font (at 5 points) to increase height to an inch (72 points). LaTeX will process it. But *xdvi* and *dvips* may not be able to handle it and then there'd be no output. Instead you will have messages such as:
   ```
   kpathsea: Appending font creation commands to missfont.log. xdvi:
   Can't find font cmr5. xdvi.bin: Not all pixel files were found
   ```

3. There is no wraparound for the text being processed by a single *textfit* command. If, say, the command is:

```
{\Large\scaletoheight{100pt}{Large programs are built from small ones.}
```

The first word and some of the second will fit on the page. The rest is chopped.

4. A page of oversized font may be too complex for the printer to print. Messages such as *Page 3 may be too complex to print* are common.

Figure 12.4: Scaling By Height. Point Scaling.

Foiltex

This is primarily intended to create slides and transparencies, but can be used for small posters and pamphlets. It prints attractive large characters in sans serif at size 20 points as default. The base sizes are 17 points, 20 points, 25 points and 30 points. The ordinary size commands are relative to the base size and will produce characters up to 51 points. Most of the usual font and positioning LaTeX commands work—if you don't write commands like *twocolumn*—except that the output is larger. There's an automatic logo that can be turned off with *\LogoOff*.

The program was developed by Jim Hafner [Hafner95] at the IBM Research Division, the Almaden Research Center in San Jose.[11] This is a new class, so it can't be inserted in another LaTeX class. Use it as a separate document. If you need to insert it in a regular document, as we do here, write and process a separate file, which you convert into a Post-Script file with **dvips -o** *<filename.ps>* *<filename.dvi>*. Insert the PostScript file in your document.

The package comes with a hefty disclaimer and a larger list of usage restrictions. If I have it right, you can use the program *and its derivative works* for your own non-commercial use. Write the author if you have questions. We used **\documentclass[25pt]{foils}** in the example shown in Figure 12.5. The textcomp symbols were written in Large.

Spreads

Call this package with a **\usepackage{letterspace}** [Taylor94] in the preamble. The spread can be made relative to the ordinary size of the text (*\naturalwidth*) or to the defined width of a line of text(*\textwidth*). Expansion does better without punctuation. A little goes a long way, but it is an easy way to emphasize or dramatize a small piece of text; e.g., the start of a new chapter. It will even compact text phrases in the multicols environment. Using it there, however, isn't cut and dried in that there's interaction between font, font size and number of columns. Some examples are:

The MarkUp:

```
\letterspace to .9\naturalwidth{Compress this.}
\letterspace to 1.5\naturalwidth{Expand this.}
\letterspace to .5\textwidth{Compress this.}
\letterspace to \textwidth{Expand this.}
\newcommand{\LS}{\letterspace to .9\naturalwidth}
\LS{Compress this.}
```

---

[11] Documentation is to be found in *foiltex.dvi* and *sampfoil.ps* in the *~/texmf/doc/latex/foiltex* directory.

The PrintOut:

Compress this.

E x p a n d   t h i s .

C o m p r e s s   t h i s .

E   x   p   a   n   d   t   h   i   s   .

Compress this.

\textdegree	°
\textcentigrade	°C
\textcentoldstyle	¢
\textsterling	£
\textyen	¥
\textflorin	f

Figure 12.5: Using Foils Large Font on Textcomp Symbols.

	'0	'1	'2	'3	'4	'5	'6	'7	
'04x		✁	✂	✃	✄	☎	✆	✇	"2x
'05x	✈	✉	☛	☞	✌	✍	✎	✏	
'06x	✐	✑	✒	✓	✔	✕	✖	✗	"3x
'07x	✘	✙	✚	✛	✜	✝	✞	✟	
'10x	✠	✡	✢	✣	✤	✥	✦	✧	"4x
'11x	★	✩	✪	✫	✬	✭	✮	✯	
'12x	✰	✱	✲	✳	✴	✵	✶	✷	"5x
'13x	✸	✹	✺	✻	✼	✽	✾	✿	
'14x	❀	❁	❂	❃	❄	❅	❆	❇	"6x
'15x	❈	❉	❊	❋	●	❍	■	❏	
'16x	❐	❑	❒	▲	▼	◆	❖	◗	"7x
'17x	❘	❙	❚	❛	❜	❝	❞		
'24x		❡	❢	❣	❤	❥	❦	❧	"Ax
'25x	♣	♦	♥	♠	①	②	③	④	
'26x	⑤	⑥	⑦	⑧	⑨	⑩	❶	❷	"Bx
'27x	❸	❹	❺	❻	❼	❽	❾	❿	
'30x	➀	➁	➂	➃	➄	➅	➆	➇	"Cx
'31x	➈	➉	➊	➋	➌	➍	➎	➏	
'32x	➐	➑	➒	➓	→	→	↔	↕	"Dx
'33x	➘	➙	➚	➛	➜	➝	➞	➟	
'34x	➠	➡	➢	➣	➤	➥	➦	➧	"Ex
'35x	➨	➩	➪	➫	➬	➭	➮	➯	
'36x		➱	➲	➳	➴	➵	➶	➷	"Fx
'37x	➸	➹	➺	➻	➼	➽	➾		
	"8	"9	"A	"B	"C	"D	"E	"F	

Figure 12.6: Dingbat Symbol Fonts

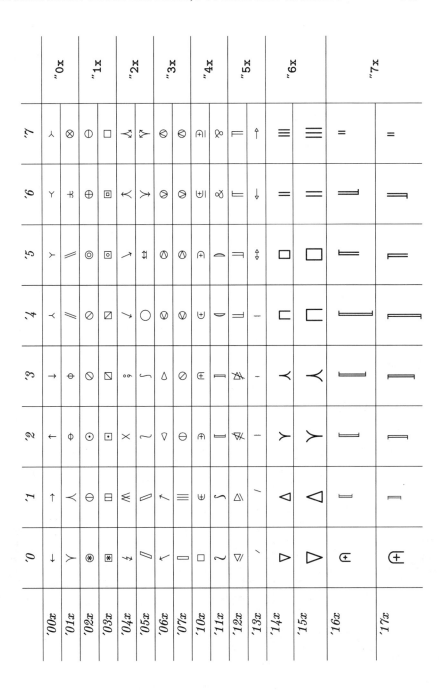

Figure 12.7: Math Symbols, St Mary Road font, Size 9

	′0	′1	′2	′3	′4	′5	′6	′7	
′00x	`	´	^	~	¨	˝	°	ˇ	"0x
′01x	˘	¯	˙	¸	˛	‚	‹	›	
′02x	``	''	„	«	»	–	—		"1x
′03x	°	ı	ȷ	ff	fi	fl	ffi	ffl	
′04x	␣	!	"	#	$	%	&	'	"2x
′05x	(	)	*	+	,	-	.	/	
′06x	0	1	2	3	4	5	6	7	"3x
′07x	8	9	:	;	<	=	>	?	
′10x	@	A	B	C	D	E	F	G	"4x
′11x	H	I	J	K	L	M	N	O	
′12x	P	Q	R	S	T	U	V	W	"5x
′13x	X	Y	Z	[	\	]	^	_	
′14x	`	a	b	c	d	e	f	g	"6x
′15x	h	i	j	k	l	m	n	o	
′16x	p	q	r	s	t	u	v	w	"7x
′17x	x	y	z	{	|	}	~	-	
′20x	Ā	Ą	Ć	Č	Ď	Ě	Ę	Ğ	"8x
′21x	Ĺ	Ľ	Ł	Ń	Ň	Ŋ	Ő	Ŕ	
′22x	Ř	Ś	Š	Ş	Ť	Ţ	Ű	Ů	"9x
′23x	Ÿ	Ź	Ž	Ż	Ĳ	İ	đ	§	
′24x	ă	ą	ć	č	ď	ě	ę	ğ	"Ax
′25x	ĺ	ľ	ł	ń	ň	ŋ	ő	ŕ	
′26x	ř	ś	š	ş	ť	ţ	ű	ů	"Bx
′27x	ÿ	ź	ž	ż	ĳ	¡	¿	£	
′30x	À	Á	Â	Ã	Ä	Å	Æ	Ç	"Cx
′31x	È	É	Ê	Ë	Ì	Í	Î	Ï	
′32x	Đ	Ñ	Ò	Ó	Ô	Õ	Ö	Œ	"Dx
′33x	Ø	Ù	Ú	Û	Ü	Ý	Þ	SS	
′34x	à	á	â	ã	ä	å	æ	ç	"Ex
′35x	è	é	ê	ë	ì	í	î	ï	
′36x	ð	ñ	ò	ó	ô	õ	ö	œ	"Fx
′37x	ø	ù	ú	û	ü	ý	þ	ß	
	"8	"9	"A	"B	"C	"D	"E	"F	

Figure 12.8: European Modern Fonts

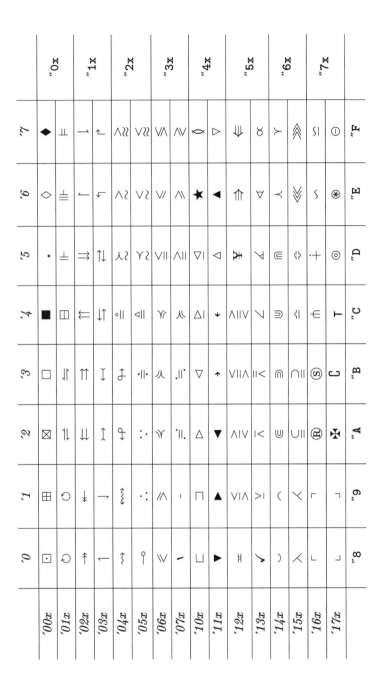

Figure 12.9: $\mathcal{AMS}$ Symbols, msam10 font.

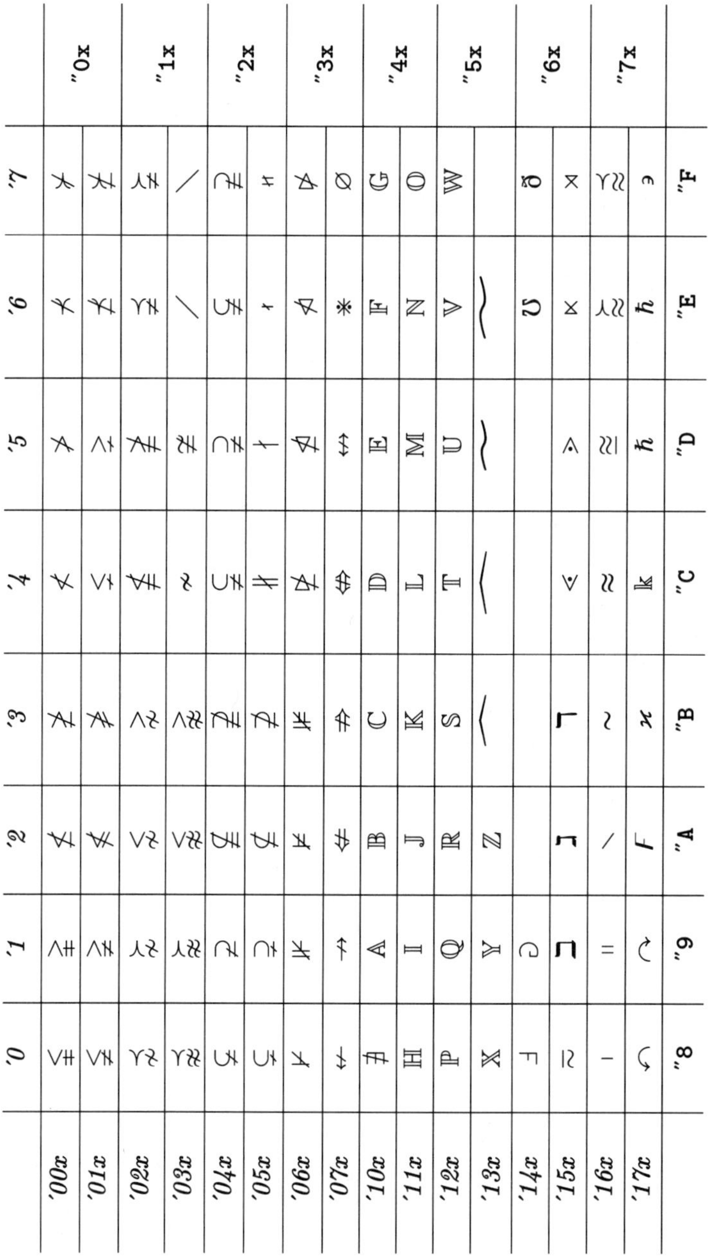

Figure 12.10: $\mathcal{AMS}$ Symbols, msbm10 font.

	′0	′1	′2	′3	′4	′5	′6	′7	
′04x		!	∀	#	∃	%	&	∋	"2x
′05x	(	)	*	+	,	−	.	/	
′06x	0	1	2	3	4	5	6	7	"3x
′07x	8	9	:	;	<	=	>	?	
′10x	≅	A	B	X	Δ	E	Φ	Γ	"4x
′11x	H	I	ϑ	K	Λ	M	N	O	
′12x	Π	Θ	P	Σ	T	Y	ς	Ω	"5x
′13x	Ξ	Ψ	Z	[	∴	]	⊥	_	
′14x	‾	α	β	χ	δ	ε	φ	γ	"6x
′15x	η	ι	φ	κ	λ	μ	ν	o	
′16x	π	θ	ρ	σ	τ	υ	ϖ	ω	"7x
′17x	ξ	ψ	ζ	{	|	}	~		
′24x		ϒ	′	≤	/	∞	f	♣	"Ax
′25x	♦	♥	♠	↔	←	↑	→	↓	
′26x	°	±	″	≥	×	∝	∂	•	"Bx
′27x	÷	≠	≡	≈	…	|	—	↵	
′30x	ℵ	ℑ	ℜ	℘	⊗	⊕	∅	∩	"Cx
′31x	∪	⊃	⊇	⊄	⊂	⊆	∈	∉	
′32x	∠	∇	®	©	™	∏	√	·	"Dx
′33x	¬	∧	∨	⇔	⇐	⇑	⇒	⇓	
′34x	◊	⟨	®	©	™	Σ	(	|	"Ex
′35x	\	⌈	|	⌊	(	{	(	|	
′36x		⟩	∫	(	|	)	)	|	"Fx
′37x	)	⌉	|	⌋	)	}	)		
	"8	"9	"A	"B	"C	"D	"E	"F	

Figure 12.11: PostScript Symbol Fonts

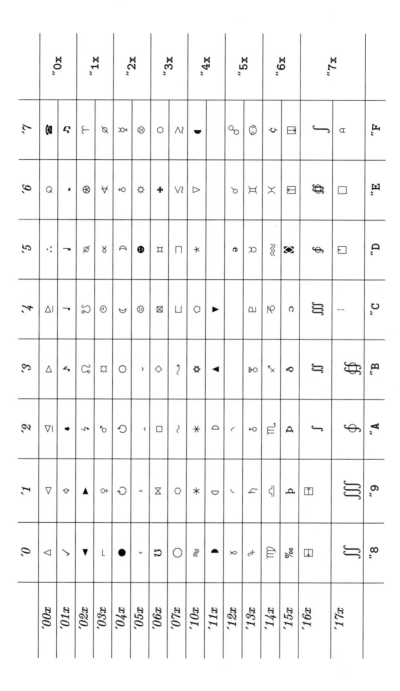

Figure 12.12: wasy Symbol Fonts

Chapter 13

MANIPULATING SPACE

13.1   Adding A Small Amount Of Space Between Characters/Words

To force a small space at the end of slanted/italicized text. If you stick to \text... commands like *textit*{...} or \textsl{...}, the text in the argument should be fine without adjustments. But, if need be, you can use \/ at the change from italicized/slanted text to upright text, *unless* the upright character is a punctuation mark.

The MarkUp:

```
''Need space after {\itshape Slanted\/} text.
{\slshape Don't need extra space before the period.}''
```

The PrintOut: "Need space after *Slanted* text. *Don't need extra space before the period.*"

To force an unbreakable space. Use a tilde. (See Section 8.1 for another example.)

The MarkUp: ``Use numbers from 1 to~10.''

The PrintOut: "Use numbers from 1 to 10."

To force a little space between single and double quotes. Use \, (a backslash followed by a comma) between a double quote and a single quote. This can be used in any mode.

The MarkUp: `She said, ''He said, 'Say hello for me.'\,''`

The PrintOut: She said, "He said, 'Say hello for me.' "

Dashes. There are the single dash, the double dash (en dash) and the triple dash (em dash).

- Use one dash for an ordinary hyphen between words.
    The MarkUp: `It belongs to the x-ray department.`
    The PrintOut: It belongs to the x-ray department.
- Use two dashes between page numbers or letters.
    The MarkUp: `It is to be found on page 10--16.`
    The PrintOut: It is to be found on page 10–16.
— Use three dashes for a true punctuation dash.
    The MarkUp: `Use three dashes---not two---for interjected text.`
    The PrintOut: Use three dashes—not two—for interjected text.

minus sign. The minus sign is the same keyboard symbol as the single dash. It is used in math mode, surrounded by math brackets.

The MarkUp: `It was $-10$ degrees Centigrade ($-$10\textdegree C).`
The PrintOut: It was -10 degrees Centigrade ($-10°$C).

dots, dots and more dots. \cdots, \ddots, \ldots and \vdots.

The MarkUp: `\prit{ldots} (\ldots) can be used in all modes.`
`\prit{cdots} ($\cdots$), \prit{ddots} ($\ddots$)`
`and \prit{vdots} ($\vdots$) work only in math mode.`

The PrintOut: *ldots* $(\ldots)$ can be used in all modes.
cdots $(\cdots)$, *ddots* $(\ddots)$ and *vdots* $(\vdots)$ work only in math mode.

13.2 Adding Significant Space Between Words With \hspace

If you leave more than one space between words, the program ignores the extra spaces, printing out a single space—or a double space after a sentence. If you need column spacing, use the tabbing commands in Section 16.3.1 or the tabular commands in Section 16.3.2. But if you need an occasional specific amount of space between words to fill out an area, add it—or subtract it—with a **\hspace{*width*}** command or the **\hspace*{*width*}** commands.

The Difference Between \hspace And \hspace*

Both \hspace and \hspace* add the argument width. For *\hspace*, if, by chance, the gap falls at the beginning or at the end of a print line, the space command is ignored. This is what you mostly want when you shift a block of text. *\hspace** will create whatever empty space you call for as it shifts the text to the right or left, no matter where it occurs.

To illustrate the difference between the space command falling at the beginning or at the end of a print line, we will use the first two print lines of this section, and the *hspace* commands. Observe the shift in the space between *spaces,* and *printing*.

The MarkUp:

```
If you leave more than one space between words, the program ignores
the extra spaces,\hspace*{.2in} printing out a single space---or a double

If you leave more than one space between words, the program ignores
the extra spaces, \hspace*{.2in}printing out a single space---or a double
```

The PrintOut:

If you leave more than one space between words, the program ignores the extra spaces,   printing out a single space—or a double

If you leave more than one space between words, the program ignores the extra spaces,   printing out a single space—or a double

Examples Of The \hspace Command Between Words

Except at the beginning or end of a print line, there is no difference in effect using *\hspace* and *\hspace**.

You can add up to a single space on either side of the *hspace*-specified width. Or you can move the space backwards to create an overwrite. A small-width backward command is also a way to adjust an occasional awkward gap between words.

If the space is 3/4 of an inch, then:

1. **exact fit.**
   The MarkUp: [WORD1]\hspace{.75in}[WORD2]
   The PrintOut: [WORD1]   [WORD2]

2. **Space prepended.**
   The MarkUp: [WORD1] \hspace{.75in}[WORD2]
   The PrintOut: [WORD1]   [WORD2]

3. **Space postpended.**
   The MarkUp: [WORD1]\hspace{.75in} [WORD2]
   The PrintOut: [WORD1]   [WORD2]

4. **Spaces prepended and postpended.**
   The MarkUp: [WORD1] \hspace{.75in} [WORD2]
   The PrintOut: [WORD1]   [WORD2]

5. **Space backwards.**
   The MarkUp: [WORD1]\hspace{-.25in}[WORD2]
   The PrintOut: [WOR[WORD2]

Creating Fixed Sized Horizontal Gaps

It is often useful to create several space wedges and use them as needed. This can be done using the complete *newcommand* command format as explained in Section 10.6. *sgap*, *mgap* and so forth will be ignored if they come at the very beginning or end of a line because they are based on \hspace. For example:

```
\newcommand{\sgap}[1][.25in]{\hspace{#1}}
\newcommand{\mgap}[1][.50in]{\hspace{#1}}
\newcommand{\lgap}[1][.75in]{\hspace{#1}}
\newcommand{\bkgap}[1][-.75in]{\hspace{#1}}
```

The MarkUp:		*The PrintOut:*		

```
This \sgap Mimics \sgap Columns          This    Mimics    Columns
1223 \sgap 233213 \sgap 12345            1223    23321     12345
```

Or try difference stretches:	*Or try difference stretches:*

```
Stretch \sgap this space.        Stretch      this space.
Stretch \mgap this space.        Stretch          this space.
Stretch \lgap this space.        Stretch              this space.
Stretch \bkgap this space.       thSitrspadce.
```

Adding Whatever Horizontal Space Is Needed

\hspace{\fill}

This will force space between words up to the limit of the text line; i.e., the total fill space is the width of a text line minus the total width of the text characters in the line. The fewer the number of characters on the line, the larger the fill space. In this next example, the space is equally divided between the words. The command is used so frequently, it has a short form: **\hfill**. For example:

The MarkUp:

```
FirstWord \hspace{\fill} MiddleWord \hfill LastWord.
```

The PrintOut: FirstWord   MiddleWord   LastWord.

LaTeX provides some variations for *\hfill*: *\dotfill* and *\hrulefill*. Thus:

The MarkUp: `The start \dotfill the end.`
The PrintOut: The start . . . . the end.

The MarkUp: `THIS \hrulefill  FILLS TWO SMALLER \hrulefill SPACES.`

The PrintOut: THIS —————————FILLS TWO SMALLER —————————SPACES.

\hspace{\stretch{number}}: This is like \hfill, except the fill space is stretched in proportion to the stretch number.

The MarkUp:

```
FirstWord\hspace{\stretch{4}} MiddleWord\hspace{\stretch{1}} LastWord.
```

The PrintOut: FirstWord   MiddleWord   LastWord.

13.3   Adding Space Between Sentences

LaTeX RULE: A sentence is a string that ends in a period (or ? or !), *unless* the character before the period is upper case. TeX puts a single space after a word; a double space after a sentence. Implicit in this rule is the command: **\nonfrenchspacing**.[1]

This creates problems under two conditions:

1. The period (or ? or !) isn't the end of the sentence; so you don't want a double space after the period.

    To force a single interword space: *immediately* after the period, write a \ followed by a space.

    The MarkUp: ``Smith et al.\ published their findings in 1960.''
    The PrintOut: "Smith et al. published their findings in 1960."

2. The Upper case character before the period really does end the sentence.

    Use \@ between the Capital Letter and the period.

    The MarkUp: `As is Grade III\@. This is the next testing date.'
    The PrintOut: 'As is Grade III. This is the next testing date.'

    More generally: to print a double space after a period, the question mark or the exclamation mark:

---

[1] Type **\frenchspacing** for a printout with only a single space after sentences.

The MarkUp: 'Yes\@. No\@? Maybe\@!'
The PrintOut: 'Yes. No? Maybe!'

13.4   Adding Vertical Space Between Two Lines In A Paragraph

13.4.1   Using \\ [length]

The double backslash is a simple way of breaking a line. But occasionally you want just a little bit more or less than the standard interline space. The double backslash has an optional length argument, so that the line is broken and extra space is added before the next line. The format is \\[+ or - <*length*>]. This is a useful feature in formatting arrays, tables and tabbed lines, where you have to mark the end of each line with a double slash. So additional space is easily added or subtracted.

For example, the appearance of this array

The MarkUp: *The PrintOut:*

```
\[ \begin{array}{cc}
25 & \frac{x+y}{1 + \frac{y}{z+1}} \\
15 & \frac{x-y}{1 + \frac{y}{z+1}}   \\
\end{array} \]
```

$$25 \quad \frac{x+y}{1+\frac{y}{z+1}}$$
$$15 \quad \frac{x-y}{1+\frac{y}{z+1}}$$

can be improved this way:

The MarkUp: *The PrintOut:*

```
\[ \begin{array}{cc}
25 & \frac{x+y}{1 + \frac{y}{z+1}} \\[.7pc]
15 & \frac{x-y}{1 + \frac{y}{z+1}}   \\
\end{array} \]
```

$$25 \quad \frac{x+y}{1+\frac{y}{z+1}}$$
$$15 \quad \frac{x-y}{1+\frac{y}{z+1}}$$

13.4.2   Using the *\vspace* command

This is an excellent way to control the exact amount of vertical space that you need. It can be set to any length measure. (See Section 30.2.) Its activity depends on where it is written. If it is set in a line within a paragraph, it does NOT have first priority. The program first finishes setting the line properly (including bringing in the words that follow after the space command as in #4 in Figure 13.1) and only then does it attend to the *vspace* command. Used between paragraphs—as in #3—it will leave the exact amount of space you write in the argument. The interactions between *vspace*, \\ and the *baselineskip* can create major visual differences in what starts out as the same text.

The MarkUp: *The PrintOut:*

```
\be
\item \LARGE A TALE OF \\ TWO CITIES\\
\normalsize by Charles Dickens
```

1. **A TALE OF TWO CITIES**
by Charles Dickens

```
\item \LARGE A TALE OF \\[5mm] TWO CITIES\\
\normalsize by Charles Dickens
```

2. **A TALE OF**

   TWO CITIES
   by Charles Dickens

```
\item \LARGE A TALE OF \vspace{5mm}

TWO CITIES\\
\normalsize by Charles Dickens
```

3. **A TALE OF**

   TWO CITIES
   by Charles Dickens

```
\item \Large A TALE OF\vspace{5mm}TWO\\CITIES:
\normalsize Charles Dickens
\ee
\caption{\textit{\BS vspace} in context}
\label{fig:dickens}
```

4. A TALE OF TWO

   CITIES: Charles Dickens

Figure 13.1: *\vspace* in context

\vspace will be ignored if the program decides to break the page at that point. To force a specific amount of vertical space, even if it is at a page break (at the bottom of a page), write an asterisk immediately after the command; e.g., **\vspace*{.2mm}**.

\addvspace adds a vertical length; e.g., **\addvspace{2in}**. This is a capacity measure rather than an absolute directive. It actually says: there should be 2 inches of vertical space

here. If some of the space has been added by another *\addvspace* command—say 1.5 inches was previously added—then the current *\addvspace* will add a half inch to bring the total space to the value written into \addvspace's argument.

13.4.3 Using fixed size vertical skips

You can define different vertical sizes by using different arguments to *\vspace*. Or you can create short names for specific sizes, just as horizontal fixed size gaps were generated in Section 13.2. In addition, as shown next, the program has defined some specific vertical gap sizes. In all cases, these commands do not have priority within a paragraph, only between paragraphs.

smallskip, medskip And bigskip. The program created these commands as shortcuts for *\vspace{ \smallskipamount}*, *\vspace{ \medskipamount}* and *\vspace{ \bigskipamount}*, respectively. The values for the short forms are:

\smallskip = one fourth of the baseline skip[2]

\medskip = one half of the baseline skip.

\bigskip = one baseline skip.

The MarkUp:

```
The printout record is stylized. A record is the abstract of a
journal article. NOTE: \textit{bigskip} is on the next line.
\bigskip
STARTING here, you might expect the rest of this paragraph would
be written after \textit{bigskip}, but it isn't. \textit{bigskip} is
ignored until the program finishes typesetting the previous line.
```

The PrintOut:

The printout record is stylized. A record is the abstract of a journal article. NOTE: *bigskip* is on the next line. STARTING here, you might expect the rest of this paragraph would be

written after *bigskip*, but it isn't. *bigskip* is ignored until the program finishes typesetting the previous line.

---

[2]The baseline skip is the spacing from the baseline of one text line to the baseline of the next. The program sets it automatically to approximately 120% the height of a text line.

13.4.4   Filling vertical space up to what's needed

If \vspace is set to \fill, then it becomes elastic and fills the available space. For example, \vspace{\fill} or its abbreviation, \vfill, shifts space vertically, thus:

The MarkUp: `The start\vfill the end.`
The PrintOut: The start

the end.

The MarkUp: `THIS\vfill  FILLS TWO SMALLER\vfill SPACES.`
The PrintOut: THIS

FILLS TWO SMALLER

SPACES.

Like the *\hspace* command, the *\vspace* command can take a stretch argument. This next will create stretches of 2 to 3 between the segments. In this example, the vertical length of the minipage holding the printout constrains it to 2.2 inches in length. The markup shows how the minipage options are filled. (See Section 23.2.2 on the minipage.)

The MarkUp: *The PrintOut:*

```
\begin{minipage}[t][2.2in]%
[t]{2.5in}
Start Line \\
\vspace{\stretch{2}}
Start The Stretch \\
\vspace{\stretch{3}}
Next Segment\\
Final Line
```

Start Line
 Start The Stretch

Next Segment

Final Line

13.4.5 The \par command

Unlike the *vspace* command, this forces an immediate blank line where it is written.

The MarkUp: `This line will be interrupted\par by a blank line.`
The PrintOut: This line will be interrupted

by a blank line.

13.5 Changing The Permanent Spacing Between Lines

LATEX conforms to the print rule that the empty space between lines should be approximately 20% of the line height; it sets the baselineskip—the distance from the bottom of one line of text to the bottom of the next line—to 120% of the font size. As example, if the font size selected is 16 points, the baselineskip will be a little over 19 points. The program sets the baselineskip automatically, but you can reset it to a different value anywhere in the document; e.g., **\setlength{\baselineskip}{20pt}**. Manipulating the amount of white space between text lines has a considerable effect on the visual appearance of the page. General macros to bypass the automatic setting of the baselineskip by the program are discussed in Size in Section 11.3.2.

13.6 Adding A Blank Line Between Paragraphs

Here again, use the *\vspace* command. The amount of space will depend on the size given in the argument. For ordinary 10 point font size, **\vspace{1pc}** should be about equal to a blank line for 10 point. **\vspace{\baselineskip}** is the same as a blank line whatever the current font size.

Do not attempt to use the \newline (\\) to force a blank line between paragraphs. The program sees this as an error.

13.7   Adding Permanent Space Between Paragraphs

The **\parskip** command controls the spacing between paragraphs. In many documents, there is no blank line between paragraphs; i.e., \parskip is zero pica. Paragraph separation is then indicated by an indentation at the start of each new paragraph. This is the default in LaTeX.

To obtain a permanent blank line between paragraphs, write the three instructions below in the preamble of the source document. The \flushbottom command must be set for this to work. (See Chapter 31.) Notice that indentation, controlled by the *\parindent* command, is reduced to zero. It isn't necessary if there's an empty line between paragraphs.

The program automatically resets the baselineskip whenever you reset font size, so that it stays approximately 120% of the current font size. As shown next, the **\setlength**{**\parskip**} command will change the interval between paragraphs to whatever the program has set the baselineskip, so this will work for any size font.

```
\flushbottom  % Stretch text to the end of a page, if possible.
\parindent=0pc % Amount of indentation from the left margin.
\setlength{\parskip}{\baselineskip} % Skip a line between paragraphs.
```

You can, if you prefer, set *\parskip* to a specific value. `\setlength{\parskip}{12pt}` would set the paragraph spacing to the default baselineskip for 10-point font. Depending on the visual appearance of the particular font, you may wish to modify the spacing between paragraphs by changing the routine setting by a fraction of a point or by one or more points.

13.8   Double Spacing A Draft Copy

To double space a document, change the **\baselinestretch** length, which has an initial size of 1, to 1.5 or 2. This should be done just after **\begin**{**document**}. To make it kick in, do a temporary change in font size. Try this:

```
\renewcommand{\baselinestretch}{2}
\tiny
\ignore{just some junk}
\normalsize
```

Setting *baselinestretch* to 1.5 or 2 will expand the space between lines—all lines—including lines in tables; the effect is not attractive. To retain table line proportion, one painful solution is to reset interline space just before each table with:
\renewcommand{\baselinestretch}{1}.

Rereset it to 2 just after the end of the table. Or use the package called *doublespace*, written by Stephen Page [Page86], which also sets the baselinestretch to 2. It also turns off double spacing in figures, tabbing and tabular environments and footnotes for you. To use it, write **\usepackage{doublespace}** in the preamble.

An alternative method—I found this in a FAQ—is to write **\linespread{1.6}** in the preamble or just after \begin{document}.

Another common demand is that all figures and tables be placed at the end of a chapter or the end of the article. The *endfloat* package by James D. McCauley and Jeff Goldberg [McCauley95] will handle that. It's documented in *endfloat.dvi* in *~/texmf/doc/latex/styles*.

Chapter 14

LISTS

Before we begin the discussion of lists, please examine these new commands. We will frequently use these aliases to create environments for the different list styles:

\bi	for	\begin{itemize}
\ei	for	\end{itemize}
\be	for	\begin{enumerate}
\ee	for	\end{enumerate}
\bd	for	\begin{description}
\ed	for	\end{description}

Each was created with a \newcommand. For example:

\newcommand{bi}{\begin{itemize}}

Basic Rules for Writing Lists

- ⋆ There are three basic list styles: itemize, enumerate and description. Each is written within a separate environment.

- ⋆ Once a list environment is asserted with a \begin{..} statement, the next statement *must* begin with **\item**.

* ★ Each item must be separately marked by an initial **\item**. But you can add additional paragraphs to an item, without labeling them as items.

* ★ Each list must terminate with an **\end{..}** statement.

* ★ Any list can be part of another, to considerable depth. A single enumerate list can have four levels. The numbers on each level are differently styled. We show the markup in outline style for clarity but it is not necessary. The program will provide indentation during processing.

The MarkUp: *The PrintOut:*

```
\begin{enumerate)
\item ABC
\item DEF
  \begin{enumerate}
  \item GHI
  \item JKL
    \begin{enumerate}
    \item MNO
    \item PQR
      \begin{enumerate}
      \item STU
      \item VWX
      \end{enumerate}
    \end{enumerate}
  \end{enumerate}
\end{enumerate}
```

1. ABC

2. DEF

  (a) GHI

  (b) JKL

    i. MNO

   ii. PQR

     A. STU

     B. VWX

14.1   The Itemize List

Basic Rules For Writing An Itemize List:

* We begin an Itemize List with a **\begin{itemize}** statement.

* We start each item on the list with **\item**.

* We end an Itemize List with an **\end{itemize}** statement.

- When printed, itemized items are preceded by a small black circle. The program prepends a bullet when it sees **\item**.

- If an itemize list contains another itemize list within it, the program uses a different type bullet for the inner list. As you can see in this example, the second level bullet is a hyphen; the third level bullet is an asterisk; the fourth level bullet is a dot.

This is a Four-Level Itemize List.

- The delimiters are used to develop an alphabetized index.

- Derivative field types are requested via the main field type:
  - To request a senior author index, type: sa/au.
    * sa is an abbreviation for senior author.
      · It is the first name in the author field.
      · It is not a regular MEDLINE field.
    * au is an abbreviation for author, a regular MEDLINE field.
  - To request a mesh subheadings index, type: ms/mh, where ms represents a mesh subfield, mh represents a mesh heading.

Except for obvious exceptions such as % and #, you may use almost any symbol as your bullet style, but you must write it each time. An empty bracket will produce a blank bullet. The default bullet is printed if there's no bracket option. (It can also be typeset using \textbullet.) You can create a newcommand such as \Star based on defined math symbols such as \star; e.g., **new command**{\Star}{\item [$\star$]}. Note that the \item token MUST be included in the definition.

The MarkUp:

```
\bi
\item [-] first
\item [\textbf{AA}] second
\item [@] third
\item [] fourth
\item fifth
\Star sixth
\ei
```

The PrintOut:

- first

AA second

@ third

    fourth

• fifth

⋆ sixth

14.2   The Enumerate List

Basic Rules For Writing An Enumerate List:

1. We begin an enumerate list with a **\begin{enumerate}** statement. And we end an enumerate list with a **\end{enumerate}** statement.

2. Each item in the enumerate environment must begin with **\item**.

3. As in any of the list styles, we can have a single word or a great deal of additional text, separated into paragraphs after a \item command. This is shown next in a section of an enumerate list.

The MarkUp:

```
\be
\item
\textit{alp} uses a log comparison to determine where an incoming
key word belongs in the chain of already alphabetized keys.

\be
\item Struct arithmetic isn't needed, because top-medium-bottom
positions are determined by using an integer for looping, NOT a
struct member.

\item The list is anchored at the top (A end) and bottom (Z end) by
two permanent structs.

pA is the pointer to the top 'goal post' struct and pZ is the
pointer to the bottom 'goal post' struct. pM points to the
midpoint struct. An entering keyword (KW) is first compared to
the keyword in the midpoint struct.

\ssgap \hfill  KW \hfill \ssgap \\
\ssgap \hfill  $\Downarrow$ \hfill \ssgap \\
pA \hrulefill pM \hrulefill pZ
\ee

\item \prit{squish} combines a sequence of records that have the
same key.
\be
```

```
\item squish consolidates or erases selected fields from a series of
records, whose key fields match.
\ee
\ee
```

The PrintOut:

1. *alp* uses a log comparison to determine where an incoming key word belongs in the chain of already alphabetized keys.

    (a) Struct arithmetic isn't needed, because top-medium-bottom positions are determined by using an integer for looping, NOT a struct member.

    (b) The list is anchored at the top (A end) and bottom (Z end) by two permanent structs.

    pA is the pointer to the top 'goal post' struct and pZ is the pointer to the bottom 'goal post' struct. pM points to the midpoint struct. An entering keyword (KW) is first compared to the keyword in the midpoint struct.

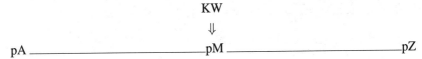

2. *squish* combines a sequence of alphabetized records that have the same key.

    (a) squish consolidates or erases selected fields from a series of records, whose key fields match.

As shown above, the default for the Enumerate List is a set of items, which the program numbers. But you can substitute words for the numbers. This can create a striking format, with the appearance of outdenting. We reuse an earlier list from Section 12.1.1, with much of the text removed.

The MarkUp:
```
\be
\item [Supplier.] The first character denotes the current supplier,
not the original designer, if the two differ. Apple fonts begin with
\textit{e}, Bitstream with \textit{b}, Adobe \PS\ with \textit{p}.

\item [Typeface.] \textit{tm} represents, of course, the Times (or
```

Roman) style. \textit{bk} is Bookman, \textit{ch} is Charter,
\textit{g3} is Garamondthree, \textit{g4} is Goudy modern,
\textit{lc} is Lucida, and \textit{zd} is Zapf Dingbat.

\item [Weight.] The thickness of a font line ranges from \textit{a},
Thin Hairline, throught \textit{m}, Medium, and goes on to
\textit{x} for ExtraBold ExtraBlack.

\item [Variants.] This is a complicated category, and includes
typeface variants such as italic and sans serif. \ee

The PrintOut:

Supplier. The first character denotes the current supplier, not the original designer, if the two differ. Apple fonts begin with *e*, Bitstream with *b*, Adobe PostScript with *p*.

Typeface. *tm* represents, of course, the Times (or Roman) style. *bk* is Bookman, *ch* is Charter, *g3* is Garamondthree, *g4* is Goudy modern, *lc* is Lucida, and *zd* is Zapf Dingbat.

Weight. The thickness of a font line ranges from *a*, Thin Hairline, throught *m*, Medium, and goes on to *x* for ExtraBold ExtraBlack.

Variants. This is a complicated category, and includes typeface variants such as italic and sans serif.

These are other ways to change list numbering: (a) the *pifont* program can be used to create eye-catching numbers for a list. (See Section 12.3.1.); and (b) additional text can be added to the list numbers. (See Section 30.1.6.)

14.3   The Description List

Basic Rules For Writing A Description List:

Format. The description environment begins with a \begin{description} statement and ends with a \end{description} statement. And each item begins with \item.

Versatility. The description list is versatile. It prepends no bullet or number, so it is the best one to use when modifying a list style to suit yourself.

Initial Bolding. It allows you to bold the first part of the text in an item, if you wish. You insert the text for bolding inside square brackets right after \item.

For example:

The MarkUp: \item [First Type.] The first type of fiberglass hull..

The PrintOut: **First Type.** The first type of fiberglass hull..

An Ambiguity. This syntax—\item follows by [—can be the occasion of an error if both these conditions obtain:

1. You choose not to bold the first part of the item text.

2. *But* you write a single left bracket immediately after \item.

For example, if the Markup is:

\item [. The left square bracket starts a text aside.

the program would assume the left bracket was the start of the text to be bolded. It would search for the terminating right bracket, which doesn't exist. The program would then call it an error (See Section 7.1 on error correction.)

Protecting Initial Text Brackets. If a left square bracket is the initial text after \item in a description list, the text needs to be protected. Do this by bracketing the text with a pair of braces.

The MarkUp: \item {[. } The left square bracket starts a text aside.

The PrintOut: [. The left square bracket starts a text aside.

The MarkUp:
```
\bd
\item [\Large\textit{Supplier}.] The first character denotes the
current supplier, not the original designer, if the two differ.
Apple fonts begin with \textit{e}, Bitstream with \textit{b},
Adobe \PS\ with \textit{p}.

\item [\Large\textit{Typeface}.] \textit{tm} represents, of course,
the Times (or Roman) style. \textit{bk} is Bookman, \textit{ch} is
Charter, \textit{g3} is Garamondthree, \textit{g4} is Goudy modern,
\textit{lc} is Lucida, and \textit{zd} is Zapf Dingbat.
\ed
```

The PrintOut:

Supplier. The first character denotes the current supplier, not the original designer, if the two differ. Apple fonts begin with *e*, Bitstream with *b*, Adobe PostScript with *p*.

Typeface. *tm* represents, of course, the Times (or Roman) style. *bk* is Bookman, *ch* is Charter, *g3* is Garamondthree, *g4* is Goudy modern, *lc* is Lucida, and *zd* is Zapf Dingbat.

14.4   Other Description List Styles

New list styles can be created by modifying a description environment as in these next examples.

Example 1:

This new environment, for example, would write each item in italic:

The MarkUp: *The PrintOut:*

```
\newenvironment{itlistA}%
{\begin{description}\itshape}
{\end{description}}
```

This is a method.

And this is another method.

```
\begin{itlistA}
\item This is a method.
\item And this is another method.
\end{itlistA}
```

Example 2:

Whereas this new command—call it *itlistB*—would italicize just the initial text of each item.

The MarkUp:

```
\newcommand{itlistB}[2]%
{\textit{#1} #2}

\begin{description}
\item \itlistB{Method 1.}%
{This is a method.}
\item \itlistB{Method 2.}%
{ And this is another method.}
\end{description}
```

The PrintOut:

Method 1. This is a method.

Method 2.   And this is another method.

Example 3:

In the Description List template, the bracketed text is called the *Label*. The distance between it and the start of the paragraph text is called \labelsep, which is set to 5 points by default. It is impossible to force the paragraph text onto a separate line by using the *vspace* command. You can, however, force a new line by resetting \labelsep to some size larger than the line width. Be sure to reset it, unless you want all the lists to start paragraph text on a separate line.

The MarkUp:

```
\setlength{\labelsep}{7in} \bd
\item [\Large\textit{Supplier}.] The first character denotes the
current supplier, not the original designer, if the two differ.
Apple fonts begin with \textit{e}, Bitstream with \textit{b},
Adobe \PS\ with \textit{p}.

\item [\Large\textit{Typeface}.] \textit{tm} represents, of course,
the Times (or Roman) style. \textit{bk} is Bookman, \textit{ch} is
Charter, \textit{g3} is Garamondthree, \textit{g4} is Goudy modern,
\textit{lc} is Lucida, and \textit{zd} is Zapf Dingbat. \ed
\setlength{\labelsep}{5pt}
```

The PrintOut:

Supplier.

The first character denotes the current supplier, not the original designer, if the two differ. Apple fonts begin with *e*, Bitstream with *b*, Adobe PostScript with *p*.

Typeface.

> *tm* represents, of course, the Times (or Roman) style. *bk* is Bookman, *ch* is Charter, *g3* is Garamondthree, *g4* is Goudy modern, *lc* is Lucida, and *zd* is Zapf Dingbat.

Example 4:

What follows is a markup for a list that is in Section 31.3.2. It nests one list within another. It was constructed to provide space for the examples and not look cramped. Because there are just a few numbers, we wrote them in 'by hand'. The example illustrates the variations that can be achieved by the judicious use of *hspace* and *vspace*.

```
\bd
\item \hspace{-.25in}\prbf{(1.) Books, reports.}\hspace{1pc}\vspace{2pt}
\bi
\item [\prtt{Even Page:}] Section HeaderText\hfill Chapter HeaderText

\item [\prtt{Odd Page:}] Chapter HeaderText\hfill Section HeaderText
\ei

\hspace{-.25in}For example: \\[.4pc]
\texttt{Even pages:} 11.1 Font Terminology\hfill Chapter 11. Fonts.\\
\texttt{Odd pages:} Chapter 11. Fonts.\hfill 11.1 Font Terminology

\item \hspace{-.25in}\textbf{(2.) Two-sided articles.}
\hspace{1pc}\vspace*{8pt}

The style will be similar to the book style. The top two divisions in
the article will be written in the header instead of Chapter HeaderText
and Section HeaderText.

\item \hspace{-.25in}\textbf{(3.) One-sided documents.}
\hspace{1pc}\vspace*{2pt}
\bi
\item [\texttt{Each page:}]\hfill Section HeaderText \textit{OR}
Subsection HeaderText
\ei

\item \hspace{-.25in}\prbf{(4.) Page number.}\hspace{1pc}\vspace*{8pt}

The page number will appear by itself in the middle of the footer on
all pages, including the start of a Chapter.
```

```
\item \hspace{-.25in}\textbf{(5.) Chapter.} \hspace{1pc}\vspace*{8pt}
```

```
The page that starts a chapter will have no header.
\ed
```

14.5   The Trivlist Environment

The usual separation between label and text is omitted, but items are separated with intervening blank lines. So it's an easy way to emphasize a set of remarks if your style is to
indent paragraphs with no blank lines between paragraphs.

The MarkUp:
```
 \begin{trivlist}
\item [\Large\textit{Supplier}.] The first character denotes the
current supplier, not the original designer, if the two differ.
Apple fonts begin with \textit{e}, Bitstream with \textit{b},
Adobe \PS\ with \textit{p}. \end{trivlist}
```

The PrintOut:

Supplier. The first character denotes the current supplier, not the original designer, if
the two differ. Apple fonts begin with *e*, Bitstream with *b*, Adobe PostScript with *p*.

Chapter 15

ALIGNING AND INDENTING TEXT

15.1 Aligning The Text Horizontally

Vertical alignment of headers and footers with respect to the top and bottom of the page is defined at the start of the document. The appearance of the page at major document divisions—chapter, section, and so forth—depends on the specific font and spacing built into the document class for that division. Spacing between paragraphs can be modified by resetting \parskip. Rotation is done in the graphics and picture packages and is discussed in Part 7. Horizontal alignment refers to the way the main body text is blocked out on the page relative to the right and left edges of the paper. This chapter examines how LATEX changes local horizontal alignment.

Text is justified by default in all document classes. When we say *justified*, we mean that the text lines within a paragraph begin at the same distance from the left edge of the paper, and, because the program hyphenates words and manipulates space on the line, they end at the same distance from the right edge of the paper.

Other alignments are possible. A text paragraph can be aligned on the left only; i.e., all the lines begin at the same distance from the edge on the left but a line can be of any length, providing it doesn't overflow the amount of space allocated to a line of text. Such an alignment is called *ragged right*. Or the lines in the paragraph can be *ragged left*, meaning that they are aligned at the right margin, but the lines can begin anywhere on the left.

Occasionally you might want ragged text, with all the lines beginning in the same column on the left—in writing blank verse, as example—or ending in the same column on the right. Combined with Courier font, ragged lines give the document a hand-typed look. (Heck, if that's what you want to achieve, be creative—overstrike a few words, use some of the whiteout that's been in the back of the desk for ten years...)

Or each line can be individually centered on the page; these are center column justified, with equal amounts of space on either side.

The available instructions for horizontal alignments other than the default alignment have a declaration form and a separate environment form. They are:

	Environment:	**Declaration:**
Aligned on the left:	\begin{flushleft} \end{flushleft}	\raggedright
Aligned on the right:	\begin{flushright} \end{flushright}	\raggedleft
Centered:	\begin{center} \end{center}	\centering

declaration. Use one of these alignment declarations early in the document to format the entire document. The text will be unjustified beginning wherever you write the declaration. The scope of the declaration will be up to the right-side bracket of the command or environment in which it is located. The alignment declarations are used in text mode and box mode. The centering declaration, declared just inside a table environment, will center the table on the page.

If you use a *raggedright* declaration, return to justified paragraphs with a **\setlength-**{**\rightskip**}{**0pt**} command. Similarly, with a *raggedleft* declaration, use a **\setlength**{**\leftskip**}{**0pt**} command. Morever, ragged or centering declarations can be controlled indirectly by inserting them inside another environment, as is done by placing *\centering* in a minipage in the next example. (Minipage, tabular and list environments automatically restore paragraph alignment when they terminate.)

environment. An alignment environment can be placed anywhere in the document to format that part of the document. An example of the center environment can be seen in Section 15.6.3.

Notice in this next example, how the boundary between the flushleft and the centering instructions is processed. While assembling the line for printing, the program is not told to stop after *does not a poem make.* It continues on until stopped by the \\ after *Not even.* By that time, the \centering declaration has taken over control. So the entire line is printed centered. Try this with a \\ after *does not a poem make.*

The MarkUp:

```
This is justified.
\begin{flushleft}
This proves that\\
Just writing some syllables\\
funny \\
does not a poem make.
\centering
Not even\\
if it is nicely centered.
\end{flushleft}
```

The PrintOut:

This is justified.

This proves that
Just writing some syllables
funny
           does not a poem make. Not even
               if it is nicely centered.

15.2   Raising Text

Text can be raised just as math expressions can:

^{...}. This raises text written in 5 point a fixed amount. For example:

> *The MarkUp:* This will ^{raise the text} within the argument.

> *The PrintOut:* This will ^{raise the text} within the argument.

\raisebox{...}. This gives you more control, in that you can raise the text different amounts. And you can change font size. For example:

> *The MarkUp:* This will \raisebox{.1in}{\tiny raise the text} within the argument.

> *The PrintOut:* This will ^{raise the text} within the argument.

> *The MarkUp:* This will \raisebox{.08in}{\large \bfseries raise the text} within the argument.

> *The PrintOut:* This will **raise the text** within the argument.

Indenting and, to a lesser extent, *outdenting* are major ways to change the general appearance of a block of text. The rest of the chapter describes ways to handle indentation in

LATEX: both line indenting/outdenting and paragraph indentation.

15.3   Outdenting

Section 13.2 described how the \hspace*{...} command shifts text horizontally. If the argument of the command is a negative value, the text line that follows the command is shifted to the left.

Using this notion, we can do outspacing or outdenting on the left for a single line, usually the first line. The first words in the outdent can be made dramatic, as we show here:

The MarkUp:

```
\hspace*{-.25in}\textbf{\LARGE Section~\ref{ss:gaps}} describes how
the \BS hspace*{...} command shifts text horizontally. If the argument
of the command is a negative value, the text line that follows the
command is shifted to the left.
```

The PrintOut:

Section 13.2 describes how the \hspace*{...} command shifts text horizontally. If the argument of the command is a negative value, the text line that follows the command is shifted to the left.

An alternative, one that works well for an enumerate list of items, is shown in Section 14.2, where you substitute words for the default numbering. The outdents can be typeset in various shapes and sizes. These are some examples:

The MarkUp:
```
 \be
\item [\textsc{\small Supplier}] The first character denotes the
current supplier, not the original designer, if the two differ.
Apple fonts begin with \textit{e}, Bitstream with \textit{b}.

\item [\textit{\Large Type.}] \textit{tm} represents, of
course, the Times (or Roman) style. \textit{bk} is Bookman,
\textit{ch} is Charter, \textit{g3} is Garamondthree, \textit{g4}
is Goudy Modern, \textit{lc} is Lucida.
```

```
\item [\textsf{Weight.}] The thickness of a font line ranges from
\textit{a}, Thin Hairline, throught \prit{m}, Medium, and goes on
to \textit{x} for ExtraBold ExtraBlack.

\item [\textbf{\itshape \footnotesize \underline{Variants.}}] This is
a complicated category, and includes typeface variants such as italic
and sans serif. If the encoding scheme (the next grouping) is 7 for
7-bit encoding, 8 for 8-bit encoding or 9 for expert encoding.
\ee
```

The PrintOut:

SUPPLIER The first character denotes the current supplier, not the original designer, if the two differ. Apple fonts begin with *e*, Bitstream with *b*.

Type. *tm* represents, of course, the Times (or Roman) style. *bk* is Bookman, *ch* is Charter, *g3* is Garamondthree, *g4* is Goudy Modern, *lc* is Lucida.

Weight. The thickness of a font line ranges from *a*, Thin Hairline, throught *m*, Medium, and goes on to *x* for ExtraBold ExtraBlack.

<u>Variants.</u> This is a complicated category, and includes typeface variants such as italic and sans serif. If the encoding scheme (the next grouping) is 7 for 7-bit encoding, 8 for 8-bit encoding or 9 for expert encoding.

15.4 Breaking Single Lines On The Right

The two ways to force an End-of-Line (EOL) are the newline and the linebreak commands.[1]

\newline. Its short form is: \\. This will break a line without justifying it. The complete format is \\[<*length*>], where the length in brackets is added to the single line break. It can only be used on lines inside a paragraph. It can NOT be used at the end of a paragraph. To add space after a paragraph, use the *\vspace* command. (See Section 13.4.2.)

[Lamport [Lamport 94a, Section C.1.6] strongly advises against using two \\ in text mode to force a couple of blank lines; he suggests you use only one \\ and a vertical

---

[1]Section 7.2 discusses the line break and its impact on the overfull or underfull line.

length in brackets. For example: \\[2pc] will break the line and create two empty lines before printing the rest of the text.

As noted in Item 20, Section 7.1, a \\ can NOT be followed by ordinary text starting with [, because the ordinary text might mistakenly be taken for the optional length value and cause the program to see the construction as an error.

To terminate a line but prevent the start of a new page, put an asterisk just after the double backslashes: `..text...` *. (See Section 31.4 for specifics of the interrelations of line and page breaks.)

\linebreak. This justifies a line and then breaks it. So this is suitable for breaking a line at the end of a page to force the rest of the paragraph to the next page. The **\nolinebreak**, on the other hand, prevents the program from breaking a line.

Both \linebreak and \nolinebreak have a demand and a request format:

Demand. The format is **\linebreak**.

Request. The format is **\linebreak[#]**. A number from 0 to 4 is placed in the square brackets. A 0 is a polite request to break the line, a 4 is equivalent to a demand. This can be used anywhere in the line, even in the middle of a word.

%. Note that the % command does not really break the line. It keeps the words that follow the %—including the End-Of-Line symbol—out of the printed document. So the next line of text is pulled in on the heels of the current line with no intervening space. Macro arguments must not be separated by gaps. If two macro arguments are long so that you wish to write them on separate lines, add a % to the end of the first line.

15.5   Creating An Outline

Attractive outlines can be made simply by using an enumerate list on the outline items; see, for example, Chapter 14. Or they can be done systematically by painstakingly shifting tab positions in a tabbing environment. (See Section 16.3.1.) A simple method, if the outline is not complicated, is to use different size spaces. This next is part of Figure 3.4 in Section 3.8. The outline indentation was created by using space wedges. (See Section 13.2.) If the indentation comes after a significant character, use the \hspace format, as in this example.

The MarkUp:

```
\newcommand{\sgap}[1][.25in]{\hspace{#1}}
\newcommand{\mgap}[1][.50in]{\hspace{#1}}
\newcommand{\lgap}[1][.75in]{\hspace{#1}}
0. \part{...} (optional) \\
1. \sgap \chapter{...} \\
2. \mgap\section{...} \\
3. \lgap\subsection{...} \\
4. \lgap\sgap\subsubsection{...} \\
5. \lgap\mgap\paragraph{...} \\
6. \lgap\lgap\subparagraph{...}
```

The PrintOut:

0. \part{...} (optional)
1.   \chapter{...}
2.   \section{...}
3.   \subsection{...}
4.   \subsubsection{...}
5.   \paragraph{...}
6.   \subparagraph{...}

If the indentation is to be first on the line, the format above won't do, because the program erases initial white noise—spaces, tabs, and so forth. So use the asterisk form, defined below. Actually, the asterisk version can be used anywheres, so the previous set of gap definitions is redundant, *unless* you don't want the program to add space at the start/end of lines.

The MarkUp:

```
\newcommand{\ssgap}[1][.25in]{\hspace*{#1}}
\newcommand{\mmgap}[1][.50in]{\hspace*{#1}}
\newcommand{\llgap}[1][.75in]{\hspace*{#1}}

\part{...} (optional) \\
\ssgap\chapter{...} \\
\mmgap\section{...} \\
\llgap\subsection{...} \\
```

```
\llgap\ssgap\subsubsection{...} \\
\llgap\mmgap\paragraph{...}  \\
\llgap\llgap\subparagraph{...}
```

The PrintOut:

\part{...} (optional)

    \chapter{...}

        \section{...}

            \subsection{...}

                \subsubsection{...}

                    \paragraph{...}

                        \subparagraph{...}

15.6   Using Displayed Paragraph Formats

LaTeX has several environments that indent text. Each is a specialized version of the list construction. Each formats text paragraphs somewhat differently. They have the disadvantage that the degree of indentation can not easily be parameterized. But they are ready to wear.

15.6.1   Quotation and quote environments

Quotation Environment: As the name would suggest, the **quotation environment** is intended to set off a quote of indefinite size, one with multiple paragraphs. It is indented from both sides and has an additional indentation at the start of each paragraph. Paragraphs follow without an intervening blank line, unless you force one. But the text is justified. In this example, it is used to indent a single paragraph from both the left and right margins.

The MarkUp:

```
\begin{quotation}
This will alphabetize \textit{In} and write the reordered records to
\textit{Out}. The record delimiter is @; the field delimiter is \#.
The first 6 visible characters in field 3 serve as key.
\end{quotation}
```

The PrintOut:

> This will alphabetize *In* and write the reordered records to *Out*. The record delimiter is @; the field delimiter is #. The first 6 visible characters in field 3 serve as key.

Quote Environment: This is intended for one liners, pithy sayings, and so forth, but it can be used to justify a set of paragraphs, without preliminary indentation. It is indented from both side margins. It has the advantage of leaving a blank line between paragraphs. Here it is used to subsume information under a major heading.

The MarkUp:

```
\prbf{USING COMMAND LINE OPTIONS:} alp -iIn -oOut -d@\# -f3 -zL6
\begin{quote}
This will alphabetize \textit{In} and write the reordered records
to \textit{Out}. The record delimiter is @; the field delimiter
is \#. The first 6 visible characters in field 3 serve as key.

Once the program has been run, all parameter values except file
names can be retrieved by writing STICKY as the first option.
\end{quote}
```

The PrintOut:

USING COMMAND LINE OPTIONS: alp -iIn -oOut -d@# -f3 -zL6

> This will alphabetize *In* and write the reordered records to *Out*. The record delimiter is @; the field delimiter is #. The first 6 visible characters in field 3 serve as key.
>
> Once the program has been run, all parameter values except filenames can be retrieved by writing STICKY as the first option.

15.6.2 Verse environment

This is intended to display short lines or run-on lines of poetry. Given a paragraph, the program will indent each line without a blank line intervening. A blank line in the output signals the start of another paragraph. Used as it is here, it is a way of producing an indented list.

The MarkUp:

```
\begin{verse}
This will alphabetize \textit{In} and write the reordered records to
\textit{Out}.

The record delimiter is @; the field delimiter is \#.

The first 6 visible characters in field 3 serves as key.

Parameter values can be retrieved by using STICKY option.
\end{verse}
```

The PrintOut:

This will alphabetize *In* and write the reordered records to *Out*.

The record delimiter is @; the field delimiter is #.

The first 6 visible characters in field 3 serves as key.

Parameter values can be retrieved by using the STICKY option.

15.6.3   Center environment

The center environment starts a new paragraph; it writes each line in its domain individually in the middle of the page. So it is a good way to customize letter headers, as is done in Section 32.6. This next illustrates output format.

The MarkUp:

```
\begin{center}
This is one length. \\
And this is a longer length. \\
And this is a longer length than the previous one. \\
But this is short.
\end{center}
```

The PrintOut:

This is one length.

And this is a longer length.

And this is a longer length than the previous one.

But this is short.

15.6.4 An ordinary description list

Not surprisingly, results using an ordinary description environment without initial bolding look like those produced by the quote environment, except that indentation is only on the right. We contributed to the similarity by making the lead line part of the *item*, and it required some added vertical space to separate it from the indented text.

The MarkUp:

```
\begin{description}
\item \textbf{USING COMMAND LINE OPTIONS:} alp -iIn -oOut -d@\# -f3
-zL6 \\[.5pc]

This will alphabetize a file named \textit{In} and put the reordered
records in
\textit{Out}. The record delimiter is @; the field delimiter is \#.
The first 6 visible characters in field 3 serve as key.

Once the program has been run, all parameter values except file
names can be retrieved by writing STICKY as the first option.
\end{description}
```

The PrintOut:

USING COMMAND LINE OPTIONS: alp -iIn -oOut -d@# -f3 -zL6

> This will alphabetize *In* and put the reordered records in *Out*. The record delimiter is @; the field delimiter is #. The first 6 visible characters in field 3 serve as key.
>
> Once the program has been run, all parameter values except file names can be retrieved by writing STICKY as the first option.

15.7   Simple Paragraph Indenting

\parindent=<*width*>   Write this command in the preamble to indent the start of each paragraph a certain amount; e.g., **\parindent=.3in** will indent the first line of each paragraph a third of an inch. The syntax of the *parindent* command is TeX, not LaTeX.

The default style for documents classes other than the slide and letter classes is: (1) the first line of each paragraph is indented; and (2) there are no empty lines between paragraphs. This command can be used to increase or decrease the size of the default paragraph indentation. Conversely, **\parindent = 0pc** will see to it that the start of each paragraph in the document is not indented. If indentation is eliminated, some other differentiation between paragraphs is needed. (See Section 13.7 above.)

Either of these next two commands can be typed at the very beginning of a paragraph. It is assumed that the document layout is such that the start of each paragraph is indented.

\indent   If, because of some other command, indenting can't occur, then this indents the start of the single paragraph the amount it usually is indented.

\noindent   This prevents indenting of the first line of the next paragraph.

15.8   Controlling The Degree Of Indentation

Letterpaper width is 8.5 inches. By default, the border inch on the inner margin is not used in LaTeX page layouts. So the typical text width of 5 to 6 inches leaves 1.5 to 2.5 inches of available side space. By default, the program shifts text on the page, resulting in a wider outside margin—i.e., the left side on even-numbered pages, the right side on odd-numbered or one-sided pages. Whether the page is odd or even, we can usually count on having at least an inch of margin on a side for marginal notes and overwide text. At worst, we can expect from 1/4 to 3/4 inch overflow writing area on each side of the text.

Extending the first paragraph into the margin(s).

For special effects, we can start the text to the left of the usual position by using the *\hspace**instruction to prepend a horizontal negative gap to a minipage.[2] In this example,

---

[2]A minipage is a rectangular area, whose size and text are under your control. When the minipage is termi-

\hspace subtracts 0.2 inches from the left margin. The minipage occupies a 5.4 inches wide area, thus overflowing .2 inches into each margin. The *bbm* font of Section 11.5.3 is used to emphasize the effect. You can enlarge the font still more or bold it or stretch it with *letterspace* for extra drama. The right margin does not need to be specified. Why?

The MarkUp:

```
\hspace*{-.2in}\begin{minipage}[t]{5.4in} \MAIN{\Large
Each field is one line long and extends the full length of a
line. The abstract field is the exception.}
\end{minipage}

Mitral cells of the main and accessory olfactory bulbs have been
shown to project monosynaptically to the supraoptic nucleus (SON)
via the lateral olfactory tract (LOT) which uses excitatory amino
acid transmitters.
```

The PrintOut:

Each field is one line long and extends the full length of a line The abstract field is the exception

Mitral cells of the main and accessory olfactory bulbs have been shown to project monosynaptically to the supraoptic nucleus (SON) via the lateral olfactory tract (LOT) which uses excitatory amino acid transmitters.

Setting off a paragraph by centering it.

This next *\hspace** instruction will add 1 inch to the original left margin. The minipage is made 3 inches wide.

The MarkUp:

```
Each field is one line long and extends the full length of a
line. The abstract field is the exception.

\hspace*{1in}\begin{minipage}[t]{3in}
Mitral cells of the main and accessory olfactory bulbs have been
shown to project monosynaptically to the supraoptic nucleus (SON)
via the lateral olfactory tract (LOT) which uses excitatory amino
```

---

nated, margin measurements immediately revert to whatever they were before the minipage took control. Minipages are explained in Section 23.2.

```
acid transmitters.
\end{minipage}
```

```
Data collected during characterization of these projections suggested
that synaptic activation of SON neurons via LOT stimulation in slices
influenced the incidence of dye-coupling.
```

The PrintOut:

Each field is one line long and extends the full length of a line. The abstract field is the exception.

> Mitral cells of the main and accessory olfactory bulbs
> have been shown to project monosynaptically to the
> supraoptic nucleus (SON) via the lateral olfactory tract
> (LOT) which uses excitatory amino acid transmitters.

Data collected during characterization of these projections suggested that synaptic activation of SON neurons via LOT stimulation in slices influenced the incidence of dye-coupling.

Cascading a group of paragraphs.

In this example, the first paragraph starts at the actual left margin. Note that second minipage starts 1.25 inches from the margin, but this is temporary; the margin snaps back to the original left margin when the *\end{minipage}* is processed. So the third paragraph starts, again, measuring from the left margin.

The MarkUp:

```
\begin{minipage}[t]{2in}
Each field is one line long and extends the full length of a line.
The abstract field is the exception.
\end{minipage}
```

```
\hspace{1.25in}\begin{minipage}[t]{2in}
Mitral cells of the main and accessory olfactory bulbs have been
shown to project monosynaptically to the supraoptic nucleus (SON)
via the lateral olfactory tract (LOT) which uses excitatory amino
acid transmitters.
\end{minipage}
```

```
\hspace{2.5in}\begin{minipage}[t]{2in}
```

```
Data collected during characterization of
these projections suggested that synaptic activation of SON
neurons via LOT stimulation in slices influenced the incidence of
dye-coupling.
\end{minipage}
```

The PrintOut:

Each field is one line long and extends the full length of a line. The abstract field is the exception.

> Mitral cells of the main and accessory olfactory bulbs have been shown to project monosynaptically to the supraoptic nucleus (SON) via the lateral olfactory tract (LOT) which uses excitatory amino acid transmitters.

> Data collected during characterization of these projections suggested that synaptic activation of SON neurons via LOT stimulation in slices influenced the incidence of dye-coupling.

Chapter 16

FLOATING OBJECTS

We want a figure or a table or even a marginal note to be undivided on the page, if at all possible. Typically, in cut-and-paste layout, we lay down figures and tables discussed locally in the text and fill the rest of the available space on the page with ordinary text.

So how do we calculate where to put these objects on the page, so they are nicely balanced by text in the remaining space? We don't. We let the program do it for us. It is called floating the object. The imagery is right on target. A figure or table will be positioned somewhere on or after the page on which it is mentioned for the first time in the text.

The process does not necessarily put the figure—or table—where you would like it and there is only one absolute override. You can, however, always try to influence the placement of a figure or table.[1]

16.1 Figures

16.1.1 General format

The figure environment can cloak almost anything—text, picture, box, math equations, so that the object, providing it isn't overlarge, is kept as an unbreakable unit that is not

---

[1] With luck. These are not the most user-friendly instructions.

chopped and displayed on more than one page. And, a most useful feature, it can be captioned. To ensure that the figure is correctly cross-referenced, label the figure after the caption. Figures enclose boxes such as minipages and other environments; they themselves can not be enclosed. The general configuration is:

```
\begin{figure}[location request]
Place text, picture or equations here.
\caption{text} \label{whatever}
\end{figure}
```

The optional argument in the brackets following \begin{figure} can be one or more of the following. If you write, say, [bp], the program will attempt to put the figure at the bottom of the same page, else on a separate page just of floats. These are the choices:

here or **h**	Put the table where this is written.
top or **t**	Put table at the top of the page.
bottom or **b**	Put table at the bottom of the page.
page or **p**	Put table on a separate page of all floats.
!	Ignore parameters that could stop placement locally.

You would write as an example: **\begin{figure}[top]**.

If you don't have a preference, the program will try to place the float at the top of the page, then at the bottom and then on a separate page, in that order.

Getting the program to place floats roughly where you want them can be frustrating, particularly when there's a large number of figures relative to the size of the text. These often work:

[!] The program has a set of values it tries to satisfy in placing a figure. This tells the program to chuck them all as long as it doesn't chop the figure.

\afterpage{\clearpage} By itself, \clearpage immediately finishes the page and forces the figure to the beginning of the next page. The preceding afterpage command tells the program to pull in whatever text it can to maintain page length. Try this format: **\afterpage{\clearpage\begin{figure}... \end{figure}}**.

The PrintOut:

The MarkUp:
```
\begin{center}
\includegraphics{sarah.ps}
\vspace{-.15in}
\caption{Sarah E.}
\label{fig:sarah}
\end{center}
```

Figure 16.1: Sarah E.

[H] This is not a LATEX placement option as such. It can be used by loading either the simple *here.sty* package or the more complex *float.sty* package discussed in Section 16.1.5. Combine it with the *afterpage* and *clearpage* commands if the page prints short.

16.1.2 Usage

Verbatim Statements. You can keep a long verbatim statement together by shrouding it in a figure environment.

Pictures and Graphics. You certainly would put a picture or graphics object in a figure environment to keep it from being spread across two pages. This requires the *graphicx* package and the *\includegraphics* command, as in Figure 16.1.

Boxed Text. Box mode keeps text intact by itself. But often boxed text is placed within an outer figure environment, so that it can be captioned as in Figure 16.2. Actually, the contents of this figure are worth reading. They discuss ways to place figures on the page in a balanced way.

Highlighted Text. You can also emphasize text and/or group paragraphs visually by graying them. The amount of white that's added to the gray increases from 0 to 1. We defined a new color **lightgrey** to be a light gray. The *colorbox* command puts a background color inside a box it creates. Ordinarily, it would operate on a single line, but we cunningly made it the surround of a minipage, so it includes all the text inside the minipage. Color is dealt with in Section 25.4.9; the minipage is explained in Section 23.2.

The Markup For Figure 16.2

```
\definecolor{lightgrey}{gray}{.8}
\begin{figure}[h]
\OUT\\
\colorbox{lightgrey}{
\begin{minipage}{3.5in}
\LaTeX\ will attempt to put the figure somewhere close to the
text that describes it. The job becomes harder as the number
of figures in the vicinity increase and if these figures
are large.
\end{minipage}
}
```

```
\vspace{1pc}\hspace{1in}
\colorbox{lightgrey}{
\begin{minipage}{3.5in}
The program deals with floats in the sequence in which
you construct them. Your request for one figure can make
for problems downstream; if, say, you request [p] for the
first figure, [t] for a neighboring second figure. If all
else fails, you can force the program to 'dump' whatever
is in the queue by writing a \clearpage. However, this
command also stops printing more text on that page
immediately, so the results may be a shortened page.
When there's no room on the page for the figure, to fill
the page with as much text as possible, use this set of
commands:
\afterpage{\clearpage\begin{figure}[t]
\ldots\end{figure}}\footnote{\afterpage was
written by David Carlisle [Carlisle95a]. You load it
with a \prbf{\usepackage{afterpage}} command in
the preamble.}
\end{minipage}
}
```

```
\vspace{1pc}\hspace{1in}
\colorbox{lightgrey}{
\begin{minipage}{3.5in}
An alternative solution is to create the figure (or table)
in another file and bring it in with the \input command,
which is discussed in Appendix~\ref{ss:rootfile}. Because
the input command automatically begins a new page, you are
guaranteed a great deal of room for the figure or table.
```

```
To forstall shortening the text on the page prior to the
figure, you would use the afterpage command. So if
you generated a figure in a file called \prit{bigfig.tex},
you would write in the appropriate place in the document:
\textbf{\afterpage{\clearpage\input{bigfig}}}.
\end{minipage}
}
\caption{Interspersing Figures and Text} \label{fig:afterpage}
\end{figure}
```

The PrintOut:

LaTeX will attempt to put the figure somewhere close to the text that describes it. The job becomes harder as the number of figures in the vicinity increase and if these figures are large.

The program deals with floats in the sequence in which you construct them. Your request for one figure can make for problems downstream; if, say, you request [p] for the first figure, [t] for a neighboring second figure. If all else fails, you can force the program to 'dump' whatever is in the queue by writing a \clearpage. However, this command also stops printing more text on that page, so the results may be a shortened page. When there's no room on the page for the figure, to fill the page with as much text as possible, use this set of commands: \afterpage{\clearpage\begin{figure}[t] ... \end{figure}}[a]

[a]\afterpage was written by David Carlisle [Carlisle95a]. You load it with a **\usepackage{afterpage}** command in the preamble.

An alternative solution is to create the figure (or table) in another file and bring it in with the \input command, which is discussed in Appendix A. Because the input command automatically begins a new page, you are guaranteed a great deal of room for the figure or table. To forstall shortening the text on the page prior to the figure, you would use the afterpage command. So if you generated a figure in a file called *bigfig.tex*, you would write in the appropriate place in the document: **\afterpage{\clearpage\input{bigfig}}** .

Figure 16.2: Interspersing Figures and Text

16.1.3 Subfigures

Figures can be subdivided sequentially into several figures with separate captions, but the whole is printed out as a unit. The subfigures can be captioned individually. There is an example in Section 18.4.2 on citations.

In addition, the *subfigure* package by Steven Cochran [Cochran95] can help create more sophisticated layouts, blending several figures and tables into a unit. *subfigure* can label all the subunits as well as the entire figure. You can load the package with general options. To produce indented captions write **\usepackage[hang]{subfigure}** in the preamble.

The format for each of the subfigures is: \subfigure[<*Caption*>]{<*Text*>}

Usually the subfigure extends the width of the body text. In this next example, the individual subfigures are limited to two inches. The captions for the subfigures are written inside the square brackets.

Figure 16.3 is a single figure that contains a frame that encloses a set of subfigures. The frame around the figure was produced using the \begin{Subs}...\end{Subs} inside the figure environment. If you delete the Subs pair, the figure will be printed unframed. The entire macro is shown as the first part of the Markup. It is a useful macro that can be generalized, as it is in Chapter 23, where boxes and frames are discussed. (See also Example 2, Section 16.1.4.)

The Markup For Figure 16.3

```
\newsavebox{\SubFrame}
\newenvironment{Subs}{\begin{lrbox}{\SubFrame}%
\begin{minipage}[t]{4.5in}}%
{\end{minipage}%
\end{lrbox}\fbox{\usebox{\SubFrame}}}

\begin{figure}[!]
\hspace*{.3in}\begin{Subs}
\subfigure[Note 1.]{
\begin{minipage}[t]{1.75in}
At its simplest, the identifier is written at the start of
the note in the same way that any other field type is written.
\end{minipage}}\hspace{.75in}
```

At its simplest, the identifier is written at the start of the note in the same way that any other field type is written.

(a) Note 1.

Multiple lines are allowed. These do not have to be indented.

(b) Note 2.

To be minimally useful, the only requirement is that the UI of that article prefaces the note about the article.

(c) Note 3.

The program will know from context what the database filename is.

(d) Note 4.

Figure 16.3: The Universal Identifier

```
\subfigure[Note 2.]{
\begin{minipage}[t]{1.75in}
Multiple lines are allowed. These do not have to be indented.
\end{minipage}}\\

\subfigure[Note 3.]{
\begin{minipage}[t]{1.75in}
To be minimally useful, the only requirement is that the
UI of that article prefaces the note about the article.
\end{minipage}}\hspace{.75in}
\subfigure[Note 4.]{
\begin{minipage}[t]{1.75in}
The program will know from context what the database filename is.
\end{minipage}}
\end{Subs}
\caption{The Universal Identifier} \label{tb:univ}
\end{figure}
```

16.1.4   Working text around a figure

There are a fair number of packages that float a figure to one side or another so that it appears to have carved space from a paragraph of text. We will call these floats *sidefloats*. Most work on figures; some handle both figures and tables.

The typical format is to write the sidefloat markup in an environment—each package of course labels the environment differently. This is followed immediately by what will become the surrounding text. They all do best with running text, especially in a short document. They all require more or less care to ensure that the sidefloat doesn't collide with a neighboring LaTeX object such as a list or a command such as \section or even, on occasion, with another sidefloat. The next section examines *wrapfig*, a robust and deservedly popular program.[2]

The wrapfig Package

The *wrapfig* package by Donald Arseneau [Arseneau95] has few restrictions. It works for both figures and tables in one- or two-column format. It lets you decide where to put the sidefloat. *wrapfig* then *wraps* text around it. *wrapfig* does best partnered with a paragraph of plain running text but, if you wish, the sidefloat can be placed inside the running text at a line break (as in Example 1) as well as between paragraphs.

Load the program with a **\usepackage[verbose]{wrapfig}**. *verbose* adds log information you'll find helpful if things don't look right in the output file. The documentation is to be found starting half way through *wrapfig.sty*.

The author warns that the sidefloat, not being a regular float, may be printed out of sequence with the regular floats. If it happens, flush the previous floats that are involved with a \afterpage{ \clearpage}} instruction. Floating is always tricky. It helps if you keep things simple.

The environment is named *wrapfigure*. \begin {wrapfigure} has two optional values in square brackets and two mandatory arguments in braces. The format, using the author's example, is:

```
\begin{wrapfigure}[12]{r}[34pt]{5cm} <figure> \end{wrapfigure}
```

where the sequence represents:

---

[2]*floatflt* by Mats Dahlgren [Dahlgren96a and Dahlgren96b] is also fairly easy to use but it takes careful handling near some LaTeX objects. It will operate in the *multicol* environment, a useful feature in landscape mode. *floatflt* is an upgrade of Thomas Kneser's *floatfig* package [Kneser90], which is described in [Goossens94, page 150].

optional number of lines. This value—12 in the example—states the number of narrow lines to allocate for the figure. An equation counts as 3 lines. Use this if you want more or less height for the short text lines (the text lines paired with the sidefloat).

mandatory placement. The options are *RLIOrlio*. The upper case letters let the figure and surrounding text float within a small range. The lower case letters say: put it right here. The author advises using exact placement, when you have a good idea of where the wrapped figure should be located.

l puts the sidefloat on the left   **r** places the sidefloat on the right

i puts it on the inner page margin   **o** puts it on the outer margin

In a two-sided document, the locations of the last two depend on whether its an even- or odd-numbered page.

optional overhang. This is the amount of space the sidefloat can push into the margin. The default is no bulge into the margin. *\width* is special in *wrapfig*; it is the width of the sidefloat. So you can let a third of the figure hang over the edge by writing *.3 \width*.

In LATEX, *marginparwidth* is the width of the marginal note and *marginparsep* the width of the space between the note and the text. If you want all the sidefloats positioned in the margin and by the same amount, write this before the first use of the program:

```
\setlength{\wrapoverhang}{\marginparwidth}
\addtolength{\wrapoverhang}{\marginparsep}
```

mandatory width. This is the width of the sidefloat, specified in any of the measurement units acceptable to LATEX. If the sidefloat includes a tabbing or a box environment with a different width, the program uses the larger one.

The restrictions are not onerous.

- You must not enclose a sidefloat in a list; separate it from a neighboring list by a blank line at the very least.

- If you put a wrapfigure in a box such as a minipage, or in another outer environment, the text surrounding the wrapfigure must be completely contained within the outer box/environment.

- The program adjusts the test width depending on sidefloat width. You can't then change the linewidth within the text surround. (By default, \linewidth is the column width of the document.)

- The *wrapfigure* environment should not be broken across pages.

Here are some examples:

Example 1. A simple format.

The Markup For Example 1.

```
\textit{wrapfig} works best with ordinary running text in
ordinary paragraphs,
\begin{wrapfigure}[3]{r}{1.75in}
\textbf{\itshape Using wrapfig in a one or two column page.}
\end{wrapfigure}
especially if the text extends beyond the length
of the float. It will work in two-column  pages,
and you can help things by making the float
narrower than the column by fiddling with
the \\ \ command.
```

wrapfig works best with ordinary running text in ordinary paragraphs, especially if the text extends beyond the length of the float. It will work in two-column pages, and you can help things by making the float narrower than the column by fiddling with the \\ command.

                                                  Using wrapfig in a one or two column page.

Example 2. A sidefloat in a framed box.

The FramePix macro is general; it will put a frame around any box. It is discussed in detail in Section 23.5. Here, it creates and frames a small minipage, placing it to the right of an ordinary minipage.

The Markup For Example 2.

```
\NC{\FramePix}[3][t]{\fbox{\begin{minipage}[#1]{#2} #3\end{minipage}}}

\begin{wrapfigure}[7]{o}[.8\width]{.96in}
\FramePix[b]{.95in}{
\begin{center}
Read \textit{wrapfig.\-sty} on finetuning space around the sidefloat.
\end{center} }
\end{wrapfigure}
\begin{minipage}{4in}
The sidefloat can be placed so far over that it becomes a marginal
note. This time we use a box macro that draws a frame around the
sidefloat.... \end{minipage}
```

The sidefloat can be placed so far over that it becomes a marginal note. This time we use a box macro that draws a frame around the sidefloat. *FramePix* is versatile and is shown as part of the markup. The three arguments are: (1) the alignment of the object on the Top, Bottom or Center of the baseline; (2) the width of the box; and (3) the text within the box. In this case, the bottom of the box is on the baseline; the box size is .95 inches. If you wanted center alignment and 4 inches, you would write **\begin{FramePix}[c]{4in}**<*text*>. If baseline alignment is not filled in, it is Top by default. (See Chapter 23 for a general discussion of boxes.)

> Read *wrapfig.sty* on how to finetune space around the sidefloat.

Example 3. Using an outer minipage.

In this example, we enclose both the text and sidefloat in a minipage. For some objects, an outer box is an excellent way to keep text and sidefloat together.

The Markup For Example 3.

```
\begin{minipage}[b]{5in}
\begin{wrapfigure}[11]{o}{2in}
\begin{center}
\includegraphics{sam.ps}
\caption{Sam E.}
\end{center}
\end{wrapfigure}
The minipage enclosure may not be necessary, because usually a
\prit{wrapfigure} environment as the...
\end{minipage}
```

The minipage enclosure may not be necessary, because usually a *wrapfigure* environment as the outer enclosure would do much the same. The outer minipage does, however, force the text to a specific size. This makes it unnecessary to do trial and error adjustments of the *wrapfigure* environment when you need an exact size for the text. With a picture, you can control the size by a width option to *\includegraphics*. (See Section 25.4.1.)

Figure 16.4: Sam E.

There is another advantage in using an outer minipage to surround the wrapfigure environment. Pictures as sidefloats can be tricky because often, depending on previous text and picture size considerations, the picture will appear below rather than next to the intended text; which happened here. To make this example visually more palatable, I redid the construction slightly and put the entire paragraph— the one you are currently reading—immediately after the *wrapfig* environment, with no intervening blank line The program saw it as text controlled by the sidefloat. So it wrapped what should have been an ordinary paragraph around the picture. Telling the program how many narrow lines to use (option 1) also helps foster the illusion that the sidefloat is sheltered within text.

Using the minipage as a surround as shown here is an easy way to keep a sidefloat connected to its text.

The picinpar Package

This package, written by Friedhelm Sowa [Sowa95], lets you place a sidefloat inside a paragraph as well as on the left or right of it. What little has survived from my highschool German is not up to reading the documentation in *picinpar.dvi* in ~/texmf/doc/latex/styles. So I rely on [Goossens94, page 53].

The *figwindow* environment takes four options in sequence:

1. **nl**. The number of long lines before the figwindow begins.

2. **align**. l for left; r for right; c for center.

3. **material**. The picture, text or equation in the window.

4. **explanation**. The caption.

We've left the final option blank in the example below. Its spot is marked by an empty pair of braces {}. We again use a gray color to highlight the center text. **\shortstack** does just what it sounds like.

The MarkUp:

The PrintOut:

```
\definecolor{lightgrey}{gray}{.8}
\newcommand{\CT}{\colorbox%
{lightgrey}%
{\sffamily\bfseries\small%
\shortstack{Captures\\%
Attention.\\No?}}}
\begin{figwindow}[2,c,\CT,{}]
This can look quite dramatic,
especially when it is also
colored. You can put a line
drawing in the middle or some
special font. Or whatever.
What do you call a side
float in the center?
A center float? A center fold?
\end{figwindow}
```

This can look quite dramatic, especially when it is also colored. You can put a line drawing in the middle or some special font. Or whatever. What do you call a side float in the center? A center float? A center fold?

Figure 16.5:

The shapepar Package

This is a novelty package written by Donald Arseneau [Arseneau93] that typesets your text in one of four shapes. Load it with a \usepackage{shapepar} command in the preamble. There is no separate documentation file, but the *shapepar.sty* file in ~/tex/latex/misc contains information and is interesting to read, should you wish to try your hand at designing some other shapes.

The MarkUp:

The PrintOut:

```
\squarepar{\tiny \sffamily This will
write the text as a square.
Notice we have set the size at 5 pica,
which is tiny but it still looks much
like a square.}
```

This will write the text as a square. Notice we have set the size at 5 pica, which is tiny but it still looks much like a square.

The MarkUp:

```
\diamondpar{\footnotesize \scshape
The font isn't
slanted. But even in footnote size,
it does look like a diamond.}
```

The PrintOut:

THE FONT
ISN'T SLANTED.
BUT EVEN IN FOOT-
NOTE SIZE, IT DOES
LOOK LIKE A DI-
AMOND.

◇

The MarkUp:

```
\shapepar\nutshape{\bfseries
Notice that this has a double
command and single set of
braces. BE CAREFUL.}

\vspace{.2in}
\heartpar{\large \itshape
Do you not think
that in a very much
larger size, this would be
great for Valentine banners?}
```

The PrintOut:

**Notice   that
this has a dou-
ble   com-
mand   and
sin-   gle set
of braces.   BE
CAREFUL.**

*Do you   not
think that in a very
much   larger   size,
this would be great
for   Valentine
banners?*
♡

16.1.5   Creating new float styles

The *float* package, written by Anselm Lingnau [Lingnau95], was mentioned earlier in that it provides a new placement category: **[H]**, which forces the program to put the figure exactly here. You can use this feature by itself, but the program's major function is to allow you to set styles for new float classes.

Essentially, there are three styles: (1) *plain* is the ordinary float; (2) boxed; and (3) ruled, where the caption comes first, enclosed inside top and bottom ruled lines. You name your new class—algorithm or computer program or whatever—and associate it with one of these styles.

The program guarantees that all members of a class will have a uniform presentation. You can even specify that the particular figure type should be placed at the top or on the bottom of the page. It is not, admittedly, the program for people who adjust float styles in part according to text context. It is well-described in Section 6.3 in [Goossens94].

rotating, a package written by Sebastian Rahtz and Leonor Barroca [Barroca95], rotates text or figures (brought in as Encapsulated PostScript files) counterclockwise in whatever degree turn you stipulate.

16.1.6 Captions

LaTeX has a shortened format for captions, just as it does for parts of the document such as \section and so forth. The complete format for the ordinary figure (or table) caption is:

\caption[<*shortform*>]{<*caption text*>}

Ordinarily, the shortform can be ignored; you just write the regular caption text. But if the regular caption text is very long, you can add a clipped version in brackets that will appear in the List of Figures.

The classic LaTeX caption is straightforward, although you can change its appearance somewhat by using sans serif or a different font shape. Two packages provide different styles: (1) *caption.sty* written by Harald Axel Sommerfeldt [Sommerfeldt95] and (2) *hangcaption.sty* by David Jones.

The *caption* package lets you create a variety of caption styles by varying font size and shape as well as location: indented, centered or normal. The author recommends loading this after packages such as *float, rotating* and *subfigure*, with which it interacts. It is documented in *caption.dvi*.

In the *hangcaption* package, you set a width that determines whether the caption is typeset centered or as a hanging indentation.

16.2   Marginal Notes

Full Format

```
\marginpar[optional text for leftside page]%
{Mandatory text, rightside page.}
```

In a report or book or a *twoside* document, a marginal note is a floating body that is printed in the left margin on a left-side page and in the right margin on a right-side page. In ordinary *oneside* articles, there are only right-side pages by default, hence only right-side marginal notes.

The note starts on the line on which the body text encloses the marginal note in the markup. It is a good idea to keep marginal notes short. LaTeX never runs a note onto the next page. If you use a long note, you may have to fiddle with it to prevent it from extending into the bottom margin. [Note: because of book size considerations, the marginal note examples shown simulate text and *real* margins.]

```
  The Markup: \NC{\BHS}[1][1.75]{\hspace*{#1in}}
\BHS This is some body text and we want \marginpar{ \textit{\BHS
Hey!\\\BHS Look\\ \BHS here.}} to \\ \BHS highlight it with a
marginal note like this one.
```

Hey!
Look
here.
 The PrintOut: This is some body text and we want to highlight it with a marginal note like this one.

Arrows and other directional symbols in marginal notes need to point right on left-side (even-numbered) pages and left on right-side (odd-numbered) pages. But revising a paper will often shift the location of a marginal note to another page. So `marginpar` lets you write two symbols, one of which will be used, depending on the page. The marginal note for even-numbered pages is written in the option; the note for odd-numbered pages is written in the argument. If there is only one symbol, write it inside the mandatory argument. For example:

The MarkUp:

```
\NC{\HS}[1][-1]{\hspace*{#1in}}
```

```
This is some body text and we want \marginpar[\HS\prit{Hey!}$\ddag
\rightarrow$\\ \prit{\HS left side\\ \HS note.}]{\prit{\HS Hey!}
$\leftarrow\ddag$\\ \prit{\HS right side\\ \HS note.}} to highlight
it\\ with a marginal note that will draw attention to it. Printed
symbols\\change depending on whether the page is right-sided or left.
```

The PrintOut: This is some body text and we want to highlight it with a marginal note that will draw attention to it. Printed symbols change depending on whether the page is right-sided or left.

> *Hey!* ← ‡
> *right side note.*

Moving The Position Of The Note

Shifting the note. You can adjust the placement of the marginal note somewhat with the \vspace command; for example, **\vspace{.5pc}**.

Shifting to the next page. If the note comes at the end of the page, you can decide to move the entire paragraph and its note to the next page with a **\newpage** command. Or reduce the body of text on the page with an negative **\enlargethispage{length}** command; e.g., **\enlargethispage{-2pc}**. Or, for appearance sake, add a couple of lines of text to the page with a **\enlargethispage*{length}** command. This not only adds the extra lines, it subtracts from the available vertical white space on the page.

16.3   Tables

The table environment lets you caption a table. And it keeps the rows of a table together on the page. Its format is:

```
\begin{table}[<location request>]
\end{table}
```

The table optional arguments are the same as the figure optional arguments. Similarly, you can prioritize locations, writing, as example: **\begin{table}[bp]**.

here or **h**	Put the table where this is written.
top or **t**	Put table at the top of the page.
bottom or **b**	Put table at the bottom of the page.
page or **p**	Put table on a separate page of all floats.
!	Ignore parameters that could stop placement locally.

A table environment doesn't itself create a table. There are two ways in LaTeX to create a table: (1) use the tabbing environment and (2) use the tabular environment. The table environment is a wrapper that makes the table into a floating object.

16.3.1   Tabs

The full format for a tabbing environment is: **\begin{tabbing}**
                                                      \end{tabbing}.

Unlike typewriter tabbing, the tabbing environment is not intended to indent a single line of text on the fly. It is, however, a major way to line up a sequence of lines into columns, so it acts as a table maker, just as the tabular environment does.

It differs from the more formal tablemaker in that: (1) it can be used only in text mode and (2) you must set column widths by yourself. Extracting the lemonade from a basic lemon, (2) also means it is simple to adjust and readjust column widths in a set of tabbed lines, simpler, certainly, than in a tabular table. The visual effect of a tabbed table can be very different from that of a tabular table with the same data. Tabbing also has the advantage—or disadvantage—that the program will split a tabbed sequence of lines across pages.

Tabbing Table Rules:

* Each line ends with a \\. This isn't needed in the last line, nor is it usually used, but it will sometimes improve the appearance of the table in the printout.

* Do tab settings using the \= command within text on the *first* line of what will become a table. The number of characters to the right of any tab determines the width of the corresponding column of the table. The first column is from the left side of the body text up to the first tab. The last column is from the last tab up to the end of the line.

* Use \> to indicate the end of a text column in succeeding lines.

* When the program determines column width, format instructions such as the \textsc surrounding NAME below do not count as characters; only the actual text in its particular font shape/size signifies.

⋆ The start position of all columns except for the first is rigidly set by the \= tabs settings. Alignment can not be changed by manipulating text elements on the succeeding lines. This has several effects:

1. An element in a column can be blank; it doesn't affect spacing for the column. But the \> separators must be written. See the Fax column for the Joel line in **Example 1.**

2. If the text in a column element is too wide for the tab setting, the next column's text will overwrite the preceding one. This occurs in the first two examples.

3. Unlike typewrite tabbing, you can't make room for a long piece of text by double tabbing. See **Example 2**.

⋆ Input spaces before the tab sign are significant *up to the limit of the column width*; spaces after the tab sign are ignored until the next non-space character. You can prepend some \ (\space) to shift text right, as in Table 16.2 before 'FIELD INFORMATION'.

⋆ The first row—the row that sets the tabs—does not have to be part of the table. Use numbers or nonsense words to give you as much space as you will need for the longest phrase that will appear in that column. End the line with **kill**. The text on the line will be ignored. This is done in **Example 3**.

⋆ Tab settings may be individually changed in a later line by writing a \= right in the text of the line. But if text elements in subsequent lines will vary in size, it is better to introduce another space control line (one that ends in **kill**). This is done in **Example 4**.

⋆ A tabbed table by itself can not be captioned. Also, because it is in text mode, the table is printed where it is written. But a table can be written inside a table environment, so that it will float and can be captioned. This is done in **Examples 3** and **4**.

⋆ Local changes in font shape must be done an item at a time. To italicize the fields in a record, for example, in the first three examples, you would write: \textit{Joel} \>\textit{5556788} \>...

⋆ Some variations are added to **Example 4**, to the point of downright ugly. Do you understand why the first | can be attached to the text, but the last | must occupy its own column? The resulting table can be compared to table 16.8 in the next section.

Example 1.

The MarkUp:

```
\begin{tabbing}
\textsc{NAME} \= Tel:        \= Fax:        \= Email: \\
Joel        \> 5556788     \>              \> jarthur@erols.com\\
Lew         \> 5551234     \> 5552323      \> lel@helix.nih.gov\\
Steven      \> 12125552345 \> 12125557867 \> se@aol.com
\end{tabbing}
```

The PrintOut:

NAME Tel: Fax: Email:

Joel   5556788 jarthur@erols.com

Lew   5551553121@helix.nih.gov

Steven   1212535296578607com

Example 2.

The MarkUp:

```
\begin{tabbing}
\textsc{NAME} \= Tel:        \= \=     Fax:    \= \= Email: \\
Joel        \> 5556788     \> \>            \> \> jarthur@erols.com\\
Lew         \> 5551234     \> \> 5552323 \> \> lel@helix.nih.gov\\
Steven      \> 12125552345 \> \> 12125557867 \> \> se@aol.com
\end{tabbing}
```

The PrintOut:

NAME Tel: Fax: Email:

Joel   5556788 jarthur@erols.com

Lew   5551553121@helix.nih.gov

Steven   1212535296578607com

Example 3. This example embeds the tabbing environment inside a table environment, allowing us to caption the table—table 16.1.

The Markup For Table 16.1

```
\begin{table}[h!]
\begin{tabbing}
NAMEfillUPwit:\=TelFillUPwit:\= FaxFillUPwit:\=EmailFillUPwith:\kill
\textbf{NAME}  \>\textbf{Tel:} \> \textbf{Fax:} \>\textbf{Email:}\\
Joel           \>5556788       \>                \>jarthur@erols.com\\
Lew            \>5551234       \> 5552323  \>lel@helix.nih.gov\\
Steven         \>12125552345   \> 12125557867 \>se@aol.com
\end{tabbing}
\caption{Phone List} \label{fig:phones}
\end{table}
```

NAME	Tel:	Fax:	Email:
Joel	5556788		jarthur@erols.com
Lew	5551234	5552323	lel@helix.nih.gov
Steven	12125552345	12125557867	se@aol.com

Table 16.1: Phone List

Example 4. This also embeds the tabbing environment in a table environment, so that we can caption the table (table 16.2). We also added multiple vertical line separators. (**\CL** is an abbreviation created in Section 8.1 for $|$). Whereas Table 16.1 is simple and pleasing, Table 16.2 looks amateurish. Compare it to Table 16.8. Full lines in the markup have been separated to make reading easier.

The Markup For Table 16.2

```
\begin{table}[h!]
\begin{tabbing}
THISISAVERYLONGCOLUMNHEADING1234 \= ANDTHISISTHESECONDLONGCOLUMNHEAD
  \= \CL \kill
\underline{\textsl{$|$ \ \ \ \ FIELD INFORMATION}} \>
\underline{\textsl{FILE INFORMATION}} \> $|$ \\
\smallskip \\
THISIS \= $|$ \= SplitColumnIntoTwoColumns \= $||$ \= AndThis1234 \=
$|$ \= SplitColumnIntoTwoX \= 12 \kill

\underline{$|$HIT} \>$|$ \> \underline{Location Information} \>\CL\>
\underline{Byte Position} \> $|$ \> \underline{Text} \> \CL \\
```

```
\CL Green B \> $|$ \> 91234565'55552'newdb'55600\TLD \> $||$
    \> byte 55552 \> $|$ \> UI - 91234565 \> \CL\\

\CL \>$|$ \>$|$ \> $||$ \>byte 55600 \>$|$ \>AU - Green B \>\CL\\

\CL Smith C \> $|$ \> 92345676'62767'newdb'63000\TLD \> $||$
    \> byte 62767 \> $|$ \> UI - 92345676  \CL\\

\CL \> $|$ \>$|$ \>$||$ \>byte 63000 \>$|$ \>AU - Smith C \>\CL\\

\CL Wells A \> $|$ \> 95123456'50025'newdb'50125\TLD \> $||$
    \> byte 50025 \> $|$ \> UI - 95123456  \CL\\

\CL \> $|$ \> $|$ \> $||$ \> byte 50125 \> $|$ \> AU - Wells A \>\CL
\end{tabbing}
\vspace{-.15in}\caption{Compare this to Table~\ref{tb:fieldinfo}}
\label{ss:comp}
\end{table}
```

FIELD INFORMATION			FILE INFORMATION	
HIT	Location Information		Byte Position	Text
Green B	91234565'55552'newdb'55600~		byte 55552	UI - 91234565
			byte 55600	AU - Green B
Smith C	92345676'62767'newdb'63000~		byte 62767	UI - 92345676
			byte 63000	AU - Smith C
Wells A	95123456'50025'newdb'50125~		byte 50025	UI - 95123456
			byte 50125	AU - Wells A

Table 16.2: Compare this to Table 16.8

Practice the tabbing environment on an example. Try one with and one without added vertical lines. Expand the space between columns. Create you own centering. Tabbing is flexible. And it is attractive if not gussied up.

16.3.2   The tabular environment

The tabular environment produces tables that are similar to math arrays, except they can be created in any of the modes, so you can mix numerical values and text. The program works out spacing for the columns by itself. Moreover, basic LaTeX won't break a table across pages.

The basic format is: \begin{tabular}{<*table column parameters*>}

. . .

\end{tabular}

If a table must be a specific width, use the *tabular** environment. Its format is

\begin{tabular*}[<*width*>]{<*table column parameters*>}

. . .

\end{tabular}

Tabular Table Rules:

* Each line ends with a \\. Even the last line.[3]

* The environment is declared to be tabular.

* The mandatory braced argument that contains the table column parameters is read left to right.

* You must provide the program with justification information about each of the columns; there are no defaults. At its simplest, a column may be left-justified (l), right-justified (r) or center-justified (c). **\begin{tabular}{lcrc}** would indicate there are four columns, the left one justified left, the second from the right justified right, and the other two centered. See **Example 1** below.

* Upright lines on either side of the justify information per column will produce full-extent vertical lines at those positions. Two upright lines together will produce a double vertical line. For example, **\begin{tabular}{||l |c |r |c ||}** would indicate the table is framed with vertical double lines; the four columns are separated from each other by single line. Creating lines to box a table is optional. Many people profess to find it easier to read an unlined table.

* Table elements are separated by **&**. An element can be blank, but the & separators must be written, to keep columns correctly spaced.

* An **\hline** after the tabular declaration and argument or after a NewLine symbol (\\) will produce a full-extent horizontal line.

---

[3] Arrays and tabbed lines do not need to add a \\ to the end of the last line.

* A \vline draws a vertical line extending the full length of the row.

* A \cline{i-j} will draw a horizontal line between columns i through j.

* A tabular or tabular* environment can be embedded inside a table environment, making it possible to caption the table and to float it on the page.

Except for the first example, a simple tabular environment, the tabular tables shown below are wrapped within *table* environments. Captions can be used with the table environment; they are not available with the tabular environment itself.

A Simple Tabular Environment. This is a simple table with default spacing. Reading from left to right, the four columns are left-aligned, centered, right-aligned, centered. The first column is bracketed by double vertical lines.

The Markup For A Simple Tabular Environment.

```
\begin{tabular}{||l||c|r|c|} \hline\hline
    Hit &    Location Information    & Byte Position & Text\\\hline
Green B & 91234565'55552'newdb'55600\~ &byte 55552 &UI - 91234565\\
                                                    \cline{3-4}
      &                          & byte 55600 & AU - Green B\\
                                                    \hline
Smith C & 92345676'62767'newdb'63000\~ &byte 62767 & UI - 92345676\\
                                                    \cline{3-4}
      &                          & byte 63000 & AU - Smith C\\
                                                    \hline
Wells A & 95123456'50025'newdb'50125\~ & byte 50025 & UI - 95123456\\
                                                    \cline{3-4}
      &                          & byte 50125 & AU - Wells A\\
                                                    \hline\hline
\end{tabular}
```

Table Information: A search program 'hit' three authors in an ASCII-delimited index. The first column lists the author. Each *Location Information* element is the last field of an index record; in packed form, it indicates where the record and the author fields start in the file *newdb*. (In each record, the tilde acting as record delimiter, the single quote as subfield delimiter.) The last two columns write the file locations of the actual data in readable form: (1) the byte position of the start of the Medline item and the text at that position; (2) the byte position of the author field and the text at that position. *UI* stands for Universal Identifier; it identifies that record over all the Medline databases in the set. *AU* is for Author.

The PrintOut:

Hit	Location Information	Byte Position	Text
Green B	91234565'55552'newdb'55600˜	byte 55552	UI - 91234565
		byte 55600	AU - Green B
Smith C	92345676'62767'newdb'63000˜	byte 62767	UI - 92345676
		byte 63000	AU - Smith C
Wells A	95123456'50025'newdb'50125˜	byte 50025	UI - 95123456
		byte 50125	AU - Wells A

Table 16.3: the p-width command. The elements of the previous table have been separated into text and math elements, with the math elements bracketed with $. Two text
columns are given specific sizes that are deliberately narrow, to illustrate how the *p* instruction causes the program to break the text into lines rather than spreading it out in a
single line. The table has been enclosed in a \table environment, so that the table can be
captioned.

The *p{width}* command sets a column that contains text to the specified width. The first
and fourth columns are obvious text and their widths are specified using the *p* command.
The numbers are uniform-sized integers, not decimals, so they can be treated either as text
or as math entities. Here, they are treated as math entities. Reading the table instructions
(see below) left to right, **\begin{tabular}{||p{.45in} ||c |c |p{.45in} |c ||c |c ||}** means
that there are seven columns, the first and fourth are each exactly .45 inches wide, and the
others vary in width depending on what they contain. Notice that the program splits *\p*
command text to fit the declared width, if there are spaces in the text. It won't split a word
it can't hyphenate.

The Markup For Table 16.3

```
\begin{table}
\begin{tabular}{||p{.45in}||c|c|p{.45in}|c||c|c||}\hline\hline
Hit &UI &UI Pos'n&Db &AU Pos'n&Byte Pos'n&Text\\\hline\hline
Green, Bartlett&$91234565$&$55552$&newdb in med&$55600$&55552&UI -\\
91234565 \cline{6-7} &   &   &   &   &55600 & AU - Green B\\ \hline
Smith, Clarence&$92345676$&$62767$&newdb in med&$63000$&62767&UI -\\
92345676 \cline{6-7} &   &   &   &   & 63000 & AU - Smith C\\ \hline
Wells, Andy&$95123456$&$&$50025$&newdb in med &$50125$ &50025&UI -\\
95123456 \cline{6-7} &   &   &   & &50125&AU - Wells A\\ \hline\hline
\end{tabular}
\caption{Splitting Wordy Text In a Column} \label{tb:wordy}
\end{table}
```

Hit	UI	UI Pos'n	Db	AU Pos'n	Byte Pos'n	Text
Green, Bartlett	91234565	55552	newdb in med	55600	55552	UI - 91234565
					55600	AU - Green B
Smith, Clarence	92345676	62767	newdb in med	63000	62767	UI - 92345676
					63000	AU - Smith C
Wells, Andy	95123456	50025	newdb in med	50125	50025	UI - 95123456
					50125	AU - Wells A

Table 16.3: Splitting Wordy Text In a Column

Table 16.4: Touching Up a Table. The material in columns 6 and 7 in Table 16.3 appear awkwardly placed. We can improve the appearance by judicious use of the \vspace command as shown in Table 16.4. The markup of the previous table is reduced to scriptsize to show each line as a unit. The printout is reduced to small to show that you can write a table in one size and then resize it for esthetic or practical reasons.

The Markup For Table 16.4

```
\begin{table}[h!]
\scriptsize
begin{tabular}{||p{.45in} || c | c | p{.45in} | c || c | c ||} \hline\hline
Hit & UI & UI Pos'n & Db & AU Pos'n & Byte Pos'n & Text\\hline\hline
Green, Bartlett&$91234565$&$55552$&newdb in med&$55600$&$55552&UI - 91234565
\vspace{-1pc} \cline{6-7} & & & & & 55600 & AU - Green B\\ \hline
Smith, Clarence&$92345676$&$62767$&newdb in med&$63000$&$62767&UI - 92345676
\vspace{-1pc} \cline{6-7} & & & & & 63000 & AU - Smith C\\ \hline
Wells, Andy&$95123456$&$50025$&newdb in med&$50125$ & 50025&UI - 95123456
\vspace{-1pc} \cline{6-7} & & & & & 50125 & AU - Wells A\\ \hline\hline
\end{tabular}
\vspace*{-.15in}\caption{Touching Up Table~\ref{tb:wordy}} \label{tb:touchup}
\end{table}
\normalsize
```

Table 16.5: the @-expression. The *@-expression* command customizes the area between columns. First, the program suppresses the default spacing between the column and its neighbor; it reduces the spacing to zero. Then it uses the *@-expression* argument to create the intercolumn. The argument may contain spacing or actual text instruction.

\hspace. The instruction **\begin{tabular}{l@{\hspace{.25in}}r}** would put a quarter inch space between the two columns, the first of which is left-aligned,the second of which is right-aligned. An actual example is shown in Table 16.5, where it forms part of a intercolumn.

Hit	UI	UI Pos'n	Db	AU Pos'n	Byte Pos'n	Text
Green,	91234565	55552	newdb in	55600	55552	UI - 91234565
Bartlett			med		55600	AU - Green B
Smith,	92345676	62767	newdb in	63000	62767	UI - 92345676
Clarence			med		63000	AU - Smith C
Wells,	95123456	50025	newdb in	50125	50025	UI - 95123456
Andy			med		50125	AU - Wells A

Table 16.4: Touching Up Table 16.3

\extracolsep space. The instruction **\extracolsep**{*width*}, puts *width* in the all columns that follow the command. **r** @{\extracolsep{**5mm**}} would add 5 mm of space after each column that follows the first (right-justified) column, unless countermanded by another \extracolsep command. *This command can be used everywhere except to indent the first column.*

Text. The intercolumn substitute can also be ordinary text, which is copied as written, including spaces; e.g., @{} or @{ =FILEA= } or @{.}. @{} would place a column smack up against the preceding column. Notice that =FILEA= includes its own outside spaces to compensate for the erasure of the default spacing.

Various intercolumn styles are shown in table 16.5. The use of the period is particularly interesting. Ordinary LaTeX tables do not line up by decimal point. But an alignment by decimal point can be faked as shown.

The Markup For Table 16.5

```
\begin{table}[h!]
\begin{tabular}%
{||p{.6in}@{}r @{[\CL\CL]\hspace{2mm}} r@{.}l @{ $\ddagger$ } r@{.}l
@{[ XX ]} r@{.}l @{$\Uparrow$} p{.5in}||}\hline\hline

Greens& B &  912345 & 65  &  555 & 52   & 0 & 55600  & 55552\\
     & &        &      &     &      &   &        & 55600\\ \hline
Smithers& C &  923456 & 76  &   6 & 2767 & 6 & 3000   & 62767\\
     & &        &      &     &      &   &        & 63000\\ \hline
Wells& A &  951234 & 56  &  50 & 025  &   & 50125  & 50025\\
     & &        &      &     &      &   &        & 50125\\ \hline\hline
\end{tabular}
```

```
\caption{Using @-expressions to form intercolumns} \label{tb:intercol}
\end{table}
```

Greens	B[‖]	912345.65 ‡ 555.52	[XX]0.55600⇑55552
	[‖]	. ‡ .	[XX] . ⇑55600
Smithers	C[‖]	923456.76 ‡ 6.2767	[XX]6.3000 ⇑62767
	[‖]	. ‡ .	[XX] . ⇑63000
Wells	A[‖]	951234.56 ‡ 50.025	[XX] .50125⇑50025
	[‖]	. ‡ .	[XX] . ⇑50125

Table 16.5: Using @-expressions to form intercolumns

Table 16.6: the dcolumn package. Note that in the previous example, the period is intercolumn material, so there is no way to suppress it when it is not wanted; e.g, when the 'decimal' number is blank. A better way to align numbers by decimal point is to make use of the *dcolumn* package, written by David Carlisle [Carlisle96b]. As usual, you make the package available to the program by a **\usepackage{dcolumn}** statement in the preamble. Using *dcolumn* is illustrated in Table 16.6.

D is the basic way to lay out a column; it has three arguments:

1. A single character that acts as separator of the integer and decimal parts of the decimal values in the column in the markup. Use a comma for European decimals, a period otherwise.

2. The decimal separator in the printout file column. For decimal values, you'd likely use a period or comma. But you can use any expression or symbol such as *\ldots* or *\ddag*, and so forth.

3. An integer value for the expected number of decimal places for the values in the column. If it's positive, the program will allocate space for these many decimal places plus some space. If the values in the table vary in their decimal portions, the program won't chop an overlong decimal part, so numerical values in a row will run together or look lopsided if the decimal portions in some of the row elements are more than the number of places the program has allocated. However, if the number is negative, the program will align the numerical values around the decimal point, no matter how long the decimal part of the numerical value.

\D{.}{.}{3} would expect a column of numeric values, each of which has up to 3 decimal places. It would be fine for *12.44* or *.012* or *123456.412*.

Each column needs a separate column specifier. To save energy, write a *newcolumntype* alias. It is analoguous to the \newcommand. For example, in this next, we define an alias called *d*, which can be used for all decimals. The third value is filled in according to the number of decimal places in the column.

\newcolumntype{d}[1]{D{.}{.}{#1}}

If some of the values in the column will be European values, you can define another column type for commas.

\newcolumntype{e}[1]{D{,}{,}{#1}}

The column definers substitute for the *c*, *l* and *r* column definers of the usual tabular environment. The | has its usual meaning.

The Markup For Table 16.6

```
\begin{table}[H]
\begin{tabular}{d{5}|d{5}|d{-2}|d{-2}|e{3}} \\
   912.34565 & .55552 & 5560.0  &  5.5552 &    91234,565 \\
   9234.5676 & 6.2767 & 630.00  &  62.767 &    923456,76 \\
   951234.56 & 500.25 & 50.125  &  5.0025 &    95123,456 \\
\end{tabular}
\caption{Using dcolumn} \label{tb:dcol}
\end{table}
```

912.34565	.55552	5560.0	5.5552	91234, 565
9234.5676	6.2767	630.00	62.767	923456, 76
951234.56	500.25	50.125	5.0025	95123, 456

Table 16.6: Using dcolumn

Table 16.7: the extracolsep instruction. Table 16.7 is actually two tables. The one on the left illustrates the use of the extracolsep instruction within a @-expression in an ordinary tabular environment; the one on the right shows its use in a tabular* environment. Using one of the box formats is generally a better way to align two charts. But using the vspace and hspace commands for layout is reasonable for simple tables such as these.

tabular environment on the left: Notice that we can't use the extracolsep to fake a decimal point. It can only add space. We disable it to add a decimal point after 912345.65.

tabular* environment on the right: This is a table whose width you specify. It usually uses a @{\extracolsep{\fill}} command to create intercolumns; i.e., the program subtracts the width of the text from the specified width of the table to determine how much space to allocate to all the intercolumns. The format for the tabular* environment includes a width measure for the total table; in this case, it is 1.8 inches.

The Markup For Table 16.7

```
\newcommand{\ECS}{\extracolsep}
\begin{table}[h!]
\begin{tabular}{l@{\ECS{1mm}}r | lr || l@{\ECS{0pt}.}r lr }
Green & B &  Johns & J   & 912345 & 65  & 555 & 52 \\
Smith & C &  Evans & D   & 923456 & 76  & 236 & 27\\
Wells & A &  Philip & R  & 951234 & 56  & 350 & 25 \\
\end{tabular}
\caption{@-expressions: tabular (on left), tabular* (on right).}
\label{tb:ECS}
\vspace{-4.8pc}\hspace{3.25in} % raises the whole table.
                % shifts it 3.25 inches to the right.
\begin{tabular*}{1.8in}{p{.3in} @{\ECS{\fill}} cl @{\ECS{0pt} = }r}
Q1: & Gr 1: & 912 & x + 45 \\
Q2: & Gr 1: & 923 & x + 67 \\
Q3: & Gr 1: & 951 & x - 71 \\
\end{tabular*}
\end{table}
```

GreenB	Johns	J	912345.65	555	52		Q1:	Gr 1:	$912 = x + 45$
SmithC	Evans	D	923456.76	236	27		Q2:	Gr 1:	$923 = x + 67$
WellsA	Philip	R	951234.56	350	25		Q3:	Gr 1:	$951 = x - 71$

Table 16.7: @-expressions: tabular (on left), tabular* (on right).

Table 16.8: the multicolumn command. A **\multicolumn** command allows a single item to extend over several columns. The multicolumn overrides some of the vertical line instructions in the tabular environment; i.e., the vertical lines do not cut through a multi-column item.

Its format is: \multicolumn{n}{pos}{item} where:

1. {n} the number of columns the text extends over.

2. {pos} justify information (e.g., l,r,c) and vertical line information.

3. {item} the actual text. This can include font commands.

As an example, we will combine:

```
\multicolumn{2}{||c|}{\textsl{FIELD INFORMATION}} \\
\multicolumn{2}{c||}{\textsl{FILE INFORMATION}}
```

with the first tabular table. In addition, we will embed the table inside a table environment, so that we can caption it, and if need be, the program can float it. The result is Table 16.8.

The Markup For Table 16.8

```
 \begin{table}[!th]
\begin{tabular}{||l||l|l|l|} \hline \hline
\multicolumn{2}{||c|}{\textsl{FIELD INFORMATION}} &
\multicolumn{2}{c|}{\textsl{FILE INFORMATION}} \\[.1in]
   HIT &   Location Information   & Byte Position & Text \\ \hline
Green B & 91234565'55552'newdb'55600\~ & byte 55552 & UI - 91234565\\
  \cline{3-4}  & &  byte 55600 & AU - Green B \\ \hline
Smith C & 92345676'62767'newdb'63000\~ & byte 62767 & UI - 92345676\\
  \cline{3-4} & &   byte 63000 & AU - Smith C \\ \hline
Wells A & 95123456'50025'newdb'50125\~ & byte 50025 & UI - 95123456\\
  \cline{3-4} & &  byte 50125 & AU - Wells A \\ \hline\hline
\end{tabular}
\caption{Field Information Relative to the File} \label{tb:fieldinfo}
\end{table}
```

Table 16.9: the longtable package. *longtable* by David Carlisle [Carlisle96a], is a very useful package that writes a long tabular environment table across pages, just the way a

FIELD INFORMATION		*FILE INFORMATION*	
HIT	Location Information	Byte Position	Text
Green B	91234565'55552'newdb'55600˜	byte 55552	UI - 91234565
		byte 55600	AU - Green B
Smith C	92345676'62767'newdb'63000˜	byte 62767	UI - 92345676
		byte 63000	AU - Smith C
Wells A	95123456'50025'newdb'50125˜	byte 50025	UI - 95123456
		byte 50125	AU - Wells A

Table 16.8: Field Information Relative to the File

tabbing environment table can be extended beyond a page. Don't be disturbed if it takes a couple of runs through LaTeX before columns line up properly, especially if you are using *multicolumns*. You can repeat the Header on each new page—an excellent idea for tables that run for pages and pages.

Footnotes are possible. And you can use the *\newpage* command within the longtable, to control where to break text within a page.

A long table can be kept in its own file and brought in with an *\input* command. Occasionally, the text near the longtable is set erratically. If this happens, load the *afterpage* packages with a *usepackage* request in the preamble if you haven't already done so. In the document, if the table file is called *TableFileA*, you would write:

```
\afterpage{\clearpage\input{TableFileA}}
```

The *input* command always starts a new page. The *afterpage* command will see to it that the current page is filled with ordinary text.

This is a versatile program and it is worth reading the documentation filed as *longtable.dvi* in ˜*/texmf/doc/latex/tools*. Additional information is in [Goossens94, Section 5.4.2].

Using Table 12.1 as example, suppose it long enough to go beyond the page. The original table was written:

```
\begin{table}
\begin{tabular}{||l|l||l|l||l|l||l|l||} \hline
Markup & Print & Markup & Print & Markup & Print &
Markup & Print \\ \hline
```

```
\V=\'{o}= & \'{o} & \V=\~{o}= & \~{o} & \V=\v{o}= & \v{o}
 & \V=\c{o}= & \c{o} \\ \hline
. . . . . . . . . .
\end{tabular}
\caption{Accents and Symbols for Foreign Languages}\label{tab:accents}
\end{table}
```

You would change it to a long table by deleting the *table* environment and substituting the longtable environment for the tabular environment. Table 16.9 shows just the first part of what could be page 1 of a multipage table. Note that the caption has been moved to the top of the first page of the table. The text up to \endfirsthead is the title of the first page. The text up to \endhead is the title of the other pages of the table.

```
\begin{longtable}{||l|l||l|l||l|l||l|l||} \hline
\caption{Accents and Symbols for Foreign Languages}\label{tbl:accents}
\\ \hline
\multicolumn{8}{||c||}{\sffamily\large ACCENTS AND SYMBOLS}
\\ \hline
\endfirsthead
\multicolumn{8}{||c||}{\sffamily\large ACCENTS AND SYMBOLS}
\\ \hline
\multicolumn{8}{||c||}{\sffamily Markup And Print Pairs}\\ \hline
\endhead
Markup & Print & Markup & Print & Markup & Print & Markup & Print
\\ \hline
\V=\'{o}= & \'{o} & \V=\~{o}= & \~{o} & \V=\v{o}= & \v{o}  &
\V=\c{o}= & \c{o} \\ \hline
. . . . . . . . . .
\end{longtable}
```

Table 16.9: Accents and Symbols for Foreign Languages

ACCENTS AND SYMBOLS							
Markup	Print	Markup	Print	Markup	Print	Markup	Print
\'{o}	ò	\~{o}	õ	\v{o}	ǒ	\c{o}	o̧
\'{o}	ò	\~{o}	õ	\v{o}	ǒ	\c{o}	o̧
\'{o}	ó	\={o}	ō	\H{o}	ő	\d{o}	o̩
\^{o}	ô	\.{o}	ȯ	\t{oo}	o͡o	\b{o}	o̲
\oe	œ	\OE	Œ	\ae	æ	\AE	Æ
\aa	å	\AA	Å	\o	ø	\O	Ø
\l	ł	\L	Ł	\ss	ß	?`	¿
\dag	†	\ddag	‡	\S	§	\P	¶

Most of the additional float programs discussed for figures apply to tables. The *wrapfig* program that wraps text around figures (discussed in Section 16.1.4) has a *wraptable* environment for tables. It has the same syntax and the same restrictions as for the *wrapfigure* environment. In addition, *hlines* above and below the sidefloat are ignored. You can reinsert them manually. Similarly, just as there is a *floatingfigure* environment for the *floatflt* package, there is a *floatingtable* environment. The *endfloat* program [McCauley95] normally places all the figures at the end of the chapter and then all the tables. This can be reversed by used the *tablesfirst* option. And Lingnau's *float* program [Lingnau95] works equally well with tables.

Marking up tables can become a complicated game. The tabular environment has been extended so that you have more control of inter- and intra- column spacing, uninterrupted and split column length, and so forth. (See, for example, *array.dvi* [Mittelbach96c].) These extensions are not examined here. When creating a table becomes like brushing dust specks from a sticky 3 foot poster, try designing it in *xspread* [Cornelius92], the spreadsheet available in Linux, or in a WYSIWYG spreadsheet. (Using Excel is discussed in Section 24.7.) Then input it as an Encapsulated PostScript file with the *includegraphics* command that is discussed in Section 25.3.

16.3.3   Floats and multiple columns

Floats—figures and tables—can be written directly in the two-column format LaTeX provides as an option. In two-column format, however, they continue to be printed as if they were in single-column mode, even if they are too large for the column. To position the float across both columns, use the asterisk variant:

```
\begin{figure*}[location] ... \end{figure*}
\begin{table*}[location] ... \end{table*}
```

The *multicol* environment can be used inside minipages and figures. Conversely, ordinary figures and tables can't be used inside a *multicol* environment, but the asterisk variant is acceptable. In this example, do NOT confuse *table** and *tabular**. The tabular* object shown is not a float; it is a table with a specific size. It is small enough to fit into a column width and will be printed in place. If it were encased in a *table** environment, it would be treated as a float and might be moved out of the text.

The MarkUp:

```
\begin{multicols}{4}
When it is necessary to pool databases, it is not necessary to
concatenate the original MEDLINE database files and realphabetize
and reconsolidate a much enlarged pooled file.

\begin{tabular*}{.1in}{p{.1in} cr}
Q1: & 912\\
Q2: & 923\\
Q3: & 951\\
\end{tabular*}

Rather than realphabetize the already alphabetized and squished
individual index files, mergealp() can be used to create a 'virtual'
concatenated database.
\end{multicols}
```

The PrintOut:

When it is necessary to pool databases, it is not necessary to concatenate the original MEDLINE database files and re- alphabetize and re- consolidate a much enlarged pooled file.

Q1: 912
Q2: 923
Q3: 951

Rather than real- phabetize the al- ready alphabetized and squished indi- vidual index files, mergealp() can be used to create a 'vir- tual' concatenated database.

Chapter 17

FOOTNOTES

Writing a footnote can be very easy or very difficult. If you let the program number the footnotes and write them only in running text, there is nothing simpler.

Commands can become complicated:

* ⋆ if you wish to label footnotes with symbols

* ⋆ if you interrupt the program-generated sequence

* ⋆ if you wish minipage footnotes to look ordinary

17.1   Footnotes In Text

Footnotes are ordinarily used just in text mode. In classic LaTeX, they can not be used inside the arguments of such commands as: \chapter, \(sub)section, \figure, \table or \mbox. A footnote is written smack up against the text it amplifies and appears in the printout at the bottom of the same page in footnote size.

Footnotes in text are numbered by ordinary numbers or by symbols. The program attends to inserting a footnote number (or symbol) in the text and prepending the same number (or symbol) to the footnote printed at the bottom of the page.

Numbering is by number unless you specifically request a symbol.

17.1.1   Footnote syntax in text

Ordinary Numerical Footnote Syntax

The most-used footnote format is the footnote command and its argument; the text in the argument will be the footnote at the bottom of the page.

\footnote{<*footnote text*>}.

The MarkUp:

```
This is numbered 1 because it is the first number the program
automatically inserts in the chapter.\footnote{This will be printed
at the bottom of the page prepended by a raised number.}
```

The PrintOut:

This is numbered 1 because it is the first number the program automatically inserts in the chapter.[1]

The program will automatically increment the footnotes from 1 on. In fact, this is the format of most footnotes in most documents. If an occasional footnote is all you need, you can stop reading this chapter right now.

The Complete Numerical Footnote Syntax

The full footnote format is the footnote command, an optional number in square brackets and a braced argument that contains the text that will be in the footnote.

\footnote[<*num*>]{<*footnote text*>}.

The MarkUp:

```
 I don't know why anyone would want to insert a footnote
number\footnote[250]{This is footnote \#250 and we are only on
the second footnote of the chapter.} but there it is.
```

---

[1] This will be printed at the bottom of the page prepended by a raised number.

The PrintOut: I don't know why anyone would want to insert a footnote number[250] but there it is.

If [<*num*>] is filled in—with 250 in the example—the program will use this value to number the footnote. A word of caution: user-determined numbers are outside the automatic numbering procedure. If the next footnote doesn't specify a number, the program returns to where it was in the numbering cycle. To reset the numbering in a permanent way, use the \setcounter command, shown in Section 17.1.4. (See Section 30.1 for a discussion of the *setcounter* command.)

17.1.2   Shifting between numbers and symbols

The program uses the variable \thefootnote to store the footnote counter's current value. You set the numbering style of the footnote this way. The default is arabic numerals. To change to numbering by symbol, write:

\renewcommand{\thefootnote}{\fnsymbol{footnote}}

To change back to numbers, write:

\renewcommand{\thefootnote}{\arabic{footnote}}

17.1.3   Numbering by symbol

Footnotes can be numbered by symbols, using the nine built-in footnote symbols shown in Figure 17.1.

Ordinary Symbol Footnote Syntax

The program rotates the footnote symbols in this order.

The program considers the asterisk symbol *1* and so on through the double ddagger, the *#9* symbol. If you only use symbols and not ordinary numbers, the program automatically

---

[250]This is footnote #250 and we are only on the second footnote of the chapter.

$$* \quad \dagger \quad \ddagger \quad \S \quad \P \quad \parallel \quad ** \quad \dagger\dagger \quad \ddagger\ddagger$$

Figure 17.1: The Nine Footnote Symbols

steps through the symbols. It will, however, refuse to do more than one cycle per chapter. It resets numbering to * for each new chapter.

If you mix numbers and symbols but use automatic numbering, the program will select the correct symbol for the sequence. If, for example, the last ordinary number was 5, then the next footnote, if it's labeled by a symbol, will be prepended by a ∥, the 6th symbol.

In order of appearance, the command names of the symbols are:

\ast   \dagger   \ddagger   \S   \P   \parallel   \ast\ast   \dagger\dagger
\ddagger\ddagger

Many of the footnote symbols are defined as math symbols. If you use them in text mode, they need to be enclosed in $ brackets. For example, write: **$\ast$**.

The Complete Symbol Footnote Syntax

The square-bracketed option must be filled in by an ordinary number from 1 to 9, not the actual symbol. The program uses the symbol associated with that number. For example, writing **\footnote[3]{See example 6.}** in the text will produce a footnote preceded by a ‡.

17.1.4   Resetting the counter

To reset the numbering in a permanent way, use the *setcounter* command.

The footnote counter, *footnote*, like most other program-counted variables, is incremented when the command is issued, just before the footnote is processed. Footnote numbers recycle to zero at the beginning of each new chapter in a book or report. The counter is incremented to one when the first footnote command is issued.

footnote can be reset to a specific number at any point in the numbering cycle by using the *setcounter* command—there is no *resetcounter*.

The format is: \setcounter{footnote}{#}, where *#* is some number. This resets the footnote counter to this value, so that the change is permanent. The program then automatically increments the number at the next *footnote* command.

The MarkUp:

```
\setcounter{footnote}{5}
This is text\footnote{This
footnote will be numbered 6.}....
```

The PrintOut: This is text[6]....

17.1.5 Examples of numbering styles

The comments in this list of items refer to the markup that follows. The single text paragraph is broken up into separate sentences. It is printed as one paragraph in the printout that follows the markup.

Line A. The option in the bracket ([*num*]) can be any integer. The program does not count it as part of cyclic incrementing; i.e., it has no effect on the footnote counter.

Line B. The optional [*num*] is missing, so the footnote is automatically numbered by the program. The previous footnote that was part of the count cycle was 6. So this automatically becomes 7. It is independent of the numbering we gave the footnote in Line A.

Line C. We want to shift to numbering footnotes by symbol. To do so, we first need to redefine the footnote variable from numeric to symbol mode, using a *renewcommand* command.

Line D. We are now in symbol mode, automatic numbering, so the program uses its symbol presentation order. The last footnote that was automatically numbered (in Line C) was 7. So the program numbers this with the 8th symbol in its list, the double dagger (††).

---

[6]This footnote will be numbered 6.

Line E. We are still in symbol mode. We choose the footnote number—the fifth item in the symbol list—so this footnote isn't part of the numbering cycle. What do you think the next footnote symbol will be, if we stay in symbol mode and *num* is not given a value next time? Reread Section 17.1.3, then try it.

Line F. We return the footnote numbering style to ordinary arabic numbers. The next footnote in the chapter will be 9, because the last automatic numbering was the 8th symbol.

The MarkUp:

```
\slshape
Each field is a single line, with the exception of the
TItle, ADdress and ABstract fields\footnote[7]{The    % Line A
abstract field is a multiline author-produced
abstract of the article.}.

The SOurce\footnote{This was multiline for          % Line B
a time in the 1970's.} field is a complex of journal
name, year, volume and page number;
it is highly stylized.

\renewcommand{\thefootnote}{\fnsymbol{footnote}}      % Line C.

Lines appear to be under 75 characters in
length.\footnote{Wrap lines if you are printing       % Line D.
in double column.}

Fields always appear in the same
order.\footnote[5]{The number of items in many of
the fields, MEsh headings as example, is              % Line E.
unrestricted.}

\renewcommand{\thefootnote}{\arabic{footnote}}        % Line F.
\upshape
```

The PrintOut:

*Each field is a single line, with the exception of the TItle, ADdress and ABstract fields[7].
The SOurce[7] field is a complex of journal name, year, volume and page number; it is highly*

---

[7]The abstract field is a multiline author-produced abstract of the article.

[7]This was multiline for a time in the 1970's.

stylized. Lines appear to be under 75 characters in length.[††] *Fields always appear in the same order.*[¶]

17.2 Footnotes In A Minipage

Footnotes in classic LaTeX cannot be put in the argument of most commands. But in a minipage,[9] a footnote can be used in any of the modes: text, box or math.

The numbering in a minipage can be made independent of the numbering in the rest of the chapter.

Keep the minipage construction simple.

Don't enclose a minipage within a minipage—this may place footnotes where you don't want them.

17.2.1 Minipage footnotes with independent numbering

Each minipage can have its own set of incremental numbers, independent of the footnotes in the regular text. You would want to keep minipage footnotes with the minipage if the enclosed table, say, has glosses not applicable to the rest of the text. To do this, you use the usual \footnote command, as in this example, which uses the table from Example 1 in Section 16.3.2 in the previous chapter.

Default Numbering Of Minipage Footnotes

Footnotes, by default, are labeled with lowercase letters.

[††] Wrap lines if you are printing in double column.

[¶] The number of items in many of the fields, MEsh headings as example, is unrestricted.

[9] A minipage environment lets you write text, a list, a figure and so forth, within a line width of your choosing. The program sets the length of the minipage to (invisibly) encase the contents. The width reverts to the default line width when the environment terminates.

Hit	Location Information	Byte Position	Text
Green B	91234565'55552[a]'newdb'55600~	byte 55552	UI - 91234565
		byte 55600	AU - Green B
Smith C	92345676'62767'newdb[b]'63000~	byte 62767	UI - 92345676
		byte 63000	AU - Smith C
Wells A[c]	95123456'50025'newdb'50125~	byte 50025	UI - 95123456
		byte 50125	AU - Wells A

[a]See [1].
[b]Revised 1978.
[c]Duplicate Reference Ignored.

Figure 17.2: Footnotes restricted to the minipage

The Markup For Figure 17.2

```
\begin{minipage}[t]{5in}
\begin{tabular}{||l||c|r|c|} \hline \hline
    Hit &    Location Information    & Byte Position & Text \\
 \hline \hline
Green B & 91234565'55552\footnote{See [1].}'newdb'55600\~ & byte
    55552 & UI - 91234565 \\ \cline{3-4}
        &                 & byte 55600 & AU - Green B \\ \hline
Smith C & 92345676'62767`newdb\footnote{Revised 1978.}'63000\~ &
    byte 62767 & UI - 92345676 \\ \cline{3-4}
        &                 & byte 63000 & AU - Smith C \\ \hline
Wells A\footnote{Duplicate Reference Ignored.} &
 95123456'50025'newdb'50125\~ & byte 50025 & UI - 95123456 \\
\cline{3-4}   & & byte 50125 & AU - Wells A \\ \hline\hline
\end{tabular}
caption{Footnotes restricted to the minipage} label\{fig:restricted}
\end{minipage}
```

Numbering Footnotes With Ordinary Numbers And Symbols

As shown in Figure 17.3, numbers and symbols can be produced in a minipage using the
mpfootnote command, which is to the minipage what *footnote* is to ordinary text.

Number by number: `\renewcommand{\thempfootnote}{\arabic{mpfootnote}}`
Number by symbol: `\renewcommand{\thempfootnote}{\fnsymbol{mpfootnote}}`
Return to default numbering: `\renewcommand{\thempfootnote}{\alph{mpfootnote}}`

Sentences are separated in the markup portion of Figure 17.3 for clarity.

The MarkUp:

```
\begin{minipage}{2.75in}
This is a minipage\footnote{Default
footnotes in a minipage are
lowercase letters.} footnote.

And here's\footnote{Second default
footnote.} another footnote.

\renewcommand{\thempfootnote}%
{\arabic{mpfootnote}}

This is written inside a
minipage.\footnote{It will
be footnoted at the bottom of the
minipage.} Notice that the
numbering is now an ordinary number.

\renewcommand{\thempfootnote}{\fnsymbol{mpfootnote}}

Now we ask to change to symbols, like
this\footnote{This should be
a symbol and it is.}.

\renewcommand{\thefootnote}{\arabic{footnote}}
\end{minipage}
\caption{Restricting footnotes to the minipage}\label{fig:footnte}
```

The PrintOut:

This is a minipage[a] footnote. And here's[b] another footnote. This is written inside a minipage.[3] Notice that the numbering is now an ordinary number. Now we ask to change to symbols, like this[§].

---

[a]Default footnotes in a minipage are lowercase letters.

[b]Second default footnote.

[3]It will be footnoted at the bottom of the minipage.

[§]This should be a symbol and it is.

Figure 17.3: Restricting footnotes to the minipage

17.2.2 Blending minipage and text footnotes

Writing a footnote in a minipage so that the numbering is continuous with the regular footnotes in location, in numbering and in style has several peculiarities.

- The *\footnote* command can not be used. Instead, two commands—*\footnotemark* and *\footnotetext*—do the work of \footnote.

- The program increments the footnote counter with each \footnotemark. But this is not coordinated with \footnotetext. You have to make adjustments with \addtocounter.

This is the general procedure. The lines referenced are for the example that follows.

1. Write a separate **\footnotemark** wherever you want footnote numbers in the text in the printout. Note that there is no text argument for the footnotemark. See Lines A, B and C.

2. Complete the minipage before writing the addtocounter and footnotetext statements. See Line D.

3. **\addtocounter**{*counter*}{NUM} synchronizes the footnote count between footnotemark and footnotetext. The program incremented the counter for every footnotemark and there are three \footnotemark commands. So we need to reduce the count by two (1 minus 3) to match the first footnote number. See Lines E. We increment the count by one after the first footnote. The \addtocounter in Lines G and I adds 1 to the count for each of the other two footnotes.

4. **\footnotetext**{<TEXT>} writes the footnote text. Write a single \footnotetext-{<text>} for each *footnotemark* in the paragraph. See Lines F, H and J.

The box in Figure 17.4 outlines the general procedure for formatting three footnotes. It applies to the example that we have been analyzing. Notice the use of % at the end of some of the lines. The % at the end of a line deletes the End of Line Mark, so the final character on one line blends with the first character on the next line. This is especially necessary in commands where there must not be a gap between components.

The MarkUp:

```
\begin{minipage}[t]{\textwidth-.5in}

A command operates only on the text in its
argument.\footnotemark                        % Line A

A declaration, on the other hand, acts up
to the limits of the territory\footnotemark\
in which it resides.                          % Line B
```

FORMAT FOR INTRODUCING THREE FOOTNOTE MARKS IN A MINI-
PAGE SO THE NOTES BLEND WITH THE REGULAR CHAPTER NOTES.

```
\begin{minipage}{<width>}
<...text>\footnotemark <text...>
<...text>\footnotemark <text...>
<...text>\footnotemark <text...>
<...rest of the text in the minipage.>
\end{minipage}
\addtocounter{footnote}{1 minus the number of footnotemarks}%
\footnotetext{Actual footnote text for 1st footnote.}
\addtocounter{footnote}{plus 1}%
\footnotetext{Actual footnote text for 2nd footnote.}
\addtocounter{footnote}{plus 1}%
\footnotetext{Actual footnote text for 3rd footnote.}
```

Figure 17.4: How To Blend Minipage and Regular Footnotes

```
An environment can be of any
size\footnotemark and complexity.              % Line C

end{minipage}                                  % Line D

\addtocounter{footnote}{-2}%                   % Line E

\footnotetext{The text within the
adjoining brace pair.}                         % Line F

\addtocounter{footnote}{+1}%                   % Line G

\footnotetext{Usually this is an               % Line H
environment, but it can be a command.}

\addtocounter{footnote}{+1}%                   % Line I

\footnotetext{Within the confines              % Line J
of \begin{document} and \end{document}.}
```

The PrintOut:

A command operates only on the text in its argument.[10]A declaration, on the other hand, acts up to the limits of the territory[11] in which it resides. An environment can be of any size[12]and complexity.

17.3   Changing Footnote Style

Two commands change the appearance of the footnote area. These commands default to the values given them when a page was composed:

1. **\footnotesep**. This controls the height of the invisible strut at the beginning of every footnote; it creates the space between footnotes. (The strut concept is discussed in Section 23.3.2.) It can be changed to .15 inches, for example, with a **\renew-command{\footnotesep}{.15in}**.

   It can also be written:

   \renewcommand{\footnotesep*}{.15in}

   The asterisk makes it permanent.

2. **\footnoterule**. This controls the appearance and length of the line that separates the text from the first footnote. It goes into effect and stays in effect from whenever it is redefined.

   It can be extended, for example, with:

   \renewcommand{\footnoterule}%

   {─────────────────────────────}

   Or it can be given a difference appearance with:

   \renewcommand{\footnoterule}{=================}

---

[10]The text within the adjoining brace pair.
[11]Usually this is an environment, but it can be a command.
[12]Within the confines of \begin{document} and \end{document}.

17.4   Footnote Modification Packages

ftnright can be used in a two-column page format. It moves all the footnotes that belong on the page in sequence to the bottom of the right column. It was written by Frank Mittelbach [Mittelbach96b] and is documented in *ftnright.dvi*.

footnpag, written by Joachim Schrod [Schrod95], will number footnotes per page, starting fresh on each new page.

fnpara, written by Dominik Wujastyk and Chris Rowley [Wujastyk95], write the footnotes as running text.

endnotes, This was written by John Lavagnino [Lavagnino91]. To put all the footnotes at the end of the document, you write the footnote as you would ordinarily but you add two sets of commands:

1. You redefine the footnote command early on:

   `\renewcommand{\footnote}{\endnote}`

2. You write this at the end of the document or chapter—wherever you want the notes to be located.

```
\newpage          % Makes sure you start on a new page.
                  % It will also write a header: Notes.
\begingroup       % \TeX\ 'environment'.
                  % Ends with \endgroup below.
\parindent=0pt    % No indenting
\setlength{\parskip}{2ex} % The spacing between notes.
\renewcommand{\enotesize}{\normalsize}
                  % Write in regular size,
                  % not footnote size.
\theendnotes      %This is the footnote counter value.
\endgroup
```

See also Section 32.10 for macros that let you write end notes in several styles. Numbering in the text can look like footnotes or not.

Several packages that lift restrictions on the presentation of the text also modify footnote usage. For example:

The **multicol** package, written by Frank Mittelbach [Mittelbach96a], allows up to 10 columns per page. Footnotes are written as they would be in single-column pages, namely, across the width of the text line.

The **longtable** package, written by David Carlisle [Carlisle96a] and discussed in Section 16.3.2, extends a tabular environment table across multiple pages. The *\footnote* command can be used in the body of the table. Use the *\footnotemark* and *\footnotetext* commands in the caption, and in the headers and footer areas.

Chapter 18

CROSS-REFERENCING

18.1   Referencing Numbered LaTeX Objects

Many LaTeX objects are automatically numbered incrementally. This includes all the document partitions from chapter to subparagraph, figures, tables, enumerate items, arrays, equations, eqnarrays and the different formal names conjured up by the \newtheorem command.

LaTeX provides a way to label them with nicknames, so that you can avoid referring to them by absolute number. Consequently, you avoid having to change *Refer to Section 5.3* to *Refer to Section 4.7* when that section becomes Section 4.7 and continue to change the reference as the Section becomes 4.8 and later Section 4.9, as document writing progresses.

Suppose, you wish to reference a section that is written in the source as:

```
\section{Labeling Objects} \label{sec:labels}
```

You would reference the section by its nickname. For example:

```
Refer to Section~\ref{sec:labels}
```

The program would make the association between the nickname and the actual section number, no matter how often the section changes number. So when Section 5.3 eventually

287

becomes Section 4.9, the text would print as: **Refer to Section 4.9**.

The reference name (the nickname) should be a label that is easy to associate with the figure or equation or section. The label is assigned using the `\label` command, immediately after the name of the chapter or equation or (sub)section is typed in. The label nickname stays with the referenced item, wherever it may move.

Because Upper and lower case are different, it is probably a good idea to write labels consistently in one case or another.

It is also a good idea to use a prefix that identifies the object type. For example, 'sec-' or 'sc:' as part of the label, is a reminder that this is a section label. You can integrated a figure, an affiliated table and a chapter by giving them all the same nickname with a initial descriptor detailing what the object is: for example a cluster of labels for such a group might be called: *chap:newdb, fig:newdb, arr:newdb*.

If you use the same label on two objects or if you use a label you haven't defined (usually a typo but maybe not), the program will tell you about it in the log file.

Do NOT place a label inside another argument.[1]

Numbering won't change to reflect the newer changes each time LaTeX is run, because the program always uses the numbering worked out the previous run. As in writing a Table of Contents, you need to run the program several times on a static document to get updated numbers.

Numbering is always sequential. But suppose you are working on only a few modules in a document whose parts are separated among several files, so several of the parts are not included in the current run. Numbering will only be piecewise accurate. If you need to know how many figures there are in the whole document, run LaTeX over all the text files that form the document by revising (or omitting) the `\includeonly{...}` command in the root file. (See Chapter A below.)

Some people like to assign a nickname as soon as an equation or figure or section is written. Others prefer adding a label only when they actually write the magic words: 'refer to ...' or 'see Figure ...'.

---

[1] Actually, you can place a label inside a \caption command or inside one of the document division commands. But why learn a complicated rule, when it is simpler to put the label just after the argument.

If you only reference a few numbered objects, it is sufficient to find the original label by searching for some odd-ball text phrase from the vicinity. For very large files with very many labels, it is very useful to have a list of the labels used, so that you know what to call a heading while writing about it. LaTeX can provide you with a beautifully formatted TOC-style label list in *lablst.dvi*. To create it:

1. Type in an xterm: **latex lablst**.

   The program will ask you:

   (a) The name of the root file, without the *.tex* extension. It expects the extension will be *.tex*. Don't argue. If your major file does not end in *.tex*, make a copy for *lablst* to use; e.g., *cp practice.doc practice.tex*. Then answer the question; for our practice file, it would be: **practice**.

   (b) The document class: article, report, book.

   (c) Other packages. You can usually ignore this by doing a CarriageReturn.
   NOTE: If you make a mistake in typing, use the DELETE key (NOT the BACK-ARROW key) to erase. Or get out and start again.

2. Run xdvi on *lablst* to view the complete label list. Or print it with **dvips lablst.dvi**.

3. There is also a set of statistics on the file in lablst.log.

If you change a nickname in a document partition, be sure to change it in all the references to it.

18.2 Page References

Labelling of the LaTeX object is the same whether reference will be by section or by page.

However, the page reference is: \pageref, rather than \ref.

The Section that begins on this very page is labeled:

\section{Page References} \label{ss:pgref}

The page reference is: `\pageref`, rather than `\ref`. Thus, we could refer to the Section that begins on this very page this way:

The MarkUp:

```
See Section~\ref{ss:pgref} on page~\pageref{ss:pgref}
for a discussion on referencing pages.
```

The PrintOut: See Section 18.2 on page 289 for a discussion on referencing pages.

18.3   Referencing Footnotes

Classic LaTeX does not reference footnotes. But Goossens et al [Goossens94, page 73] demonstrate a clever way to reference footnotes. This example is an adaptation.

It consists of three parts:

1. Writing a new command to cut down on tricky typing. They used:

   `\newcommand{\fnref}[1]{~\ref{#1}}`

2. Incorporating a label in the footnote.

   This is preliminary text.\footnote{This footnote includes a label.\label{fn:EXftn}} And this follows the footnote.

3. Referencing the footnote.

   ......(See footnote\fnref{fn:EXftn} on page~\pageref{fn:EXftn} for further details.)

The PrintOut: This is preliminary text[2]. And this follows the footnote.

........(See footnote 2 on page 290 for further details.)

---

[2]This footnote includes a label.

18.4 Positioning The Label

Some numbered LaTeX objects, such as the section heading, have a stylized appearance. Other numbered objects, such as the figure, have no specific style. This affects where to place the label.

18.4.1 The LaTeX object is stylized

part, chapter, section, subsection,... are counters that have commands associated with their names. *chapter* numbers chapters. It is associated with the command *\chapter*. When the command is issued, the text in its argument is automatically printed in a particular font in a particular size. The label obviously belongs directly after the header.

This particular chapter is entitled 'Cross-Referencing' and is labeled *ss:Xref*. It appears in the source document as: `\chapter{CROSS-REFERENCING} \label{ss:Xref}`

The section we are in is labeled *ss:Xcmd*. It appears in the source document as: `\section{ The LaTeX object is stylized} \label{ss:Xcmd}`.

It might be referenced this way in the source text: `See Chapter~\ref{ss:Xref}, Section~\ref{ss:Xcmd} for details.`

which would be printed as: See Chapter 18, Section 18.4.1 for details.

The tilde before the \ref command ensures an unbreakable space. This way, the chapter number is printed as a unit on the same line as the Chapter name.

If you change a partition in a document, you do not have to change the label. If a section becomes a subsection, the program takes the object with its associated label out of the section numbering stack and puts it in the subsection numbering stack. How does it know? Because you have to change the associated command from \section to \subsection.

18.4.2 The LaTeX object is not stylized

Many LaTeX objects—tables, figures, equations—do not have a specific repertoire of print features. Two objects, both called figures, can look very different from each other, be very different in length and composition, have very different font shapes. In addition, a figure often contains a set of equations, so it is not always obvious where the different labels for the components of the figure belong.

Put the label for a specific equation in the eqnarray environment after the equation and before the \\. The final equation can be labeled before the \end{eqnarray}.

If an equation is part of a figure environment, do NOT place the figure label right after the equation or some other numbered object, because the program will assign the label to the equation, not to the figure.

In a figure environment, it is a good idea to put the label right after the \caption command argument.

LaTeX lets you use multiple captions to partition the figure as you partition a document. But each caption automatically increments the figure count, so in simple figure or single-subject figures, only use one caption command (\caption).

This next is an example where you might want to break up a figure into subfigures, each with its own caption. The advantage is that the subfigures will be printed as a unit.

The Markup For Figures 18.1–18.3

```
\begin{figure}[H]
Today Pythagorus is remembered for his mathematical contributions.
It is hard to reconstruct the excitement and the connotations that
arose around what today seems so pragmatic an idea.
\caption{Life of Pythagorus} \label{fig:life}
\vspace{.07in}
The pythagoreans made mystical interpretations of what today's
school children see as another dreary formula to memorize.
\caption{Talking About Mystical Equations} \label{fig:myst}
\vspace{.07in} This is the famous equation:
\begin{equation}
x^{2} + y^{2} = z^{2} \label{eq:pyth}
```

```
\end{equation}
\caption{Pythagorus and His Equation} \label{fig:pyfig}
\end{figure}
```

The PrintOut:

Today Pythagorus is remembered for his mathematical contributions. It is hard to reconstruct the excitement and the connotations that arose around what today seems so pragmatic an idea.

Figure 18.1: Life of Pythagorus

The pythagoreans made mystical interpretations of what today's school children see as another dreary formula to memorize.

Figure 18.2: Talking About Mystical Equations

This is the famous equation:

$$x^2 + y^2 = z^2 \tag{18.1}$$

Figure 18.3: Pythagorus and His Equation

The current number associated with a labeled object will show up in the printout, if you use the \ref command.

The MarkUp:

```
Compare this to Figure~\ref{fig:pyfig} on page~\pageref{fig:pyfig}.\\
Refer to Equation~\ref{eq:pyth} for details. \\
His life, as shown in Figure~\ref{fig:life}.... \\
In the section containing Figure~\ref{fig:myst}, notice that...
```

The PrintOut: Compare this to Figure 18.3 on page 293.

Refer to Equation 18.1 for details.

His life, as shown in Figure 18.1....

In the section containing Figure 18.2, notice that...

Chapter 19

LITERAL TEXT AND SILENT TEXT

19.1 Verbatim Text

There are times you need the program to treat its special characters and formatting instructions as ordinary text.

You have a set of short lines that you do NOT want the program to run together as a paragraph. It is of course possible to type in a NewLine (\\) command at the end of each line to force the program to treat them as independent lines, but it is inconvenient.

You are writing and discussing programming code. Many of the LaTeX special characters are constantly used in programming. As example, the intersection with C programming symbols is extensive. If there were no way to write a special character as an ordinary one, you would be forced to convert each brace pair separately into literal characters. And each `%s, \n, \t, --, &&, _, and #` would require special handling.

You need to show the original markup commands.

There are several ways to make the program print your text exactly as you typed it, with formating and special characters treated as ordinary characters and each and every space output exactly as typed.

1. **\verb.** The verb command does not take a braced argument. Instead, the command is followed **immediately** by any character that is NOT a space, asterisk or an alphabetic character; for example: `\verb=10% of (7x3)=`. This bracket character, the equal sign in our example, is used on the left- and on the right-side to enclose the literal text. All the text that follows up to another plus sign is treated as ordinary text. If = is in the body of the text that is to be displayed, use another bracketing symbol such as a **+**.

   The **\verb** command and its text have the advantage of fitting into any environment. You can intersperse it in ordinary text. It also does nicely as an item in a list.

   The disadvantage is that the **\verb** and its enclosed text must fit on a single line. If on printout the literal statement pokes out, either split the literal text in two and issue two verb commands, or move the entire verb command and its text to the next line.

   ATTENTION: The **\verb** command should NOT be used inside the argument of some other command. This is illegal: `\section{Using the \verb=?= command}`.

   As a variant, there is the **\verb*** as in `\verb*+this and that+`. This replace spaces with ⎵ marks in the printout, making it easier to pick out all the spaces in the literal text, if you are making a point about spacing.

   A useful abbreviation is this: **\newcommand{\V}{\verb}**.

   Or better: **\newcommand{\L¹}[1]{\verb+#1+}**.

   Supposed you wished to write this sentence as is, without enclosing the angle brackets in math delimiters or constructing an alias:

   Use < and > as delimiters.

   To use the \V command, you would write: **\V**, the + symbols and enclose the sentence in the middle: **\V+Use < and > as delimiters.+**

   To use the \L command, you would write: **\L{Use < and > as delimiters.}**

2. **verbatim.** The verbatim environment is used for large chunks of text. Most of the markup and printout illustrations in this book use the verbatim environment for the markup. For example, this verbatim chunk:

---

¹I hope it is clear that you can name new commands whatever you wish. I picked V for *verb* and L for *literal*.

```
\begin{verbatim}
\textbf{SHOW FAMILIES:}
\textsf{of the previous and }
\textrm{next structs in the list,}
\texttt{respectively. So the keys are always in alphabetic order}
\end{verbatim}
```

was used to show the markup of this printout:

SHOW FAMILIES: of the previous and next structs in the list, `respectively`.
`So the keys are always in alphabetic order`

As with the Verb command, there is an asterisk variant: *\begin{verbatim*}*, which will print each space in the text it controls as ␣.

This is a useful abbreviations: `\newcommand{\bv}{\begin{verbatim}}`

The corresponding: `\newcommand{\ev}{\end{verbatim}}` does NOT work. The program doesn't snap out of literal mode until it encounters an actual `\end{verbatim}` statement. It accepts no substitutes. Moreover, there must be NO space between the end command and the left brace that begins its argument.

Like the `\verb` command, the `\begin{verbatim}` .. `\end{verbatim}` can not be used in another command's argument. Moreover, it has the flavor of an indented quote (see Section 15.6.1), in that it forces an empty line before writing out the literal text.

3. **alltt.** This package [Lamport96] is an upgrade of *verbatim.sty* in which \, { and } continue to act as command delimiters; write **\begin{alltt} ... \end{alltt}** in place of **\begin{verbatim} ... \end{verbatim}**. This is an excellent way to format lists that come in from an optical character reader or straight ASCII, where you don't want the individual lines pulled together into a paragraph. At the same time, it is easy to dress them in whatever font you wish. With the insertion of a few LaTeX commands, you can make a straight ASCII document PostScript print-ready and forgo the need to format it in Printer Command Language (PCL) for printing. If you have a PostScript printer and set up a skeleton LaTeX file into which you insert the ASCII manuscript, you might eliminate the need to maintain a dual printing system; i.e., one that is responsive both to PCL for ASCII printing and to PostScript. See the recording of a nfssfont session in Section 12.1.3 for a example of *alltt* usage. What is printed was wrapped in:

```
\footnotesize
\begin{alltt}
\textbf{\textsl{latex nfssfont}}

***********************************************\\
. . . . . . . . . . . . . .
Output written on nfssfont.dvi (2 page, 22212 bytes).\\
Transcript written on nfssfont.log.
\end{alltt}
\normalsize
```

4. moreverb. This package, written by Robin Fairbairns [Fairbairns96], is another useful addition to verbatim text, particularly if you need to refer to line numbers in a legal brief or in a computer program. Load it with a **\usepackage{moreverb}** command in the preamble. You use the *listing* environment in lieu of the *verbatim* environment. The second argument is the starting line number. For example:

The MarkUp: \begin{listing}{1}

```
<filename>.mh = alphabetized/compressed mesh headings
<filename>.ms = alphabetized/compressed mesh subheadings
<filename>.ui = alphabetized/compressed unique identifiers
<filename>.au = alphabetized/compressed authors
<filename>.sa = alphabetized/compressed senior authors
```

\end{listing}

The PrintOut:

```
1    <filename>.mh = alphabetized/compressed mesh headings
2    <filename>.ms = alphabetized/compressed mesh subheadings
3    <filename>.ui = alphabetized/compressed unique identifiers
4    <filename>.au = alphabetized/compressed authors
5    <filename>.sa = alphabetized/compressed senior authors
```

19.2   Writing Notes To Yourself

19.2.1   Using the %

In writing a file that will be processed by *LATEX*, the % is a signal that the rest of the text on the line will not show up on printout; thus:

```
...in file secB %did i call this B or BB?.
```

19.2.2   Invisible reminders

The simplest is to have some acronym such as **cbh** for *come back here*. It reminds you that you aren't done until you attend to this part of the document. You would create it by writing:

```
\newcommand{\cbh}{}
```

Writing **\cbh** in the document will not show up in a xdvi display or in the printout. To find the *\cbh's*, you would use the ordinary *Emacs* search mechanism; for example:

CTRLs \cbh

You could differentiate several types of reminders by different acronyms:

\cbh for *Come Back Here*
\can for *Compare Against Newest*
\bsa for *Bring to So and so's Attention*
\cit for *Change Index Term*

and so forth. This is rather like using different color highlighters.

The notion can be expanded by rewriting *\cbh* so that it takes an argument; i.e., **\renew-command**{\cbh}[1]{...}. This format supports the writing of actual notes in the argument of the acronym such as: **\cbh{..in file secB did i call this B or BB?}**. This would differentiate a note about unfinished business from a note such as **\can{Use this chart in feb paper as basis for pop gen figs}**, which is a general comment about an object in the text.

Other useful commands are:

```
\newcommand{\ignore}[1]{}     % The argument text won't be printed.
\newcommand{\redo}[1]{}       % The argument text won't be printed.
\newcommand{\spellchk}[1]{}   % The argument text won't be printed.
\newcommand{\addhyph}[1]{}    % The argument text won't be printed.
\newcommand{\newthunk[1]{}    % The argument text won't be printed.
```

where *spellchk* is a reminder to check spelling and *addhyph* identifies a place that may need special hyphenation, and so forth.

Fill the argument of any of these commands with text. The text will NOT appear on output. Recall that when you write a macro with placeholders, text can be written in the command *as part of the definition.* Otherwise, it can be inserted later only as substitute for a placeholder.

So if you type text into the argument of any of these new commands, the text will be ignored by the program because it wasn't there when the command was born and it can't substitute for the non-existent placeholder. Neither of these will show up in the printout or in the screen version:

```
\redo{Revise 1st para in 'Correcting \LaTeX\ Box Errors'.}

\spellchk{apparent? apparant.}
```

\ignore{...} is also very useful if you want to 'cut a section of text' to see what the surround looks like.

```
\ignore{
<text>
}
```

19.2.3 Visible reminders

You may want to gloss a portion of the text so that you or some other reader will find problem areas easily. This draws a frame around a note, using the *cbh* acronym as a base.

```
\newsavebox{\CBHbox}
\newenvironment{CBH}{\begin{lrbox}{\CBHbox}%
\begin{minipage}[t]{1in}\scriptsize}%
{\end{minipage}%
\end{lrbox}\fbox{\usebox{\CBHbox}}}

\newcommand{\BCBH}{\begin{CBH}}
\newcommand{\ECBH}{\end{CBH}}
```

You would use it, for example, this way:

```
The other example is this: \BCBH{Combo these examples. Condense.}\ECBH
```

It would print as: The other example is this: | Combo these examples. Condense. |

19.2.4   The LaTeX \typeout and \typein commands

The text argument of each \typeout and \typein command will appear on the screen when LaTeX is processing the document.

1. *\typeout*. While you are working on a file, you can insert a note into an ordinary text paragraph. When you run LaTeX, the message will appear on the screen when LaTeX gets to that point in the file. If there is no error, the information will appear on the screen and rapidly disappear. For example, type this at the start of the *chap1* file:

   ```
   \typeout{THIS IS THE START OF CHAPTER 1, PART 1}
   ```

   Scatter a few more such messages in your source document.

   If you run LaTeX in a batch or quiet mode, where LaTeX doesn't stop for errors, the message will still appear in the log.

   The typeout facility is useful in that you can insert messages that identify each module at the beginning of each of the files that make up your document. (See Appendix A.) In this way, each file identifies itself as it is brought in for processing. If LaTeX announces an error, or a warning about an overfull box, you immediately know in which module the error occurred. The message text does NOT become part of the printout.

2. *\typein.* You can type a message as argument to the \typein command, in any source file that will be processed by LATEX. The \typein command differs from the \typeout command, in that (1) the program stops for keyboard input; and (2) the text you type will become part of the file that is being processed and will be in the printout.

Do NOT use a typein command with batch or quiet modes.

The typein can serve as a primitive command line option for varying the specific text files you wish to view or print. (See Appendix A.) For example: In the preamble of the root file, install:

\typein{Please type in the current working file(s).}

When the message appears during LATEX processing, type for example:

\includeonly{chap1,chap2}.

The program will process all the input files but only two include files: *chap1.tex* and *chap2.tex.*

3. *\typein and placeholder text.* This is a variant of the regular typein command. The text you type is substituted, rather like placeholder text, within previously written text. Note however, that the placeholder name is an instruction to LATEX. So a backslash must prepend it.

The format is:

```
\typein[\PlaceHolderName]{<Screen Message>}
<text> \PlaceHolderName\ text.
```

For example:

```
 \protect \typein[\Recipient]%
{Enter Recipient's name now, please.}
 ATTENTION: Send this copy to: \Recipient\.
```

Suppose this typein appears at the beginning of the root file, right below the line that reads: **\begin{document}**. And you type in: **Dr. R. Smith**.

The top of the printout will read:

ATTENTION: Send this copy to Dr. R. Smith.

Part V.

FORMATTING IN MATH MODE.

This section deals with handling mathematical objects—equations, arrays, matrices—of the kind to be found in largely non-mathematical papers. It makes no attempt to enter the complex world of formatting complex mathematical formulae. It presents some common math symbols and layouts; these should be sufficient for most papers. In addition, some of the symbols from the American Mathematical Society ($\mathcal{AMS}$) specialized packages for serious math layouts are shown in Section 12.3.5. Chapter 8 in Goossens et al [Goossens94] is an excellent guide to the markup of intricate equations.

Another way of writing a complicated formula is to construct it in a graphics package such as *xfig*. Then transfer the design over in an Encapsulated PostScript file. This is discussed in Chapter 25.

Chapter 20

MATH SYMBOLS, ALPHABETS AND GRAMMAR

Mathematical symbols and formulae in TeX have their own vocabulary, equation formats, font shapes, even spacing. The default math fonts are typically different from the default text fonts, and the general layout and spacing most certainly is, so math mode output is automatically distinct from text mode. As we saw in Section 11.5.2, math alphabetic fonts and symbols can be woven into ordinary text. But the design of fonts and rules of symbol/alphanumeric concatenations in TeX, and hence in LaTeX, were dictated by the desire to express any mathematical relationship, no matter how complex.

LaTeX automatically enters math mode when it reads the start of a math bracket—$...$ or \(...\) or \[...\]—or one of the reserved math environments such as \begin{equation}...\end{equation}. LaTeX makes a distinction between alphanumeric characters and symbols in math mode, just as it does in text mode. A symbol has no keyboard key equivalent. An individual symbol is written in the source document as a command name (a defined alias), or, if the appropriate font is in control, as the argument of the \symbol command. LaTeX has predefined command names for a large group of math symbols (see Section 20.1); i.e., the command names work no matter what font is in control. So there is no need to bring in the font source of the symbol in order to use the symbol.

Alphanumeric characters participate in equations and conform to their rules of construction. They differ from the other math symbols in that they can be written directly from the keyboard. They can shift shape—e.g., from bold to italic—just as in text mode. But alphabet characters are deliberately less malleable. Several shape commands can operate on the same text in text mode; so a word can be printed both in slant and bold. In math mode, the inner command—the one immediately adjacent to the text—is in control; outer shape commands are ignored. User-supplied spaces are ignored, except to indicate natural breaks; i.e., spaces between adjacent letters are ignored, letters are pulled together. Space wedge commands can be used to modify spacing.

20.1   Built-in Symbols

20.1.1   Greek letters, booleans, integrals and sums

Using a variety of font sources, LaTeX includes a large group of named math symbols. These can be used immediately in your document without the need to summon any of the math font packages. Some of these symbols were discussed in Section 12.2.1 with the focus on using them together with ordinary fonts in running text. In this chapter, we emphasize their utilization in equations. As with their intermittent use in running text, these symbols need to be bracketed with math delimiters or used inside a math environment. This section details some of the built-in symbols. See Section 3.3 in Lamport [Lamport94a], Section 8.2 in Goossens et al [Goossens94] and Warbrick [Warbrick94] for complete lists of the predefined symbols.

As the table illustrates, you can prepend a backslash to the name of any Greek symbol to turn it into a command name to print that symbol. Make it Upper case by capitalizing the first letter.

Markup	Print	Markup	Print	Markup	Print	Markup	Print
`$\gamma$`	γ	`$\delta$`	δ	`$\sigma$`	σ	`$\theta$`	θ
`$\Gamma$`	Γ	`$\Delta$`	Δ	`$\Sigma$`	Σ	`$\Theta$`	Θ

These are the command names for some boolean symbols.

Markup	Print	Markup	Print	Markup	Print	Markup	Print
`$\forall$`	$\forall$	`$\exists$`	$\exists$	`$\cap$`	$\cap$	`$\cup$`	$\cup$
`$\in$`	$\in$	`$\emptyset$`	$\emptyset$	`$\equiv$`	$\equiv$	`$\notin$`	$\notin$

These next print as integrals and sums. Default size will vary, depending on whether the symbol is part of an in-text equation or is in an equation that is displayed on a separate line. Note that in math mode, the circumflex translates to a superscript, the underscore to a subscript. Examples in this section and the next are taken from Lamport, Section 3.3 [Lamport94a].

The MarkUp:

```
\textbf{In displaymath mode:} \\
\[ \sum_{i=1}^{n} x_{i} = \int_{0}^{1} f \]
\[ \lim_{n \rightarrow \infty} x = 0 \]
\vspace{.25in}

\textbf{In running text:} \\
$ \sum_{i=1}^{n} x_{i} = \int_{0}^{1} f$
$ \lim_{n \rightarrow \infty} x = 0 $
```

The PrintOut:

In displaymath mode:

$$\sum_{i=1}^{n} x_i = \int_0^1 f$$

$$\lim_{n \to \infty} x = 0$$

In running text:

$\sum_{i=1}^n x_i = \int_0^1 f$

$\lim_{n \to \infty} x = 0$

20.1.2 Some common mathematical operators

This is a list of common mathematical operators, all immediately available for use. Again, the circumflex is the markup symbol for a superscript, the underscore for a subscript. Levels are denoted by the appropriate use of braces in the markup.

The MarkUp:

```
\begin{tabbing}
1234567890abcdefghijkl \= 13453464364574756858588 \kill
OPERATOR:     \>  EXAMPLE \\
Superscript: \>  $ z = x^{2y} +  x^{y^{2}} - x^{y}_{1}$ \\
Subscript:   \>  $ z = x_{2y} +  x_{y_{2}}  $ \\
Fractions:   \>  $  x = \frac{y+z/2}{y^{2}+1}  $ \\
             \>  \( r^t-1 = \frac{x+y}{1 + \frac{y}{z+1}} \) \\
Square Root: \>  \( \sqrt{x+y} \)  \\
Log:         \>  \( \log\; (xy) = \log x + \log y \) \\
Mod:         \>  binary form: $ a \bmod b $; paren form:
                 $\pmod{a+b}$\\
Not:         \>  If $ x \not< y$ then $ x \not\leq y-1 $ \\
Stacking:    \>  $ A \stackrel{a'}{\rightarrow}
                 B \stackrel{b'}{\rightarrow} C$ \\
Low ellipsis: \> $ n^{5}, n^{4}, \ldots, n^{1} $ \\
Centered ellipsis: \> $ b = ar +  2ar \cdots + 6ar $  \\
```

```
Labeled Braces:   \> $\underbrace{a +\overbrace{b +
                     \cdots + y}^{24}}_{25}$ \\[.1in]
Overline:      \>  $ \overline{a^{2} + 1} $  \\
Underline:     \>  The \underline{value} is $\underline{10}$.
   NOTE: Underline works in all modes.
\end{tabbing}
```

The PrintOut:

OPERATOR:	EXAMPLE
Superscript:	$z = x^{2y} + x^{y^2} - x_1^y$
Subscript:	$z = x_{2y} + x_{y_2}$
Fractions:	$x = \frac{y+z/2}{y^2+1}$
	$r^t - 1 = \frac{x+y}{1+\frac{y}{z+1}}$
Square Root:	$\sqrt{x+y}$
Log:	$\log(xy) = \log x + \log y$
Mod:	binary form: $a \bmod b$; paren form: $(\bmod\ a+b)$.
Not:	If $x \not< y$ then $x \not\leq y-1$
Stacking:	$A \xrightarrow{a'} B \xrightarrow{b'} C$
Low ellipsis:	$n^5, n^4, \ldots, n^1$
Centered ellipsis:	$b = ar + 2ar \cdots + 6ar$
Labeled Braces:	$a + \underbrace{b + \cdots + y}_{25}^{24}$
Overline:	$\overline{a^2 + 1}$
Underline:	The value is 10. NOTE: Underline works in all modes.

To use the log operator in a LATEX math format, you simply prepend a backslash to the operator name and bracket the expression. Other operators in this class include all the geometric operators (e.g., sin, arcsin and sinh) as well as: lim, arg, min, max, gcd and deg.

20.1.3 Math accents

The MarkUp:

```
\begin{tabbing}
1234567890abcdefghijkl \= 134534643645747568586588 \kill
```

```
OPERATOR:    \>  EXAMPLE \\
hat          \>  $\hat{x} + \hat{y}$ \\
widehat      \>  $\widehat{-y} {=} \widehat{x+y}$ \\
tilde        \>  $\tilde{\imath} + \tilde{\jmath}$ (\imath and \jmath
   are dotless.) \\
widetilde \> $\widetilde{-\imath} = \widetilde{\imath + \jmath}$ \\
acute and grave \>  $\acute{a} -\grave{e}$ \\
dot and ddot    \>  $\dot{a} + \ddot{b}$ \\
bar and vec     \>  $\bar{a} + \vec{b}$
\end{tabbing}
```

The PrintOut:

OPERATOR:	EXAMPLE
hat	$\hat{x} + \hat{y}$
widehat	$\widehat{-y}=\widehat{x+y}$
tilde	$\tilde{\imath} + \tilde{\jmath}$ (\imath and \jmath are dotless.)
widetilde	$\widetilde{\imath + \jmath}$
acute and grave	$\acute{a} - \grave{e}$
dot and ddot	$\dot{a} + \ddot{b}$
bar and vec	$\bar{a} + \vec{b}$

20.1.4 Adding ordinary text in math mode

By ordinary text, we mean text within math mode that you do not want treated as part of the equation. See the next chapter for ways to write text surrounding math mode material.

In Running Text. Ordinary text and equations bracketed in $ can be mixed in running text; e.g. `Use $a^i \textit{ and }\ b^i$ instead.` prints as: Use a^i *and* b^j instead.

In *displaymath* Mode. Ordinary text can be used in single line displayed equations carefully. Note that the text italic font 'works'; the math italic font, which is actually the same font in Computer Modern, does not because spaces are ignored.

The MarkUp: `\[ x^{y} \textit{ and } y^{z} \mathit{ and } x_i \]`
The PrintOut:

$$x^y \ and \ y^z \ and x_i$$

In A Math Environment. Again, text roman and math roman may be the same font, but the effects are different. In addition, the newline commands are ignored.

The MarkUp:

```
\begin{equation}
\textrm{If } a = s \mathrm{ and } b = t \\
\textrm{ and } l > m \mathrm{ and } r < v \\
\textrm{ then } n^{\psi} < m^{\alpha} < o^{\beta}
\end{equation}
```

The PrintOut:

$$\text{If } a = s \text{and} b = t \text{ and } l > m \text{and} r < v \text{ then } n^{\psi} < m^{\alpha} < o^{\beta} \qquad (20.1)$$

The $\mathcal{AMS}$ packages offer a rich selection of alignment possibilities, including the \intertext command, which aligns interspersed ordinary text between full equations. Use it with the *amstex* package. An example is shown in Figure 20.1.

20.2   Modifying The Appearance Of Equations

20.2.1   Changing math type style

Math mode has its own font commands for stylized alphanumerics and symbols: *mathnormal, mathrm, mathsf, mathit, boldmath, mathtt* and *mathcal* for upper case letters. These shapes, predefined by the program, are from different font families. They always modify the appearance of letters and numbers in equations. They generally don't modify symbols, except to bold them.

The first expression in each statement shows how the type style operates on letters/digits. The \mbox command keeps the second expression together in running text.

The MarkUp:

```
\begin{tabbing}
123456789012345 \= 1234567890123456789012 \= 123456789012345 \kill
Math Normal:      \> (1.)\ $\mathnormal{Normal\ 012345.}$ %
```

```
\> (2.)\ \mbox{$\mathnormal{\sum 7-\overline{st}\alpha\beta\gamma}$}\\
Math Roman:       \> (1.)\ $\mathrm{Roman\ 012345.}$ %
\> (2.)\ \mbox{$\mathrm{\sum 7-\overline{st}\alpha\beta\gamma}$}\\
Math SansSerif:     \> (1.)\ $\mathsf{Sans\ Serif\ 012345.}$ %
\> (2.)\ \mbox{$\mathsf{\sum 7-\overline{st}\alpha\beta\gamma}$}\\
Math Italic:    \> (1.)\ $\mathit{Italic\ 012345.}$ %
\> (2.)\ \mbox{$\mathit{\sum 7-\overline{st}\alpha\beta\gamma}$}\\
Math Bold:       \> (1.)\ $\mathbf{Bold\ 012345.}$ %
\> (2.)\ \mbox{\boldmath $\sum 7-\overline{st}\alpha\beta\gamma$}\\
Math Typewriter: \> (1.)\ $\mathtt{Typewriter\ 012345.}$ %
\> (2.)\ \mbox{$\mathtt{\sum 7-\overline{st}\alpha\beta\gamma}$}\\
Math Script: \> $\mathcal{UPPER CASE \; \{abcde\} \; \{12345\}\;%
\{|-@!\}\; LETTERS\ ONLY}$
\end{tabbing}
```

The PrintOut:

Math Normal:	(1.) $Normal\ 012345.$	(2.) $\sum 7 - \overline{st}\alpha\beta\gamma$
Math Roman:	(1.) Roman 012345.	(2.) $\sum 7 - \overline{st}\alpha\beta\gamma$
Math SansSerif:	(1.) Sans Serif 012345.	(2.) $\sum 7 - \overline{st}\alpha\beta\gamma$
Math Italic:	(1.) $Italic\ 012345.$	(2.) $\sum 7 - \overline{st}\alpha\beta\gamma$
Math Bold:	(1.) **Bold 012345.**	(2.) $\sum \mathbf{7 - \overline{st}\alpha\beta\gamma}$
Math Typewriter:	(1.) Typewriter 012345.	(2.) $\sum 7 - \overline{st}\alpha\beta\gamma$
Math Script:	$\mathcal{UPPERCASE}$ $\{⊣⊔⊓\}$ $\{\infty\in\ni\triangle\triangledown\}$ $\{|-@!\}$ $\mathcal{LETTERS\ ONLY}$	

In text mode, sans serif (without feet style) is a different feature than bold or italic. So you can have a sans serif bold or a sans serif italic, or even a sans serif bold italic, if the particular typeface has that font in its repertoire. But you don't have that in math mode; aside from size, single features can not be contextually changed. Notice in this next statement that the italic is footed, even though it is in the domain of the sans serif font.

The MarkUp:

```
\large $\mathsf{Sans serif 12345 \mathit{Italic012345}
\mathbf{Bold012345} \mathtt{Typewriter012345}}$ \normalsize
```

The PrintOut: Sansserif12345*Italic012345***Bold012345**Typewriter012345

You can write an entire set of equations with everything in bold—letters, digits, symbols, brackets—by a preceding declaration: **\mathversion{bold}**. Shift back to the default with

The MarkUp:

```
\begin{align}
\intertext{If it can be shown that}
a = sb   \\
\intertext{and}
l > m + r < v \\
\intertext{then it follows that}
n^{\psi} < m^{\alpha} < o^{\beta}
\end{align}
```

The PrintOut:

If it can be shown that

$$a = sb \tag{0.1}$$

and

$$l > m + r < v \tag{0.2}$$

then it follows that

$$n^{\psi} < m^{\alpha} < o^{\beta} \tag{0.3}$$

Figure 20.1: Using the $\mathcal{AMS}$ *intertext* command.

a **mathversion**{**normal**} statement. The **boldmath** and **unboldmath** declarations also effect the switch from all bold to no bold; see the material in the *mbox* in the *Math Bold* example in the previous table. The math alphabet *mathbf*, shown in the same example, also bolds the material within its argument.

20.2.2 Space wedges

These spacing wedges can act on components of the equation. They allow you to add the final touches in creating a visually esthetic equation.

```
\, (thin space)                  \!    (thin negative space)
\: (medium space)                \quad (equal to width of an em)
```

\; (thick space)   \qquad (equal to width of 2 em)
\ (interword space)

The MarkUp:

```
$(1.)\ \sqrt{x+y} = (2.)\ \sqrt{\,x+\,y} \!= (3.)\ \sqrt{\:x+\:y} \;= %
(4.)\ \sqrt{\;x+\;y} = (5.)\ \sqrt{x\quad +y} = (6.)\ \sqrt{x+\qquad y}$
```

The PrintOut: (1.) $\sqrt{x+y}$ = (2.) $\sqrt{x+y}$ = (3.) $\sqrt{x+y}$ = (4.) $\sqrt{x+y}$ = (5.) $\sqrt{x\ +y}$ = (6.) $\sqrt{x+\quad y}$

20.2.3 Size

To Change Default Symbol Sizes

There are four styles that LaTeX routines use to size math mode symbols:

display   the normal mode for equations displayed by themselves on a line
text   for math symbols inside running text
script   for subscripts and superscripts
scriptscript   for second level and higher order subscripts and superscripts

These have declarative forms that you can access to vary size, should you wish; namely, *\displaystyle, \textstyle, \scriptstyle,* and *\scriptscriptstyle,* respectively. In this example, we reversed ordinary size progression, switching *\scriptscriptstyle* and *\scriptstyle,* which gives the output a somewhat odd appearance.

Markup:`\[\textstyle a*b\Psi^{{\scriptscriptstyle i}^{\scriptstyle j}}\]`
The PrintOut:

$$a * b\Psi^{i^j}$$

You can set specific sizes for the four size styles by declaring them in the preamble with a **\DeclareMathSize** statement. You can use any set of sizes that exist in the current math font and in all the math fonts that you use anywheres in the document.

This will set the display style at 12 points, the text style at 10, the script style at 9 and the scriptscript style at 8.

```
\DeclareMathSizes{12}{10}{9}{8}
```

To Change Overall Size Of The Equation

exscale, written by Frank Mittelbach and Rainer Schöpf, is a package that operates on Computer Modern Math Extension (cmex). It can scale an equation from 7 points to 25 points. Call it with a **\usepackage{exscale}** command.

More generally, you can write a macro to increase size within the font's size limits. We illustrate usage by increasing the size of the example shown in Section 20.1.1 to 20 points from its original 10 points.

The MarkUp:

```
\newcommand{\INC}[1]%
{\fontsize{20}{25}%
\selectfont #1
normalsize\normalsize}

\textbf{In displaymath mode:} \\
\INC{\[\sum_{i=1}^{n}x_{i}%
=\int_{0}^{1}f\]}
\INC{\[\lim_{n\rightarrow%
 \infty}x=0\]}

\textbf{In running text:} \\
\INC{$\sum_{i=1}^{n}x_{i}%
=\int_{0}^{1}f$}
\INC{$\lim_{n \rightarrow%
 \infty}x=0$}
```

The PrintOut:

In displaymath mode:

$$\sum_{i=1}^{n} x_i = \int_0^1 f$$

$$\lim_{n \to \infty} x = 0$$

In running text:

$$\Sigma_{i=1}^n x_i = \int_0^1 f$$
$$\lim_{n \to \infty} x = 0$$

20.2.4   Creating a New Math Alphabet Command Name

Several of the math packages include some unusual-looking alphanumerics and symbols in their tables. For example, the *bbm* double strike fonts can be used in text mode (see Figures 11.1 and 11.2 in Section 11.5.3) and, with different commands, in math mode (see Section 12.3.5). When the package is loaded with a *\usepackage{bbm}*, the math commands become available so you can print characters in upright (*\mathbbm{...}*), sans serif (*\mathbbmss{...}*) and typewriter (*\mathbbmtt{...}*); e.g., **$mathbbmss{abc}$**.

There is an upper limit (16) on the number of math fonts—alphabet and symbol—that can be in use at one time. You will know you've reached it, when sometime way down the road, LATEX reports an error such as this: *Font OT1/pss/b/n/17.28=pnssb10 at 17.28pt not loaded: Not enough room left.* A solution that works particularly well if the material is consolidated is to write the segment in another document and bring it in with an *\include-graphics* command. See Section 25.4.1 on how to 'trim' the insert so that it fits directly into the major document.

Alternatively, if you have only a few spots in which you need the font and the number of math fonts is getting close to the limit, don't load the package. Instead, write macro substitutes—the font doesn't 'count' when it isn't being used. This uses the *bbm* font as illustration. The command names mimic those assigned by the *bbm* package to math commands. But they are actually defined in *bbm* text mode, so they don't use math brackets.

```
\newcommand{\mathbbm}[1]{\fontencoding{U}\fontfamily{bbm}%
\fontseries{m}\fontshape{n}\fontsize{10}{12}\selectfont #1
\normalfont\normalsize}

\newcommand{\mathbbmss}[1]{\fontencoding{U}\fontfamily{bbmss}%
\fontseries{m}\fontshape{n}\fontsize{10}{12}\selectfont #1
\normalfont\normalsize}

\newcommand{\mathbbmtt}[1]{\fontencoding{U}\fontfamily{bbmtt}%
\fontseries{m}\fontshape{n}\fontsize{10}{12}\selectfont #1
\normalfont\normalsize}
```

MarkUp: \mathbbm{ABCDEabcde} PrintOut: $\mathbb{ABCDEabcde}$
MarkUp: \mathbbmss{ABCDEabcde} PrintOut: $\mathbb{ABCDEabcde}$
MarkUp: \mathbbmtt{ABCDEabcde} PrintOut: $\mathbb{ABCDEabcde}$

This approach works well for running text containing simple mathematical enclosures; e.g., writing \mathbbmss{AB} $ +\quad\mathsf{R_{i}}$ would print as: 𝔸𝔹 +   R$_i$.

It is more work if you wish to make use of an alphabet font that isn't part of a package that sets it up for you. The many fonts discussed in Chapter 11 can easily replace Computer Modern text fonts, but they can't automatically function as math fonts. For an alphabetic font to take its place along side \mathit{...} and \mathsf{...} or the other commands that call built-in math alphabet fonts, it has to be declared as a Math Alphabet. This is the general procedure to add a new math style.

1. Find a style you like. Section 11.3.3 is a good place to start looking. Classic Computer Modern is the style most often used in LaTeX. But there are other families and newer members of Computer Modern available on your machine: Pandora, Computer Modern Dunhill, Euler, Computer Modern Fibonacci and the many Adobe PostScript fonts. Sometimes there will be several styles that have the features you want, sometimes only one, sometimes none.

2. Recall that the NFSS is the way LaTeX defines a font. As a quick review: a NFSS definition has four components: (1) encoding; (2) typeface plus family; (3) font series; and (4) font shape. Thus, OT1/cm/m/i describes Computer Modern math italic in the original TeX encoding. (See Section 11.3.2 for more details on using NFSS to specify fonts.)

3. The shapes, weights and sizes available in any font family are part of the family's Font Definition (FD) file. Make sure the font you want is available; i.e., that its features are listed in the FD file.

   Suppose we decide we want to use the Pandora Sans Serif bold size 10 style. (We can double check font availability by using the system *locate* command: *pnssb10.tfm* in *˜/texmf/fonts/tfm/public/pandora*.)

4. We construct a *\DeclareMathAlphabet* statement. *\DeclareMathAlphabet* is a command that acts very much like *\usefont* for text, except that it is used only in math mode. You make up a command name for the new font and you state the values of its four NFSS components. In this example, the values are: *OT1* (the coding scheme), *pss* (the Pandora clan and sans serif family), *b* (bold series) and *n* (upright shape).

Suppose we call this new font *mathusb*. *DeclareMathAlphabet* defines the new command name. The definition must be written in the preamble after Symbol Font declarations (if any). This would declare a new alphabet *mathusb*, which prints in Pandora Sans Serif bold upright:

\DeclareMathAlphabet{\mathusb}{OT1}{pss}{b}{n}

> *The MarkUp:*
>
> ```
> \begin{equation}
> \mathusb{A^{\alpha} + B^{\beta} = C^{\gamma}}
> \end{equation}
> ```
>
> *The PrintOut:*

$$\mathbf{A}^{\alpha} + \mathbf{B}^{\beta} = \mathbf{C}^{\gamma}$$

5. If you are going to be using *mathversion* to go back and forth between upright and bold in the new font (see Section 20.2.1, declare both the normal and bold forms in the preamble:

\DeclareMathAlphabet{\mathusb}{OT1}{pss}{m}{n}
\SetMathAlphabet{\mathusb}{bold}{OT1}{pss}{b}{n}

Writing: \mathversion{bold} $\mathusb{A^{\alpha} + B^{\beta} = C^{\gamma}}$\mathversion{normal} would output the math expression in bold.

6. The same technique allows you to substitute a new math alphabet for the current one. This would change the current math sans serif to Pandora Sans Serif slant. You simply write in the preamble:

\DeclareMathAlphabet{\mathsf}{OT1}{pss}{m}{sl}

After that, whenever you use the *mathsf* command, the printed version will be in Pandora Sans Serif Slant.

7. The new math style will work in all math modes.

20.2.5   Adding Math Symbols

Symbols Named As Part of A Math Font Package.   Section 20.1 talked about built-in symbols. Many more symbols, however, require the installation of a particular math font. As an example, to use symbols such as ⋈ (**$\Join$**), ⊏ (**$\sqsubset$**) or ℧ (**$\mho$**), you need *latexsym* or *amsfonts* in memory. Once this is done, all their preassembled symbol names are available to you.

Many of the math font packages are to be found in Linux in subdirectories under ˜*/texmf/fonts* and in the *misc*, *base*, *amsfonts* and *amslatex* subdirectories under ˜*/texmf/tex/latex*. Declaring, say, *\usepackage{amsfonts}* or *\usepackage{amssymb}* or *\usepackage{latexsym}* in the preamble immediately enlarges the repertoire of symbols that can be used to express mathematical notions.[1]

Some $\mathcal{AMS}$ packages, such as *amssymb*, are largely a set of symbol declarations. Other such prepackaged files include *mathbbol.sty*, a package developed by Jörg Knappen. It can be found in ˜/texmf/tex/latex/misc. The package creates symbol names from *bbold* and *Saint Mary Road* codes. If you call the *mathbbol* package in the preamble, all the symbol names in the package are immediately usable. *\bbalpha, \bbbeta* and *\bbgamma* are three symbols defined in *mathbbol.sty*.

MarkUp: `$\bbalpha\quad\bbbeta\quad\bbgamma$`
PrintOut: α   β   ℸ

The Markup Rules for Math Symbol Command Names.   If the command name is used in `math mode` as part of an equation, surround the entire equation with math delimiters; the specific symbol names do not need additional delimiters. If the command name is an individual symbol in `running text`, use the command name surrounded by $ brackets.

Using *\usefont*.   Section 12.3 devoted considerable space illustrating how to define symbols by using their table codes in a *\usefont* macro. It remains a simple way to introduce individual math symbols and expressions within a document that is primarily in text mode,

---

[1]Recall from Section 12.1.3 that you can use the *nfssfont* program to view all the symbols in a font table you may wish to add to your font wardrobe.

and mathematical elegance is not an issue. For documents heavy with mathematical equations, use the method discussed below—*Declaring A Symbol Font*. To illustrate the difference between the two methods, we use a symbol shown in Figure 12.9. \EqqDot in this section is the same symbol as \EqDot in the next section, but it is defined in text mode.

`\NC{\EqqDot}{\fontsize{10}{12}\usefont{U}{msa}{m}{n}\symbol{"24}}`

MarkUp: `$a^i$ \EqqDot $b^j$`
PrintOut: $a^i \doteq b^j$

Declaring A Symbol Font. This is the method used in LaTeX to create math symbol command names (aliases) that can be included within all the math brackets and environments.

Adding a symbol command name is procedurally similar to adding a new text font by way of the \usepackage command or a new math alphabet using *DeclareMathAlphabet*. It is however more convoluted and involves declaring the font in which the symbol is defined.

1. Do NOT add a \usepackage{<Source Font>} in the preamble.

2. Declare the specific font that is the source of the symbol in the preamble. <Name> represents your nickname for the font. The other values are NFSS values. The format is:

   `\DeclareSymbolFont{<Name>}{<coding>}{<family>}%`
   `{<series>}{<shape>}`

   We again use the msam font used in the definition of the \EqqDot symbol above and pictured in Figure 12.9. Its FD file is called *Umsa.fd* and can be found in ~/texmf/tex/latex/amsfonts. Our nickname will be *amsa*. So we'd fill in the Symbol Font declaration this way:

   `\DeclareSymbolFont{amsa}{U}{msa}{m}{n}`

3. Next we fill in the declaration for the symbol's command name. (Note that the Symbol Font—nicknamed *amsa* in this example—counts toward the upper limit of sixteen math fonts in use. But then you can declare any number of math symbols in that font without restriction.) This is placed in the preamble after its symbol font declaration. The format is:

```
\DeclareMathSymbol{<\SymbolAlias>}{<\SymbolType>}%
{<SymbolFont>}{<Code>}
```

This is how to fill in the Math Symbol Declaration:

(a) The first value is our nickname for the math symbol. We shall call it *\EqDot*.

(b) Check what sort of symbol the symbol is. LaTeX has a set of defined symbol types, each of which provides different spacing for the symbol. This reproduces Table 7.13 in [Goossens94].

Type	Meaning	Example	Type	Meaning	Example
\mathord	Ordinary	/	\mathop	Large operator	\sum
\mathbin	Binary operator	+	\mathrel	Relation	=
\mathopen	Opening	(	\mathclose	Closing	)
\mathpunct	Punctuation	,	\mathalpha	Alphabet character	A

Suppose we decide that the symbol is going to be used as an unusual binary operator for some code we'll write. This makes the second argument *\mathbin*.

(c) The third parameter is the nickname we assigned the particular symbol font; in this case it is *amsa*.

(d) The last argument is the actual code for the symbol in the *msam10* font. This is 24 in hex ("24), 36 in decimal (36) and 44 in octal ('44). So the Symbol Font Declaration would look like this:

```
\DeclareMathSymbol{\EqDot}{\mathbin}{amsa}{"24}
```

4. Usage: MarkUp: $ a^i \EqDot b^j $ PrintOut: $a^i \stackrel{\circ}{=} b^j$

20.3 Writing, Protecting And Revising Math Macros

20.3.1 Writing a math macro

As we know, some symbols and commands, *pi* and the superscript in this next expression, can only be used in math mode.

The MarkUp:

```
%We put circ in caps because 'circ' is already spoken for.
\newcommand{\CIRC}{$\pi r^{2}$}
The area of a circle is: \CIRC.
```

The PrintOut: The area of a circle is: πr^2.

Protecting The Math Macro

The program rewrites \CIRC as `$\pi r^{2}$`. The math bracket is $, a toggle. So, given a math new command inside a math expression—see `$a = \CIRC$` below—you would toggle out of math mode at the $ before the \pi, just as you need to be in it. The *ensuremath* command ensures that the command is always properly set in math mode and that the math expression can be used in text, math and box modes. The ensuremath version is:

The MarkUp:

```
\renewcommand{\CIRC}{\ensuremath{\pi r^{2}} }
As we know, \CIRC\ is the area of a circle.
If $a = \CIRC$, how much would we need to increase
the radius, to double the size of $a$?
```

The PrintOut:

As we know, πr^2 is the area of a circle. If $a = \pi r^2$, how much would we need to increase the radius to double the size of a?

20.3.2 Redefining the math macro

As in ordinary text mode, a math new command can be written expanding another command. For example, this would typeset the alphanumeric characters in the previous command in boldface.

The MarkUp:

```
\newcommand{\Bcirc}{\ensuremath{\mathbf{\pi r^{2}}}}
\Bcirc\ is the area of a circle.
```

The PrintOut: $\pi \mathbf{r}^2$ is the area of a circle.

Even more useful is a macro that allows variable text to be entered in a math expression:

The MarkUp:

```
\newcommand{\REZ}[3]{\ensuremath{#1\ \times \ #2 = \mathbf{#3}}}
Multiplication is commutative: \REZ{2}{3}{6} and \REZ{3}{2}{6}.
```

The PrintOut: Multiplication is commutative: $2 \times 3 = \mathbf{6}$ and $3 \times 2 = \mathbf{6}$.

As with text mode macros, the program removes the outer braces of the newcommand argument before substituting text. So the scope of declarations such as **\scriptstyle** and **\boldmath** has to be delimited. Otherwise, a declaration will bleed into later text.

The MarkUp:

```
\renewcommand{\REZ}[3]{\ensuremath{{\scriptstyle #1\ \mathrm{x}
\ #2}% = {\boldmath #3 }}}
In multiplication, \REZ{2}{3}{6} and \REZ{3}{2}{6}. Why?
```

The PrintOut: In multiplication, $_{2\ \mathrm{x}\ 3} = 6$ and $_{3\ \mathrm{x}\ 2} = 6$. Why?

20.4   Lemmas, Axioms And Conjectures

Math mode uses a special command, **\newtheorem**, to define environments for conjectures, lemmas, axioms, postulations and rules-of-thumb. The command has two arguments: (1) the name of the environment and (2) the text name.[2] Use this environment if you have axioms, etc, scattered throughout the document. When you use the newtheorem command, you can annotate it with a name or a reference as shown.

For example: *The MarkUp:*

```
\newtheorem{callax}{Axiom}
\begin{callax}[20th cent. wisdom]
All laws are chancy except Murphy's.
\end{callax}
```

---

[2]An extension to the theorem environment can be loaded in the preamble with a **\usepackage{theorem}** command. See [Mittelbach96d].

The PrintOut:

Axiom 1 (20th cent. wisdom) *All laws are chancy except Murphy's.*

If the axioms are grouped in a single section or chapter, there is an optional third argument in the newtheorem command, so that the section or chapter number becomes part of the axiom number. For example, you could write this at the beginning of the chapter.

The MarkUp:

```
\newtheorem{chapax}{Axiom}[chapter].
\begin{chapax}
All laws are chancy except Murphy's.
\end{chapax}
```

The PrintOut:

Axiom 20.1 *All laws are chancy except Murphy's.*

You can force two classes to share the same numbering sequence. Define a class—*lemma*. Define another class—*conjecture*. Link the two classes by writing the name of the first newtheorem in optional brackets as part of the definition of the second. If you omit the square bracket, the classes will be numbered independently. Except for the semantics, it doesn't matter in which order you define the classes or use them.

The MarkUp:

```
\newtheorem{lemma}{Lemma}
\newtheorem{conjecture}[lemma]{Conjecture}
\begin{lemma}
All laws are chancy except Murphy's.
\begin{conjecture}
And even that is not guaranteed.
\end{conjecture}
\end{lemma}
```

The PrintOut:

Lemma 1 *All laws are chancy except Murphy's.*

Conjecture 2 *And even that is not guaranteed.*

You need not stick to accepted rubrics. You can define your own. This establishes a new category called *bureaucratese*. People have been known to squelch departmental grumblings for years using either #1 or #2.

The MarkUp:

```
\newtheorem{govt}{bureaucratese}
\begin{govt} No one else has complained about
\textit{\LT whatever\RT}. So why are you complaining? \end{govt}

\begin{govt} Everyone else is also \textit{\LT whatever\RT}.
So why are you complaining? \end{govt}
```

The PrintOut:

bureaucratese 1 *No one else has complained about <whatever>. So why are you complaining?*

bureaucratese 2 *Everyone else is also <whatever>. So why are you complaining?*

Chapter 21

SINGLE LINE MATH MODES

21.1   Unnumbered Equation In Running Text

Ordinary text is written as usual. Equations are written between math delimiters and can be distributed in the text. Enclose values that are superscripted or subscripted in braces.

A short equation can be enclosed in either one of the two bracketing formats: \(... \) and $ ... $. Extra spaces within the equation are disregarded. The line can be broken within the equation.

The MarkUp:

```
This is followed by $y^{2} = z_{j}^{2}$ in the first model. The
second version suggests that $y^{j*2} = z_{j}^{2}$ is
more accurate.\\[.2pc]
Note that the caret prints as superscript:
 \(x^{y^{2}}\).  \\
The backspace prints as subscript: $x_{2y}$. \\
Observe the difference between: $y^{2}_j = z_{j}^{2}$
and $y^{{2}_j} = z_{{j}^{2}}$. \\[.2pc]
Primes ( \(y' < x''\) ) are produced using the single-quote
character on the keyboard.
```

The PrintOut: This is followed by $y^2 = z_j^2$ in the first model. The second version suggests

325

that $y^{j*2} = z_j^2$ is more accurate.

Note that the caret prints as superscript: x^{y^2}.

The backspace prints as subscript: x_{2y}.

Observe the difference between: $y_j^2 = z_j^2$ and $y^{2j} = z_{j^2}$.

Primes ($y' < x''$) are produced using the single-quote character on the keyboard.

A long equation can be enclosed in a **\begin{math}..{\end{math}**. Use the math environment to write a very long equation within running text.

The MarkUp:

```
Given that
\begin{math}
\mathit{r\tau = a^\omega + \sigma s^\psi + t_\eta*i}
\end{math},
it is clear that ...
```

The PrintOut: Given that $r\tau = a^\omega + \sigma s^\psi + t_\eta * i$, it is clear that ...

21.2 *displaymath* For A Single Unnumbered Equation On A Separate Line

The displaymath environment is used for a single unnumbered equation that is too long to fit easily in a text sentence. The equation is written separately on a line.

The MarkUp:

```
The first model suggests that
\begin{displaymath}
x_{3i} = y^{\psi*t}
\end{displaymath}
can be used more extensively than it is.
```

The PrintOut: The first model suggests that

$$x_{3i} = y^{\psi*t}$$

can be used more extensively than it is.

There is a short form that substitutes \[and \] for the environment brackets. It displays a single unnumbered equation on a separate line this way.

The MarkUp: `Equation 10: \[ y^{2} = z_{i}^{2} + 7 \]`
The PrintOut: Equation 10:

$$y^2 = z_i^2 + 7$$

21.3 A Numbered Equation On A Separate Line

The equation environment is used to place a numbered equation on a separate line, thus:

The MarkUp:

```
Equation~\ref{eq:sq} has been shown to handle this nicely.
\begin{equation}
\mathbf{y^{2} = z_{{{i}^{2}}^{3} + 7} \label{eq:sq}
\end{equation}
```

The PrintOut: Equation 21.1 has been shown to handle this nicely.

$$\mathbf{y^2 = z_{i^2}^3 + 7} \tag{21.1}$$

LaTeX numbers equations on the far right by default. To display the numbers of equations within the *equation* or *eqnarray* environments always on the far left throughout the entire document—an article in this example—write **leqno** in the preamble as one of the bracketed options. For example:

`\documentclass[leqno,11pt,twocolumn]{article}`

This next preamble command places displayed equations at a fixed distance from the left margin rather than centering them.

`\documentclass[fleqn]{article}`

Both **fleqn** and **leqno** can also be used in report and book classes.

Chapter 22

ARRAYS: MULTI-LINE MATH MODE

22.1   Creating An Array

The array environment is used to write a set of equations, or an array of numbers or, with the addition of math parentheses, a matrix.

The full format for an array is:

```
\[ \begin{array}[bct]{|clr}
# &  # ... \\
....
\end{array} \]
```

Rules For Writing Arrays:

1. The entire array is bracketed by in-text delimiters, \(and \), or, more reasonably, by displaymath delimiters, \[and \].

2. The array environment takes a single mandatory argument, which indicates: (1) the number of columns, (2) their print justification and (3) whether lines are to be drawn on the sides of the column.

Justification commands are chosen by you from the set: **clr**, where **c** indicates the column number should be centered; **l** is flush left; **r** is flush right. Thus: **clcr** would indicate that numbers in the first and third columns should be centered, numbers in the second column will print flush left and numbers in the fourth column will print flush right.

Drawing full vertical lines is optional. If you want them, indicate their locations by using |'s next to the justification information for the columns. Indicate the position of a double line by ||, as in Example 3.

3. Numbers between columns are separated by a **&**. There is no **&** at the end of a row.

4. A \\ indicates the end of a row. There is no final \\ in the last row.

5. Don't put extra spaces between numbers in a column; for example, write '4-x', not '4 - x'. Extra spaces between columns are ignored.

6. As in the minipage format, several arrays—or expressions and arrays—can be associated horizontally. By default, the vertical centers (**c** of the group are aligned in a row. As with the minipage environment, relative positioning can be manipulated by writing a **t** for top or **b** for bottom in the optional square bracket argument. This aligns the top or bottom of the array with the vertical center of the row of arrays. See Example 4.

7. Arrays can appear inside arrays. See Example 5.

Example 1. A single simple 5-column array, first column centered, 2nd and 5th columns flush left, 3rd and 4th columns flush right. Note that basic LaTeX does not do decimal alignment.[1] The array is bracketed by in-text delimiters. Note that the word *Printout* is anchored to the middle of the array, the default in Rule 6.

The MarkUp:

```
\( \begin{array}{clrrl}
\mathcal{A} & 10^{2}   & \mathbf{12.4} & 14.05  & 16\\
\mathcal{B} & 10^{1.4} & \mathbf{2.2}  & 124.05 & .0026\\
\mathcal{C} & 10^{5}   & \mathbf{323}  & 7.2    & 36
\end{array} \)
```

---

[1]See Table 16.6, Section 16.3.2 for an example of how to use the *dcolumn* package to align decimal numbers in a column.

$$
\begin{array}{llll}
\mathcal{A} & 10^2 & \mathbf{12.4} & 14.05 & 16 \\
\textit{The PrintOut:} \quad \mathcal{B} & 10^{1.4} & \mathbf{2.2} & 124.05 & .0026 \\
\mathcal{C} & 10^5 & \mathbf{323} & 7.2 & 36
\end{array}
$$

Example 2. The same array as in Example 1. Lines will be drawn as indicated. As a variation from example 1, some text, protected by a mbox so it won't be split, prepends the array.

The MarkUp:

```
\mbox{The results are as follows:}  \\[.5pc]
$ \begin{array}{|c|lrrl|}
\mbox{The results are as follows:}  \\
\mathcal{A} & 10^{2}   & \mathbf{12.4} & 14.05  & 16 \\
\mathcal{B} & 10^{1.4} & \mathbf{2.2}  & 124.05 & .0026 \\
\mathcal{C} &   10^{5  & \mathbf{323}  &   7.2     & 36 \\
\end{array} $
```

The PrintOut: The results are as follows:

$$
\left|\begin{array}{llll}
\mathcal{A} & 10^2 & \mathbf{12.4} & 14.05 & 16 \\
\mathcal{B} & 10^{1.4} & \mathbf{2.2} & 124.05 & .0026 \\
\mathcal{C} & 10^5 & \mathbf{323} & 7.2 & 36
\end{array}\right|
$$

Example 3. If a constantly used pattern format has multiple font changes, it is often simpler to type in row numbers with a skeleton macro such as this. (The lines in Examples 3, 4 and 5 were added to make partitions clear.)

The MarkUp:

```
\NC{\SKELa}[5]{\mathcal{#1} & \mathbf{#2} & #3 & %
\mathit{#4} & #5}
$ \begin{array}{||c|l|r|r|l||}
\SKELa{A}{.02}{3}{33}{.05} \\
\SKELa{B}{1.03}{22}{33}{3} \\
\SKELa{C}{4.4}{2}{-11}{49a}
\end{array} $
```

The PrintOut:
$$
\left\|\begin{array}{c|l|r|r|l}
\mathcal{A} & .02 & 3 & \mathit{33} & .05 \\
\mathcal{B} & 1.03 & 22 & \mathit{33} & 3 \\
\mathcal{C} & 4.4 & 2 & \mathit{-11} & 49a
\end{array}\right\|
$$

Example 4. In this 5-array chain, the top of the 2nd array is forced level with the midpoint of the 1st array. The centers of the 3rd and 4th arrays are by default at the same height as the center of the group of arrays. The bottom of the 5th array is aligned with the group center. Notice that the displaymath brackets surround the entire group of arrays.

The MarkUp:

```
\[
\begin{array}{||r|r||}
1 & 22 \\
2 & 34 \\
3 & 46
\end{array}
- \begin{array}[t]{||r|r||}
11 & 22 \\
22 & 34 \\
33 & 46
\end{array}
+ \begin{array}{||r|r||}
13 & 22 \\
24 & 34 \\
35 & 46
\end{array}
 - \begin{array}{||r|r||}
33 & 22 \\
74 & 34 \\
95 & 46
\end{array}
+ \begin{array}[b]{||r|r||}
23 & 22 \\
44 & 34 \\
55 & 46
\end{array}
\]
```

The PrintOut:

$$
\left\|\begin{array}{|r|r|} 1 & 22 \\ 2 & 34 \\ 3 & 46 \end{array}\right\| - \left\|\begin{array}{|r|r|} 11 & 22 \\ 22 & 34 \\ 33 & 46 \end{array}\right\| - \left\|\begin{array}{|r|r|} 13 & 22 \\ 24 & 34 \\ 35 & 46 \end{array}\right\| + \left\|\begin{array}{|r|r|} 33 & 22 \\ 74 & 34 \\ 95 & 46 \end{array}\right\| + \left\|\begin{array}{|r|r|} 23 & 22 \\ 44 & 34 \\ 55 & 46 \end{array}\right\|
$$

Example 5. If a small array is written within a larger array, **t** (or **b**) in the optional argument of the smaller array has a different meaning than when an array is aligned in a chain of independent arrays. When one array is inside another, **t** in the small array aligns its top line with the row in which it will reside; **b** aligns its bottom line with the rest of the row.

Note that the big array announces it has 3 columns, because a small array uses one column slot. Note also that the second line is "b & 34 &", not "b & 34". This appears to contradict rule 3, but otherwise, there would be a gap in the right-side double line.

The MarkUp: *The PrintOut:*

```
\[
\begin{array}{||r|r|r||}
a & 22 &
        \begin{array}[b]{|rr|}
        \prit{9} & \prit{8}\\[-.3pc]
        \prit{-4} & \prit{2} \\[-.3pc]
        \prit{3} & \prit{5}
        \end{array}
b & 34 & \\
c & 46 &
        \begin{array}[t]{|ll|}
        \prbf{2} & \prbf{3} \\[-.3pc]
        \prbf{7} & \prbf{8} \\[-.3pc]
        \prbf{6} & \prbf{3}
        \end{array}
\end{array}
\]
```

$$
\left\|\left|\begin{array}{c|c|cc}
 & & 9 & 8 \\
 & & \text{-4} & 2 \\
a & 22 & 3 & 5 \\
b & 34 & & \\
c & 46 & \mathbf{2} & \mathbf{3} \\
 & & \mathbf{7} & \mathbf{8} \\
 & & \mathbf{6} & \mathbf{3}
\end{array}\right|\right\|
$$

Example 6. To write matrices and oddball styles.

TEX makes available a variety of delimiters to bracket arrays.[2] The master touch is that all of these delimiters are printed in a size sufficient to embrace the elements of the array.

Two other commands, **\left** and **\right**, indicate side. You can attach any of the symbols in the table to the \left and \right commands, without space intervening. The \right and \left commands must be paired. If, however, you need only one of

---

[2]To write these individually in ordinary text, bracket them this way, using rceil as example: **$\rceil$**.

them—the left one, say—you can make the right one invisible by writing a dot as the symbol; i.e., **\right.**, as is done in the second array in Example 6.

Markup	Print	Markup	Print	Markup	Print
(	(	)	)	[	[
]	]	\{	{	\}	}
/	/	\backslash	\	|	|
|	||	\lfloor	⌊	rfloor	⌋
\lceil	⌈	\rceil	⌉	\langle	⟨
\rangle	⟩	\uparrow	↑	\downarrow	↓
\Uparrow	⇑	\Downarrow	⇓	\Updownarrow	⇕

Complex patterns are possible—complete arrays or small clusters can be written within arrays to considerable depth. Here are two examples, taken from [Lamport94a, page 47].

The MarkUp:
```
\[ \left( \begin{array}{c}
   \left| \begin{array}{cc}
           x_{11} & x_{12} \\
           x_{21} & x_{22}
           \end{array}
   \right| \\
   y \\ z
\end{array}  \right) \]
```

The PrintOut:

$$\left(\begin{array}{c} \left| \begin{array}{cc} x_{11} & x_{12} \\ x_{21} & x_{22} \end{array} \right| \\ y \\ z \end{array} \right)$$

The MarkUp:
```
\[ \left{ \begin{array}{ll}
           y & \mbox{if $y>0$} \\
           z+y & \mbox{otherwise}
           \end{array}
   \right. \]
```

The PrintOut:

$$x = \left\{ \begin{array}{ll} y & \text{if } y > 0 \\ z + y & \text{otherwise} \end{array} \right.$$

Example 7. To write a series of numbered equations.

The eqnarray environment is used to write a sequence of equations, each individually numbered. eqnarray* is used to write an unnumbered sequence. Write **\nonumber** if you don't want an equation in a particular line; this is particularly useful if you have spread a long equation across two lines. Control the positioning of the end of the extralong equation by using the & & tabs.

The MarkUp:

```
\begin{eqnarray}
x  & =    & \sum -y_{i}^{3}     \\
y  & >    & a+b+c-(e+f)  \nonumber \\
z  & <=   & k+o+p^{2}
\end{eqnarray}
```

The PrintOut:

$$x \quad = \quad \sum -y_i^3 \qquad\qquad (22.1)$$

$$y \quad > \quad a+b+c-(e+f)$$

$$z \quad <= \quad k+o+p^2 \qquad\qquad (22.2)$$

Example 8. Style Variations include adding frame lines (see Example 2, Section 23.5), changing spacing between rows and/or columns and adding footnotes.

- If the rows of the array are too far apart, write, for example, \\[-.3pc] at the end of each row, instead of \\, as we did in example 5. An example of increasing space between rows is shown in Subsection 13.4.1.

- Various amounts of space between columns can be added using the space adding commands shown in Subsection 20.2.2.

- As with equations displayed on separate lines such as the equation shown in Section 21.2, *eqnarray* numbering is by default on the right. You can use *leqno* as a \documentclass option to position array numbers on the left. Similarly, you use the *fleqn* option to display the set of equations themselves on the left side of the page rather than in the center.

Part VI.

FORMATTING IN BOX MODE.

We have become familiar with environments and commands that compose boxes *en passant*. In typesetting text on a line, LaTeX treats each letter of each word as a box to be positioned according to its size and reference point. When we bind a set of lines together and call them a figure, the program, as part of its activities, seals the figure in a box and finds it enough space on the current page or on a later one. In the same way, the program treats a table and an array of numbers as indivisible entities.

In this chapter, we focus on ways that we can make and size boxes ourselves, rather than having the program fashion them as just one of the activities involved in placing figures, tables and arrays on the page.

LaTeX has a rich set of tools to construct different kinds of boxes and place them. The very versatile minipage is particularly useful. It has already appeared over and over again in this book. It is also important to have the ability to create a frame around text or around a set of equations.

Section 23.5 focuses on saving a macro in a savebox. This is necessary for using a picture or icon over and over again in a document. Please do not skip this. In the next chapter it will serve as the basis for saving an Encapsulated PostScript figure just once and reusing it repeatedly.

338

Chapter 23

BOX MODE

We now come to **BOX MODE** the third way in which LaTeX deals with text. It is called Left-Right or LR mode in LaTeX.

Text mode procedures are involved in most of what we do when we mark up text for LaTeX to process: we change font appearance or we manipulate the space on the page or we compose familiar entities such as letters, lists, tables, outlines.

In math mode we convert mathematical expressions, which have their own symbols and syntax, into well-formed printed equations.

Box mode is our entry into frames and boxes, graphics and pictures. The major activity in this mode is to create two-dimensional structures, variously called boxes, frames, paragraph containers, rectangular enclosures, bins, sidebars. Once composed, the box is an object that the program will not split either horizontally or vertically. The boundaries of the box are most frequently invisible. But the text and/or mathematical symbols it contains are treated as an unbreakable unit.

The program provides us with three basic box styles, each of which has variants:

1. the single-line box

2. the multi-line (paragraph) box

3. the inked rectangle and the strut

23.1   The Single Line Box: *\makebox*, *\framebox*

23.1.1   The *\makebox* and *\mbox* commands

\makebox creates a single-line box, whose size can be varied. It prevents the program from splitting the contents of its argument across lines. The argument can be in text mode or math mode, or both. If you chose to make a box with this command 20 inches wide, the program wouldn't stop you. Of course, it would run out of space on the line well before most of the text in the box could be printed.

The complete format for the makebox command is:

\makebox[<*width*>**][lrcs]{**<*text*>**}**

As options, it allows you to vary two values: box width and text shift within the box.

width. The horizontal extent of the constructed box. The measure is independent of the actual size of the text; i.e., if the box is smaller, the text will bulge out of the box. This won't matter usually if the box is by itself on the line. Placing the box between text neighbors, however, shows the overflow.

lrcs. Each letter is a different way to shift the text. **l** shifts the contents in the box to the left, **r** shifts them to the right, **s** stretches the text from left to right and **c** moves the text to the center, with center the default.

One or both of these—width and shift—can be omitted. If you omit a value, remove its brackets.

Notice that width is an option and precedes the shift option. Different formats are used for the other box types—multiline and inked rectangle—that are discussed below.

The MarkUp: BOX 1: `\makebox[.5in][l]{This box is too small.}` DESIGN

The PrintOut: BOX 1: This box DESIGNmall.

The MarkUp: `BOX 2: \makebox[3in][r]{This box is too large.} DESIGN`

The PrintOut: BOX 2:   This box is too large. DESIGN

The MarkUp: `BOX 3:\makebox[1.75in][c]{This box is just about right.} DESIGN`

The PrintOut: BOX 3:   This box is just about right.   DESIGN

\mbox is a pared down version of \makebox. It is \makebox without options. It makes a box just wide enough to hold the text, which is centered in the box. This is what it would do with the previous example.

The MarkUp: `BOX 4: \mbox{This mbox is just right.} DESIGN`

The PrintOut: BOX 4: This mbox is just right. DESIGN

It can be used to keep a name intact on a line or to keep a mathematical expression together in an equation. For example:

The MarkUp: `Mr~\mbox{Hemsley-Smith} will arrive tomorrow.`

The PrintOut: Mr Hemsley-Smith will arrive tomorrow.

The MarkUp: `If \mbox{ $x^{2}$ }, then \mbox{$y > z$}.`

The PrintOut: If x^2 , then $y > z$.

23.1.2   *\framebox* and *\fbox* commands

\framebox is \makebox with visible borders. It works in all modes.

The MarkUp: `BOX 5: \framebox[.5in][r]{This box is too small.} DESIGN`

The PrintOut: BOX 5: This box is too small. DESIGN

The MarkUp: `BOX 6: \framebox[3in][s]{This box is too large.} DESIGN`

The PrintOut: BOX 6: This   box   is   too   large. DESIGN

The MarkUp: `BOX 7:\framebox[1.75in]{This box is just about right.} DESIGN`

The PrintOut: BOX 7: | This box is just about right. | DESIGN

\framebox has a reduced version called **\fbox**. It is \mbox with boundary lines. Like \mbox, it makes a box just wide enough to hold the text, which is centered in the box.

The MarkUp: BOX 8: \fbox{This fbox is just right.} DESIGN

The PrintOut: BOX 8: | This fbox is just right. | DESIGN

23.1.3   Changing the appearance of the frame

\fboxrule is the thickness of the frame line. By default it is set to 0.4 points. But it can be
reset with the setlength command, which takes two arguments. Note it is *\setlength*.
There is no *re*setlength command any more than there is a *re*setcounter command.
This will create a 3 mm thick frame.

\setlength{\fboxrule}{3mm}

Because frame thickness usually needs to be reset to default after a use, it is a good
idea to have a simple command such as *\thin* to reset the thickness to the default. If
you use some thicknesses often, it pays to give them individual names. Otherwise,
create a general command such as *\Fany*.

The MarkUp:

```
\newcommand{\Thin}{\setlength{\fboxrule}{0.4pt}}
\newcommand{\Fthree}{\setlength{\fboxrule}{3mm}}
\newcommand{\Fany}[1]{\setlength{\fboxrule}{#1}}

\Fany{1pc}
BOX 9: \fbox{This fbox is just right.} DESIGN\\[.1in]
\Fthree
Box 10: \fbox{This fbox is just right.} DESIGN\\[.1in]
\Thin
BOX 11: \fbox{This fbox is just right.} DESIGN
```

The PrintOut:

BOX 9: | This fbox is just right. | DESIGN

BOX 10:   This fbox is just right.   DESIGN

BOX 11: | This fbox is just right. | DESIGN

\fboxsep is the space between the frame line and the text. The default is 3 points (3pt). It can be reset if need be; e.g., \setlength{\fboxsep}{6pc}, as in this example.

The MarkUp:

```
\Fthree
\setlength{\fboxsep}{6pc}
BOX 12: \fbox{This fbox is just right.} DESIGN
\Thin
\setlength{\fboxsep}{3pt}
```

The PrintOut: BOX 12:

This fbox is just right.

DESIGN

The raisebox command \raisebox{distance}[extend-above][extend-below]{text}

The optional shift value in makebox or framebox commands shifts the text left or right within the box. It is also possible to raise or lower all the text in the box with the raisebox command. The simple raisebox command acts as if it operated on a mbox, in that the text is not framed and the box fits the text exactly. For example,

The MarkUp: LEVEL \raisebox{.4pc}{\textbf{UP}} LEVEL
  \raisebox{-.4pc}{\textbf{DOWN}} LEVEL

The PrintOut: LEVEL ^{UP} LEVEL _{DOWN} LEVEL

If you use *raisebox* in the argument of a *fbox* command, the raised text is framed. In this next example, both options are used for each of the boxes that frame the text; the first option increases the upward extent of the box above the current line; the second stretches the extent of the box below the reference point. This action is independent of how much the boxed text is raised or lowered.

The MarkUp:
```
LEVEL \fbox{\raisebox{.4pc}[.8pc][.01pc]{\textbf{UP}}} LEVEL
\fbox{\raisebox{-.4pc}[.1pc][.4pc]{\textbf{DOWN}}} LEVEL
```

The PrintOut: LEVEL ┌──┐ LEVEL ┌────────┐ LEVEL
                     │ UP │   │ DOWN │
                     └──┘   └────────┘

23.1.4 Fancy frames

The fancybox package, written by Timothy Van Zandt [Zandt93a], presents you with a variety of \fbox styles. They are: the shadow box, the double box, the thinlined oval box and the thicklined oval box.

The MarkUp:

```
\shadowbox{The shadow defaults to 4 pt.}
\vspace{.2in}

\doublebox{This has a double frame.}
\vspace{.2in}

\ovalbox{This is an oval box.}
\vspace{.2in}

\Ovalbox{Oval with thick frame.}
```

The PrintOut:

The shadow defaults to 4 pt.

This has a double frame.

This is an oval box.

Oval with thick frame.

The boxes can be nested. This may be a bit much.

MarkUp:
```
{\LARGE\sffamily\shadowbox{\doublebox{\Ovalbox{\ovalbox{This is a
box  within boxes.}}}}}
```

Printout:

```
This is a box within boxes.
```

23.2 The Paragraph Box: Parboxes And Minipages

23.2.1 The parbox

The parbox command creates a 2-dimensional box, whose size can be varied. It operates on the braced text that is its argument, so it works best when applied to a small amount of text. As its name would suggest, it can only be used in text mode, but it will accept equations bracketed for running text.

Ordinary Parbox Syntax

\parbox[<*box alignment*>]{<*box width*>}{<*text*>}

You must specify box width. As an option, you can vary the vertical alignment of the box to the baseline.

- *alignment*. You can specify how to align a parbox on the baseline. **t** will align the top of box with the print line; **c** will use the center of the box as the alignment point; **b** will place the bottom of the box on the line; and **s** stretches the text relative to the height of the box. **s** is used with the complete *parbox* format, when the text is insufficient for the height of the box (see below).
- *width*. This is the horizontal extent of the box. The vertical extent depends on the number of lines it takes to print the text in the parbox.

In this example, three boxes are written so they are printed one after another in a column down the page. Notice we can interleave ordinary text. To stack boxes in a column, leave a blank line between them; it's analogous to signalling the end of a paragraph.

The MarkUp:

```
\textbf{1: }
\parbox[t]{1.5in}{THE FIRST\\
BOX DESIGN}\vspace{2mm}


\textbf{2: }
\parbox[t]{1.5in}{\prit{This text
is boxed in a parbox. It is in
italic font.}}\vspace{2mm}


\textbf{3: }
\parbox[t]{1.5in}
{\llgap$\Downarrow\Downarrow$\\
\llgap\fbox{LOGO} \\
\ssgap\llgap\ddag\ddag}\vspace{2mm}
```

The PrintOut:

1: THE FIRST
   BOX DESIGN

2: *This text is boxed in a parbox. It is in italic font.*

3:   ⇓⇓
                  LOGO
                   ‡‡

In this example, the same three boxes are written without blank lines intervening between the parboxes. Sequencing a set of parboxes in the source document without gaps produces a row of parboxes across the printed page. Again, you can interleave ordinary text.

The MarkUp:

```
\textbf{1: }
\parbox[t]{1in}{THE FIRST \\ BOX DESIGN}
\textbf{2: }
\parbox[t]{1.5in}{\textit{This text is
boxed in a parbox.
It is in italic font.}}
\textbf{\ 3:}
\parbox[t]{1in}{\llgap$\Downarrow%
\Downarrow$\\
\llgap\fbox{LOGO} \\
\ssgap\llgap\ddag\ddag}
```

The PrintOut:

1: THE FIRST   **2:** *This text is boxed in a par-* **3:**   ⇓⇓
   BOX DESIGN   *box. It is in italic font.*   LOGO
                                                                  ‡‡

The Complete Parbox Syntax

\parbox[*<box alignment>*][*<box height>*][*<inner position of text>*]{*<width>*}%
{*<text>*}

The second and third options allow you to control two more variables than does the usual way of writing a parbox. You can set the height of the box using the second option. If you exercise the third option, you can align the text within the box with the same positions as aligning it with neighboring parboxes; i.e., **t**, **b**, **c** or **s**.

This example sets the height of the box to the actual height of the box plus some. (The program determines box height automatically; the value is held in *height*.) Doing this prevents the text from underfilling the box; at the same time, the small amount of extra space between the text and the box perimeter enhances appearances. Were you to use a very high box and a small amount of text, you'd likely need to intersperse some **vspace**{**stretch**}{**#**} commands within the text to help stretch the text. The box is framed to show the effect.

Notice that the entire parbox is written as a single argument of the framebox command.

The MarkUp: *The PrintOut:*

```
\textbf{1: }
\framebox{\parbox[c]%
[\height+.3\baselineskip][c]%
{1.5in}{THE FIRST\\ BOX DESIGN}}

\textbf{2: }
\framebox{\parbox[c]%
[\height+.3\baselineskip][c]%
{1.5in}{\prit{This text is boxed in
a parbox. It is in italic font.}}}

\textbf{3: }
\framebox{\parbox[c]%
[\height+.3\baselineskip][c]%
{1.5in}{\llgap $\Downarrow\Downarrow$\\
\llgap\fbox{LOGO}\\
\ssgap\llgap\ddag\ddag}}
```

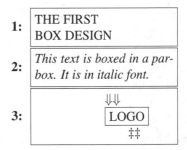

23.2.2   The minipage environment

The parbox and the minipage both create unbreakable containers for their contents. The parbox is a command that operates on whatever is within its argument. The minipage is an environment. Unlike the parbox, the minipage, as its name suggests, acts like a variable-sized page that can hold any LaTeX object that a regular page can hold.

The minipage and the parbox have the same syntax: the box is aligned at its center by default, but the top of the box or the bottom of the box can be on the baseline. Indicating the width of the box is mandatory. In the ordinary way of writing the minipage, the length of the box will depend on the number of lines printed.

Ordinary Minipage Syntax

\begin{minipage}[<*box alignment*>: **tbcs**]{<*box width*>}
...whatever...
\end{minipage}

The Complete Minipage Syntax

The box alignment option of the minipage format that is most frequently used is actually the first option of the three options available in the complete minipage format. The complete syntax of the minipage allows you to set the height of the box and position the text within the box as well as to align the box with neighboring text or boxes on the same print line.

\begin{minipage}[<*box alignment*>][<*box height*>][<*text position*>]%
{<*box width*>}
...whatever....
\end{minipage}

The first option aligns the minipage vis a vis the baseline. The third option uses the same possibilities—**t** for top, **b** for bottom, **c** for center, **s** for stretch—to position the text in the minipage. The optional height value is seldom used, because the minipage creates a box just sufficient to hold the text. But if the text looks cramped or too loose, you can try to manipulate this variable.

To compare the minipage to the parbox, this minipage repeats the last parbox example. Each complete minipage is the argument of a framebox command.

The MarkUp: *The PrintOut:*

```
\textbf{1: }
\framebox{\begin{minipage}[c]%
[\height+.3\baselineskip][c]%
{1.5in}{THE FIRST\\ BOX DESIGN}
\end{minipage} }

\textbf{2: }
\framebox{\begin{minipage}[c]%
[\height+.3\baselineskip][c]{1.5in}%
{\prit{This text is boxed in
a minipage. It is in italic font.}
\end{minipage} }

\textbf{3: }
\framebox{\begin{minipage}[c]%
[\height+.3\baselineskip][c]{1.5in}%
{\llgap$\Downarrow\Downarrow$\\
\llgap\fbox{LOGO}\\
\ssgap\llgap\ddag\ddag}
\end{minipage}}
```

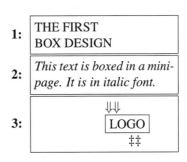

The results are identical to those produced by the parbox. And the same rule applies: if two or more minipage objects follow each other without blank lines intervening, they will be printed side by side across the page. Otherwise they appear as a stack. Note that this does not restrict the innards of the box in any way. It refers to the linkage of the \end minipage of one box and the \begin minipage of another.

Compared to the parbox, the minipage is the more efficient way to create a unitary print object or to join together a set of boxes. It is particularly well suited for unifying large chunks of running text. It acts as a containerized hold for equations, boxes, lists, pictures and tabbing/tabular environments.

Example 1:

Linking Text Units.

Minipages are useful for pairing linked text units—*before* and *after*; *wrong way* and *right way*. Minipages have been used throughout this book to show a *Markup* and its *PrintOut*, side by side or as a stack.

The minipage is versatile—it can be used both as an outer enclosure and an inner enclosure. In this example, it is an inner environment enclosed by a figure environment. (A figure can only be an outermost enclosure.) This next shows a complete set of instructions for writing two minipages that will appear side by side in print: a markup and printout pair. The instructions are encased in a figure, so the unit can be shifted on the page by the program. The code is followed by Figure 23.1, which shows what appears on the page when the instructions are processed by LaTeX. *\IN* is an alias for MarkUp; *\OUT* is an alias for PrintOut.

```
\begin{figure}[t]
\begin{minipage}[t]{3in}
\IN \begin{verbatim}
\includegraphics{esther.ps}
\caption{Esther E.} \label{fig:esther}
\end{verbatim}
\end{minipage}
\begin{minipage}[t]{2in}
\OUT
\includegraphics{esther.ps}
\caption{Esther E.}\label{fig:esther}
\end{minipage}
\end{figure}
```

The MarkUp:

```
\includegraphics{esther.ps}
\caption{Esther E.}\label{fig:esther}
```

The PrintOut:

Figure 23.1: Esther E.

Example 2:

Surrounding A Table.

In the tabbing environment, table width is the sum of the column widths, each sized according to the size and type font used; it is not an absolute number. So the minipage, where you must specify a width, and the table are likely to be telling the program to make the box different widths. If you embed a tab table inside a minipage, the program will make the minipage as wide as the longest line in the table; the minipage width you set is ignored.

Don't try to put a tabbing or tabular environment that is embedded in a table environment inside a minipage. Use either the minipage environment or the table environment, not both. The table environment allows you to add a caption to the table. The minipage environment is better for placing two tables next to each other, so you can compare them or merge them.

The MarkUp:

```
\begin{minipage}[t]{2.5in}
\begin{tabbing}
NAMEfil: \= TelFillUP: \= FaxFill: \= \CL \kill
\prsc{NAME}    \> Tel:        \> Fax:      \> \CL\\
Joel           \> 5556788     \>           \> \CL\\
Lew            \> 5551234     \> 5552323 \> \CL\\
Sandra         \> 5552345     \> 5557867 \> \CL
\end{tabbing}
\end{minipage}\BLSK\PAR
\hspace{.3in}
\begin{minipage}[t]{2.5in}
\begin{tabbing}
NAMEfil: \= TelFillUP: \=EmailFillTHIS IN: \= \CL \kill
\prsc{NAME}    \> Tel:       \> Email: \> \CL \\
Joel           \> 5556788    \> jarthur@erols.com  \> \CL\\
Lew            \> 5551234    \> lel@helix.nih.gov  \> \CL\\
Sandra         \> 5552345    \> san@aol.com   \> \CL
\end{tabbing}
\end{minipage}
```

The PrintOut:

NAME	Tel:	Fax:		NAME	Tel:	Email:	
Joel	5556788			Joel	5556788	jarthur@erols.com	
Lew	5551234	5552323		Lew	5551234	lel@helix.nih.gov	
Sandra	5552345	5557867		Sandra	5552345	san@aol.com	

Example 3:

Structuring Columns On A Page. Complex text and math typesetting can be handled by the minipage. It can even be footnoted independently. (See Section 17.2.) It can hold a variety of text objects, forcing them into a unit that LaTeX will not break across lines or pages. This next is three columns wide. The second column is a description list; its first item is made level (well, almost level) with the other columns with the **\vspace** command. Distances between columns are set with **\hspace** commands.

The MarkUp:

```
\begin{minipage}[t]{1.5in}
\textbf{Define a New Length}\\[.15pc]
\textbf{\newlength} defines a new measure and gives
it a value of zero. \new\-length{KEEP} defines
a new mea\-sure \textit{\KEEP} that can be given a
value by the \textbf{set\-length} command;
for example, \set\-length{\KEEP}{1in}.
\end{minipage}
\hspace{.02in}
\begin{minipage}[t]{2in}
\textbf{\textit{setto} Commands}
\vspace{-.35pc}
\bd
\item [\settodepth] sets a length metric to the length
a particular letter ex\-tends be\-low the bottom edge of a
text line. \vspace{-.12in}

\item [\settoheight] sets
the length metric to the ver\-tical extent of a particular
letter.
\vspace{-.3in}

\item [\settowidth] set the length metric equal
to the width of some text.
\ed
```

```
\end{minipage}
\hspace{.02in}
\begin{minipage}[t]{1.5in}
\textbf{Change Length} \\[.15pc]
\textbf{\add\-to\-length} increases or decreases an
existing length. Given an existing paragraph skip of 1 pica,
\add\-to\-length{\par\-skip}{-1pt} would change
the vertical space between paragraphs to just over 11 points.
\end{minipage}
```

The PrintOut:

Define a New Length

\newlength defines a new measure and gives it a value of zero. \newlength{\KEEP} defines a new measure \KEEP that can be given a value by the **setlength** command; for example, \setlength{\KEEP}{1in}.

setto **Commands**

\settodepth sets a length metric to the length a particular letter extends below the bottom edge of a text line.

\settoheight sets the length metric to the vertical extent of a particular letter.

\settowidth set the length metric equal to the width of some text.

Change Length

\addtolength increases or decreases an existing length. Given an existing paragraph skip of 1 pica, \addtolength{\parskip}-{-1pt} would change the vertical space between paragraphs to just over 11 points.

Example 4:

Minipages Within Minipages Within Minipages.

Section 23.3.2 illustrates the strut. To create the illustration, we used several sets of minipages. The minipages enclosing the markup and the printout are 'twinned'; moreover, the individual boxes a and b are themselves in a minipage; as are c and d. This next shows the way the strut design was written. The only changes we make here are to: (1) disable the middle verbatim statements, so that the whole design is written as a single verbatim statement. and (2) write the instructions in two columns instead of running text. \INV is a macro name for MarkUp; \OUT is a macro name for PrintOut.

```
\begin{minipage}[t]{3in}
\INV
  % \begin {verbatim}
```

```
\begin{minipage}[c]{2.05in}
   \begin{minipage}[c]{1in}
   \textbf{a: }%
   \fbox{\rule{0in}{.6in}
```

```
        Design A}
      \end{minipage}
\hfill
      \begin{minipage}[c]{1in}
      \textbf{b: }%
      \fbox{\rule{.005in}{.6in}
        Design B}
      \end{minipage}
    \end{minipage}
\vspace{.4in}

    \begin{minipage}[c]{2.05in}
    \begin{minipage}[c]{1in}
    \textbf{c: }%
    \fbox{\rule[-.4in]{.005in}%
    {.6in} Design C}
    \end{minipage}
\hfill
      \begin{minipage}[c]{1in}
      \textbf{d: }%
      \fbox{\rule[+.4in]{.005in}%
      {.6in} Design D}
      \end{minipage}
    \end{minipage}
  % \ end {verbatim}
\end{minipage}
\hfill
\begin{minipage}[t]{2.05in}
\OUT \\[.3in]
```

```
\begin{minipage}[c]{2.05in}
  \begin{minipage}[c]{1in}
  \textbf{a: }%
  \fbox{\rule{0in}{.6in}
    Design A}
  \end{minipage}
\hfill
  \begin{minipage}[c]{1in}
  \textbf{b: }%
  \fbox{\rule{.005in}{.6in}
    Design B}
  \end{minipage}
  \end{minipage}
\vspace{.4in}

  \begin{minipage}[c]{2.05in}
  \begin{minipage}[c]{1in}
  \textbf{c: }%
  \fbox{\rule[-.4in]{.005in}%
    {.6in} Design C}
  \end{minipage}
\hfill
  \begin{minipage}[c]{1in}
  \textbf{d: }%
  \fbox{\rule[+.4in]{.005in}%
    {.6in} Design D}
  \end{minipage}
  \end{minipage}
\end{minipage}
```

23.2.3   Framing the minipage

Using framebox Or fbox.

Recall from Section 23.1.2 that *\framebox* and its reduced version *\fbox* can be used to frame a single line box. They can just as well be used to frame a minipage. The two aliases (*\bmp* and *\emp*) cut down on typing.

```
\newcommand{\bmp}[2][t]{\begin{minipage}[#1]{#2}}
\newcommand{\emp}{\end{minipage}}
```

Example 1. Using \framebox

The MarkUp:

```
\framebox{\bmp{2.45in}
\itshape
\prit{\BS framebox} will frame
a parbox or a minipage. Note that
it takes the entire minipage and
the contents of the minipage as
argument. This outputs the text
in italics.
\emp }
```

The PrintOut:

> *\framebox will frame a parbox or a mini-page. Note that it takes the entire minipage and the contents of the minipage as argument. This outputs the text in italics.*

Example 2. Using \fbox

The MarkUp:

```
\fbox{\bmp{2.35in} \scshape
\textit{\BS fbox} will also frame a
parbox or a minipage. It takes the
entire minipage and the contents
of the minipage as argument. Note
the use of \textit{\BS bmp} and
\textit{\BS emp} as substitutes for
\textit{\BS begin{minipage}}
and \textit{\BS end{minipage}}.
This outputs the text in smallcaps.
\emp }
```

The PrintOut:

> *\fbox* WILL ALSO FRAME A PARBOX OR A MINIPAGE. IT TAKES THE ENTIRE MINI-PAGE AND THE CONTENTS OF THE MINI-PAGE AS ARGUMENT. NOTE THE USE OF *\bmp* AND *\emp* AS SUBSTITUTES FOR *\begin{minipage}* AND *\end{minipage}*. THIS OUTPUTS THE TEXT IN SMALL-CAPS.

Example 3. Using a macro rewrite of \fbox

The MarkUp:

```
\newcommand{\FB}[2]{\fbox{\bmp{#1}
\itshape #2 \emp}}
```

\BS FB is a 2-argument macro that can substitute for the fbox frame around a minipage containing italicized text.

The PrintOut:

\FB is a 2-argument macro that can substitute for the fbox frame around a minipage containing italicized text.

```
This is an example of usage:
```
This is an example of usage:

```
\vspace{1pc}
\FB{2.35in}{You may want to expand
the \textit{\BS FB} macro to a
3-argument macro, making font shape
a variable. }
```

> *You may want to expand the \FB macro to*
> *a 3-argument macro, making font shape a*
> *variable.*

Using The boxedminipage Package

The *boxedminipage* environment composes a framed minipage. It was written by Mario Wolczko. Call it with a *\usepackage{boxedminipage}* in the preamble.

The MarkUp: *The PrintOut:*

```
\begin{boxedminipage}[t]{2.45in}
Write material inside just as you
would in an ordinary minipage.
You can place the top, center or
bottom of the box on the baseline.
And you must set width.
\end{boxedminipage}
```

> Write material inside just as you would in
> an ordinary minipage. You can place the
> top, center or bottom of the box on the
> baseline. And you must set width.

23.3   The Inked Rectangle: The Rulebox

23.3.1   Solid boxes

Any box that (1) is created by the *\rule* command and (2) has non-zero width and height prints as a solid box. As with other boxes, its reference point is at the left bottom of the box. Width and height dimensions are mandatory. There is an optional argument to raise or lower the box. The complete format is: `\rule[+- verticalshift]{<width>}{<height>}`.

Rule boxes can not be shifted sidewards by built-in directives. However, these next boxes can be shifted because each is within its own minipage, which carves out a piece of territory for it and allows alignment vis a vis neighboring minipages.

By writing the minipage environments without gaps, we are guaranteed the boxes will be side by side.[1] The \hspace and vspace commands shift the minipage enclosures for cosmetic reasons. Note **e:** especially. The vspace command shifts the text upward a half inch within the minipage. The first of the two boxes (the upper horizontal line) should appear next to it, because there is no intervening line. But because the minipage isn't wide enough, the box is forced to the next line. There's a blank line before the directions for forming the second box. This guarantees that it will be printed below the first box.

The MarkUp:

```
\begin{minipage}[t]{.9in}
\textbf{a:} \rule{.7in}{.1in}
\end{minipage}
\hspace*{.08in}
\begin{minipage}[t]{.9in}
\textbf{b:} \rule[.3in]{.7in}{.1in}
\end{minipage}
\hspace*{.08in}
\begin{minipage}[t]{.9in}
\textbf{c:} \rule{.1in}{.7in}
\end{minipage}
\hspace*{.08in}
\begin{minipage}[t]{.9in}
\textbf{d:} \rule[.3in]{.1in}{.7in}
\end{minipage}
\begin{minipage}[t]{.9in}
\vspace*{-.5in}\textbf{e:}
\rule{.8in}{1mm}\vspace*{.5mm}

\rule{.8in}{1mm}
\end{minipage}
```

The PrintOut:

---

[1]For two minipages to be side by side, the *\end{ minipage}* command of the first minipage must be followed immediately by the *\begin{ minipage}* command of the next minipage. *But*, the contents of the minipage can have blank lines.

23.3.2   Struts

A *strut* is a rulebox with zero width. It acts as an invisible stilt that can used to change the vertical extent of a box. Like all rule boxes, it can be shifted up or down, but not sidewards. The first rectangle shows the effect of an unshifted invisible strut. The other three make effects visible by using a very thin almost-strut, one with a width of .005in; and the boxes are framed by way of the *\fbox* command. *b* is *a* with a visible strut. In **c**, a negative shift of the strut pushes the box down from the center; in **d**, a positive shift extends the top of the box up from the center.

The MarkUp: *The PrintOut:*

```
\begin{minipage}[c]{2.05in}
\begin{minipage}[c]{1in}
\textbf{a: }%
\fbox{\rule{0in}{.6in} Design A}
\end{minipage}
\hfill\begin{minipage}[c]{1in}
\textbf{b: }%
\fbox{\rule{.005in}{.6in} Design B}
\end{minipage}
\end{minipage}
\vspace{.4in}

\begin{minipage}[c]{2.05in}
\begin{minipage}[c]{1in}
\textbf{c: }%
\fbox{\rule[-.4in]{.005in}{.6in} Design C}
\end{minipage}
\hfill\begin{minipage}[c]{1in}
\textbf{d: }%
\fbox{\rule[+.4in]{.005in}{.6in} Design D}
\end{minipage}
\end{minipage}
```

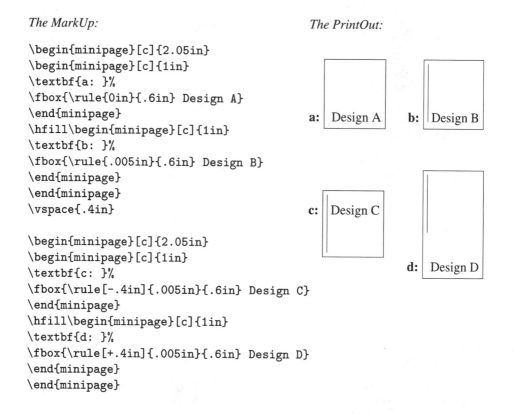

23.4   Sizing The Box In Relative Terms

Recall the way letter size is measured by width, height and depth from its reference point. (See Section 11.5.5.) The same concept applies to box measurements. It has a reference point: the point where the left side and bottom of the box intersect. It has a total height comprised of the height above the reference point and the depth below the reference point. A box 'at rest' has height, not depth. And it has width. As in a tetris game, you can pack the box any way you wish. But the contents of the box can only be moved on the page as a single object, not as an assemblage of individual objects.

Four measurements are defined for a box; i.e., the program determines the values for these variables.

\width	width of box.
\height	height of box from reference point up.
\depth	height of box from reference point down.
\totalheight	height plus depth.

These values are accessible. Box size need not be given in absolute measurements. Commands that produce boxes accept measurements relative to the contents of the box, or the length of a line, and so forth. A previous example in Section 23.2.1 illustrated using the actual height of the box plus a third of the baselineskip to make the appearance more attractive.

Here are some examples:

1. **To enclose symbols in a framed box.** Height, of course, depends on the length of the contents of the box. The width is equal to 2 times *totalheight*.

   The MarkUp: `\framebox[2\totalheight][c]{\textbf{\S\textbullet\S}}`

   The PrintOut: §•§

2. **To frame half a line of text.**

   The MarkUp:
   ```
   \framebox[.5\width][l]{\bfseries This is half of
   a short line of text.}
   ```

   The PrintOut: This is half of a short line of text.

3. **To put a frame around a line of text of any length.**

   The MarkUp:

   ```
   \fbox{The \textit{framebox} operation on a line overrides
   the width set in \textwidth.}
   ```

   The PrintOut:

   > The *framebox* operation on a line overrides the width set in \textwidth.

4. **To frame a minipage whose size is relative to a strip of text.**

   Create a variable (*\bwide* in this example) with *\newlength*. Use *\settowidth* to make the width of bwide equal to the phrase: "THIS IS NOT VERY WIDE, IS IT?", *printed in tiny letters.* This width becomes the width of the minipage.

   ```
   \newlength{\bwide}
   \settowidth{\bwide}{\tiny THIS IS NOT VERY WIDE, IS IT?}
   ```

   The unusual syntax of the FRM macro is discussed in the next section. The first placeholder defaults to **t** alignment (See Section 10.6.) *bwide* is PlaceHolder #2.

   The MarkUp:

   ```
   \newsavebox{\FrameIt}
   \newenvironment{FRM}[2]{\begin{lrbox}{\FrameIt}%
   \begin{minipage}[#1][t]{#2}}%
   {\end{minipage}\end{lrbox}\fbox{\usebox{\FrameIt}}}
   ```

   ```
   \begin{FRM}{\bwide}
   Put this in the minipage, please. The box will be as wide as
   the tiny strip of text that is the argument of bwide.
   \end{FRM}
   ```

   The PrintOut:

   > Put this in the minipage, please. The box will be as wide as the tiny strip of text that is the argument of bwide.

5. **To make a page mask.** This will print an entirely black rectangle the exact size of the text page. This is the markup; we won't bother with the printout, which, printed on a transparency, is an alternative to declaring the document in draft mode to find and correct overwide lines.

```
\rule{\textwidth}{\textheight}
```

6. **To draw a frame around a page.**

It is easy enough to frame a single page by writing text in a large enough minipage. Two ways to write such a command are shown. The first is simple; it stretches the width to enclose whatever text is the argument of \rule. We show its markup. The second uses the lrbox construction, and is precisely the width and height set in \textwidth and \textheight.

The MarkUp: 1.

```
\fbox{\rule{0pt}{\textheight}
The length of a page is set by \BS textheight.
It was set at 7.4 inches for this book.}
```

The MarkUp: 2.

```
\newsavebox{\FPageIt}
\newenvironment{FP}{\begin{lrbox}{\FPageIt}%
\begin{minipage}[t][\textheight][s]{\textwidth}}%
{\emp\end{lrbox}\fbox{\usebox{\FPageIt}}}
```

It uses the **s** option that stretches the text out in the box. If the text isn't sufficient for the page, interleave a couple of \vspace*{stretch}{1} statements judiciously.

```
Usage:
```

```
\begin{FP}
lots of text
\end{FP}
```

The procedure is shown framing the next page.

23.5   Saving Designs

To save time rewriting a pattern, you could name a sequence of formatting instructions and save it with a \newcommand macro. You would then use it with little effort by writing its command name. Unfortunately, the program would still need to retrace the separate steps in typesetting the format, a time-consuming procedure. Moreover, this can become an enormous drain on memory, especially if you wanted to introduce another file that contained a specially-designed icon to typeset on each page of a 300-page book.

To save both yourself and the program construction time, energy and memory, do two things:

Step 1. LaTeX has several specific commands for constructing a new box that is to be saved—\savebox, \sbox and \lrbox. \savebox and \sbox are commands; \lrbox is an environment. Use one of these commands to typeset the box. The formatting instructions to create the box are its definition. It is addressed via its storage area.

Step 2. The box will be preserved in permanent memory storage if the command name of the storage area is written as argument to a **\newsavebox** command.

Actually, you do steps 1 and 2 in reverse order; that is, you first create and name storage space for a yet-to-be constructed box using \newsavebox. Then you write the formatting instruction that will create that box. Note that no matter where you write the \newsavebox command, it is a global command, as if you'd written it in the preamble. The markup that creates the box follows ordinary scope rules.

In this section, we focus on constructing and saving boxes—first simple boxes, then framed logos and finally framed sidebars.

Versions of the instructions that create a framed sidebar have been shown earlier in the book, once to frame a set of subfigures in Section 16.1.3 and once to frame a sidefloat in Example 2, Section 16.1.4. It is a important utility that will be used again in the next part of the book to frame pictures and graphics.

Please DO NOT SKIP this section. You will only have to return to it when we get to importing an Encapsulated PostScript file that will be used multiple times in the document. To produce a single box from such an EPS file, there is an additional step: the PostScript file is separated into *Header* and *Body*. This cuts down the number of times the description of how to compose the graphics must be written into the document. Section 25.4.10 outlines the procedure.

Example 1. **Using savebox**. This is a simple construction that can create and save single-line boxes, a 3-inch wide box in this example.

Step 1. Create a storage bin for a box to be typeset. The command name of the bin is *Stamp*.

```
\newsavebox{\Stamp}
```

Step 2. Create the box and save it using the \savebox command. It has the same syntax as the \makebox command: an optional width for the box and a mandatory argument that holds the text that will be put in the box. The constructed box is saved in *Stamp*.

```
\savebox{\Stamp}[3in]{\today\mgap\textbf{Findings:}\dotfill\\}
```

Usage. Whenever you want to insert the text in the document, write a \usebox command. The name of the storage bin is argument to the usebox command; the contents of \Stamp are printed.

The MarkUp: `\usebox{\Stamp}`

The PrintOut: July 11, 1998   **Findings:** . . . .

Example 2. **Using sbox**. In this example, we use the short form of \savebox; it is to savebox as mbox is to makebox. It has no optional arguments; the program determines the best fit box for the text. Again, a storage area is first set up. Then \sbox constructs the box that will reside in the storage area named in the first step. Like example 1, this is used to create a single-line box.

Step 1. Create the storage bin for a box; the bin is called \LEL.

```
\newsavebox{\LEL}
```

Step 2. Use sbox to define the typesetting of the box; i.e., the markup instructions that produce the box are the definition of the box.

```
\sbox{\LEL\}{\tiny $\Diamond\heartsuit%
\Diamond$ lel $\Diamond\heartsuit\Diamond$ \normalsize\}
```

Usage. Again, whenever you wish to print the box, issue a \usebox command. The name of the storage bin is the argument; i.e., the constructed box is referenced through the memory area in which it is stored. In this example, the \Ovalbox and \fbox commands will frame the box.

The MarkUp: `Use \Ovalbox{\fbox{\usebox{\LEL}}} as a`
`miniature logo.`

The PrintOut: Use ◇♡◇ lel ◇♡◇ as a miniature logo.

Example 3. Using sbox and a macro. This creates a box much like the one in Example 2. It also constructs an ordinary macro, \useLogo, that uses the box twice. The macro has a placeholder, so different text phrases can be substituted in the box.

Step 1. Create storage for a box; call it, say, \Logo.

`\newsavebox{\Logo}`

Step 2. Using \savebox, write the prescription for typesetting the box and storing it in its preassigned storage bin.

`\savebox{\Logo}{\tiny $\overline{\Diamond\heartsuit\Diamond}$}`

Step 3. Create the macro. Note that the first *Logo* is underlined, not the second—the printout will make clear what happens.

```
\newcommand{\useLogo}[1]{\underline{\usebox{\Logo}%
#1 \usebox{\Logo}}}
```

Usage. *The MarkUp:* `Use \useLogo{lel} as a miniature logo.`

The PrintOut: Use ◇◇◇ lel ◇◇◇ as a miniature logo.

Example 4. Using lrbox. This example shows another way to create a box. \savebox and \sbox are commands. **\lrbox** is very similar to \sbox, except that: (1) it is a environment, so you can create other environment from it by modifying it; and (2) initial and final spaces in the text are ignored.

Step 1. Name a storage bin (\SmallBox) that will reference a box to be constructed.

`\newsavebox{\SmallBox}`

Step 2. Create a new environment by modifying the lrbox environment by the name of the bin stored in step 1. Name the new environment, *SmallBoxEnv* in this case.

```
\newenvironment{SmallBoxEnv}%
{\begin{lrbox}\SmallBox}%
{\end{lrbox}\fbox{\usebox{\SmallBox}}}
```

The procedure is analogous to the way an ordinary new environment is created. For example, this ordinary environment called *NewName* will list any items you insert into the environment in bold.

```
\newenvironment{NewName}%
{\begin{itemize}\bfseries}%
{\end{itemize}}
```

There are, however, major differences.

1. *\bfseries* is a general command. *\SmallBox* is specific; it the command name of the storage bin.

2. The \end term, which is usually kept free of extraneous text and other commands, is concatenated with the \usebox command. And the argument of *\usebox* is the name of the storage container.

Usage. *The MarkUp:*

```
\begin{SmallBoxEnv}
Fill this with a line of text.
\end{SmallBoxEnv}
```

The PrintOut: | Fill this with a line of text. |

Example 5. **Using lrbox and a minipage.** *lrbox* is an extremely versatile construction. For example, we can redo the previous example and make the lrbox contain a minipage, which then can hold tab tables or pictures or a sizable chunk of ordinary text. Notice that the *begins* for both lrbox and minipage are contained in the begin argument. Similarly, the *ends* for both the minipage and lrbox are contained in the end argument. The minipage environment is enclosed by the lrbox environment. The argument of the lrbox is the name of the storage bin.

An environment inside the minipage would be written in the usual fashion—see the centering environment inside a lrbox construction in Section 16.1.4.

Step 1. Set aside memory area for a storage bin.

```
\newsavebox{\MiniBox}
```

Step 2. Create a new lrbox environment that includes a minipage.

```
\newenvironment{MSBox}{\begin{lrbox}{\MiniBox}%
\begin{minipage}[t]{2in}}
{\end{minipage}%
\end{lrbox}\fbox{\usebox{\MiniBox}}}
```

Usage. *The MarkUp:*   *The PrintOut:*

```
\begin{MSBox}
The box construction can be
used in text OR math modes.
It prevents the program from
breaking the contents of the box
either horizontally or vertically.
The fbox command frames the box.
\end{MSBox}
```

> The box construction can be used in text OR math modes. It prevents the program from breaking the contents of the box either horizontally or vertically. The fbox command frames the box.

Example 6. Generalizing the lrbox environment. A new environment made from the lrbox environment can be generalized. In this example, the width of the minipage is a variable. As part of the demonstration, we show the box used as a sidebar.

Step 1. Set up and name a storage area, whose contents will be the typeset box.

```
\newsavebox{\SideBar}
```

Step 2. Create a new lrbox environment that includes a minipage.

```
\newenvironment{SBar}[1]{\begin{lrbox}{\SideBar}%
\begin{minipage}[t]{#1}}
{\end{minipage}%
\end{lrbox}\fbox{\usebox{\SideBar}}}
```

Usage.

```
\definecolor{lightgrey}{gray}{.8}
\begin{minipage}[t]{2in}
\IN
This is ordinary text put in a minipage. The box construction
can be used in text OR math modes. It prevents the program
from breaking the contents of the box either horizontally
or vertically. The fbox command frames the box. Adding color
makes the material stand out from the rest of the text.
\end{minipage}
\hfill
\begin{minipage}[t]{1.5in}
\OUT
\colorbox{lightgrey{
```

```
\begin{SBar}{1.4in}
\textbf{HIGHLIGHTS:}
\be
\item The program typesets the box once only.
\item You can use it many times with no additional
cost in time or memory.
\item Just master the syntax. \ee
\end{SBar}}
\end{minipage}
```

The PrintOut: This is ordinary text put in a minipage. The box construction can be used in text OR math modes. It prevents the program from breaking the contents of the box either horizontally or vertically. The fbox command frames the box. Adding color makes the material stand out from the rest of the text.

HIGHLIGHTS:

1. The program typesets the box once only.

2. You can use it many times with no additional cost in time or memory.

3. Just master the syntax.

Part VII.

ENHANCEMENTS TO THE TEXT.

LaTeX itself contains commands to compose graphs, draw complex curves and create grids. The first chapter in this part starts with LaTeX's picture environment. It then describes several packages that come with Linux or are readily obtainable from the Net that let you create a design, do a drawing or enhance (or distort) a picture. This is, by no means, a comprehensive survey. Just the opposite. But the programs are solid and cover the range of what you need to produce and/or reformat and/or modify art objects—be they graphs, charts, drawings, images, paintings, sketches, stick figure drawings, CAM/CAD diagrams, logo designs, clip art, photographs—so they can become part of your printed document. The programs discussed have one essential feature: they can output images as Encapsulated PostScript (EPS) files.

A graphics or picture file must be converted into EPS to be accepted into a LaTeX document. An Encapsulated PostScript file is a one-page PostScript file with stylized information about the size of the entering image and a reduced set of PostScript operators. Chapter 25 covers this. It lays out the steps whereby the *graphicx* package and the *includegraphics* command integrate the EPS file into the document. It discusses how to add size information to an ordinary PostScript file and how to manipulate size information to 'crop' the picture. It talks about factors—width, height, scaling, framing, the origin and angle of rotation—that influence the positioning and the appearance of the drawing on the page.

Chapter 24

CREATING PICTURES AND GRAPHICS

This chapter is devoted to programs that let you convert a list of coordinates to an image; chart condensed data; and draw, paint, colorize, solarize and otherwise modify scientific constructions and artistic creations in a digital environment. The first Section describes the LaTeX picture environment and ancillary graphics programs that work directly in the picture environment. Xy-pic works directly in LaTeX and MetaPost graphics can be added. The other sections describe WYSIWYG graphical design and image processing programs, whose products can be incorporated into LaTeX as Encapsulated PostScript files.

24.1   Creating Pictures In LaTeX

LaTeX provides an environment that produce an invisible box within which you can write text and draw plain lines and arrows, some curves and different-sized circles. It is called a *picture environment*, which connotes gray-scaled or colored pixels and paintings and density and perspective and *story*, but that isn't what LaTeX does. Moreover, each type of creatable object requires a different command. If you can visualize an image from a set of x,y coordinates, this is a program you will enjoy.

24.1.1   Positioning the picture

A picture environment creates a box in which you can draw objects. The reference point of the box is, as usual, its lower left corner. The size of the box—its width and height in points from the reference point—is the first argument. To size the box and to locate the reference point and points within the box, we use the vocabulary of simple coordinate geometry. Unless otherwise specified, the reference point is taken as the origin (the 0,0 position). You can move the origin from the reference point; the distance from the reference point to the origin is then the second argument.

```
\begin{picture}
(picture width, picture height) %Argument 1.
(x,y coordinates of left lower corner of box) %Optional Argument 2.
\end{picture}
```

This would make a box that was 100 points wide, 200 points high. The distance of the reference point from the origin is 10 points on the x axis and 20 points on the y axis.

```
\begin{picture}(100,200)(10,20)
'draw' picture here
\end{picture}
```

24.1.2   Picture commands

The available commands are: \put, \multiput, \qbezier, \graphpaper, \line, \circle. *multiput* lays down a sequence of objects; the syntax is: \multiput(<*the starting x,y*>)% (<*the increment x,y*>){<*the object*>}. There are facilities to label the drawing.

A Bezier curve is important for vector graphics. It is usually described in terms of an envelope polygon, its *control polygon*. The curve extends along the vertices of the polygon, starting at the start point and ending at the end vertex; these vertices are called *control points*. Bezier curves can be connected by concatenation—the start point of the second being the last point of the first. The curve is invariant under shear, scale, rotation and scaling transformations; so transforming the control points is the same as transforming the curve itself. LATEX calculates the curve from the values you give it. Some Bezier curves are shown in Figure 24.1. The arguments to the *qbezier* (quadratic Bezier curve) command are the start and end points and the intermediate control point.

The MarkUp: *The PrintOut:*

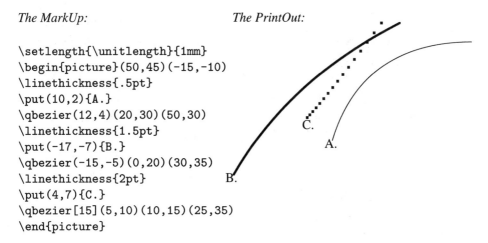

```
\setlength{\unitlength}{1mm}
\begin{picture}(50,45)(-15,-10)
\linethickness{.5pt}
\put(10,2){A.}
\qbezier(12,4)(20,30)(50,30)
\linethickness{1.5pt}
\put(-17,-7){B.}
\qbezier(-15,-5)(0,20)(30,35)
\linethickness{2pt}
\put(4,7){C.}
\qbezier[15](5,10)(10,15)(25,35)
\end{picture}
```

Figure 24.1: Bezier curves in the picture environment

```
\begin{picture}(50,50)
\setlength{\unitlength}{2mm}
\graphpaper[12](-1,-4)(36,36)
\put(2,25){\small\textsl%
{Salvador, do not dali.}}
\put(0,-3){\textsf{Line A.}}
\linethickness{2pt}
\put(-1,0){\line(1,0){21}}
\linethickness{.4pt}
\put(10,5){\circle*{1}}
\put(10,10){\circle{2}}
\put(10,15){\circle{3}}
\put(10,20){\circle{4}}
\put(28,20){\circle*{1}}
\put(32,20){\circle*{1}}
\put(25,5){\oval(5,1)}
\put(25,10){\oval(8,15)}
\put(25,15){\oval(12,5)}
\put(25,20){\oval(16,7)}
\put(20,0){\vector(0,1){25}}
\put(20,28){\textsf{Line B.}}
\linethickness{2pt}
\put(20,25){\line(1,0){15}}
\end{picture}
```

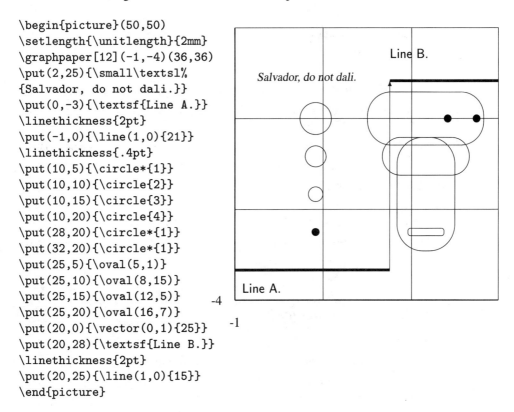

Figure 24.2: Picture environment primitives

Unit length is set to 1 point by default. We have reset it to 1 mm. Note that line thickness can be specified. In Curve C, the number in the square bracket specifies the number of points the program should calculate.

Various LaTeX picture environment primitives have been combined in Figure 24.2. A line is defined by a slope and a length. The *put* command lays down its starting point. A vector is a line that ends in an arrow. The argument of the *circle* command is its diameter. The argument of the *oval* command provides its width and height. The *graphpap* package by Leslie Lamport was used to draw the graphpaper in the second drawing. The default is a line every 10 units; here it is set at every 12 units.

Packages For The LaTeX Picture Environment

trees by Peter Vanroose [Vanroose90] adds commands within the LaTeX picture environment that draw binary or ternary trees. The number of nodes is unrestricted.

bar by J. Bleser and E. Land [Bleser92] produces bar charts within the picture environment. Its primitives are a set of differently striped and solid bars, similar to those in Xpaint.

curves by Ian Maclaine-cross [Maclaine95] draws accurate curves and graphics, useful where precision counts. Examples are drawn from mechanical engineering. This runs under the LaTeX picture environment.

epic, an extensive program written by Sunil Podar [Podar86], helps calculate the coordinates for graphic objects in the LaTeX picture environment. Additional macros have been written by others for the package.

24.1.3   Additional graphics packages

Several programs have been developed as adjuncts to LaTeX either for general typesetting of mathematical functions or for specific tasks.

The Xy-pic Package

This is a layout and typesetting program for complex diagrams and charts, which allows mathematical objects to be linked or positioned by a variety of connections. The program is organized as a 'kernel' (a small number of essential operations) and options that include different objects and structures. Objects can be square or circular boxes and various arcs. Special notation lets you describe rotation, scaling, color, and line thickness. The different modes of operations include: a graph-combining mode; a matrix-like mode where diagram entries are aligned in a matrix; a polygon mode for writing diagrams in polygon enclosures and a mode for typesetting knots and links.

To use the program, write **\usepackage{xy}** in the preamble. The program was written by Kristoffer H. Rose; program documentation can be found in *xyguide.dvi* [Rose95a] and *xyref.dvi* [Rose95b].

The Gnuplot Package

Gnuplot is a simple but useful program that plots functions and shows the results graphically, as an aid in visualizing complex functions. *Gnuplot*, a part of GNU, was written by Thomas Williams and Colin Kelley. Russell Lang, Dave Kotz, John Campbell and Gershon Elber wrote additions to the upgrades.

Gnuplot plots functions and shows the results graphically. It works in Linux, Unix, DOS, and VMS. It works on a variety of terminals, plotters, and printers. And it can output in XFig format, so it can be put directly into LATEX.

/usr/lib/gnuplot/gnuplot.gih has detailed information on the program. There is also a man page and well-designed demo programs in the gnuplot directory. They can be seen by typing the demo name; e.g., **gnuplot animate.dem**. A DEM file is a script demonstrating how you can set a data structure, calculate the function and display the result.

MetaPost

MetaPost [Hobby96] is a versatile programming language for manipulating pictures and drawing graphs. It was written by John D. Hobby and is based on Knuth's METAFONT. Its large set of drawing commands create and manipulate geometric objects. It functions as a 'higher level language' for writing PostScript commands. The MetaPost commands you write in a (*.mp*) file are interpreted by MetaPost. The output PostScript can be integrated with an ordinary TEX or LATEX DVI file via *dvips*. Its graph program includes formats for data entry and processing. It can handle large numbers; and it can label and prettify graphs for output.

24.2   The *xv* Package

xv is shareware and was developed by John Bradley [Bradley94]. A manual is available from the author. This discussion references Version 3.10a, release 6, 21 nov 1996.

xv is an interactive image display system that works on both color and grayscale. It is not a freeform drawing program, but it does allow freehand contouring and smudging. It loads an existing picture from any of a number of formats—GIF, BMP, JPEG, and so forth. You can load a set of pictures, which have the same extension or format, but view them one at at a time. Once a picture is loaded, there is a large group of operations you can perform on a rectangular region that you select.

Use the algorithms. Oil painting, Blur, Blend, Despeckle, Pixelize (obscures rather than smooths) and Spread are smoothers. Edge sharpen, Edge detect and Emboss are contrast enhancers. Each operation runs on the results of the previous one.

Increase or decrease size within wide limits, shift picture position, rotate it 90°, use portrait or landscape mode.

Crop a region.

Cut or Copy a region. You can then Paste it into another region.

Save a picture in color, grayscale or black and white with changes in size, height, width, paper size, orientation. The picture can be saved from 72 to 300 dpi, with 72 dpi by

72 dpi the default. To reset this to 300 dpi, set the scale factor to 25%; set it to 12% for 600 dpi. You can play some tricks for upgrading dpi by blowing the picture up as large as possible, requesting Grayscale printing and resetting the dials to a smaller size. As size decreases, dpi increases.

The Undo undoes all the operations, not just the previous one; so it's a good idea to save frequently, especially before starting an operation that might botch things.

The image can be output as an Encapsulated PostScript file. As part of the save, you can stipulate position—Center, Max, Left, Top. If you aren't sure where the picture will finally be positioned, align it with Origin (the left bottom corner of the image.) Running an image through *xv* to crop, size and output it as a Encapsulated PostScript file is a painless way to prepare an image for a LaTeX document.

The program includes *Visual Schnauzer*, a file manager for viewing, deleting, shifting directories, and so forth. The contents of an image directory are viewed as pictorial icons. To inspect a particular directory of images, be in it when you call *xv*; e.g., cd /home/images/weddingpix.

Figure 24.3 is a old picture of a friend. The original photograph was viewed through the lens of a Canon[TM]Hi-8 camcorder. Snappy[TM]transmitted the frame to a DOS program, which converted it to JPEG format. It was brought into *xv* as a JPEG file. The photograph was in poor condition, with many breaks where the paper had torn.[1] It was cropped, zoomed and smoothed mostly by blending[2] and despeckling.[3]

It's interesting how quickly you develop procedural algorithms; for example:

Blending a small area into a large monotone area is a good way to reduce contrast in the small area. Despeckling is best used with a small mask size.

Anything that breaks a tear line helps.

---

[1] Some operations are slow, so it's a good idea to have another window open in which you can be doing something else. Restoring pictures is not a job for the impatient.

[2] This nicely blends the inside of the rectangle less than the edges, so edges don't become sharp.

[3] Despeckling removes minor random noise, without involving the edges of the rectangle.

Figure 24.3: Repairing A Torn Picture. Top: before. Bottom: after.

24.3   The XFig Package

XFig is an acronym for *Facility for Interactive Generation of figures under X11*. It is an versatile computer-aided design (CAD) package that is easy to use. The more I use it, the more I appreciate its drawing and layout capabilities. Documentation is available as a man page. Or read *An Introduction to XFIG*, [Solenka95]. XFig is distributed by the X Consortium as freeware. The program was first copyright in 1985 by Supoj Sutanthavibul; later copyrights are held by Paul King in 1991 and by Brian V. Smith in 1994. The referenced version is xfig 3.1.4.

Call XFig by typing **xfig** in an xterm. The program presents as a blackboard with a set of pull-down menus on top and bottom and an enormous number of tool icons on the side. Orientation, background, color, fonts for directives and fonts for display, the number of buttons in a row and the default outout format can all be customized. Type **xfig -help** in an xterm for the complete list of options.

xfig deals with graphical objects. The *primitives* of the system are: arc, circle, closed spline, ellipse, polyline, polygon, picture, box, arc-box, spline and text. These can be copied, rotated, scaled, moved, erased and, except for *text*, flipped vertically or horizontally. Line thickness can be varied. A group of *primitives* can be assembled into a *compound object*, which, thereafter, is treated as a single object, subject to the various xfig transforms.

Layering of objects is allowed. Objects with lower depth numbers obscure or, depending on size and location, overlap objects with higher depth numbers. This is a simple example, using the program to design different styles of business cards. The program supplies grids and rulers. The logo is adapted from *logo.eps.Z*, that comes with the program. The Escher knot is from the X11/pixmaps subdirectory. xfig comes with a variety of fonts, some of which are shown in Figure 24.4.

For designs such as this one, XFig quickly achieves what can take substantial time in LaTeX. The process can, however, be made more rapid by using text placeholders to modify text with spelling errors, etc. This is a portion of the very end of the file; i.e., the material after the solid block of numbers. You can replace *Tel, Rue* and *hack* with the actual text. Font style can also be changed.

Sarah Engle

Third Vice President

Paris Office
Rue Michel-Ange, 2000

Tel: 454534

Sarah Engle

Third Vice President

Paris Office
Rue

Tel

Sarah Engle

We Hack It.

Rue Michel-Ange,2000   Tel: 454534

Paris 750016   Fax: 454543

Sarah Engle

hack,

Rue   Tel

Paris 750016   Fax: 454543

HACK, Ltd

Sarah ENGLE

Paris Office
Rue Michel-Ange, 2000

By Appointment   TEL: 454543

HACK, Ltd

Sarah ENGLE

Paris Office
Rue

By Appointment   Tel

(a) Complete Design.   (b) Placeholder Text.

Figure 24.4: Text in an XFig Drawing

```
gs 1 -1 sc (hack.) col-1 sh gr
/Times-Roman ff 180.00 scf sf
4350 2625 m
gs 1 -1 sc (Tel) col-1 sh gr
/Courier ff 210.00 scf sf
3450 9300 m
gs 1 -1 sc (Tel) col-1 sh gr
/Courier-Bold ff 150.00 scf sf
1425 5625 m
gs 1 -1 sc (Rue    Tel) col-1 sh gr
/Palatino-Roman ff 180.00 scf sf
1575 2775 m
gs 1 -1 sc (Rue) col-1 sh gr
/Times-Roman ff 180.00 scf sf
2400 9000 m
gs 1 -1 sc (Rue) col-1 sh gr
$F2psEnd
rs
```

This is analogous to using the *psfrag* package to change math fonts in an EPS file. The first argument of a \psfrag command is Xfig text, the second argument is the replacement text, which takes advantage of LATEX math fonts.

In an xterm you run *ps2frag* on the file; in this example, you'd run **ps2frag foo.eps**. *PSfrag* was written by Craig Barratt and Michael C Grant; documentation is available in [Barratt95]. You include replacement text in the LATEX document this way:

```
\documentclass[<options>]{<document type>}
\begin{document}
. . . . . . . . . . . . .
\begin{figure}[t]
\psfrag{xy}{$x_{2} + y_{3}$}
\psfrag{xyz}{$\overline{xyz}$}
\includegraphics{foo.eps}
\end{figure}
\end{document}
```

24.4   The XPaint Package

This is a multi-featured paint program that was authored by David Koblos and is maintained by Torsten Martinsen. The version discussed is V 2.4.9, 31 may 1997. It provides the canvas, menus, color palettes and a variety of pencil, brush and geometric operations. You can crop the input, leaving only a particular area. Or you can cut out a region and store it on the clipboard, to be copied in one or more areas later. These are features that we have come to expect from a useful paint program. XPaint does them very nicely. In addition, it lets you work on several images simultaneously; cutting and pasting between them. It accepts TIFF, PPM, GIF, XBM, XPM and XWD formats. It outputs these formats as well as Encapsulated PostScript, so you can transfer pictures to LaTeX documents.

The number of fonts is large. You can select by size, weight, boldness and color them at will. The program has an excellent online help file as well as a man page.

The canvas is 640x480 pixels by default, but it can be sized. Figure 24.5 is a composite that uses scenes from Lewis Carroll's *Alice in Wonderland*. The illustrations were obtained from Project Guttenberg, which has been engaged in placing ASCII-coded classics in the public domain.[4] The original art work is by Teniel. This is the scene of the cards painting the flowers, with the addition of the queen from the courtroom scene on the right. A third image was introduced to add the vertical fence texture at the bottom. Text and pencilled 'charcoaling' was added. The pieces were added to an initially blank canvas by using the *Load Clipboard* in the FILE menu. They were then *Pasted*, an option in the EDIT menu, either to the whole canvas or to a region. Adding text and pencilling were done last.

24.5   ImageMagick

The discussion references version 3.8.3, Release 1, 25 march 1997, which has been placed in the public domain as freeware. It runs on multiple platforms that use X11 and has recently been compiled for Linux. The author and copyright holder is John Christy of E. I. du Pont de Nemours and Company. Check the documentation for legal restrictions involving the Company name; the program is unencumbered.

---

[4]You can reach them at http://sailor.gutenberg.org. Michael Hart directs the project.

Figure 24.5: A composite of three Teniel sketches for *Alice in Wonderland.*

ImageMagick doesn't necessarily come with Linux, but can be downloaded from the Net. The program has become easier to install in just a few months, so it may be trivial by the time you read this. At this writing, these are the installation steps:

1. Get into the Net and download from:
   ftp://ftp.wizards.dupont.com/pub/ImageMagick/linux.
   Get the latest tar version that works for Linux.

2. tar -zvxf ImageMagick....(whatever number is the latest version) It will create a sub-directory called ImageMagick.

3. ImageMagick has GIF and other formats built-in. But if you will want to use JPEG, TIFF, HDEF and/or MPEG formats but didn't include one or more of these when you built Linux, add them now from the Net. There is a list of where to get the different formats in the ImageMagick README file. They have to be individually unzipped.

4. Follow the directions. They are fairly straightforward, considering the size of the program and its complexity. You do have to know whether your machine has shared memory and shared libraries. Whoever set up Linux should know.

The major operations are under *display*.

In an xterm, type **display**. The screen fills with an image of Planet Earth. A menu appears when you click to the left of the map. Each item leads to a submenu. The operations are noncommutative, so if you're not sure what to expect, SAVE OFTEN. The procedures and their combinations make for endless possibilities in reshaping a picture. In addition, you can *launch* Xpaint from ImageMagick. The core of the patterns shown in Figure 24.6 and Figure 24.7 is an Israeli stamp that depicts a detail from a copper engraving from 1741: *The Jewish Postal Courier of Prague*.

Other classes of operations are: import, animate, montage, convert, mogrify, identify and combine. In addition to the many ways ImageMagick encourages you to exercise your imagination in creating designs and wall-worthy art, the program is capable of serious image analysis. It finds the grayscale differences pixel-wise between two similar pictures. It provides variable-threshold histograms created by the application of the fuzzy c-Means contrast gradient algorithm; images can be segmented and classified on the basis of their histogram differences. It performs boolean operations on composite images.

Figure 24.6: Pattern 1. ImageMagick

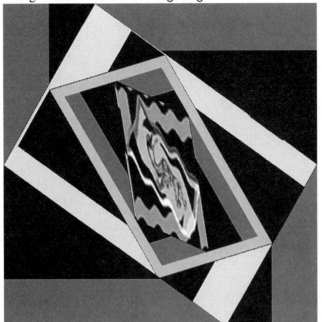

The image of this stamp was

twisted, sheared, rolled, rotated and spiffed. Several borders were added.

Figure 24.7: Pattern 2. ImageMagick

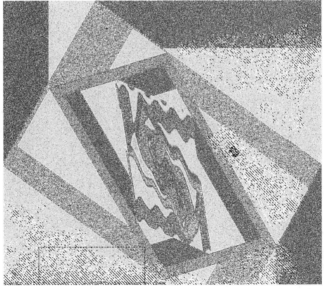

Noise was added to Figure 24.6. The image was solarized, brightened, color reversed (negation) with reduced saturation and hue. It was also lightly penciled with an Xpaint brush. And a border was cropped.

24.6 GIMP

GIMP (an acronym for GNU Image Manipulation Program) is an exceedingly rich image processing and graphics manipulation program that seems capable of handling everything from line drawings to 3-D sculpted textures. It can generate elaborate diffraction and wave patterns and it can produce animated graphics for Web pages to catch the surfer's eye. It works in Linux and Unix.

As of this writing, the program is still in pre-release; we reference Version 0.99.15. GIMP was written by Spencer Kimball and Peter Mattis, both at U California, Berkeley. GIMP's home page[5] is at *http://www.gimp.org*. Its automated plug-in registry for new plug-ins is located at *http://gimp.foebud.org/registry*.

There are several sources of information:

1. Spencer Kimball's article [Kimball97] on Script-Fu, is included in the GIMP download; it describes Script-Fu, the GIMP scripting language that does the computations to present the graphical outcomes.

2. *GIMP User Manual* V 0.7, 1997, by Karin Kylander and Olof S Kylander [Kylander97]. You can ftp it from ftp://ftp.frozenriver.ale.se/pub/Gimpmanual. Using this manual to explore the program will get you up to speed painlessly. It's carefully crafted and as thorough as it can be, considering it's writing about a moving target.

3. A 4-part article by Michael J. Hammel [Hammel97] in the *Linux Journal*. This was not completed at the time of this writing.

4. There is a Documentation Section in *http://www.gimp.org*. It has an excellent discussion of basics and some more advanced techniques. It also points to other sources. For example

   Nem W. Schlecht maintains a list of links to tutorials.

   Miles O'Neal maintains and updates a GIMP FAQ.

5. Each time you run GIMP, a TIPS window opens, revealing another helpful hint on running the program.

---

[5]These Gimp Web sites are functional as I write. But it's a time of flux and rapid change. New sites spring up. Old sites change address.

Installation even now is simple. The only trick is installing the gtk library first. Download GIMP and the *gtk* library. Make sure that a *gdk* library is formed as a result. Configure and make the library BEFORE you install GIMP.

Assuming GIMP is installed, you run it by typing **gimp** in an xterm. You will be presented with a *Toolbox*, which is a narrow box of pushbutton icons and two pulldown menus: Files and *Xtns*. Calling for a new or old image opens the *Image Window(s)*. Clicking with the left mouse button in the Image Window opens a large set of options, including among many others: tools (another way of selecting from the Toolbox), layers, filters and script-fu. *Tools* has a subsidiary set of menu items that let you select rectangular or elliptical areas, do most of what a paint program does, clone and convolve. *Filters* controls animation, mosaic and cubist artistic renditions, edge detection, textures and transforms, each of which in turn has still another set of options. *Script-fu* adds bevelling, shadows, weaving, and so forth. Submenus in the Image Window can go to considerable depth. Many of the transformations engage you in interaction with a Dialog window to set values or preview consequences. In addition to PostScript output, GIMP handles a variety of formats, including GIF, JPEG, PCX, TIFF and (shortly) PNG.

An important part of GIMP's personality is its notion that a visual image can be built up from a stack of individual layers.

Layers A segment of what will be a whole picture can be created separately and located in its own layer. Creating 3-D effects is simplified when segments in the same locale of the image are in neighboring layers, each contributing to the final effect.

Channels These are the bits devoted to each pixel in a segment in any layer. To characterize color, for example, there are four 8-bit channels: red, green, blue and *Alpha*, a grayscale mask that describes the pixel's transparency. Grayscale images use 24 bits, and have no transparency descriptor.

Besides giving you a vocabulary to address and manipulate the separate layers that you create, GIMP has a number of operators concerned solely with increasing, decreasing and combining the number of layers that are being processed.

Saving an image should be done frequently, because an operation, even previewed, can produce unwanted results, as with any other interactive graphics program. It is true that you can set the number of undo's to some number greater than 1, but each undo is costly in memory. An ordinary save saves the layer you're currently manipulating; the XCF format saves all the layers in the image.

Examples can be found in the GIMP web pages that combines 3D text and interesting background texture.

24.7   Packages For Ready Money

You are not restricted to using packages that run under Linux. You can create a finished product with your favorite product that runs under Windows or Mac. The real issue is the encoding. Ideally, your favorite tablemaker, paint, draw or CAD program can also output your handiwork as a Encapsulated PostScript (or the equivalent PostScript) file portable across systems. Check. It may be one of the options. Alternatively, a JPEG or GIF or TIFF or even a BMP[6]-encoded file can be brought into *xv* or *ImageMagick* and output as a PostScript file that LaTeX will accept.

My husband, Dr. Lewis Lipkin, keeps a DOS-Windows partition in our Linux machines, mostly so he can use Excel^{TM}. The examples, a table and a chart, were both done by him in Excel. (Excel files in Linux may look bad on the screen, but they print beautifully.)

We made several assumptions when we first tried bringing an Excel image into Linux: (1) all PostScript files are device-independent and can be easily moved between operating systems; and (2) if you had to move an image between operating systems, you were better doing it closer to the printing end of the process. These are both wrong.

First, the EPS file is incomplete. Microsoft Windows writes an EPS file that summons a dictionary. At printing time, the Windows dictionary (which is not part of the file) will supply the printer with directions on how to write the print characters. (It is rather like writing C code with requests to include some utility files. Until link time, the utility files are not utilized.) The result is that the Excel EPS file can NOT be printed by a printer under Linux or Unix. This holds true whether you send it to the PostScript printer directly, play games redirecting the printer name or use the PRINTER TO FILE option supplied by the Print Manager.

---

[6]A BMP file is bitmapped; the other files are compressed.

Issue	Value	Scott	Bale	State	Date	Note
Festival 49	05pr	28	18	24	20-Sep-49	; Air Force Insignia
Festival 49	10pr	29	19	25	20-Sep-49	; Navy Insignia
Festival 49	35pr	30	20	26	20-Sep-49	; Israel Defence Army
Postage Due	02pr	J6	PD6	33	18-Dec-49	; orange
Postage Due	05pr	J7	PD7	34	18-Dec-49	; violet
Postage Due	10pr	J8	PD8	35	18-Dec-49	; green
Postage Due	20pr	J9	PD9	36	18-Dec-49	; red
Postage Due	30pr	J10	PD1	37	18-Dec-49	; blue
Postage Due	50pr	J11	PD1	38	18-Dec-49	; brown
Univ.Postal U	40pr	31	27	39	26-Mar-50	; Running Stag over Globe
Univ.Postal U	80pr	32	28	40	26-Mar-50	; Running Stag over Globe
2nd Independ.	20pr	33	29	41	23-Apr-50	; preindependence immigration
2nd Independ.	40pr	34	30	42	23-Apr-50	; immigration to new State
Hebrew Univ.	100pr	23	31	43	9-May-50	; Library on Mt Scopus
Festival 50	05pr	35	38	50	31-Aug-50	; Arthur Szyk- 4 species
Festival 50	15pr	36	39	51	31-Aug-50	; Arthur Szyk- 4 species
Coins 1950	10pr	41	43	55	19-Sep-50	; green
Coins 1950	15pr	42	44	56	22-Sep-50	; red
Coins 1950	05pr	40	42	54	4-Oct-50	; violet
Coins 1950	03pr	39	41	53	24-Oct-50	; ?grey
Coins 1950	50pr	59	46	58	13-Dec-50	; brown
Negev	500pr	25	47	59	26-Dec-50	; Camels drinking from pipe
Coins 1950	30pr	56	45	57	31-Dec-50	; blue
Tel Aviv	40pr	44	48	64	22-Mar-51	; 40th Anniversary
Independ Bnds	80pr	45	49	65	30-Apr-51	; Worker, outline map
3rd Independ.	15pr	46	50	66	9-May-51	; Metsudat Yesha
3rd Independ.	40pr	47	51	67	9-May-51	; The Castel
KerenKayemet	15pr	48	52	68	24-Jun-51	; Tractor
KerenKayemet	25pr	49	53	69	24-Jun-51	; Tree

Example 1: A table.
This is a cutout of an Israeli stamp listing formatted in Excel. It was loaded to the Windows clipboard. In Paintbrush it was pasted to a canvas and converted to a BMP file. In *xv* in Linux, the BMP file was reduced in size, borders were cropped and the file reformatted as a PS file.

Figure 24.8: A Partial List of Israeli Stamps

Example 2: A chart.
Excel has excellent 2-D and 3-D chart-making facilities. Data were plotted, charted and captioned. The chart was loaded to the Windows clipboard. It was pasted to a canvas in Paintbrush and converted to a BMP file. In Linux, it was reduced in size and reformatted in *xv* as a PS file.

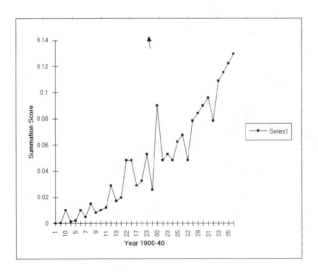

Figure 24.9: Summary

Second, you can't do a PCL-ghostscript-EPS end around. If you declare that your printer is Hewlett-Packard (it might actually be one), Windows will format your Excel file in the Hewlett-Packard PCL language and it will indeed print on a non-PostScript printer when you shift out of Windows to Linux. The catch is that the file is in binary, not ASCII, so ghostscript can't handle it.

So we shifted away from the printing process. Using the Excel copy command, a copy of a subsection of the file was put on the Windows clipboard. A new file was opened in Windows Paintbrush and the Excel image was pasted into it. It was saved as a BMP file— not our first choice—but it does provide a channel between Windows and Linux.[7] It can be translated to PostScript in *xv* or *ImageMagick*.

As a gedanken experiment, we think you may be able to move *formatted* pieces from Word or WordPerfect to Paintbrush in the same way, but we haven't tried.

---

[7]I understand that PCX is another Paintbrush format; this would permit file transfer to ImageMagick. But it is not available on our Windows 3.11.

Chapter 25

INSERTING COMPLETED PICTURES AND GRAPHICS

As we have seen, LaTeX creates a device-independent version of your source document. *dvips* then creates a PostScript version for printing. What is of interest is that another Post-Script file can be inserted into the raw document and become a seamless part of it. The insert can be text or an image or some combination of the two.

Actually, the insert is not physically brought in to the device independent file. LaTeX checks that it is present and leaves space and a marker to show where the insert belongs—it may have been shifted on the page, if it is part of a float object. Whenever *xdvi*, the screening program, is invoked, it brings in the insert on the fly. If you delete the PostScript file between two screenings, *xdvi* will screen what it has, with a note to you that it can't open the PS file. If you use *dvips* on a DVI file with a missing insert, the program will complain; it will, however, print the file without the insert.

Naturally, you can create a PostScript file for printing the whole document by using the -o option while the PostScript insert is available. The insert will be incorporated into the print-ready file, so your document will have a copy of it, even if you later physically delete the insert file.

The rest of this chapter talks about how to incorporate the insert.

The actual insertion of the completed drawing requires three operations:

1. You load *graphicx*,[1] a package written by David Carlisle and Sebastian Rahtz, by writing **\usepackage{graphicx}** in the preamble. *graphicx* needs to know the name of the printer driver.

2. The completed drawing must be an Encapsulated PostScript file or a single-page PostScript file with BoundingBox information.[2] The BoundingBox values tell *graphicx* how much space to allocate for the insert.

3. You select the spot where the program is to print the PostScript file in the document. Or you can bring it in as a float object and let the program place it amid the text.

25.1   Step 1: Linking The Printer Driver And *graphicx*

The actual inclusion of a graphics file into the LaTeX document is done by the printer driver. The printer driver is the program that converts your DVI file to PostScript. *dvips* handles files to be printed on a PostScript printer. *ghostscript* converts files to the right format so they can be printed on a non-PostScript printer. *graphicx* needs to know which printer driver you are using, so that it can load the correct instructions into the DVI file for including EPS graphics.

You involve the driver by loading the *graphicx package* with the driver name.

```
\usepackage[<printer driver>]{graphicx}
```

For example: `\usepackage[dvips]{graphicx}`

A better solution, because the name of the printer driver is necessary in several packages, is to write the name as an option in the *documentclass* command, this way:

---

[1]*epsf* and *psfig* are older packages that enable the inclusion of an EPS graphic into a document. They use the BoundingBox size to typeset a properly-sized box. The user can override this by issuing his own size specifications. A later package, *epsfig*, is a composite of *epsf* and *psfig*. In the current version of LaTeX, the syntax of the older packages persist in two newer packages: *graphics* and *graphicx*. *graphicx*—the **x** is for eXtended—has simpler syntax, so we use it here.

[2]An EPS file *is* a PostScript file with BoundingBox information and the elimination of certain PostScript commands.

```
\documentclass[dvips,10pt...]{article}
```

25.2   Step 2: Size Information In The EPS File

LATEX can insert a file written in Encapsulated PostScript; i.e., the file is in PostScript
format and somewhere near the top of the file it contains boundary box information. Or it
can insert a PostScript file with the same size information, as long as particular PostScript
commands are omitted. These are two examples of usable PS files; both were created in
Linux, both print in Linux. The second one is independent of TEX dictionary resources and
can be tranferred across platforms.

Example 1: exlet1.ps

```
%!PS-Adobe-2.0
%%Creator: dvipsk 5.58f Copyright 1986, 1994 Radical Eye Software
%%Title: exlet1.dvi
%%Pages: 1
%%PageOrder: Ascend
%%BoundingBox: 0 0 612 792
%%DocumentPaperSizes: Letter
%%EndComments
%DVIPSCommandLine: dvips -o exlet1.ps exlet1.dvi
%DVIPSParameters: dpi=1200, comments removed
%DVIPSSource:  TeX output 1997.08.30:2238
%%BeginProcSet: tex.pro
/TeXDict 250 dict def TeXDict begin /N{def}def /B{bind def}N /S{exch}N
/X{S N}B /TR{translate}N /isls false N /vsize 11 72 mul N /hsize 8.5 72
....
%%EndProlog
%%BeginSetup
%%Feature: *Resolution 1200dpi
TeXDict begin
%%PaperSize: Letter
..............
%%EndSetup
%%Page: 1 1
1 0 bop 5026 2824 a Fa(W)-14 b(riter's)56 b(street)e(address)5026
...........
%%Trailer
end
```

```
userdict /end-hook known{end-hook}if
%%EOF
```

```
Example 2: alice05a.ps
```

```
%!PS-Adobe-2.0 EPSF-2.0
%%Title: /usr/local/images/alice05a.ps
%%Creator: XV Version 3.10a  Rev: 12/29/94  -  by John Bradley
%%BoundingBox: 223 311 388 481
%%Pages: 1
%%DocumentFonts:
%%EndComments
%%EndProlog
%%Page: 1 1
% remember original state
/origstate save def
........
```

25.2.1   The BoundingBox

LaTeX needs to know the size of the incoming image. The information is transmitted by the four number following *%%BoundingBox*. If the PostScript file doesn't have this information, you can try adding it; this will often produce a file LaTeX can handle.

The four numbers in the BoundingBox describe the x,y coordinates of the bottom left corner of the insert and the x,y coordinates of the top right corner. They are given in points, so the measurement unit is omitted.

BottomLeft x   BottomLeft y   TopRight x   TopRight y

In *exlet1.ps* above, these are: 0 0 612 792. The inches measurement is obtained by dividing the points measure by 72. 0 0 612 792 are routine with 8.5 x 11 inch paper, when the whole page is included in the PostScript image.

If you have a printout of the insert, you can measure the actual image yourself. Say it is a 5 by 7 inch picture centered on 8.5 by 11 inch paper. You can do the measurements in inches and then convert the numbers to points by multiplying by 72.[3]

---

[3]This is one of the times a little knowledge will mislead you. Do NOT try for enhanced accuracy by multiply-

1. **Bottom x.** Measure the distance across from the left side of the paper to the bottom left corner of the picture. It should be 1.75 inches. 1.75 x 72 is 126.

2. **Bottom y.** Measure the distance up from the bottom of the paper to the bottom left corner of the picture. It should be 2 inches. 2 x 72 is 144.

3. **Top x.** Measure the distance from the left side of the paper across to the top right corner of the picture. It should be 6.75 inches. 6.75 x 72 is 486.

4. **Top y.** Measure the distance from the bottom of the paper up to the top right corner of the picture. It should be 9 inches. 9 x 72 is 648.

The BoundingBox dimensions for the image are: 126 144 486 648. It is just as simple to capture a part of the image. These are some of the ways to determine picture location so that you can crop the picture out of the white space or chop out a small region.

⋆ Actually measure a printed copy of the picture as we did above. Change the BoundingBox information in the PostScript file, or add it as an option to the \includegraphics command, as shown in Section 25.4.1.

⋆ Use *ghostview*, which continuously tracks the position of the cursor in pixels. Just move the cursor to the points you wish to measure. This may not be quite as accurate, but it's seldom that a few pixels more or less matter. Change the BoundingBox information in the PostScript file, or add it as an option to the \includegraphics command. (See Section 25.4.1.)

⋆ Perhaps the simplest way is to bring the image while it is still formatted in JPEG or GIF or whatever into *xv*, crop and size the image and change its orientation while continuously viewing the effect(s) on the image. Shaping the picture can be done fairly quickly. When you are satisfied, ship it out of *xv* as a PostScript file.

xv outputs Encapsulated PostScript; but it doesn't input an EPS file for processing. So you can't use *xv* to shape a small text document you wrote in LaTeX and want to include in your larger document. (See Section 3.4.) Moreover, there are times that you can not prepare the image(s) exactly ahead of time. In a page layout involving several images, you may need

---

ing by 72.27. It's true that there are 72.27 points in an inch. But we need to use EPS points, which are exactly 72 points to the inch. These are also known as Big Points (bp).

several trials to place them, resize and reorient them in context and rearrange them.[4] At
these times, you may prefer to make last-minute changes with the commands available in
graphicx. The only catch is that TEX doesn't do floating point arithmetic. Fortunately, the
calc package makes it possible to handle the simple values you need in order to size and
orient figures.

25.2.2   The *calc* package

LATEX accepts only simple values in the arguments of commands such as *setcounter*, *addtocounter*, *setlength* and *addtolength*. The *calc* program [Thorup95] lets you use concaten-
tated expressions and real values.

The usual operators are used: + - / and *. Use () parentheses to group values if the precedence rules don't lump the values as you would wish.

The precedence rules are:

1. The program reads from left to right.

2. Multiplication and division are done before addition and subtraction.

We define a counter and a length for our examples. A *counter* has a simple name, a *length*
a command name.


```
\newcounter{CountO} %This ends in Uppercase o, not zero.
\newlength{\LenO}    %This ends Uppercase o, not zero.
```


Addition and subtraction. In counters, you add undimensioned values. In lengths, you
add and subtract dimensioned values; e.g., 5cm + 7mm. When the program expects
dimensions, you can not add a dimensioned value and a non-dimensioned value,
or two non-dimensioned values; *5cm + 7* is not acceptable. As in Section 17.1.2,
prepending a *the* to a particular counter or length produces a variable that stores the
current value of the counter/length.

---

[4]Some of the graphic packages discussed in the previous chapter are efficient if you can use them. Aside from
shaping single pictures in *xv*, with a little practice, you can layout a simple composition of picture objects in Xfig.

The MarkUp: *The PrintOut:*

```
\setcounter{Count0}{(4 + 3) * 5}
\setlength{\Len0}{(4mm + 3pt) * 5}
What is Count0? \textbf{\theCount0}\\
What is Len0? \textbf{\the\Len0}\\
\setcounter{Count0}{300 - \value{page}}
What is Count0? \textbf{\theCount0}\\
```

What is Count0? **35**
What is Len0? **71.90544pt**
What is Count0? **-96**

Without the parenthesis, the program would multiply 3 by 5 and then add 4. With the parentheses, 4 and 3 are first added and the result multiplied by 5.

Multiplication/division by an integer. You can multiply and divide a dimensioned value by an integer; e.g., 5cm * 6 * 7. Write the dimensioned value first.

The MarkUp: *The PrintOut:*
                 Vertical Length:

```
Vertical Length:%
\setlength{\vspace}{9pc/4/ 2 * 2}\\

\setlength{\Len0}{9pc / 2 / 4 * 3}\\
What is Len0? \prbf{\the\Len0}\\
What is the framebox?
\framebox[9cm/2/4 * 3]{}
```

What is Len0? **40.5pt**
What is the framebox?

Multiplication/division by a real number. You multiple or divide a dimensioned value by *real* or by *ratio*.

1. <dimensioned quantity> * \real{number}—a number with a fractional or decimal component. The command \SpaceO below produces a vertical distance.

   The MarkUp: *The PrintOut:*

   ```
   What is SpaceO?
   \newcommand{\SpaceO}{\setlength%
   {\vspace}{4pc / \real{1.2}}} \SpaceO

   \setlength{\Len0}{4pt * \real{1.7}}
   What is Len0? \prbf{\the\Len0}
   ```

   What is SpaceO?

   What is Len0? **6.79999pt**

2. <dimensioned quantity> * \ratio{dimensioned num1}{dimensioned num2}.

The MarkUp: *The PrintOut:*

```
\setlength{\Len0}%
{4pt * \ratio{\textwidth}{100pt}}
What is Len0? \prbf{\the\Len0}
```

What is Len0? **6.50427pt**

25.3   Step 3: Using The graphicx *\includegraphics* Command

The **\includegraphics** command in *graphicx* [Carlisle95b] allows you to insert a photo or picture or graphics or drawing or stylized text produced by other programs into a LaTeX document.

A figure that is full-page will, of course, take a page of its own. Otherwise, it will take the space of its box-size equivalent. If the figure is small enough, it can be added to the words on a line of text.

This *Mona Lisa* came from the set of the minilogos in the X11R6 *pixmaps* directory; it was further reduced in size and formatted as a PostScript file.

If you have manipulated the figure in a graphics package so that it is the right size and orientation, just give the *includegraphics* command wherever you want to position it in the document. These next markups demonstrate how to include a image. A complete markup is shown for the first example. The others show just the special formatting.

As a picture in a figure: Insert the image within a figure so it will float.

```
\documentclass[dvips,10pt,twoside,letterpaper]{article}
\includepackage{graphicx,color}
\begin{document}
. . . . . . . . . . . . . . . .
\begin{figure}[!]
\centering
\includegraphics{max.ps}
\caption{A frame from a camcorder movie. }
\end{figure}
. . . . . . . . . . . . . . . .
\end{document}
```

In a pair of minipages in a figure: Insert the image within a minipage so that notes can be written next to the picture. The pair of minipages are placed within a figure so they can be floated.

```
\begin{figure}[!]
\begin{minipage}{2in}
\itshape This picture derives from a Snappy\TM\ capture of a
single frame from a Hi-8 camcorder movie. The picture was
brought into \prit{xv} as a GIF file, reduced in size,
cropped and converted to an EPS file.
\end{minipage}
\hfill
\begin{minipage}[2.5in]
\includegraphics{max.ps}
\end{minipage}
\caption{A frame from a camcorder movie.}
\end{figure}
```

In a minipage using a newcommand macro: Use new commands such as *InPix* or *FramePix*, where *InPix* brings in an unframed picture, *FramePix* a framed picture. Each has three arguments. The first establishes where the figure should meet the current baseline. If you don't fill in the first argument, the top of the image will be on the baseline. The second argument is the size of the frame. You can fill the third argument with text and an includegraphics command. (*bmp* and *emp* are aliases for \begin{minipage} and \end{minipage}, respectively.) These macros can of course be enclosed in a float as in the previous example.

```
\newcommand{\InPix}[3][t]{\bmp[#1]{#2} #3 \emp }
\newcommand{\FramePix}[3][t]{\fbox{\bmp[#1]{#2} #3 \emp }}
```

As example, this will frame an image, resting the center of the image on the current text line. Instead of encapsulating it in a float, we add some text.

```
\FramePix[c]{3in}{\centering\includegraphics{max.ps}\\
Max L. \\ multiscan.\\ no compression.}
```

In a minipage using a newenvironment macro:

If the image format will be used throughout the report or book (as a page logo, say) then it is better to use one of these two macros because they save the format, thus cutting the time it takes the program to recreate it. (See Section 23.5 for an explanation of the lrbox environment.) Moreover, a new environment macro is easier to use than a command if the text is expansive. The first macro encloses text and image in a minipage, the second in a framed minipage.

```
\newsavebox{\PlainPixer}
\newenvironment{PlainPix}[2][t]%
{\begin{lrbox}{\PlainPixer}\begin{minipage}[#1]{#2} }%
{\end{minipage}\end{lrbox}\usebox{\PlainPixer}}

\newsavebox{\FrameIt}
\newenvironment{FRM}[2][t]%
{\begin{lrbox}{\FrameIt}\begin{minipage}[#1]{#2} }%
{\end{minipage}\end{lrbox}\fbox{\usebox{\FrameIt}}}
```

This for example would put an unframed picture by the side of some text within a float. *\PlainPix* is made 4 inches wide, sufficient for the text plus an inch wide picture. It rests on the current text line. We put a minipage inside the PlainPix box to limit the width of the text and rest its bottom on the text page—so the text and picture will be aligned. *\hfill* fills the area between the minipage and the picture with empty space, thus separating them. Because it is a float, we can caption the two parts of the PlainPix box with one caption.

The Markup For Figure 25.1

```
\bfig[h]
\begin{PlainPix}[t]{4in}
\bmp[b]{2.8in}
Max L.\\
This was a color photograph that was viewed through a Hi-8
camcorder and digitized by Snappy\TM as a GIF file.
\emp
\hfill\centering
\includegraphics[width=1in]{max.ps}
\end{PlainPix}
```

```
\caption{Image Capture} \label{fig:Icapture}
\efig
```

Max L.
This was a color photograph that was viewed through a Hi-8 camcorder and transmitted as a GIF file using Snappy.

Figure 25.1: Image Capture

25.4 *\includegraphics* **Options**

This section and much of the rest of this Chapter owe a debt to Keith Reckdahl's very readable discussion of EPS Graphics [Reckdahl96]. D.P. Carlisle's *Packages in the 'graphics' bundle* [Carlisle95b] is also must reading.

A graphic object is characterized, as is any box in LaTeX, by a reference point and three length measurements. There is also a composite measure, *totalheight*, that is the sum of *height* and *depth*. This figure shows the Box sizes for a figure rotated from its upright position; **B–D** is the bottom of the figure when it is at rest. At rest, the figure has no depth; i.e., totalheight is the same as height.

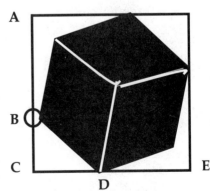

B. *reference point* is the lower left corner of the image when the figure is upright.

B–A. *height* is the distance from the reference point to the top of the space taken by the figure.

B–C. *depth* is the distance from the reference point to the bottom of space taken by the figure. Failure to take *depth* into account in a rotated picture can lead to incorrectly-placed objects.

C–E. *width* is the distance across the figure.

Figure 25.2: Measuring the Picture.

With no optional values, graphicx will bring in the picture and deposit it according to the size stipulated in the BoundingBox values and the orientation it had when it was formatted as an EPS file.

25.4.1   Resetting the BoundingBox

This is an important feature. If the PostScript file don't have BoundingBox parameters, you can set them here. This is also a way to reset the BoundingBox without having to bring a hefty PS file into the editor.

Use *bb* as the options parameter. If, for example, a picture is sized as [0 0 200 300], then **\includegraphics[bb=72 72 200 300,clip]{sarah.ps}** would delete an inch from the left and bottom margins of the image, leaving the rest of the image intact.

You can also change individual coordinates. Use *bbllx, bblly, bburx* and *bbury*. For example, **\includegraphics[bbllx=72,bblly=72]** would remove an inch from the left and bottom margins of the image, leaving the rest of the image intact.

If you need to check that you have the exact area of the image that you want, write a macro such as *\testpix*, which frames the image. *\testpix* has one argument: the *\includegraphics* statement. Correct the BoundingBox values and view the results in a simplified document such as this.

```
\documentclass[10pt]{article}
\usepackage[dvips]{graphicx}
. . . . . . . . . . . . . . .
\begin{document}
\newcommand{\testpix}[1]{\fbox{\begin{minipage}[c]{\textwidth}
  #1 \end{minipage} }}

\begin{figure}[!]
\testpix{\includegraphics[bb=95 220 625 550,clip]{exslide1.ps}}
\caption{A framed image.}
\end{figure}
\end{document}
```

25.4.2 *viewport*: resetting the part of the picture to exhibit

This is relative to the left bottom corner of the current BoundingBox. If the BoundingBox is [100 100 300 400], then **\includegraphics[\viewport=100 100 172 172,clip]{sarah.eps}** would exhibit the corner inch of the picture.

25.4.3 Resetting exhibition width

If you specify a new width and not a height, the picture will be adjusted in width so the proportions stay accurate; i.e., the aspect ratio remains constant. Similarly, if the picture is changed just in height, the width will be changed to keep things in proportion. But if you change both, you're on your way to writing your own morph program.

If you exhibit the same sorts of pictures in different but fixed sizes, you can save typing and enforce consistency by defining some size names. They can be set to specific sizes that you fine tune for different layouts.

These define and set three command names for small, medium and large picture sizes (relative to a book page). They will exhibit the same input picture in three different sizes.

```
\newlength{\spix}\setlength{\spix}{1.5in}
\includegraphics[width=\spix]{sam.ps}

\newlength{\mpix}\setlength{\mpix}{2.5in}
\includegraphics[width=\mpix]{sam.ps}

\newlength{\lpix}\setlength{\lpix}{5in}
\includegraphics[width=\lpix]{sam.ps}
```

These are five different ways of requesting the same width—assuming you've loaded the *calc* package. The *\textwidth* of a text line was defined for this book as 5 inches; so these all allow 2.5 inches for the width of the picture. The program adjusts the height to maintain picture proportion.

```
\includegraphics[width=2.5in]{sam.ps}
\includegraphics[width=.5\textwidth]{sam.ps}
```

```
\includegraphics[width=\textwidth-2.5in]{sam.ps}
\includegraphics[width=\mpix]{sam.ps}
\includegraphics[width=\lpix-2.5in]{sam.ps}
```

25.4.4　Resetting exhibition height

You can also request LATEX to zoom or shrink the picture by manipulating its height rather than its width. You can indicate the exhibition height in the same way you describe width changes. These are three ways to zoom the input picture to the same size. The third entry uses totalheight, rather than height. This makes no difference in ordinary upright pictures. It does with rotated pictures.

```
\includegraphics[height=3.5in]{sam.ps}
\includegraphics[height=\mpix+1in]{sam.ps}
\includegraphics[totalheight=\lpix-1.5in]{sam.ps}
```

Figure 25.3 shows how to define the exhibition size of a picture stored as an EPS file. If you tell the program to change both height and width, it will; the picture will likely be distorted.

The Markup For Figure 25.3

```
\subfigure[width: 1.5"]{\includegraphics[width=1.5in]{sam.ps}}
\hspace{.25in}
\subfigure[height: 1"]{\includegraphics[height=1in]{sam.ps}}
\hspace{.25in}
\subfigure[width: 1.5"; height: 1"]%
{\includegraphics[width=1.5in,height=1in]{sam.ps}}
\caption{Changing the size of the input picture}\label{fig:size}
```

25.4.5　Scaling: another way to reset size

The optional *width and height* parameters exhibit the picture at specific sizes, no matter what the original size is. Scaling increases/decreases the size of the picture relative to the original size. Thus, **[scale=2]** would double the size of the picture.

The PrintOut:

(a) width: 1.5"   (b)   (c) width: 1.5"; height: 1"
                      height:
                      1"

Figure 25.3: Changing the size of the input picture

25.4.6   Resetting exhibition orientation

Units must be integer and at least as large as the original. You can't use this *\includegraph-ics* option to decrease the size of the original picture—the program informs you that you are attempting to divide by zero.

Figure 25.4 shows changes in orientation. The exhibited picture retains the size of the stored image. Notice that shifts are done counterclockwise. A 45°[5] shift is at 11 o'clock, not 1 o'clock.

The Markup For Figure 25.4

```
\newcommand{\td}{\textdegree }
\bfig[!]
\subfigure[Angle: 0\td.]{\hspace{1.65in}\bmp[c]{2.5in}
\includegraphics[angle=0]{esther.ps}\emp}
```

---

[5]The degree sign was made using the *\textdegree* symbol in the *textcomp* package. To save space in the markup, it was given the alias: *\td*. Similarly, *\bfig* and *\efig* stand for begin and end figure. And *\bmp* and *\emp* are replacements for begin and end minipage.

```
\vspace{-.75in}
\subfigure[Angle: 45\td.]{\bmp[c]{1.5in}
\includegraphics[angle=45]{esther.ps}\emp}
\hfill
\subfigure[Angle: 315\td.]{\bmp[c]{1.5in}
\includegraphics[angle=315]{esther.ps}\emp}
\vspace{.25in}

\subfigure[Angle: 90\td.]{\bmp[c]{1.5in}
\includegraphics[angle=90]{esther.ps}\emp}
\hfill
\subfigure[Angle: 270\td.]{\bmp[c]{1.5in}
\includegraphics[angle=270]{esther.ps}\emp}

\subfigure[Angle: 135\td.]{\bmp[c]{1.5in}
\includegraphics[angle=135]{esther.ps}\emp}
\hfill
\subfigure[Angle: 225\td.]{\bmp[c]{1.5in}
\includegraphics[angle=225]{esther.ps}
\vspace{.2in}\emp}

\vspace{-.75in}\hspace{1.65in}
\subfigure[Angle: 180\td.]{\bmp{1.5in}
\includegraphics[angle=180]{esther.ps}\emp}

\caption{Picture Rotation.}\label{fig:rotate}
\efig
```

In Figure 25.4, the input picture retained its size through the entire set of rotations. On the
other hand, if we tell the program to maintain a particular width, the picture changes actual
size at different orientations. Because the width that is maintained is the BoundingBox
width at that angle, not the width of the original picture. Figure 25.2 shows the Bounding-
Box at a 30°angle; the width is **C–E**. When the object is at rest—when **B–D** are horizontal
and run along the BoundingBox—then **B–D** is the width. At positions 0° and 180°, the
picture measures 1" across; at 90° and 270°, the side of the picture measures 1" across. In
the other orientations, the picture measures 1" across its widest extent.

The PrintOut:

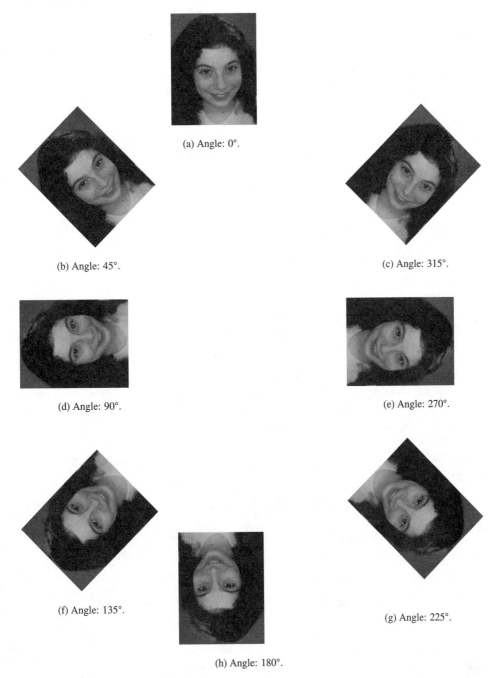

(a) Angle: 0°.

(b) Angle: 45°.

(c) Angle: 315°.

(d) Angle: 90°.

(e) Angle: 270°.

(f) Angle: 135°.

(g) Angle: 225°.

(h) Angle: 180°.

Figure 25.4: Picture Rotation.

The Markup For Figure 25.5

```
\NC{\td}{\textdegree }
\bfig[!]
\subfigure[Angle:  0\td.]{\hspace{1.65in}\bmp[c]{2.5in}
\includegraphics[angle=0,width=1in]{sarah.ps}\emp}

\vspace{-.75in}
\subfigure[Angle:  45\td.]{\bmp[c]{1.5in}
\includegraphics[angle=45,width=1in]{sarah.ps}\emp}
\hfill
\subfigure[Angle:  315\td.]{\bmp[c]{1.5in}
\includegraphics[angle=315,width=1in]{sarah.ps}
\emp
\vspace{.25in}

\subfigure[Angle:  90\td.]{\bmp[c]{1.5in}
\includegraphics[angle=90,width=1in]{sarah.ps}\emp}
\hfill
\subfigure[Angle:  270\td.]{\bmp[c]{1.5in}
\includegraphics[angle=270,width=1in]{sarah.ps}\emp}

\subfigure[Angle:  135\td.]{\bmp[c]{1.5in}
\includegraphics[angle=135,width=1in]{sarah.ps}\emp}
\hfill
\subfigure[Angle:  225\td.]{\bmp[c]{1.5in}
\includegraphics[angle=225,width=1in]{sarah.ps}
\vspace{.2in}\emp}

\vspace{-.75in}\hspace{1.65in}
\subfigure[Angle:  180\td.]{\bmp{1.75in}
\includegraphics[angle=180,width=1in]{sarah.ps}\emp}

\caption{Rotating a picture 1" wide.}\label{fig:keepwidth}
\efig
```

25.4.7   The interaction between size and orientation

Figure 25.6 sums up the interactions between size and orientation. The rule is: width/height AND angle are not commutative; i.e., it matters which option you write first. Scale and angle are commutative.

The PrintOut:

(a) Angle: 0°. Width: 1".

(b) Angle: 45°. Width: 1". (c) Angle: 315°. Width: 1".

(d) Angle: 90°. Width: 1". (e) Angle: 270°. Width: 1".

(f) Angle: 135°. Width: 1". (g) Angle: 225°. Width: 1".

(h) Angle: 180°. Width: 1".

Figure 25.5: Rotating a picture 1" wide.

The Original Picture

Changing Size OR Angle

Width is 1.2 in.

Scale is 1.2.

Angle is 30°.

Changing Size AND Angle

| Width is 1.2 in.
Angle is 30°. | Angle is 30°.
Width is 1.2 in. | Scale is 1.2.
Angle is 30°. | Angle is 30°.
Scale is 1.2 |

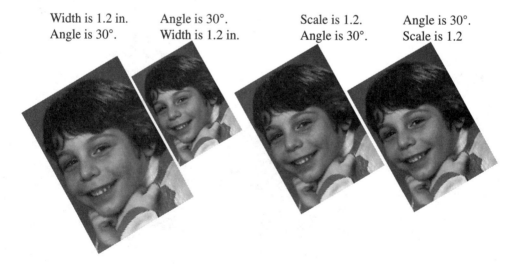

Figure 25.6: Interactions between Size and Orientation

25.4.8   Resetting the origin of rotation

By default, rotation is around the reference point, the figure's baseline. (See Figure 25.2.) But the origin can also be the exact center of the picture. Actually, it can be rotated around any box point that can be described by one member from each of these two groups:

Left/Right/Center (l/r/c)
Top/Bottom/Baseline (t/b/B)

Using Figure 25.2 as an example, **A** is tl; **B** is lB; **C** is lb; **D** is cb; **E** is rb.

To demonstrate the difference the origin makes in positioning a picture, in Figure 25.7 we first superimposed two copies of a picture, both rotated around A. That's the pair of figures on the left. Then pictures rotated around A and E were shifted by the same amount. If origin of rotation had no effect, the A and E pictures would also be superimposed.

The MarkUp:

```
\bmp{2in}
A: \includegraphics[origin=tl,angle=30]{max.ps}
\vspace{-1.33in}\hspace{-1.62in}
A: \includegraphics[origin=tl,angle=30]{max.ps}
\emp
\bmp{2in}
A: \includegraphics[origin=tl,angle=30]{max.ps}
\vspace{-1.33in}\hspace{-1.62in}
E: \includegraphics[origin=br,angle=30]{max.ps}
\emp
```

25.4.9   Color

Load the *color* package by writing a *\usepackage{color}* command in the preamble.

A: A:

Figure 25.7: Demonstrating Origin of Rotation

Color Models

The graphics packages can handle instructions that allow you to describe colors in terms of any one of these color models.

rgb The Red Green Blue model is additive. A defined color is specified by three numbers that represent the three primary colors: R G B. Numbers are separated by commas, and each number has a value between 0 and 1.

cmyk The Cyan Magenta Yellow Black model is used in the printing industry, especially in halftones. The surface color is the result of the proportion of tiny balls of the four colors. (Remember the Sunday comics?) Its values are specified by four numbers, each between 0 and 1, and separated by commas, for the four colors: C M Y B.

gray Gray scale is denoted by a single number between 0 and 1. The closer the number to zero, the darker the gray.

named These colors are accessed by name. With appropriate instructions, they can come from many models, including colors from the XWindows System. (*dvips* itself contributes over 60 named colors.) See [Carlisle95b] for the various options for hooking in colors from different models or ignoring them.

To Define A Color

Primary colors are predefined: red, green, blue, cyan, magenta, yellow, black and white.

In addition, you can mix your own colors using the \definecolor command. A color definition command takes three arguments:

Syntax: \definecolor{<*name*>}{<*model*>}{<*color specification*>}

The name is equivalent to an alias. It is your terminology. The model is one of the ones LaTeX accepts. The color specification indicates how much each of the color primaries should contribute to the new color.

There is nothing to stop you from overwriting a predefined color. For example, you could write:

\definecolor{red}{rgb}{0,0,1}

This would color the text blue, whenever you asked for red. These examples are more likely.

```
\definecolor{LBlue}{rgb}{0.7,0.8,1}  %Light Blue
\definecolor{DBlue}{rgb}{0.4,0.3,1}  %Dark Blue
\definecolor{LGreen}{rgb}{0.9,1,.8}  %Light Green
\definecolor{DGreen}{rgb}{.2,1,.2}   %Dark Green
\definecolor{SideBar}{gray}{0.75}    %SideBar Gray
\definecolor{LGray}{gray}{.80}       %Light Gray
\definecolor{MGray}{gray}{0.6}       %Medium Gray
\definecolor{DGray}{gray}{0.1}       %Dark Gray
```

As with fonts, there is a command format for coloring a small area of the text and there is a declaration format for coloring larger areas of text. And there's a way to paint the background and boxes.

Command Format To Color Text.

Syntax: \textcolor{<*colorname*>}{<*text*>}

The MarkUp: *The PrintOut:*

```
\textcolor{DGray}{This is dark gray}
\textcolor{LGray}{followed by light gray.}
```

This is dark gray followed by light gray.

Declaration Format To Color Text.

Syntax: \color{<*colorname*>}

The MarkUp: *The PrintOut:*

```
\color{DGray}
This is dark gray that could go
on for a long while, except we
override it with light gray.
\color{LGray}
The rest of the text that
follows is in light gray.
Now let's go back to
ordinary black font.
\color{black}
```

This is dark gray that could go on for a long while, except we override it with light gray. The rest of the text that follows is in light gray. Now let's go back to ordinary black font.

Declaration Format To Color A Page

The page color is white by default. Otherwise, it is the last color declared on the page—in the next example, a Dark Gray page color is overridden by Medium Gray. It is global so it continues until the end of the document, unless you declare another page color before the page ends.

Syntax: \pagecolor{<*colorname*>}

The MarkUp: *The PrintOut:*

```
\pagecolor{DGray}
This is a way to color the
background paper. The font
is black because we haven't
assigned it a color.
\pagecolor{MGray}
```

This is a way to color the background paper. The font is black because we haven't assigned it a color.

Command Format To Color A Box

There is a command for coloring a box and another for coloring a framed box. Moreover, you can use *\fboxrule* and *\fboxsep* to modify the appearance of the framed box. (See Section 23.1.3.) The colored and framed box is shown.

Syntax:

```
\colorbox{<boxcolor>}{<text>}
\fcolorbox{<framecolor>}{<boxcolor>}{<text>}
```

The MarkUp:

The PrintOut:

```
\fcolorbox{DGray}{MGray}{
\begin{minipage}{1.45in}
Write the colorbox around the
minipage, not inside the
minipage. The minipage controls
the width of the box. If the
colorbox is the inner box,
the text will run on.
\end{minipage}
}
```

Write the colorbox around the minipage, not inside the minipage. The minipage controls the width of the box. If the colorbox is the inner box, the text will run on.

Macros To Frame And Highlight Text

These two macros frame and highlight text. The first uses the previous construction—a *\fcolorbox* command as the outer brackets to a framed minipage; the second uses a colorbox and framebox construction. The first does not save the template. So every time you use it, it takes time for it to operate and it takes memory. The second saves the box template, so that memory storage is reduced. As is the time it takes the program to redraw the box. Both widen the distance from text to frame.

To frame and highlight a minipage.

The FCM command has two placeholders: (1) the width of the box and (2) the contents of the box. The height of the constructed box is increased by 40% of the baselineskip to improve appearance.

Syntax:

```
\definecolor{LGray}{gray}{.80}
```

```
\definecolor{DGray}{gray}{.10}

\newcommand{\FCM}[2]{\fcolorbox{DGray}{LGray}%
{\begin{minipage}[t]%
[\height+.4\baselineskip][t]{#1} #2
\end{minipage}} }
```

The MarkUp: *The PrintOut:*

```
\FCM{1.5in}{
\textbf{HIGHLIGHTS:}
\be
\item fcolorbox has 2 arguments:
the frame is dark gray;
the box background is light gray.

\item The argument of the minipage
controls the width.

\item There's a little extra space
between the frame and the start
of the text.
\ee
}
```

> **HIGHLIGHTS:**
>
> 1. fcolorbox has 2 arguments: the frame is dark gray; the box background is light gray.
>
> 2. The argument of the minipage controls the width.
>
> 3. There's a little extra space between the frame and the start of the text.

To save, frame and highlight a minipage.

The program is instructed to find storage for a box called *FPage*, whose length will be increased by a 1/3 of a text line, once it is constructed. The width of this box is a variable; i.e., you fill it with whatever width you want the box to be. The macro is very similar to the one constructed in Example 6, Section 23.5.

The command \FC brackets the box with a outer color directive. This template is of interest in that, like the first one above, it has two variables—placeholders—(1) the width of the box; and (2) the contents. The first variable belongs to the new environment *FPP*, which contains the minibox which is given that width. We notify the program that *FC* has two placeholders, but the first is an argument of *FPP*. The second is an ordinary placehold, pinpointing where the contents of the box will be written.

Syntax:

```
\newsavebox{\FPage}
\newenvironment{FPP}[1]%
{\begin{lrbox}{\FPage}%
\begin{minipage}[t]%
[\height+.3\baselineskip][s]{#1}}%
{\end{minipage}\end{lrbox}%
\fbox{\usebox{\FPage}}}

\newcommand{\FC}[2]%
{\colorbox{LGray}{\begin{FPP}{#1} #2
\end{FPP} }}
```

The MarkUp: *The PrintOut:*

```
\FC{2.6in}{
\textbf{HIGHLIGHTS:}
\be
\item The lrbox and minipage frame
a large chunk of text.

\item The program writes the box
once only.

\item You can use it many times
with no additional cost in time
or \LaTeX\ memory.

\item Just master the syntax.
\ee
}
```

HIGHLIGHTS:

1. The lrbox and minipage frame a large chunk of text.

2. The program writes the box once only.

3. You can use it many times with no additional cost in time or LaTeX memory.

4. Just master the syntax.

25.4.10   Saving space with a EPS repetitive image

The previous section recapitulated the technique first discussed in Section 23.5 for saving a box format that is used often. It is useful for boxes created in LaTeX, and can be used for the LaTeX picture environment. As Section 25.3 demonstrates, it can even be used to save time and LaTeX memory with inserted Encapsulated PostScript files.

However, we also need to consider the burden an EPS file imposes on printer memory. When you run *dvips* to create a PostScript file for printing, each inserted EPS file must be completely stored. If, say, you include an clipart icon as part of the header or a GIMP image in the corner of every page, the printer may run out of memory.

A solution is to divide up the much used EPS file so that the major part of it needs to be read by the printer only once. I am indebted to Keith Reckdahl [Reckdahl96] for the technique; he, in turn, credits Jim Hafner, author of the *FoilTEX* package (see Section 12.4).

A well-structured PostScript file basically consists of two parts: (1) an initial *Prolog*, which contains a set of procedure definitions appropriate to the application; followed by (2) a *Script* that contains the page data as well as references to PostScript operators and Prolog definitions.

The Prolog itself starts with a set of Comments, which includes the BoundingBox information and other environmental conditions—precisely the information that LATEX needs. The rest of the PostScript file isn't needed until print time. *exlet1.ps*, Example 1, Section 25.2 (the PS file of a demonstration letter from Section 3.5) conforms to this model. The Comment Section is:

```
%!PS-Adobe-2.0
. . . . . . . . . . . . . .
%%EndComments
```

The rest of the Prolog starts the line after **%%EndComments**:

%DVIPSCommandLine: dvips -o exlet1.ps exlet1.dvi

It continues until the line that reads: **%%EndProlog**. TeXDict is the dictionary utility that provides the information to actually print the file; i.e., it can't be printed on a machine that doesn't have access to that particular dictionary.

The Script begins immediately after the Prolog with a **%%BeginSetup-%%EndSetup** section followed by a Page section that continues to the end of the file. (In *xv* and *Xpaint* Encapsulated PostScript files, the Page section may follow immediately after the Prolog.)

To use *exlet1.ps* many times in the document, save a copy of the file out of harm's way, should you ever need the original. Then in Emacs, chop the master file in two separate files. Using *exlet1.ps* as example:

exlet1.ps This file will contain the initial Comments. Actually, it does no harm to keep the few lines that start with %% after the %%EndComments with the Comments. This file is used as the argument of an *\includegraphics* command, just as the complete .ps file was.

exlet1.h This will contain the bulk of the file; i.e., the rest of the Prolog and the Script. This file is declared in the preamble as a *special* file.

```
\documentclass[dvips,10pt]{article}
\usepackage{graphicx}
\usepackage{color}
\special{header=exlet1.h}
...........
\begin{document}
...
\includegraphics{exlet1.ps}
............
\newpage
\includegraphics{exlet1.ps} %Use it as often as you wish.
\end{document}
```

Some cautionary notes.

- This is a useful technique for a single image that is used over an entire book. So select that image carefully.

- LaTeX essentially ignores the special header. So it will not record an error, even if you do things wrong in separating the master file. If there's a problem, you'll get error messages when you run the *xdvi* program. Separated properly or not, the image won't appear on the screen. To view the image, create a PS file for your document and view that with ghostview or print it.

- An alternate technique is discussed in [Reckdahl96, Section 10.2]. The Script in enclosed in a user-chosen command name. The dictionary that operates on the Script is then named on the last line of the file containing the Comments (exlet1.ps in our example). If /NEWLET is the command name, the last line of *exlet1.ps* would read: **TeXDict begin /NEWLET end**.

25.4.11   Draft version

If the insert is complex and takes a long time to appear on the screen and you are still in the process of debugging the manuscript, you can use the draft option in *documentclass*; e.g. **\documentclass[draft,dvips]{book}**. Or you can put just the insert in draft mode; e.g. **\usepackage[draft,dvips]{graphicx}**. In both cases the program will print the outline of a box the size of the insert.

25.4.12   Other *graphicx* commands

As an option in *includegraphics*, you can write graphical rules to handle various classes of files, even compressed files. You can write rules, say, to transform GIF and TIFF files into EPS files while running LaTeX. And there is an entire set of separate commands in graphicx that size and scale text. (See [Reckdahl96] for a thorough discussion.)

Part VIII.

COMPLETING
THE DOCUMENT.

Your have completed your manuscript. This part is about the finishing touches: the table of contents (TOC) at the beginning of the document, the bibliography, glossary and index at the end. LaTeX creates a TOC that needs little or no modification. The bibliographic resources are: BibTeX, which is a complete bibliographic list maker from database entry to output but may be too restrictive for some tastes; and *thebibliography*, which formats the output but leaves data entry (mostly) to you. Creating an index or glossary is no easier than in any system that forces the user to tag each and every index item.

Chapter 26

BIBLIOGRAPHIC REFERENCES

These are some commonly-used ways to identify references in a bibliographic list.

1. **Provide an alphabetic accession number.** Usually, this means alphabetizing the reference list first and assigning the alphabetized citations accession numbers. Then these numbers are inserted into the document, replacing a marker or placeholder. Initially, you might write "Smith [get his 94 paper] demonstrated ...". After you have sorted the references alphabetically, this internal reference might read: "Smith [3] demonstrated ...". The list of references might look like this:

   1. Green, T. et al., 1995, *Gene Theories*, **Mol Biol.**, 120-129.

   2. Joneston, R.T., 1995, *Genetic Code Breaking*, **Mol Biol.**, 135-140.

   3. Smith, A.L., 1994, *Adaptive Models*, **JOSA**, 120-150.

2. **Provide a 'chronological' accession number.** The first article discussed in the document is listed first. The second paper cited is listed second, and so forth. An internal reference might read: "Smith [1] demonstrated ...". The numbers can be installed in the document in an ongoing fashion, if you don't expect to move material around much. Or you can wait until the paper is finished, rearrange the reference list 'chronologically', then write in the numbers in sequence both in the list and in the document. The list of references might look like this:

1. Smith, A.L., 1994, *Adaptive Models*, **JOSA**, 120-150.

2. Joneston, R.T., 1995, *Genetic Code Breaking*, **Mol Biol.**, 135-140.

3. Green, T. et al., 1995, *Gene Theories*, **Mol Biol.**, 120-129.

3. **Use a permanent tag.** Construct it, say, from the first 5 letters of the last name of the senior author welded to the last 2 digits of the date. (Currently, millennium-conscious authors favor a 4-digit date.) A final 'a', 'b', etc., differentiates papers written in the same year by a prolific author. An internal reference to the citation would read, say: "Smith [SMITH94] showed.." References can be alphabetized when the paper is finished without disturbing the internal organization of the paper.

[GREEN95b] Green, T. et al., 1995, *Gene Theories*, **Mol Biol.**, 120-129.

[JONES95] Joneston, R.T., 1995, *Genetic Code Breaking*, **Mol Biol.**, 135-140.

[SMITH94] Smith, A.L., 1994, *Adaptive Models*, **JOSA**, 120-150.

LaTeX handles the problem of developing a digitized bibliographic database that can be cross-referenced by constructing a special environment, the *thebibliography* environment, in which citations are written as *bibitems*. This environment can be generated automatically by BibTeX.[1] Or you can write the *thebibliography* items yourself, either writing them directly in the document or loading them from another file with an *\input{...}* command. The markup styles differ slightly, but this doesn't affect the printout. Both ways shape the initial database and force a label on each item so that LaTeX can replace citation labels in the document with associated numbers or name tags.

LaTeX handles references to these bibliographic items in a manner similar to how it handles cross-references to equations or figures or chapters. In analogy to the **\ref** or **\pageref** commands, bibliographic items are cited this way:

The MarkUp: `Green~\cite{bib:tom95} was the first..`
The PrintOut: Green [1] was the first...

In the next sections, first we will discuss the bibliography development methods that can be used with LaTeX. Then we will discuss elaborations of the *\cite* command.

---

[1] BibTeX was written by Oren Patashnik at Stanford University. The description of BibTeX presented here is cursory, but more complete information is available in the BibTeX documentation files, [Patashnik88a] and [Patashnik88b], and in the man file. The manuals and construction files for the different styles are subsumed under */usr/lib/teTeX*. The manuals on BibTeX have been consolidated in: *~/texmf/doc/bibtex*. The *btxdoc.tex* and *btxhak.tex* files can be run through LaTeX and the *.dvi* output read by *xdvi*.

26.1 BIBTEX

BIBTEX[2] handles a bibliographic database through the various stages involved in developing and writing a bibliography. It provides templates so that you can input citations in an organized fashion; it utilizes citation nicknames; and it creates a reference list in your document. BIBTEX is a comprehensive system that can be used to handle all your bibliographic databases and provide proper citation formats for journal papers, book listings, technical articles and conference references. The present writeup is cursory; you should read the BIBTEX documentation before using the program.

Writing the database(s). You create one or more separate bibliographic databases of citations. Each item has an initial entry type, followed by an argument within which fields are listed by type and content. A bibliographic file must have a *bib* extension.

The first line of a citation contains the entry type and the label for cross-referencing. The right-side brace is delayed; it becomes the last character in the record. Each field starts with a field descriptor followed by an equal sign; e.g., YEAR =. The print text is enclosed within double quotes or braces. The field, except for the last one, terminates in a comma. Except for the first line, fields may be listed in random order; the program will order them in a specific way. The entry on the left could be an actual BIBTEX entry. The item on the right is how it would eventually appear as a markup item in the *thebibliography* environment that BIBTEX generates and stores in *<document root name>.bbl*.

```
@ARTICLE{bib:tom95,                \bibitem{bib:tom95}
AUTHOR = "Green et al, T.",        T.~Green~et al.
TITLE = "\prit{Gene Theories}",    \newblock \prit{Gene Theories}.
JOURNAL = "Mol Biol",             \newblock {\em Mol Biol.},
YEAR = "1995",                     pages 120--129, 1995.
PAGES = "120-129" }
```

The first information in any raw entry is *entry type*. BIBTEX has a variety of entry types: book, booklet, conference, inbook, incollection, inproceedings, manual, mastersthesis, misc, phdthesis, proceedings, techreport, unpublished.

Each type requires certain field types and allows other field types. The required fields are appropriate for the type of document.

---

[2]The BIBTEX logo is produced by the *texnames* package written by Nelson H.F. Beebe at U of Utah. The original package was written in the 1980s by Richard Furuta, U of Maryland.

BIBTEX also has a variety of author field formats and many ways to indicate what parts of the field should appear in Upper or lower case.

The bib file can also write abbreviations for oft-used text phrases; for example:

```
@string(jmb="Molecular Biology")
```

These aliases are written at the top of the file, before the actual phrase appears in the text. Another shortcut is applicable to a compilation of separate papers, such as a conference proceedings, so that you don't have to repeat the information specific to the conference in each item. The down side is that the citation will be incomplete, if you use it outside of BIBTEX.

Commands in the Main Document. You write two instructions in your document on how to handle the citations that reside in one or more BIBTEX databases: \bibliography{...} and \bibliographystyle{...}. Write them sequentially where you want the bibliographic references to appear. This is usually at the end of an article just before the \end {document} or in the appendix of a book.

1. The argument of the **\bibliography** command tells the program what databases to bring in. This, for example, would bring in two databases, *molbiol94.bib* and *molbiol95.bib*: **\bibliography{molbiol94,molbiol95}**.

2. **\bibliographystyle{...}** tells the program how to list and number the items. The styles available can be found with a **locate .bst** command in an xterm. These are some popular ones.

   (a) **\bibliographystyle{plain}**. The sort of the citations is alphabetic. Accession numbers are attached to the sorted citations.

   (b) **\bibliographystyle{unsrt}**. Citations are listed in the order in which they appear in the document. Accession numbers are attached to the list of references.

   (c) **\bibliographystyle{alpha}**. Sorting of the reference list is by Identification Label (ID). Citations are usually identified by the Author's Name and Year of Publication. BIBTEX composes the tag.

   (d) **\bibliographystyle{abbrv}**. Authors' first names and journal names are abbreviated. Citations are sorted by these new ID's. BIBTEX composes the tag.

Referencing Papers as You Write. Cite authors as you write, using the **\cite** command and the nickname for the citations; e.g., **It was Lister~\cite{bugs:lister}** who ....

Creating the Reference List. When you complete your document, BIBTEX can write a sorted bibliography, listing all the bibliographic items you have cited. In addition, you can include references to articles you have not cited by writing their database labels as argument to a **\nocite{...}** command somewhere after *\begin{document}*; e.g., **\nocite{bib:jonesy,bib:graham}**. Similarly, if you write **\nocite{*}**, all the items in the database(s) will be listed. This is how to produce a Bibliography in your document:

1. Run LATEX on the actual document file. If it is called *mol.paper*, write **latex mol.paper**. It will produce an *.aux* file that lists the citation style, the bibliographic database(s) and the specific references.

2. Run BIBTEX once on the root filename; in this example, run: **bibtex mol**. BIBTEX sorts the references and rearranges fields, using the information in the AUX file. BIBTEX writes these results into a file based on the root name, with *bbl* as the extension. In this example, it would be called `mol.bbl`. The BBL file holds a single *thebibliography* environment containing the sorted bibliographic items and formatting instructions that will generate a print-ready bibliographic list in the print version of the document. If need be, this file can be edited.

3. Rerun LATEX a couple of times. *mol.dvi* now contains the bibliography.

26.2 The *thebibliography* Environment

BIBTEX is a rich and complex system, but perhaps a tad over-organized. LATEX lets you create a *thebibliography* environment directly so you can reference papers stored electronically in any format that suits you. The *thebibliography* environment behaves somewhat like a cross between an enumerate list and a cross-reference, with the **\bibitem** command substituting for the **\item** command used in regular lists. The list of citations is written directly in the document inside a *thebibliography* environment. Write it where you want the list printed. Numbering follows in whatever order you have listed the references. Citing a reference in the paper is done as it is in BIBTEX; i.e., using *\cite{<label>}*. *thebibliography* is particularly useful if you have a large investment in an already stylized database and it requires no time to learn. On the other hand, you are responsible for checking case consistency, field order and font style. And you need to sort alphabetic items yourself. (The GNU *sort* program is probably sufficient; consult the man page.)

26.2.1   Components of a *thebibliography* item

A bibliographic item has these components

\bibitem. Note, this is \bibitem not \item, the way objects are listed in the ordinary enumerate environment.

\Optional Name. An optional name is put in brackets. Many authors prefer a LastName-Year tag, to an accession number. If you use the bracket option, its contents will be used in the printout instead of the accession number.

\Label. The label is built into the \bibitem format, and needs no special command.

This could be the markup of a *thebibliography* item:

```
\bibitem[JONES95]{bib:bob95} Joneston, R.T., 1995,
\textit{Genetic Code Breaking}, \textbf{Mol Biol.}, 135-140.
```

Usually, all the references are assembled in a single *thebibliography* environment that is placed at the end of the document. In a book, the program confines the items in a separate section entitled: **Bibliography**, written large and bold, and always beginning, like a chapter, on a right-side page.

26.2.2   Putting a reference list at the end of each chapter

If you want to append a separate reference list at the end of each chapter in a book or report without a break, you need to modify the header slightly in the appropriate CLS file. For a book, you need to change *chapter* to *section* in *book.cls*, the file that defines the book class.[3] However, *book.cls* is copyright, so do NOT change anything in it. Instead, make a copy of book.cls to, say, *mybook.cls*. Feel free to change *mybook.cls*.

---

[3]*book.cls* is in a subdirectory of the LaTeX document; look in the ~/texmf/tex/latex/base directory.

Change *mybook.cls* this way.

```
\newenvironment{thebibliography}[1]
    {\chapter*{\bibname
        \@mkboth{\MakeUppercase\bibname}{\MakeUppercase\bibname}}%
```

to

```
\newenvironment{thebibliography}[1]
    {\section*{\bibname
        \@mkboth{\MakeUppercase\bibname}{\MakeUppercase\bibname}}%
```

In an article, you can change "\section*{\bibname" to "\subsection*{\bibname" in a copy of *article.cls*.

You can change the line that defines `bibname` as *Bibliography* to *List of References*:
$$\newcommand\{ \backslash bibname\}\{List\ of\ References\}$$

To complete the procedure of modifying a class definition, make a copy of *book.sty*[4] to, say, *mybook.sty*. At the end of *mybook.sty*, there are these lines:

```
\@obsoletefile{book.cls}{book.sty}
\LoadClass{book}
```

Change them to read:

```
\@obsoletefile{mybook.cls}{mybook.sty}
\LoadClass{mybook}
```

There is one other thing you must do: in an xterm, type: **texhash**. It may take a few minutes. The teTeX system is updating its personal list of files that are part of the system. It doesn't actually search the system; it only searches its index. So you MUST make sure the system knows about your new class.

The next time you want to use the revised bibliographic definitions in a book, you would write

---

[4]It should be in the same directory as *book.cls*.

\documentclass{mybook}

instead of

\documentclass{book}

26.2.3   The *thebibliography* reference list

Prepending A Name-Year Tag. If the Name-Year tag will identify the reference, our sample three items would be written this way. Note how we tell the program the size of the largest tag we have in an argument appended to **\begin{thebibliography}**: by writing enough characters just as we would for a tabbing environment. In this example, we need 8 places: up to 5 spaces for the name, 2 for the date and 1 space for a final a,b,... when there's more than one article by the author in that year.

The MarkUp:

```
\begin{thebibliography}{ABCDE97a}
\bibitem[GREEN95b]{bib:tom95} Green, T. \prit{et al.}, 1995,
\textit{Gene Theories}, \textbf{Mol
Biol.}, 120-129.

\bibitem[JONES95]{bib:bob95} Joneston, R.T., 1995,
\textit{Genetic Code Breaking}, \textbf{Mol
Biol.}, 135-140.

\bibitem[SMITH94]{bib:abe94}  Smith, A.L., 1994,
\textit{Adaptive Models}, \textbf{JOSA}, 120-150.
\end{thebibliography}
```

The PrintOut:

List of References

[GREEN95b] Green, T. *et al.*, 1995, *Gene Theories*, **Mol Biol.**, 120-129.

[JONES95]   Joneston, R.T., 1995, *Genetic Code Breaking*, **Mol Biol.**, 135-140.

[SMITH94]   Smith, A.L., 1994, *Adaptive Models*, **JOSA**, 120-150.

Prepending An Accession Number. *thebibliography* needs to know how much space to allow for accession numbers, just as it does for tags. If there's fewer than 100 citations, append two digits, '99' say, to the *thebibliography* environment; if there are more than 99 references but less than 1000, append '999'.

The MarkUp:

```
\begin{thebibliography}{99}
\bibitem {bib:tom95} Green, T. \prit{et al.}, 1995, \textit{Gene
Theories}, \textbf{Mol Biol.}, 120-129.
\end{thebibliography}

\bibitem {bib:bob95} Joneston, R.T., 1995, \textit{Genetic Code
Breaking}, \textbf{Mol Biol.}, 135-140.

\bibitem {bib:abe94}  Smith, A.L., 1994, \textit{Adaptive Models},
 \textbf{JOSA}, 120-150.
\end{thebibliography}
```

The PrintOut:

List of References

[1] Green, T. *et al.*, 1995, *Gene Theories*, **Mol Biol.**, 120-129.

[2] Joneston, R.T., 1995, *Genetic Code Breaking*, **Mol Biol.**, 135-140.

[3] Smith, A.L., 1994, *Adaptive Models*, **JOSA**, 120-150.

If chronological numbering is used, LaTeX will do the numbering automatically and correctly. If you want alphabetic ordering, you will first need to alphabetize the citations in the *thebibliography* environment. LaTeX will add the accession number.

The *thebibliography* environment lets you construct your own set of bibliographic references in your own way. This has the advantage that you continue to maintain your bibliographic references as you wish. It also means that you need to add font instructions, the *\bibitem* command and a label to each existing citation, jobs BIBTeX can save you.

In developing your database, one way to save typing is to create an item template that you fill in; for example,

```
\bibitem[]{bib:} ,19, \textit{}, \textbf{}, ''', pp .\\
\bibitem[]{bib:} ,19, \textit{}, \textbf{}, ''', pp .\\
```

26.3   Citing A Reference

- Once there is a bibliographic database and an association between a citation number and a permanent nickname—whether it does this in BIBTEX or in the *thebibliography* environment—LATEX can reference any item in the citation list by number or Name-Year tag.

  Inserting bibliographic citation numbers in the body of the document is done with a \cite command, not a \ref command, thus:

  ``Smith et al~\cite{bib:abe94 } demonstrated..''

  If the optional argument, e.g., [SMITH94], is part of the Smith \bibitem, it will appear this way:

  "Smith [SMITH94] demonstrated..."

  Otherwise, it will look like this:

  "Smith [3] demonstrated ..."

- Multiple papers can be referenced in a single \cite{...}. For example, you can write:

  ``Several groups~\cite{bib:tom95, bib:bob95, bib:abe94} have reached this conclusion...''

  This would print as: "Several groups [1,2,3] have reached this conclusion."

- If there is a cite optional argument, it is used this way:

  The MarkUp:

  Smith~\cite[page 10: experimental notes]{bib:abe94}
  has commented that..."

  The PrintOut: Smith [1, page 10: experimental notes] has commented that...

Chapter 27

MAKING A TABLE OF CONTENTS

27.1 The *\tableofcontents* Command

Command Format: If you issue a **\tableofcontents** instruction—this can be anywhere after the **\begin{document}** statement—the program does two things:

1. The program creates a new file with the root name of the document file and a toc extension. It fills the new file with the information from the previous Table of Contents (TOC) file (if any). So to create an up-to-date TOC file, run LaTeX twice on the document. On the other hand, if you have a TOC you want to preserve from further revision by the program, write: **\nofiles** in the preamble. Otherwise, if later in revising some of the text you interrupt a program run, the previous TOC file is likely to be wiped out.

2. The program inserts the TOC into the printed document at the point where the table of contents command is written in the source file. It is customary to print the TOC before the preface, but you can insert it afterwards.

The program generates a List of Figures (LOF) and a List of Tables (LOT) files in exactly the same way. A LOF file is created (using the root name and a lof extension) and inserted

433

in the text where a **\listoffigures** statement is issued in the source file. Similarly, a LOT file is created (the file has a lot extension) and inserted into the text where a **\listoftables** command is issued.

Any of these lists can be modified. We will illustrate this by discussing modifications in TOC.

27.2   Modifying And Deleting Items From TOC

Any of the hierarchical partitions in a document can use different text in the TOC than in the document itself. The complete form for a document division is:

<partition>[<TOC entry>]{<heading text>}

where *<partition>* can be any of the document divisions that apply to the document class, from \part, through \section down to \subparagraph.

If the [TOC entry] is missing—and it usually is—the program uses the actual heading text in TOC. But, occasionally, the optional TOC entry can be useful for clipping text that runs on too long. For example: \section[Sentence Structure]{How a Complete Sentence Is Parsed in basic LaTeX} would use *Sentence Structure* for the text of that section in TOC and *How a Complete Sentence Is Parsed in basic LaTeX* in the document.

You can suppress writing all levels below the SubSection, say, in TOC, by writing the lowest levels this way:

\subsubsection*{*<text for subsection header>*}
\paragraph*{*<text for paragraph header>*}
\subparagraph*{*<text for subparagraph header>*}

Unfortunately, this also suppresses numbering in the document. So you may need to edit the TOC file itself, deleting items on lower levels.

An easier way is to define the number of levels prior to writing the *\tableofcontents* command this way: **\setcounter{tocdepth}{<NumberOfLevels>}**.

27.3   Adding Items To TOC

If you are pretty much satisfied with the looks of one of these tables, but want some slight changes, you can tell the program to add information if necessary, but not to destroy the version you are working with. This is done by inserting **\addtocontents** and **\addcontentsline** commands in the appropriate places in the source document; i.e., if you wish an additional item in the TOC just after a particular section, put the command in the source text just after the **\section{whatever}** statement. The first argument in either of these commands tells *toc* to edit a toc file, *lof* to edit a lof file and *lot* to edit a lot file.

As example, I used a different format for the *part* command, calling it *NewPart*. Naturally, the TOC program didn't find a \part command. So I added information about Part divisions in the source file, just after the NewPart statements; for example:

\addcontentsline{toc}{part}{PART III. WRITING LaTeX}

The only difficulty is that the page numbering in TOC for the Part page was not correct. It is not possible, for example, to use \NewPart in place of *part*. Nor does it work to define *NewPart* as a new counter and try to use it. In fact, the simplest way is to wait until the document is completely done and do a last TOC. Modify this in Emacs. You may also want to add some spacing after the Chapter numbers. When you're satisfied with appearances, use \nofiles in the preamble. Or create a permanent backup file from this; if your TOC file is *practice.toc*, call this, say, *practice.toc.keep*. You can still make minor adjustments in the document, but you have a file than can act as the permanent TOC for the document; just copy it into *practice.toc* as needed.

As another example, suppose you are writing a section called *Editing Picture Files* and you wish to add allusions to particular pictures that appear on the same page as the section heading. You would write addcontentsline commands just after the section command, giving each addition a subsection level so the picture files would be indented. The document would read, say:

The MarkUp:

```
\section{Editing Picture Files}
\addcontentsline{toc}{subsection}{A Typical Picture File}
\addcontentsline{toc}{subsection}{A Modified Picture File}
```

The TOC would correctly indent these items and give them the same page number as the Section.

You can, if you wish, add an ID or figure number or picture number in the \addcontentsline command. As usual, the % at the end of a line links the previous argument to the argument on the next line without a space.

```
\addcontentsline{toc}{subsection}%
{\protect \numberline{\itshape 1a}{A Typical Picture File}}
\addcontentsline{toc}{subsection}%
{\protect \numberline{\itshape 1b}{A Modified Picture File}}
```

Notice that all the text after the right brace terminating the {subsection} argument is one large argument.

This will appear in TOC indented just after the Section Heading: *Editing Picture Files*. The Picture number is italicized. The rest of the line—Name and Page Number—are in regular font.

27.4 Editing the TOC (or LOF or LOT) file directly under Emacs

This is done:

- to modify a font shape or size.

- to reduce the overly generous spacing between items in the printout. Write, say, **\addtolength**{**\baselineskip**}{**-10pt**} at the top of the TOC file.

- you have subdivided your document down to the subparagraph level, but you don't want the TOC to go to a depth beyond the subsection. You need to delete the unwanted items.

- you reformat and rename one of the document's standard divisions. I added a revised *\part* item with a **\addtocontents** command. I could as easily have added it by 'by hand.'

- A modified document division doesn't produce the right page number. Change it.

Chapter 28

MAKING AN INDEX

28.1   Tagging Index Items

An index is an alphabetized list of words and text phrases that are important in the document as concepts or as critical elements of the subject matter of the document or as words with specialized meaning or as words reserved by the subject matter. Depending on the subject, the index item can be a single text phrase, *programming languages*, or it can warrant a hierarchical list, where it is itself chunked into subsidiary categories:

languages, programming
>   *C*
>   *C++*
>   *Fortran*

28.2   Using The *makeindex* Program

LaTeX does not provide a particularly great way to make an index, in that the program doesn't reuse tagged words. If you tag a word for the index on page 10, you need to retag it, when it appears again on another page.

This is the way to use the *makeindex* program

1. Write \textbf{\textbackslash usepackage}\{\textbf{makeidx}\} in the preamble.

2. Write \texttt{\textbackslash makeindex} command in the preamble.

3. Tag the entries. Suppose this piece of text:

> These commands are written within the document; i.e., there is no command line option. You may need to run the
> file through LaTeX several times.

You would mark each word you want with an **\index** command in this way. (The %
ending some items is an attempt to keep the indexed words from throwing off page
count, which might happen if the indexed word begins/ends a page.)

```
''These commands \index{commands} are written within the document;
\index{document}%
\index{\LaTeX, document}%
i.e., there is no command line option. You may need to run the
file through \LaTeX\ several times.''
```

Take special care when the tagged text phrase contains one of the ten special characters, such as \or $. If it does, do not write a tagged item within the argument of
another command.

4. When LaTeX processes the document, it will write the tagged items into a file with
the root name and an *idx* extension. Each entry in the IDX file has the format
\texttt{\textbackslash indexentry\{text\}\{page \#\}}, and there's one entry per line. For example:

```
\indexentry{commands}{198}
\indexentry{document}{198}
\indexentry{\LaTeX\ document}{198}
\indexentry{index}{223}
\indexentry{specialized meaning}{223}
```

5. At the prompt in an xterm, type: **makeindex <filename>**. In our example, we
would type: **makeindex practice.idx**. The output is an alphabetized file that has

consolidated the multiple page numbers for any word. The file has an *ind* extension. Operating on *practice.idx*, the index would be written into *practice.ind*. A spacing instruction—**\indexspace**—that adds a blank line is written at the start of the list for each new alphabetic letter. For example:

The MarkUp:

```
\begin{theindex}
  \item alphabetized, 198, 223

\indexspace
  \item index, 198, 223

  \indexspace
  \item specialized meaning, 223

  \indexspace
  \item text phrases, 198
\end{theindex}
```

6. Insert the actual IND file where you wish the index to be printed in the document with a **\input**{<*filename*>*.ind*}. You can make modifications on its font shape, if you wish.

7. The program will format the index, prepend it with a chapter-sized **INDEX**, which is treated like a chapter in that it begins on a right-side page. It outputs the index in two columns.

28.3 Using Just The *theindex* Environment

The \makeindex program requires so much work tucking in the index reference so that the page numbers stay correct, you might find it simpler to do part of indexing yourself, particularly for a short index. You can take still take advantage of the *theindex* environment. Doing it this way is certainly more thorough.

1. In a separate file—call it *practice.ndx*—jot down the items you wish to index, one per line and each beginning with *item*. Do NOT repeat an item because it occurs on

several pages. In fact, you should not repeat any item.

For example:

The MarkUp:

```
\item subsidiary files
\item programming
\item ASCII files
```

2. Sort the items in the NDX file. The system sort program does well with a one level alphabetizing this way:

```
sort -o practice.srt -k2 practice.ndx
```

3. Insert the subsidiaries, using **\subitem** and **\subsubitem**. Insert all the index items in a *theindex* environment.

The MarkUp:

```
\begin{theindex}
\item ASCII files
\indexspace
\item programming
\subitem languages
\subsubitem C
\subsubitem C++
\subsubitem Fortran
\subitem history
\indexspace
\item subsidiary files
\end{theindex}
```

4. Review the alphabetized list, making sure you didn't repeat an item. Delete the repeats.

5. Keep the list in one window. In another window, create a viewing copy of the document. In still another, keep a copy of your source module. The *less* program is useful in that it highlights each copy of the item you select for searching. Go through the tortuous process of searching for each item in the source file, viewing its analogue

in the DVI file, and writing the page numbers for all the pages in which it appears in the index file. For example

```
\item programming, languages 10, 18-22, 27-30, 42
\item programming, history of  15-27
```

6. Insert the NDX file in the document in the appropriate place. The program will write out an INDEX chapter in two columns.

The MarkUp:

```
\begin{theindex}
\item ASCII files 15,43
\indexspace
\item programming
\subitem languages 10, 18-22, 27-30, 42
\subsubitem C 18-20, 42
\subsubitem C++ 20-22, 42
\subsubitem Fortran 27-30
\subitem history 15-27
\indexspace
\item Subsidiary files 4-7
\end{theindex}
```

Index

Chapter 29

CREATING A GLOSSARY

A glossary is usually a listing of important terms and their definitions, rather like a dictionary. Glossary items can be brief or discursive.

An index can include definitions of some of the terms as well as page and/or section numbers. To make an index that includes a glossary, use the `\makeindex` method.

Making an ordinary glossary is the same as making an index, except that the general command in the preamble is called `\makeglossary`. Glossary words are tagged by `\glossary-`{text item}. Entries are stored in a file with the root name and a *glo* extension. Entries in *<root>.glo* are written as `\glossaryentry{text}{page}`.

There is no `\theglossary` environment as there is for indices. But you can create an attractive list using an ordinary description environment, after sorting the items in <filename>.glo. Use **\chapter*{GLOSSARY}** in the appropriate place in the source file and insert the sorted GLO file.

ALGOL Languages. The earliest higher level languages were procedural. By 1958 the ALGOL(Algorithmic Language) Committee of the Association for Computing Machinery issued a preliminary report on emerging ideas for implementing assertions and primarily numerical procedures.

Programming Languages. Initially instructions to the machine were directly in terms of electronic traffic patterns. Assembly languages detailed how to ship a value from one register to another. In time, higher level languages were developed. One could now say: **c = a + b;** in a single instruction, instead of: **put a in xreg. Move a to yreg. Put b in xreg. Add b to yreg. Put the yreg value in zreg...**

Part IX.

DESIGNING STYLE SHEETS.

Until now, we have had little need to change default values. Although you know how to reset the footnote counter and style, it's likely you use the default version most of the time. There's been even less reason to change something as important as the general appearance of a page. In fact, for most jobs, minor changes incorporated into a few macros are more than sufficient.

This part is about designing and redesigning documents LaTeX handles—letters—and documents LaTeX doesn't handle as specific classes—title pages, chapter headings, memo headers, faxes. To have the tools to redesign documents, you need to know more about counters and lengths. And that's what the first section of this part of the book is about.

A counter is an entity whose value changes by one (usually)—1, 2, 3 or 3, 2, 1—each time it is hit, ticked, entered, clicked, used, snagged. We start with how to change the value of a counter, how to add to the current value and how to designate new counters. In contrast, length measures are those you measure on a ruler. They include width measurements and any geometric measure based on x,y coordinates. Like a counter, a new length can be defined and an existing length can be reset.

Next we devote a chapter to the page and its parts. The page has many components—header, footer, body height and width, inner and outer margin widths—that don't change location or size from one page to the next, no matter what the text or structural articulation (e.g., *chapter* or *subparagraph*). Each of these components can be separately measured and set to a particular size in the preamble of the document.

We then examine some resources that are currently available for customizing templates.

Finally, we go on to actual documents that you can use as models. Better still, sniff at them and do your own.

Chapter 30

MEASUREMENTS: COUNTERS AND LENGTHS

Simple counting and ruler-unit sizing are the main arithmetic operations that LaTeX needs to do. In this chapter we examine these two tasks. Note that certain commands are global; i.e., no matter where they are defined, they are 'sticky'. Their scope extends from the point of definition throughout the document, no matter whether they are contained in a command argument or in an environment. They may, however, be redefined. These include these counter commands: *\newcounter, \setcounter, \addtocounter*. Similarly, the *\newlength* command is global.

30.1   Counters

We have already seen several instances of counters in action—chapters, sections and other divisions of the document are automatically numbered sequentially; figures, tables and footnotes are incremented, their numbering restarted with each new chapter; cross-references are linked to page or document partition. LaTeX maintains separate counters for all the divisions in a document from the *part* down to the *subparagraph*. It also tracks figures, tables, equations, footnotes, the newtheorem names and four levels for items in an enumerate list. Each of these counters has a simple name such as *footnote* or *section*. The name is NOT prepended by a backslash. Associated with the counter is a LaTeX command that has a defined print activity and increments the counter. The rule for composing the command is simple: it is the name of the counter prepended with a backslash; e.g., \footnote and \section.

Referring to Figure 3.4, note that each document division is incremented within the confines of the next division up in the hierarchy. As an example, suppose that in Chapter 3 of some book, there are 20 sections, each one separately numbered from 1 to 20. Within Section 1 of Chapter 3, there are 24 subsections, each one separately numbered from 1 to 24. After the 24th subsection, section 2 starts because you issue a \section{<text>} command. LaTeX resets the subsection counter to zero. It will be incremented from 1 on for each subsection in Section 2. If a subsection has subsubsections, the subsubsections will be incremented from 1 on, until the subsection is completed. LaTeX numbers the separate division in the document by concatenating the hierarchy of division numbers.

LaTeX numbers divisions for as many levels as you specify. Otherwise four levels are numbered—for a book: chapter, section, subsection and subsubsection. \secnumdepth controls depth of numbering. To number levels from chapter through subparagraph, write this:

\setcounter{secnumdepth}{5}

If all divisions are numbered in the printout, the 8th subparagraph of the 2nd paragraph of the 6th subsubsection of the 5th subsection of the 3rd section of the 7th chapter would be numbered: 7.3.5.6.2.8. The \part command does not interfere with the consecutive numbering of chapters. If you don't want a document division numbered, but you do want it as a separate entity printed in its usual size and font, use the asterisk form. Write, for example, **\subsection*{New Methods}**.

In most cases, these LaTeX counters recycle to zero. More generally, they are automatically set to one less than what will be the first number in the next counting cycle. In the chapter on footnotes, recall that to revise a footnote number, we set it one less than the number we wanted, just before we wrote the footnote command. Part of the \footnote activity is to increment the footnote value.

Page counting is an exception. The page is counted when the program has all the material in hand to snip off the page and is ready to start the next page. To reset a page counter to 20, we would write somewhere in the middle of the current page after \chapter and \section commands have had their say:

\setcounter{page}{20}

In this section, we discuss how you can determine the value of counters created by LATEX, and how you can create your own counters.

30.1.1 Determining the current value of a counter

For every counter, the program creates a specific variable to store the counter's current value. It is simply the concatenation of *the* and the counter name; e.g., \thefootnote. Recall from Section 17.1.5:

\renewcommand{\thefootnote}{\fnsymbol{footnote}}.

Read this as: the variable *thefootnote* holds the numeric value of the counter named *footnote* and this value is printed in symbol.

The **\the...** format is used to find out current values. For example:

The MarkUp:

```
What section is it? \textbf{\thesection}. \\
What chapter is it? \textsf{\thechapter}. \\
What is the page number? \textsl{\thepage}.
```

The PrintOut: What section is it? **30.1**.
What chapter is it? 30.
What is the page number? *449*.

30.1.2 Creating a new counter

A new counter is fashioned using the \newcounter{<CounterName>} command. It is a global variable, unrestrained by command braces or an environment. The initial count is zero. By default, it will be printed in ordinary numbers, as in this example.

The MarkUp:	*The PrintOut:*

```
\newcounter{KeepTabs}
What is the value of KeepTabs?
\textbf{\theKeepTabs}
```
What is the value of KeepTabs? **0**

```
\newcounter{NewSection}
What is the value of NewSection?
\textbf{\theNewSection}
```
What is the value of NewSection? **0**

This next illustrates how a new counter can be slaved to an existing variable. After the new counter is set, whenever the older variable is incremented by \stepcounter or \refstep-counter,[1] the new one is reset to zero—which is exactly what happens with the numbering of the document's divisions. Notice that the prior variable (*subsection* in the example) is written in square brackets.

\newcounter{NewSubSection}[subsection]

Notice below that the first argument to the counter commands is the name of the counter, NOT the associated command.

30.1.3   Using \setcounter to give the counter a value

Use the \setcounter command to give the new variable a numerical value. It too is global in scope. If the value is in terms of another variable, use the \value command. Formats for assigning a value are:

Actual Numbers: `\setcounter{<NewCounter>}{<numerical value>}`

The \value command: `\setcounter{<NewCounter>}{\value{<OldCounter>}}`

The MarkUp:

```
\setcounter{KeepTabs}{20}
\setcounter{NewSection}{\value{section} + 5}
```

---

[1] *\stepcounter* increases the count by one. *\refstepcounter* forces the specified \ref to be the counter value.

```
The value for \textit{NewSection} is the value for \textit{section}
incremented by 5.\footnote{You need to load the \textit{calc} package
to be able to do much arithmetic. See Section~\ref{ss:calcpack}.}\\
What is the value of NewSection? \textbf{\theNewSection}.\\
What is the value of KeepTabs? \textbf{\theKeepTabs}.
```

The PrintOut:

The value for *NewSection* is the value for *section* incremented by 5.[2]

What is the value of NewSection? **6**.

What is the value of KeepTabs? **20**.

30.1.4   Using *\addtocounter* to increment a counter

\addtocounter will add (or subtract) a numerical value. It has global scope. If the added value is in terms of another variable, use the *\value* command. Formats are:

Actual Numbers: \addtocounter{<*NewCounter*>}{<*numerical value*>}

The *\value* command: \addtocounter{<*NewCounter*>}{\value{<*OldCounter*>}}

The MarkUp:
```
\addtocounter{chapter}{-3} \\
What is the value of chapter if we subtract 3? \textbf{\thechapter}.\\
\addtocounter{footnote}{\value{chapter}}
If we allowed the revised addtocounter to remain,\footnote{The
previous footnote was 2. Adding 28 makes it 30 just before the
current footnote command increments it.} the next section would
be 28.1.5; the next chapter would be Chapter 29.
```

The PrintOut:

What is the value of chapter if we subtract 3? **27**.

If we allowed the revised addtocounter to remain,[30] the next section would be 28.1.5; the next chapter would be Chapter 29.

---

[2]You need to load the *calc* package to be able to do much arithmetic. See Section 25.2.2.

[30]The previous footnote was 2. Adding 28 makes it 30 just before the current footnote increments it.

30.1.5   Setting the style of a counter

These are the styles available for all counters:

\arabic Ordinary numbers

\roman Lower case roman numerals

\Roman Upper case roman numerals

\alph Lower case ordinary alphabet letters (Up to 26)

\Alph Upper case ordinary alphabet letters (Up to 26)

\fnsymbol{*A number from 1 to 9, each linked to a different footnote symbol.*}}

The MarkUp:

```
What is the page? \textbf{\thepage}. \\
Print the number in roman: \roman{page}.\\
\renewcommand{\thechapter}{\Roman{chapter}}
What chapter is this? \thechapter \\
\renewcommand{\thechapter}{\arabic{chapter}}
```

The PrintOut: What is the page? **452**.

Print the number in roman: cdlii.

What chapter is this? XXX

Any one of the counter styles can be changed from the default value; e.g., **\renewcommand**{**\thesection**}{**\Alph**{**section**}} would change the Section numbering style to Upper case alphabet letters. Numbering would be reset automatically each new chapter.

A numbering style can be set in the preamble for the entire document. It can be reset later in the document. It is sticky, unless reset.

30.1.6 Using \usecounter to style list item numbering

The special environment, *list*, is an addition to the more common lists formats. In it, you can modify the appearance of the list's accession numbers by creating a counter–*acct* in this example. Pick one of the available styles; the accession numbers will be numbered in that style.

The first argument of the environment contains the text that will be prepended to item numbers, and the style of the counter. The second argument, *\usecounter*, forces the list to be numbered by the counter.

The MarkUp:

```
\newcounter{acct}

\begin{list}
{ACCOUNT--\Roman{acct}}{\usecounter{acct}}

\item (\#A1234567.) Xref:   Smith et al | SmithAB.
\item (\#A23456678.) Xref:  Green, T | GreenT.


\item (\#A34567890.) Xref:  Black, C | BlackC.
\end{list}
```

The PrintOut:

ACCOUNT–I (#A1234567.) Xref: Smith et al |SmithAB.

ACCOUNT–II (#A23456678.) Xref: Green, T |GreenT.

ACCOUNT–III (#A34567890.) Xref: Black, C |BlackC.

30.2   Length Measures

30.2.1   Defining a new length

\newlength defines a new measurement variable. It can be declared anywhere in the document. Thus:

\newlength{\etc}

\etc is now a length measure set at zero points.

Note that the first argument in length measures is a command name prepended by a backslash, not a name as in counter definitions.

30.2.2   Setting a length command

The format is: \setlength{\<*length*>}{<*amount*>}. For example:

```
\setlength{\textwidth}{5in}
\setlength{\parskip}{\baselineskip}
```

The length of a variable can be set to a specific number or to the value of another variable. Setting *\parskip* to *\baselineskip* is an example we encountered early on, when setting up a practice document. The space between paragraphs (*parskip*) was set to be equal to the distance from one baseline to the next. If line height increases because the font is reset to a larger size, the space between paragraphs will increase proportionally.

Length can be expressed in exact amounts: pt for points, in for inches, cm for centimeters, pc for picas. You can mix and match, but it is simpler to measure font size in picas and points, and to layout margins and minipages in inches and centimeters.

1 inch (1in) = 2.54 centimeters (2.54cm) = 25.4 millimeters (25.4mm) = 72.27 points (72.27pt) = 6.022 picas (6.022pc). Abbreviate measurement units as shown here—inches as **in**, centimeters as **cm** and so forth. Leave no separation between the value and the measurement unit; e.g., \hspace{.75in}.

A zero length is written as 0in or 0pt. There is no dimensionless zero.

Global commands that layout the page such as *\textwidth* should be set once, in the preamble, if the default width is not acceptable. Lengths such as *parindent* that indent the start of a paragraph can be changed throughout the document.

30.2.3   Increasing/Decreasing a length

\addtolength increases or decreases an existing length by a certain amount.

Given an existing paragraph skip of 1 lines (1 pc): \addtolength{\parskip}{-.15pc} will change the vertical space between paragraphs to .85 pica.

30.2.4   *setto* commands

\settodepth sets the length metric to the length a particular letter extends below the bottom edge of a text line. For example: **\settodepth{\parskip}{g}** sets *\parskip* equal to the drop from the text line to the lowest edge of the character **g**. (See Section 11.5.5.)

\settoheight sets the length metric from the line for the vertical extent of a particular letter. For example: **\settoheight{\parindent}{G}** sets the paragraph indentation to the vertical size of the letter **G**.

\settowidth set the length metric equal to the width of a some piece of text in its current shape and size. For example: **\settowidth{\parindent}{\NUMBER}** sets the initial indentation in each paragraph to the size of the printed word: NUMBER.

The *setto* commands depend on the size font in use. If you make the mistake of attempting to set a *setto* command to an actual numerical value, the length will be set to the size of the printed text, not to the number. For example, if you write: **\settowidth{\parindent}{2in}**, the indentation will not be 2 inches. It will be the few mm it takes to print the text: 2in.

30.2.5 Finding out the current size of a length measure

Recall from Section 30.1.1 that the program creates a variable called *the<counter>* to hold the current value of the associated counter.

The same syntax is used for length measurements, taking into account that length measures are command names, not plain names.

The MarkUp:

```
\newlength{\TestNum}
\setlength{\TestNum}{4pc}
\addtolength{\TestNum}{3\testwidth}
What is the size of TestNum? \the\TestNum
```

The PrintOut:

What is the size of TestNum? 1132.04997pt

30.2.6 Rigid versus relative versus rubber measurements

In TEX-talk, length measurements are considered either as rigid or rubber. Either the value is a fixed amount, or like the *fill* command, it spreads or contracts to fill the available space. Actually, a measurement can also be relative in that it can be the size of a printed character, and the size of the character depends on the font in use.

As we have seen, **\hspace** and **\vspace** are two very useful measures. We have used them mostly as fixed measurements, but they can, be rigid, relative or rubber, depending on their values. As can any length variable.

Rigid: An exact metric is of course rigid, absolute. Thus, `\hspace{1mm}` or `\vspace{2pc}` are absolute measures.

Relative: The *ex* and *em* measures introduce flexibility because they are relative to **x** and **M**, respectively, in the current type style and size. 1 ex is the height of an **x** and 1 em is the width of an **M**. Similarly, **\vspace{\baselineskip}** will skip an amount of space equal to the distance from one line of text to the next, but the size of *baselineskip* depends on the font in use.

The MarkUp: *The PrintOut:*

```
\scriptsize
\newlength{\tskip}
\setlength{\tskip}{\baselineskip}
What is the value of baselineskip?
\the\baselineskip \\
What is the value of tskip?
\the\tskip \\
\newlength{\smallM}
\setlength{\smallM}{10em}
What is the value of smallM?
\the\smallM \\
\vspace{.4in}\Large

What is the value of baselineskip?
\the\baselineskip \\
What is the value of tskip?
\the\tskip \\
\setlength{\smallM}{10em}
What is the value of smallM? \the\smallM
\normalsize
```

What is the value of baselineskip? 8.0pt

What is the value of tskip? 8.0pt

What is the value of smallM? 70.0pt

What is the value of baselineskip? 18.0pt
What is the value of tskip? 8.0pt
What is the value of smallM? 143.99994pt

Figure 30.1: Relative Changes in Font Size

Note in Figure 30.1 that, once set, user-created values don't change by themselves. *baselineskip* is changed automatically by the program when font size changes, but *tskip* doesn't change with it. *smallM* is relative to the current font and is reset automatically when font size changes from *small* to *Large*.

Rubber: The \fill command is elastic. It has a length of zero but it can expand and contract to fill the available space. But multiplying the rubber length makes it rigid; thus, *.5 \fill* is no longer rubber; it is the equivalent of zero inches.

If \flushbottom is set, the program attempts to keep the size of each page the same. It does this by increasing or decreasing the space between words on a line and the space between headers and the text that follows the header. And it manipulates the space surrounding floating objects.

On a fundamental level, the imagery—elastic, stretchable—helps convey the notion that typesetting is not a simple laying down of box characters. It is a creative art that requires numerous decisions on every page. Given the many possibilities of how print features interact in a local situation, the program almost certainly will need to stretch or compress text features or space or lines. The process is in a sense interactive in that many of the program's decisions and priorities depend on decisions you make either by global instructions written into the preamble or in response to a particular local crisis (The overfull and underfull alerts in the log file).

How much you allow the program to deviate from the various default and defined lengths will aid or hamper TEX's ability to set each page close to its most precise, ideal *goodness of fit*, while taking practicalities into account. Conversely, even though it is dogma that you can concentrate exclusively on developing ideas in your document and ignore prettiness until the finishing touches, you will find yourself often rewriting a paragraph to help the presentation and reorganizing sections to help floats drift properly.

Chapter 31

A PAGE TEMPLATE

31.1 Page Measurements

A page in many of the paperback textbooks and references is 7 to 7 1/4 inches across and around 9 to 9 1/4 high. When you open a book, odd-numbered pages are on the right; even-numbered pages are on the left. The text—usually around 5 inches across by 7 1/2 inches to 7 3/4 inches high—can look very different in different books, depending on whether the outside margin is exaggerated at the expense of the margin near the binding and whether the Book/Chapter/Section Identification text is in the *header*[1] or the *footer*,[2] or both. The font sizes of the header and footer are important. Books are usually longer than wider (*portrait* mode) but some subjects—wide tables, graphics, children's books—are better done in *landscape* mode, where the book is relatively wide. The increased use of small icons and symbols in the margins must also be factored into the appearance of a page.

Theses are assumed to be printed on 8.5 x 11 inches paper. Sizes are usually rigidly arbitrated. Some university departments allow thesis text to vary a little in length as long as the top and side margins are fixed, say, at 1 inch, and the bottom margin comes close to an inch, graphs and tables accounting for most of the variability. Articles will vary in size or, more likely, in number of words, depending on the journal or magazine. Double spacing is

---

[1] The header is the first line of text separated from the body. The body is the main bulk of text.
[2] The footer is a final line or two of text separated from the body of the text.

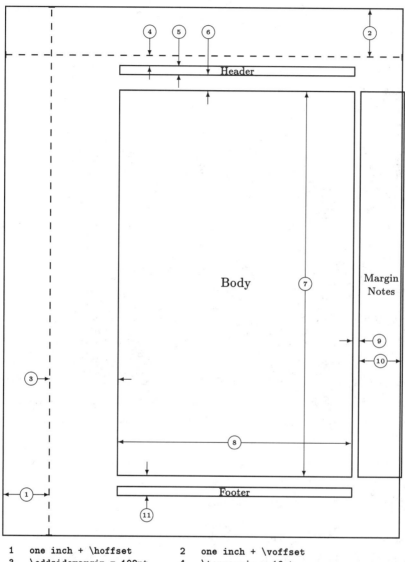

1   one inch + \hoffset   2   one inch + \voffset
3   \oddsidemargin = 108pt   4   \topmargin = 16pt
5   \headheight = 12pt   6   \headsep = 25pt
7   \textheight = 578pt   8   \textwidth = 361pt
9   \marginparsep = 11pt   10   \marginparwidth = 65pt
11 \footskip = 30pt   \marginparpush = 5pt (not shown)
    \hoffset = 0pt   \voffset = 0pt

Figure 31.1: McPherson's Page Layout

still widely enforced, but things may change as more and more journals accept entries on disk and reviewers send in their comments on disk.

To decide on a page layout, it helps to know the actual sizes of the different labeled parts of the print page. The *layout* package shown here is an aid in doing this. Call the package in the preamble and then write **\layout**, where you wish to see it. The table was designed by Kent McPherson and is documented in *Displaying page layout variables* [McPherson95]. Assuming one column per page, the critical measurements for the look of the page are the margins and other globs of white space, the appearance of the header and/or footer, font size and the bulk area allowed for the body. These are obviously not independent parameters. It helps that LaTeX is designed so that most of the global parameters change in proportion as paper size changes.

No matter for what size book or journal the text is destined, you likely will print it and submit it on ordinary paper. Most sheet paper in the States comes 8.5 by 11 inches; it is called *letterpaper* in LaTeX and is the default. By default, the 1 inch inner border on the page is not used.[3] So in an 8.5 inch width, you have 7.5 inches to play in. Most of this—around 5 inches[4]—will be for text.

The rest is additional margin. In a book, you want the margins of the stack of pages aligned; i.e., were you to push a pin through the right margins of a right-side page, you'd also be hitting the left margins of the even-side pages underneath. This usually occurs automatically—the *size10.clo* file sets the *\oddsidemargin* at 44 points, the *\evensidemargin* at 82 points for 10 point font. If need be, in a two-sided article or book, you can change these parameters. These can be set preferably in the preamble or just after the *\begin{document}* statement. For example:

\setlength{\oddsidemargin}{30pt} would push odd-numbered pages from the left an additional 30 points towards the right margin.

Similarly, **\setlength{\evensidemargin}{.5in}** would push even-numbered pages from the left an additional half inch towards the right margin.

---

[3]The dash line in the Layout diagram. You can, however, shift the entire layout on the paper, if need be, by shifting *\hoffset* and *\voffset*, which are set to zero in the diagram.

[4]Unless, of course, you do much of your writing as marginal notes. If so, decrease text width.

In one-sided documents, the default for articles, all the pages are treated like odd-numbered pages.

These next are additional global measurements that are set for the typical page layout either by default or in the preamble. They can be set by a *setlength* command; e.g., **\setlength{textheight}{10in}**. Or by an *\addtolength* command, which adds or subtracts from the current length. Note, however, that if you change the width, say, to 3 inches and include a table that is 4 inches wide, it will not shrink to the new width.

Usually the default sizes are adequate for most jobs. But these next parameters are the most likely to be changed. Put statements—with size values that suit you—in the preamble. This is an example that is useful for draft unbound copies.

```
%PAGE STYLE
\setlength{\textheight}{7.5in}
\setlength{\textwidth}{5in}
\setlength{\oddsidemargin}{1in}
\setlength{\evensidemargin}{1in}
```

\textheight. The vertical extent of the text on a page, not including the header and footer. For a book, this is typically 7.5 to 8 inches, including footnotes. The header adds a quarter of an inch or so.

\textwidth. The horizontal extent of the text from left margin to right margin. For a book, this is typically 5 inches across. Reports and articles vary, depending on local conditions and whether the article is a separate or will join others in a journal or magazine. Theses are printed on quality paper stock and are later bound by the university. Occasionally, a narrower text line is required. To force a four inch text line, write this next command in the preamble:

```
\setlength{\textwidth}{4in}
```

If you use the *calc* package that enables you to do ordinary arithmetic, you can write statements like this:

```
\setlength{\textwidth}{.5\textheight + 2mm}
```

\headheight, \headsep. *headheight* is the height of the header line. *headsep* is the distance from the baseline of the header to the start of the body. (*Baseline* and *baselineskip* are defined in Section 11.5.5.)

\footskip. *footskip* is the distance from the baseline of the last line in the body to the baseline of the footer.

\baselineskip. The distance between the baseline of one line to the bottom edge of the next in a paragraph. You can get a rough estimate of how many ordinary lines would fit on the page by dividing textheight by baselineskip—minus a line or two.

\parindent. Paragraph Indentation. This is the amount of space at the start of a paragraph, measuring from where the first character in the line would otherwise be placed. The default is about the length of three characters. If you wish the text to begin at the margin in each paragraph, write: **\parindent=0pc**[5] in the preamble. Use a negative number to extend the text into the left margin.

\flushbottom. The options are **\flushbottom** versus **\raggedbottom**. If text runs out and **\flushbottom** is set, the program adds vertical spacing to the space between lines so that the text is approximately the same height on all pages.[6] It is typically used in books. It is also the default when the **twoside** option is selected. Otherwise, *raggedbottom* is the default; i.e., when text runs out, there's no vertical stretching and the page is short.

\parskip. This determines the amount of space between paragraphs. Except in the letter class, the default skip length is zero; i.e., the default page text has no empty lines between paragraphs.

An alternative style—starting each paragraph at the left margin and leaving a blank line between paragraphs—is obtained by changing **parskip** and **indent**. This will only work if the page text can be extended so that text per page is approximately uniform; i.e., the *\flushbottom* command must also be set, as shown here. Write this in the preamble. The distance between paragraphs is usually 20% more than line height, so the parskip measure for 10 point font is set to 1 pica (equal to around 12 points).

```
\flushbottom
\parindent=0pc
\setlength{\parskip}{1pc}
```

---

[5]This is a TeX command, not a LaTeX command.

[6]The stretching can on occasion be excessive, with large gaps in the text, so that you will need to interfere, by writing **\raggedbottom** on the page and **\flushbottom** on the next page.

\marginparwidth The width of the marginal note. This quantity can be used to extend the
length of the header in the *fancyhdr* package. To be more precise, you can also add
\marginparsep, the area that separates the text from the note. (See Section 31.3.2
below.)

31.2   Rules Of Thumb

The empty space between lines of text is usually around 20% of the thickness of a line.
For 10-point font, this means the distance from the base of one line of text to the base
of the next line (the *baselineskip*) is around 12 points.

Depending on the font, the characters involved and inter-character widths, a 5-inch text
line may hold anywhere from 65 characters to 100 characters, assuming a font size
of 10 point. Reading difficulty increases with longer lines and smaller type.

Defaults:

Lines of text per inch	6.
Margin widths	1 inch.
Start of paragraph indentation	1/4 inch.
normal \baselineskip	12 points, if font size is 10 point.

31.3   Headers And Footers

31.3.1   The built-in LaTeX formats

Set the style with a **\pagestyle{...}** declaration in the preamble for the entire document,
using one of these options. If it is the default for your document class, you don't need to
do anything.[7]

\pagestyle{plain} Page numbers are in the foot. The header is empty. This is the default
for articles and reports.

---

[7]Note that the style of the page number is set by a separate command. What the pagestyle command does is
to set where the number will appear, if it appears at all.

\pagestyle{empty} No number is visible on the page, although the program still keeps track of the page number. This should be used for single-paged letters.

\pagestyle{headings} In the book class, all the page and chapter/section information is in the header. The footer is empty.

In two-sided documents, in a book or report, each left-side (even) page header shows the Chapter number and text; each right-side (odd) page header shows the Section number and text. In an article, the left side is devoted to Section information, the right side to Subsection information. In both cases, the page is on the outside of the header.

In one-sided documents, book and report headers show Chapter information, article information show Section information.

\pagestyle{myheadings} Page information is in the header. The other information in the header is specified by the *markright* or *markboth* commands, in which you can write text that will be repeated. The full syntax is:

two-sided document: \pagestyle{myheadings}\markboth{$<left\text{-}header>$}%
    {$<right\text{-}header>$}

one-sided document: \pagestyle{myheadings}\markright{$<right\text{-}header>$}

For example, a thesis could repeat the title and author or administrative necessities, thus:

```
\pagestyle{myheadings}\markboth{\textsc{A New Technique for
Splitting MacroMolecules}}{Libbe A. Stevens}
```

```
\pagestyle{myheadings}
\markboth{\textbf{DATE OF SUBMISSION}: 2 May 1997}%
{\textbf{CANDIDATE}: JOEL ARTHUR MAXWELL,
 \textit{History Department}}
```

If you want modifications only for several introductory modules, begin with the **\pagestyle-{myheadings}** material. Then put a **\pagestyle{headings}** at the start of the rest of the document.

Pagestyle instructions kick in just before the page is shipped to the output file. These commands can be modified for a particular page by introducing a **\thispagestyle** command before the *chapter* or *section* command that starts a new page, or somewhere within the page you wish to modify. If you want a particular page to have no header and footer, you would write: **\thispagestyle{empty}**. After the page is printed, the style reverts to the global style chosen for the whole file.

If one chapter ends on an odd page, the default for a book is an empty page before the next chapter begins. Or you can choose this style by writing **openright** in the square brackets of the *documentclass* statement. The alternative option is **openany**.

31.3.2   Using *fancyhdr*

This package, written by Piet van Oostrum [Oostrum98], increases the number of styles available for headers and footers. To use *fancyhdr* (previously called *fancyheadings*), write **\usepackage{fancyhdr}** and **\pagestyle{fancy}** in the preamble. **\pagestyle{fancy}** must be reissued whenever *textwidth* is changed. You can shift between *fancyhdr* headers and the ones produced by LaTeX by changing the *pagestyle* argument; but results may be disconcerting. We cover the major points here, but you should really read the documentation, which discusses how to create dictionary style headers, 'this is page # of # pages' fax style, and thumb indexes.

fancyhdr lets you divide both the header and the footer into three areas: left, center and right. And the text in each of these areas can vary, depending on whether the page is odd or even. The rule that books and reports are by default two-sided, articles one-sided, applies.

The default layout

You get the default layout for fancyhdr if you do nothing but write this in the preamble.

```
\usepackage{fancyhdr}
\pagestyle{fancy}
```

The program will fill the headers/footers as follows (assuming there are Chapter and Section divisions). *HeaderText* is shorthand for 'the text that is the argument of the Chapter or

Section command'; e.g. in \chapter{Fonts}, 'Fonts' is HeaderText. The text is written in slanted upper case.

(1.) Books, reports.

`Even Page:` Section HeaderText   Chapter HeaderText

`Odd Page:` Chapter HeaderText   Section HeaderText

    For example:

        `Even pages:` 11.1 Font Terminology   Chapter 11. Fonts.

        `Odd pages:` Chapter 11. Fonts.   11.1 Font Terminology

(2.) Two-sided articles.

The style will be similar to the book style. The top two divisions in the article will be written in the header instead of Chapter HeaderText and Section HeaderText.

(3.) One-sided articles.

`Each page:`   Section HeaderText *OR* Subsection HeaderText

(4.) Page number.

The page number will appear by itself in the middle of the footer on all pages, including the start of a Chapter.

(5.) Chapter.

The page that starts a chapter will have no header.

Header areas

These three commands—*\rhead, \chead* and *\lhead*—govern the text in the three components of a header. In each case, text in the square brackets is optional, text in the braced argument is mandatory. In any document, if you invoke a header command, you must attach the braced argument. For books, reports and two-sided articles, you can also write different text for even-sided pages.

It is important to realize that where *fancyhdr* inserts default information (see the default layout above), it will continue to do so *unless* you override the insertion with your own directive.

This is the command format.

Left-side component format:

```
\lhead[even page: left-side text]{odd page: left-side text}
```

Center component format:

```
\chead[even page: center text]{odd page: center text}
```

Right-side component format:

```
\rhead[even page: right-side text]{odd page: right-side text}
```

Here are some memo headers as examples. They declare a two-sided layout, to illustrate the different effects on odd and even pages. Write header and footer instructions in the preamble. Example (a.) is complete. If you don't issue *\rhead* and *\chead* commands, the program will write in Chapter and Section HeaderText or Section and Subsection Header-Text. If you don't issue *footer* instructions, the page number will be written in the center of the footer. The other examples present only the specific text that is wanted.

(a.) This will appear on the left in the header on *every* page, with a thick underline.

```
\lhead{\Large From the desk of \textit{Miriam Samuels}}
\setlength{\footrulewidth}{2pt}
\rhead[]{}
\chead[]{}
\lfoot[]{}
\cfoot[]{}
\rfoot[]{}
```

(b.) In this example, the text will appear on the left in the header on odd pages. The square brackets are used, so the blank text inside the brackets becomes the left component on even pages.

```
\lhead[]{\Large\textit{From the desk of Miriam Samuels}
```

(c.) This will write the previous text as the left component on even pages. The right bracket is mandatory. It writes an empty space as the left component on odd pages.

```
\lhead[\Large From the desk of \textsl{Miriam Samuels}]{}
```

(d.) This will write the previous text on the left on even pages. *Meeting Notes* will be the left component on odd pages.

```
\lhead[\LARGE\bfseries From the desk of Miriam Samuels]%
{\bfseries Meeting\\ Notes}
```

Footer areas

The footer areas have the same syntax as the header areas. They are called: *\lfoot, \cfoot* and *\rfoot*. This example will typeset the footer on the even page differently that the footer on the odd page. It overwrites the program's page number with its own. *\thepage* is the page count. In this example, only odd pages are numbered. Multiple lines are created by splitting the text with \\.

```
\lfoot[DRAFT\\COPY]{\textbf{DO\\NOT\\COPY}}
\rfoot[Version 3\\ \today]{Last Update:\\ \today}
\cfoot[]{\large\textbf{\textsf{\thepage}}}
```

Header size

Headers and footers are by default set in a box as wide as *\textwidth*. They never extend into the inner margin. But the header can be extended into the outer margin by changing the length of *\headwidth*. And it can be reduced in size. The footer is the same size as the header; i.e., it too is controlled by *\headwidth*. These are some examples.

(a.) This reduces the default size of the header by an inch.

```
\setlength{\headwidth}{\textwidth-1in}
```

(b.) This extends the header so that it lies above the marginal note.

```
\setlength{\headwidth}{\textwidth+\marginparwidth+\marginparsep}
```

(c.) This reduces the current length of the footer by 10 points.

```
\addtolength{\footwidth}{-10pt}
```

(d.) This runs the footer 10 inches across. Do this in landscape mode.

```
\setlength{\footwidth}{10in}
```

Rule width

The *\headrulewidth* command controls header rule thickness, with .4 point the default. The *footrulewidth* command controls footer rule thickness, with 0 points the default; i.e., the rule is invisible by default. Use the *\setlength* and *\addtolength* commands. These are some examples.

```
\setlength{\headrulewidth}{5pt}
\setlength{\footrulewidth}{0pt}
\addtolength{\footrulewidth}{.5ex}
```

Writing location information

Any counter has an associated value. The number of the current page is to be found in *\thepage*. This can be placed in any area of the header or footer, in any available size or shape.

Apparently LaTeX saves the current Chapter header contents in *\leftmark* and the current Section header contents in *\rightmark*. So you can write:

```
\rhead[\textsf{\rightmark}]{\large\textbf{\thepage}} %section
\lhead[\large\textbf{\thepage}]{\textsf{\leftmark}}  %chapter
```

This will put the section number and text on the right on even pages. It will put the Chapter number and text on the left on odd pages. The page number is the other piece of information in a header. This is also the default format for ordinary LaTeX headers.

There isn't usually enough space for center text. But you can change the appearance of the text in the header: Chapter or CHAPTER, and so forth. (See [Oostrum98] for the details.)

Mixing fancy and plain styles

In classic LaTeX, the first page of a chapter is automatically printed in a particular style called *plain*: i.e., there is no header and the page number in the center is the only information in the footer. Similarly, *fancyhdr* will by default write the first page of chapters with no header and a simple page number in the center of the footer.

There is, however, another mode called fancyplain, which you invoke in the preamble as the argument of *pagestyle*. You write **pagestyle**{**fancyplain**} instead of **pagestyle**{**fancy**}.

In fancyplain mode, *fancyhdr* accepts initial directions for two ways of dressing up the same component; it calls them *plain* and *fancy* formats. In point of fact, each can be as (over)elaborate as you wish. *plain* is automatically used to start chapters and you can enable it whenever you wish within the document. In keeping with its expanded layout possibilities, *fancyhdr* lets you design different plain formats for odd and even pages. And the plain designs and the fancy designs for a single component can be written as a single command. You issue the **fancyplain** command in the preamble or early on, and, unless you reissue the command, it will hold throughout the document. The format for writing the two is:

```
\fancyplain{Plain text}{Fancy text}
```

If you use separate text for all the areas, this is the overall syntax. In this, we use FET for Fancy Even-page <text>; *FOT* for Fancy Odd-page <text>; *PET* for Plain Even-page <text>; and *POT* for Plain Odd-page <text>. The rest of the syntax is familiar: text for even pages is written into the square brackets; text for odd pages is written into the braces.

The important thing to note is that you can completely describe how to write the headers and footers in one place for the entire document; then you 'toggle' between the plain and fancy versions by changing the argument of the *pagestyle* command. You switch to *plain* by writing **pagestyle**{**plain**}. You return to fancy mode with a **pagestyle**{**fancy**} command.

The plain format can be put into operation for just the current page with a **\thispage-style{plain}** command. The program will automatically return to the fancy form. **\this-pagestyle{empty}** works just as it does in LaTeX.

```
\lhead[\fancyplain{PET}{FET}]{\fancyplain{POT}{FOT}}
\chead[\fancyplain{PET}{FET}]{\fancyplain{POT}{FOT}}
\rhead[\fancyplain{PET}{FET}]{\fancyplain{POT}{FOT}}

\lfoot[\fancyplain{PET}{FET}]{\fancyplain{POT}{FOT}}
\cfoot[\fancyplain{PET}{FET}]{\fancyplain{POT}{FOT}}
\rfoot[\fancyplain{PET}{FET}]{\fancyplain{POT}{FOT}}
```

The thickness of the plain rules can also be controlled with these two commands: *\plainheadrulewidth* and *\plainfootrulewidth*. They are zero thickness by default.

In the tradition of Al Capp's Five Dollar Wedding, let's use them all. Suppose this describes our document layout. We are starting with a fancy style. This sets the text until the plain style command is issued.

Because the word *fancyplain* takes room in what can be a complex statement, we write a new command to provide us a short alias.

```
\newcommand{\fp}{\fancyplain}
```

```
\documentclass{report}
\usepackage{fancyhdr}
....                       % other packages
\pagenumbering{arabic}
\setcounter{page}{1}
\pagestyle{fancyplain}   % This enables you to write your own plain.
\setlength{\headwidth}{.85\textwidth}
\setlength{\headrulewidth}{3pt}
\setlength{\footrulewidth}{2pt}
\setlength{\plainheadrulewidth}{0pt}
\setlength{\plainfootrulewidth}{0pc}
```

```
\lhead[\fp{}{\large\prbf{\thepage}}]{\fp{}{\prbf{SOFTWARE PLANS}}}
\chead[\fp{}{Chair:\\ Mr. Chips}]{\fp{}{Secretary:\\ Dr. Septium}}
\rhead[\fp{}{\prsf{Meeting Minutes}}]{\fp{}{\prbf{\thepage}}}
\lfoot[\fp{CONFIDENTIAL}{CONFIDENTIAL}]{\fp{DO\\NOT\\COPY}{DO\\NOT\\COPY}}
\cfoot[\fp{\textbf{\thepage}}{}]{\fp{\large\textbf{\thepage}}{}}
\rfoot[\fp{}{Minutes Filed:\\ \today}]{\fp{}{Previous Meeting:\\5May97}}


\begin{document}
\thispagestyle{empty}
\NewPart{}{}{}{}{} %A variation on Part.


\pagestyle{fancy}
\chapter{} % The page will be in plain, but the setting stays at fancy.
. . . . . . . . .


\end{document}
```

31.3.3 Ensuring empty pages are empty of headers

Because of the way LaTeX configures headers, you may find that the empty page between chapters may not be empty. It may have a header and page number. In articles and books that use the openright option, this macro should erase the header.

```
\newcommand{\EMPTYPAGE}{\clearpage\thispagestyle{empty}\cleardoublepage}
```

Write the macro just before the start of a new chapter. If it isn't needed it will do no harm.

For example:

```
\EMPTYPAGE
\chapter{CREATING A STYLE SHEET}
```

If you have chosen or it has defaulted to the *openany* option—where a new chapter starts the next page after the last chapter—you can use this:

```
\newcommand{\EMPTYPAGE}{\clearpage\thispagestyle{empty}\clearpage}
```

Either one will ensure the empty page has no spurious header. And it will move the document on to the start of the next chapter.

The same principle holds after any unit in which one format with a header is separated from the next articulated unit. I wrote a macro to use at the beginning of each new part of this book.

```
\EMPTYPAGE
\pagestyle{myheadings}
\markboth{}{}
```

31.4   Forcing A Page Break

You can break a page where the program might not ordinarily do so in one of several ways. Note that the page breaking commands work only in text mode. If you're in two-column mode, the *\newpage* and *\pagebreak* commands start a new column; the *\clearpage* and *\cleardoublepage* start a new page. Contrariwise, the *\nopagebreak* prevents the program from breaking the page at that point.

\pagebreak This has a request and a demand format. Written by itself it is a demand that TeX finish justifying the current line and then break the page at that point. Written as **\pagebreak[#]**, where the optional number in the bracket can be from 0 to 4, it is a request. Zero is a very mild suggestion to please break the page and 4 is the same as a demand.

You can place this anywhere in a paragraph, except in a box or in an equation within the paragraph. This is very useful for forcing the last line on a page to the next page so the next page doesn't begin with a single isolated line.

\newpage This enforces an immediate page break, without line justification; i.e., it acts like the \\ on a line. It is useful just after a short full sentence, which might otherwise be stretched out by a *\pagebreak* command. This works immediately, even if the *\flushbottom* is set.

Writing a bunch of **\newpage** commands is the same as writing a single one. If you really want some blank pages, write invisible text after each *\newpage* command. Finish with a *\newpage* command.

```
%This sequence of commands creates two blank pages.
\newpage
\mbox{ }
\newpage
\mbox{ }
\newpage
```

\clearpage If the page contains figures or tables that will be pushed forward by the command, use this instead of *\newpage*. It will place the figures on the next page or pages by themselves. So this command is good for terminating a chapter or a section. It is more effective if combined with the *\afterpage* command as shown in Figure 16.2 in Section 16.1.2.

\cleardoublepage is a clearpage command for two-sided printing. It makes sure the next chapter begins on a right-side page. It can also be used to force the next section onto the next right-side page.

\enlargethispage{*<amount>*} Place this command where you want to enlarge (or reduce) the body of text on the page. It forces *amount* more (or less) print space. The previous lines are not affected. To reduce the last paragraph by two lines, for example, write **\enlargethispage{-22pt}** just before or inside the last paragraph. In increasing space, if you are not sure how much room to leave, you can request an overly generous amount of space. Just after the specific lines you want to see on that page, write a *\pagebreak* or *\newpage* command, depending on whether you do or do not want line justification for the last line on the current page. Combined with a page break command, the *\enlargethispage* command is very useful for preventing an isolated single line at the bottom of the page.

\enlargethispage*{*<amount>*} This command enlarges the print area and also deletes some of the vertical white space. If you aren't sure how much space to ask for, request more than enough. For example, **\enlargethispage*{100pt}** should certainly be enough to add a couple more print lines. Then write a *\pagebreak* or *\newpage* command in the right place in the text.

31.5   Numbering Pages

31.5.1   Styles for numbering pages

The styles available for numbering pages are the same styles that are available for all the counters:

  \arabic Ordinary numbers

  \roman Lower case roman numerals

  \Roman Upper case roman numerals

  \alph Lower case ordinary alphabet letters

  \Alph Upper case ordinary alphabet letters

A style is set in the preamble for the entire document with the **\pagenumbering**{*style*} command.

It can be reset later in the document with another style, which is sticky, unless reset.

In a book, **\pagenumbering{roman}** is usually used for the table of contents, the list of figures, acknowledgements, disclaimers, the preface and foreword.

\pagenumbering{arabic} is the default for the rest of the document.

31.5.2   Resetting the page number

The page is counted after the page number is written. This means that even though all the other counters recycle to zero, the page counter resets to one. If you need to reset the page number to 7, you would write **\setcounter**{**page**{**7**}} somewhere in the middle of the page, not **\setcounter**{**page**{**6**}}. Compare this to resetting footnote numbers.

Suppose in a book, we have all the preliminary material out of the way and want to reset numbering so that the first page of Chapter 1 is 1 in ordinary numbers. We could write:

```
\begin{document}
\pagenumbering{roman}
%text sections in Roman: TOC, PREFACE, etc.
\EMPTYPAGE
\part{I:...}
\pagenumbering{arabic}
\EMPTYPAGE
\chapter{Introduction}
\setcounter{page}{1}
```

31.6   Special Pages

If you wish a special insert or a novelty page or if a style doesn't suit you for a particular document division, you will need to design your own.

A Preface Page

This is the way I redid the Preface in simple fashion:

```
\pagestyle{myheadings}
\markboth{Preface}{Preface}
\EMPTYPAGE
\chapter*{\Huge\slshape PREFACE}
\hspace*{.01in}\vspace{.5in}
\addcontentsline{toc}{part}{\normalsize PREFACE}
```

Starting A New Part

The Part page was also redone. I did the numbering by hand for the first placeholder. The second and third placeholders are the title and subtitle. The fourth is a short text introduction to NewPart. The fifth is a mini table of contents; it lists the names of the chapters and sections in the part. It was 'lifted' from the LaTeX TOC and edited.

```
\newcommand{\NewPart}[5]{\EMPTYPAGE \raggedbottom
{\protect \begin{center}
\textbf{\huge Part {#1}} \\[2pc]
\textbf{\Huge {#2}} \\[3pc]
```

```
\textbf{\Huge {#3}} \\[3pc]
\protect \end{center}}
\normalsize {#4} \bigskip {#5}
\newpage \thispagestyle{empty} \cleardoublepage}
```

This begins the *\NewPart* for Part 3.

It is important that the braces surrounding the arguments are 'joined' without a gap; hence the %.

```
\EMPTYPAGE
\pagestyle{myheadings}
\markboth{}{}
\NewPart{III.}{WRITING \LaTeX.}{Markup\\[.2in] Instructions}%
{Open your practice file: \prit{practice.tex}.

The first significant line (\prbf{\BS documentclass\{article\}})
marks the beginning of the  preamble. The preamble is the region
between that line and the line that reads:
\prbf{\BS begin\{document\}}. Store new commands in the preamble..
```

Alternatively, it is also an error if this next were to occur, when you rejustify a paragraph. The % now acts to remove the start of the next argument from the printout.

```
\NewPart{III.}{WRITING \LaTeX.}{Markup \\[.2in]Instructions}%{Open
your practice file: \prit{practice.tex}.
```

This is a piece from the fifth argument from the same Part 3.

```
{\bd
\item LaTeX-RESERVED SINGLE CHARACTER COMMANDS \dotfill \ref{ss:10single}
\bi
\item Single Character Command Symbols \dotfill \ref{ss:10chars}
\item Writing Special Symbols as Ordinary Text \dotfill \ref{ss:ordinary}
\item Aliases For Single Character Commands \dotfill \ref{ss:alias}
\item Meta Level Mimicking of Text Commands \dotfill \ref{ss:mimic}
\ei
\item SINGLE-WORD INSTRUCTIONS \dotfill \ref{ss:symbols}
\bi
\item Font Features \dotfill \ref{ss:fontfeatures}
```

```
. . . . . .
\ei
\ed
. . . . .
```

An Appendix Page

The appendix introductory page was also redone as an abbreviated NewPart command.

```
\newcommand{\NewAppendix}[2]{\EMPTYPAGE \raggedbottom
{\protect \begin{center}
\textbf{\huge APPENDIX} \\[2pc]
\protect \end{center}}
\normalsize {#1} \bigskip {#2}
\newpage \thispagestyle{empty} \cleardoublepage}
```

Chapter numbering was changed to Upper case letters just after the use of the \NewAppendix command. Section and subsection numbering continued in ordinary numbers. As did page numbering.

```
\NewAppendix%
{ }%
{ }
\addcontentsline{toc}{part}{\normalsize APPENDIX}

\EMPTYPAGE
\renewcommand{\thechapter}{\Alph{chapter}}
\setcounter{chapter}{0}
```

Chapter 32

CREATING A STYLE SHEET

32.1   Resources For Creating Style Sheets

You can do a great deal by using the forms and templates available in LaTeX as is or by elaborating existing styles. You can create dramatically different appearances in the text by writing new commands that are minor or ambitious modifications of the built-in constructions. You can change fonts for emphasis or for added interest. You can indent, outdent, do center minipages, side floats, sidebars and margin comments. You can write the text in one column, or two, or even three. You can add icons, bullets and images. The workhorse LaTeX objects—lists, tables, figures, arrays—can be adapted for almost any publication task.

What is a style sheet? The particular layout instructions for the general appearance of the page, the values in the macros you contribute, the specific spacings of the partitions that divide the document, the LaTeX entities you modify, the enrichments added to your repertoire by the packages distributed with LaTeX, the small local changes you consistently make to emphasize a word or two—all these taken together become the style sheet for a particular document. The real trick is not finding additional constructions and styles but making sure they contribute to helping the text 'talk'. You don't want the message lost in a dazzling medium.

Should you need a particular feature or structure, explore. There is a wealth of material available, which is almost automatically usable, once it's on disk. This is because packages

481

that are accepted as ancillary LATEX files must conform to the general stylistic and grammatical practices of the LATEX community, must be written in TEX and must be capable of being accessed via the *usepackage* command. The ones listed below are available in the Linux distribution and many of them have served to illustrate particular print tasks in this book.

★ The *.*sty* files are packages that extend or enhance or fix an annoyance in a LATEX command. They can be used in your document by writing **\usepackage{**<*PackageName*>**}** in the preamble. Do NOT use the *sty* extension of the package in the argument; e.g., write **\usepackage{alltt}**, not **\usepackage{alltt.sty}**. These packages are routinely distributed with LATEX. Except for the ones like *babel* and *amslatex* that are so large they have their own subdirectory, these packages are mostly in: ˜*/texmf/tex/latex/base*; still others are in ˜*/texmf/tex/latex/misc*. Consult the files in ˜*/doc/latex/styles* for documentation of the different packages in ˜*/texmf/tex/latex-/misc*.

Section 32.3, contains a list of some of these packages.

★ Check the CTAN sites to see if there's a package out there that will mostly do what you want. You can modify it if need be in the same way you modify the files that are installed with LATEX.

★ For major changes in the structure of your document class, go to the directory where the LATEX **.cls** and **.sty** files are kept.[1] As usual, you can find the directory by doing a **locate**; e.g., *locate book.cls*.

1. Suppose you are using the book class. Make copies of *book.cls* and *book.sty*. Call them, say, *newbook.cls* and *newbook.sty*. Do NOT modify the originals; they are copyright.

2. Change a font or a module in *newbook.cls*. Remember that internal commands in a package usually begin with a @ to avoid conflict with potential user-created commands. To redo a new environment, you may run into the TEX **\def** command instead of **\newenvironment**. Section 26.2.2 illustrates a modification in naming the bibliographic section.

3. At the bottom of the newbook.sty file, there is a line that reads:

---

[1]The *.cls* files refer to LATEX classes—book, slide, and so forth. The class for the document is declared in the preamble using the **\documentclass{**<*class*>**}** command. Do NOT use the *cls* extension in the Class argument.

```
\@obsoletefile{book.cls}{book.sty}
\LoadClass{book}
```

Change it to:

```
\@obsoletefile{newbook.cls}{newbook.sty}
\LoadClass{newbook}
```

4. In the preamble of your document, change: *\documentclass{book}* to *\documentclass{newbook}*.

5. Run **texhash**, the program that updates the list of files the program knows where to find. *texhash* adds *newbook.cls* and *newbook.sty* to the list. The next time you run LATEX on the document, the program will use your definition of the book class.

32.2   Large Software Packages That Are LATEX-related

Software packages such as *amslatex* or *babel* are massive and come complete with multiple files. To use a package, write a **\usepackage**{<*PackageName*>} statement in the preamble.

★ **amslatex.** AMS stands for *American Mathematical Society*. *amslatex* is supported by AMS and is described in the *AMS* LATEX Users Guide as "miscellaneous enhancements for superior information structure of mathematical documents and superior printed output." This is not an exaggeration. It is an impressive package that provides a rich menu of commands for typesetting mathematical formulae. Some of their symbols can be seen in Part V on formatting in math mode. See also Figures 12.9 and 12.10 in Chapter 12.

★ **babel.** The complete command to use this package is **\usepackage**[<*language*>]-{**babel**}, where you fill the square brackets with *french* for french, *polish* for polish, and so forth. See *babel.sty* in ˜/texmf/tex/generic/babel for the list of supported languages. This package, written by Johannes Braams [Braams96], is essential for typesetting in various languages. The package works with whatever font(s) you pick for the document. Babel commands produce sensible vocabulary results. For example: the \today command with the French option outputs *Janvier*, not *January*. Document partition commands, such as \chapter and \section, are written in the particular language; necessary accents used by the language are provided.

⋆ **graphicx** This is the enhanced graphics program written by David Carlisle and Sebastian Rahtz [Carlisle95b] that lets you insert graphics and pictures that were produced using any paint and image processing program capable of outputting a product in Encapsulated PostScript. See Chapter 25. The accompanying **color** package will format the page to print color versions of graphics, designs and pictures on a color printer.

⋆ **mfnfss.** This directory contains packages and font definition files for bitmapped METAFONT fonts such as Old German and Pandora. See Section 11.3.2 on the NFSS scheme for cataloguing these fonts.

⋆ **psnfss.** The packages in this directory print a variety of Type 1 Adobe PostScript fonts. See Section 11.5.5.

32.3   Packages That Are Bundled With LATEX

These packages are included with the current LATEX program.[2] *tools* consists of a group of font and test programs and useful additions to the LATEX markup commands. Miscellaneous packages are in *~/texmf/doc/latex/styles*. Some of the packages have documentation—see *List of References* below. The several packages listed here do not reference all the packages that come with a Linux distribution. And there is much larger group of packages maintained by CTAN. Look at */doc/help/Catalogue* for the list of CTAN tools and packages that can be downloaded from the Net. See the Preface for the list of CTAN locations.

To use a package, write a **\usepackage**{<*PackageName*>} statement in the preamble.

⋆ **alltt.** A very useful verbatim package by Leslie Lamport and Johannes Braams [Lamport96] in which \, { and } continue to act as command delimiters. See Section 19.1 for a discussion.

---

[2]The list is taken from the latest version of *usrguide.dvi* by the LATEX3 Project Team and entitled *LATEX2ε For Authors* [Latex3PT95].

⋆ **exscale.** This is a package written by Frank Mittelbach and Rainer Schöpf, It will scale the math extension font. It is one of ways to change the overall size of an equation; see Section 20.2.3.

⋆ **fontenc.** This will specify the font encoding scheme for LATEX to use. It is by default OT1. See Section 11.3.2 for an example of usage with Cork encoding.

⋆ **graphpap.** This package, written by Leslie Lamport, lets you use the **\graphpaper** command within the LATEX picture environment. See Section 24.1.2 for an example of usage.

⋆ **ifthen.** This package by Leslie Lamport lets you write **if then...else...** statements.

⋆ **inputenc.** This will specify the input encoding for LATEX to use, if the encoding is other than the default 0T1.

⋆ **latexsym.** This provides shadow math fonts and additional symbols. See Section 20.1 for a list of some of these symbols.

⋆ **makeidx.** This is used to make LATEX indices. See Chapter 28.

⋆ **moreverb.** This package, written by Robin Fairbairns [Fairbairns96], extends the verbatim command. See Section 19.1 for an example of usage.

⋆ **showidx.** This will print each word that you have indexed on the page where it occurred.

⋆ **subfigure** by Steven Douglas Cochran [Cochran95] presents multiple figures, with, if you wish, separate captions in a single unified layout. See the figure in Section 16.1.3 for an example of usage.

⋆ **syntonly.** This will process a document through LATEX without typesetting it.

⋆ **tools.** This consists of a number of miscellaneous packages that act as enhancements to LATEX. For example, **layout** draws an excellent diagram of the different components of a page layout; it was written by Kent McPherson [McPherson95]; see Section 31.1. The **multicol** package by Frank Mittelbach [Mittelbach96a] extends the two-columns option previously available; see Section 16.3.3 for an example of its use. The **\dcolumn** program, written by David Carlisle [Carlisle96b], aligns decimal numbers properly in a column; see Section 16.3.2 for an example of usage.

afterpage, a program written by David Carlisle [Carlisle95a], coupled with \clearpage, fills the current page with text before moving the float to the next page. This is a very useful resource, given the difficult task of providing a float the space it needs, yet placing it somewhat near the text it illustrates. See Figure 16.2.

array by Frank Mittelbach extends the array and tabular environments. **longtable** by David Carlisle [Carlisle96a] lets you write a tabular environment across pages. See Section 16.3.2 for an example of usage. **enumerate** by David Carlisle extends the enumerate list features to use different number styles; **varioref** by David Carlisle handles page references so that, should you be on page 75, you don't instruct the reader to 'see figure 2.5 on page 75'. **verbatim** by Rainer Schöpf, Bernd Raichle and Chris Rowley extends the verbatim environment; it now includes a *comment* environment, where the text within the comment is not printed. **xr** by David Carlisle is useful in cross-referencing several documents that may have the same label. **fontsmpl** shows you different fonts, even if you are in Computer Modern Roman, which doesn't have the ability to reproduce the DC fonts. If you write **latex fontsmpl** in an xterm, the output will be a small file printed in that particular font.

32.4   Modular Packages Versus Do-It-Yourself

As the previous sections demonstrate, there is a wealth of packages to help you format your document. The advantages in using a prefab package are many, not the least of which is that some one else has worked out major bugs and worried about interactions with other commands. It could take you a long time to get it right.

There is no argument that some packages are indispensable. Were I a mathematician, I wouldn't like to do without the $\mathcal{A}_{\mathcal{M}}\mathcal{S}$ packages. Nor do I want to try to import pictures and graphics without the *graphicx* package. Some programs make formatting much more convenient than it would otherwise be. It is worth familiarizing yourself with what is available. There's bound to be several packages out there that you will soon find indispensable.

On the other hand, few packages are simple—*multicol* and *alltt* being delightful exceptions. It is seldom that you write a command, fill in a couple of arguments and get exactly what you want. In the group of packages that deal with tables, there are stated interactions with other packages, so you have to decide which one you call before the other. More likely, there are unspoken rules of context and grammar and reasoning. To take an example from a LaTeX command rather than a package—I spent time figuring out why a \secnumdepth of 4 also numbered the paragraph, when I assumed it would stop numbering with the subsubsection. Obviously, I had assumed the command started incrementing from zero, not from one.

Many programs come with their own vocabulary, set of rules, set of precedence rules, list of restrictions, and so forth, so there can be a sizable amount of effect involved in learning to use them properly. Many are flaky, not because they are poorly-written, but because they are sitting on top of a complex package that imposes severe limits on them.

Many have been designed for one type of environment, and you may find yourself working very hard to get it right in another type of situation. Side floats, for example, are particularly difficult to get right. They get swallowed up or they overwrite lists and other LaTeX object. *wrapfig* is robust, but it didn't always do what I wanted with pictures. After experimenting, I found it helped to put the float in a minipage. Rule of thumb. No real understanding.

If, on the other hand, you decide to write your own formatting solution, it may take time to get it just right. But constructing your own has the virtue that you become practiced in particular commands and 'understand' them. *vspace, hspace* and *minipage* are particularly high on my list.

Constructing your own design for a LaTeX design object may also mean some inconvenience. It may also put you in conflict with another LaTeX command. As an example, I redesigned the Preface, Part and Appendix. (See Section 31.6.) It worked well, except that

     I needed to write the list of Chapters and Sections myself in the last argument of NewPart, my substitute for Part. It is not onerous in Emacs, but it does take a little time.

     The page numbering of NewPart in the table of contents was incorrect. So I needed to get into the TOC file to renumber the 9 NewPart pages. Again, not difficult, but another side effect that needed handling.

You may prefer these available alternatives.

\minitoc [Drucbert94] is an alternative way to write multiple table of contents for the book or report document classes. A minitable prepends the start of each Chapter and lists the (sub)sections in the chapter and their page numbers. Call the program with a **\usepackage{minitoc}** in the preamble. Associated packages such as *mtccroatian.sty,* *mtcczech.sty* and *mtcdanish.sty* add titles in the language chosen. Different commands let you determine the font, the number of headings to be displayed and the size of the indentation.

LaTeX has a document division layout, so that you can systematically change font, spacing and indentation. It is discussed by Goossens et al in [Goossens94, Section 2.3]. This may be the way to go if you want to change the style of a frequently-used header such as Section or Subsection.

The rest of this chapter illustrates ways, not previously considered, of redesigning some basic formats and adding new ones. I assume you have designed the pictorial components—the logos, the patterns, the diagrams, the photographs—with the aid of the programs in Chapter 24.

32.5   Slides

The single slide was discussed in Section 3.4. It is reintroduced here to show another feature of the slide class: a slide can have one or more overlays. You can use the color commands from Section 25.4.9, if you first request the *graphicx* and *color* packages. The white color is used to blank a line. Recall that the FoilTeX package (see Section 12.4) will produce color slides. There is also an advanced slides program written by Van Zandt [Zandt93b].

You would write a slide and overlay(s) as a separate document as shown next. The output, Figure 32.1, is a PostScript file generated from a slides class document.

```
\documentclass[dvips]{slides}
\usepackage{color,graphicx}
\begin{document}
The Markup For the Slide
\begin{slide}
\begin{center}
\textcolor{DGray}{This is an example of a}
\textcolor{white}{\LaTeX\ instruction.}
\textcolor{DGray}{Text is embedded within a center environment.}
\end{center}
\end{slide}
```

```
The Markup For The Overlay
\begin{overlay}
\begin{center}
\textcolor{white}{This is an example of a}
\textcolor{LGray}{\LaTeX\ instruction.}
\textcolor{white}{Text is embedded within a center environment.}
\end{center}
\end{overlay}
\end{document}
```

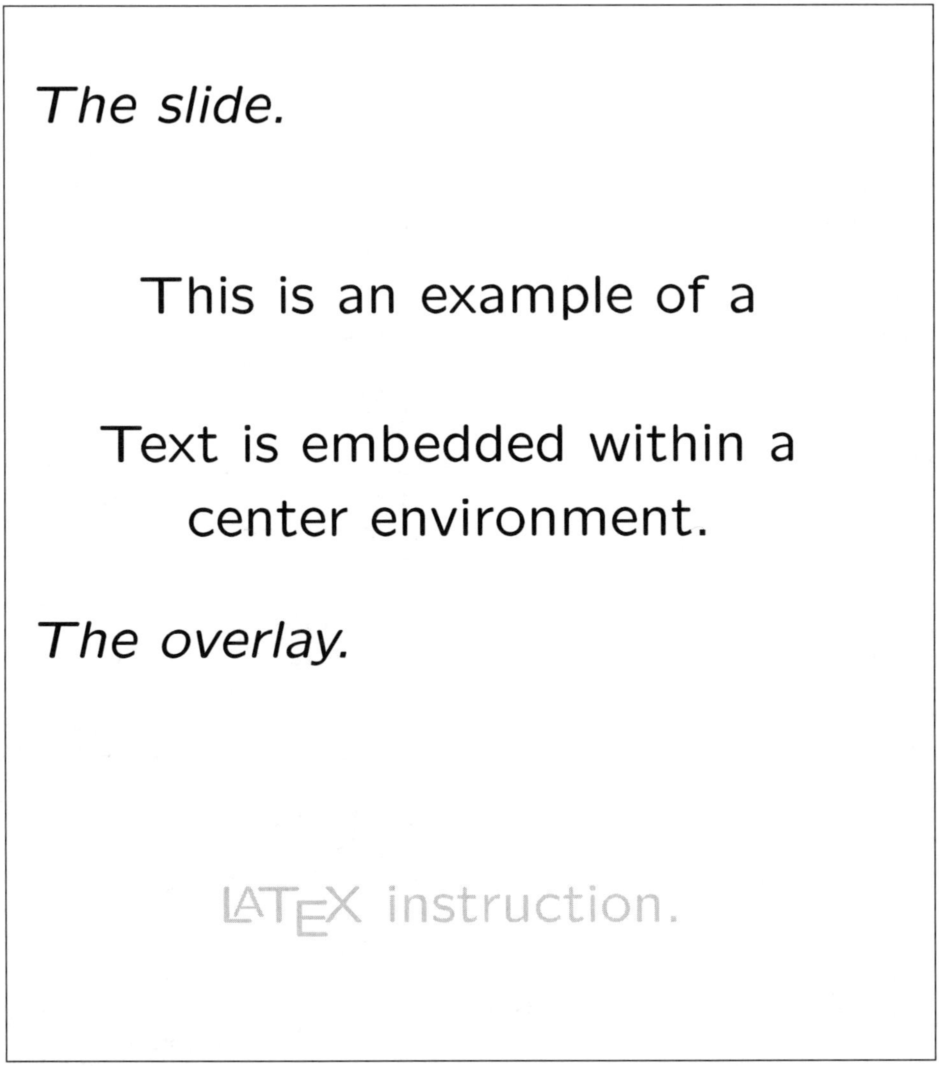

The slide.

This is an example of a

Text is embedded within a
center environment.

The overlay.

LaTeX instruction.

Figure 32.1: Two transparencies: a slide and its overlay

32.6 Letters

The basic LaTeX letter shown in Section 3.5 places the writer's name and the date on the far right. We can create various letter styles by writing the letter in the article class and creating our own headers. In fact, we can create different letter templates for different occasions. In imitation of stationery headers, this next template centers the writer's name and address; the rest of the letter is left-sided. The directives on *parindent* and *parskip* make sure there's an empty line between paragraphs. The main font has been reset to PS Times Roman. Changing font and size of font are major ways of creating different visual impacts.

To write multiple letters in a single file, use a single \begin{document} and \end{document}. Write the global directives in the preamble. If you use smaller than 8.5x11 inch paper, adjust *textheight, textwidth* and *hoffset. hoffset* shifts the body text horizontally; in this case, the body of the text is shifted to the left for better symmetry.

Write a **\newpage** command after each letter. Begin each letter with a another copy of these commands: **\setcounter{page}{1}** and **\thispagestyle{empty}**. Follow with a new copy of the header and so forth.

```
\documentclass[11pt]{article}    % Uses an 11 point font.
\input macros.tex                % Assuming you have a file of macros.
\flushbottom                     % Paragraphs will be separated
\parindent=0pc                   % by blank lines. Paragraphs will
\setlength{\parskip}{1pc}        % not be indented.

\setlength{\textheight}{8.5in}   % For ordinary 8.5x11" paper.
\setlength{\textwidth}{6in}      % Width of text across a line.
\setlength{\hoffset}{-.75in}     % Horizontal offset.
\setlength{\voffset}{-1in}       % Use this if the start of each
                                 % page is too low on the page.

\pagestyle{plain}                % Numbering will be at the bottom
                                 % of the page
\pagenumbering{arabic}           % Numbering will be in ordinary
                                 % numbers.
\renewcommand{\rmdefault}{ptm}   % Letter will be in PS Times Roman.
\renewcommand{\familydefault}{ptm}
\renewcommand{\sfdefault}{cmss}  % Print Sans Serif in Computer Modern.
\renewcommand{\ttdefault}{cmtt}  % Print Verbatim in Computer Modern.
\fontencoding{OT1}\fontfamily{ptm}\fontseries{m}% Sets the size, etc.
```

```
\fontshape{n}\fontsize{10pt}{13pt}\selectfont    % of the main font.
\normalfont\normalsize

\begin{document}

\setcounter{page}{1}                    % Starts each letter at page 1.
\thispagestyle{empty}                   % Do not number the 1st page of
                                        % the letter.
\begin{center}
\textsl{\Large Name of Writer\\
\normalsize Street Address\\
City STATE ZIP\\
TEL: <fill in>\\
FAX: <fill in> \\ }
\upshape Email: <fill in>
\end{center}

\today

Name of Recipient\\
Title of Recipient\\
Address of Recipient\\
TEL: <fill in>\\
FAX: <fill in> \\
Email: <fill in>

BODY OF LETTER

Sincerely\\[4pc]
Name of Writer
\newpage
\setcounter{page}{1}                    % Starts each letter at page 1.
\thispagestyle{empty}                   % Do not number the 1st page.
NEXT LETTER STARTS HERE.
\newpage
.....................
\end{document}
```

The header can be generalized so it can be used for different people—just fill in the blanks in the new command name *\addr* as shown. The examples below are modifications of the basic style.

The MarkUp:

```
\newcommand{\addr}[3]%
{\begin{center}
\textsl{\Large #1 \\
\normalsize #2 } \\
\upshape #3
\end{center}}


\addr{Max L. Joels}%
{99 Arthur Road \\
Bethesda MD 20817 \\
TEL: 301 555 3234\\
FAX: 301 555 1234 }%
{Email: Max@erols.com}
```

The PrintOut:

> **Max L. Joels**
> *99 Arthur Road*
> *Bethesda MD 20817*
> *TEL: 301 555 3234*
> *FAX: 301 555 1234*
> Email: Max@erols.com

The MarkUp:

```
\begin{center}
\bfseries
\vspace{.5pc}
\Huge Max L. Joels\\
\vspace{.5pc}
\large 99 Arthur Road\\
Bethesda MD 20817 \\
TEL: 301 555 3234\\
FAX: 301 555 1234 \\
Email: Max@erols.com
\end{center}
```

The PrintOut:

> # ***Max L. Joels***
>
> ***99 Arthur Road***
> ***Bethesda MD 20817***
> ***TEL: 301 555 3234***
> ***FAX: 301 555 1234***
> ***Email: Max@erols.com***

The MarkUp:

```
\definecolor{lightgrey}{gray}{.8}
\colorbox{lightgrey}{\bmp{3in}
\letterspace to
.5\textwidth{MAX L. JOELS}
\vspace{.5pc}\letterspace to
.4\textwidth{99 Arthur Road}
\letterspace to
.4\textwidth{Bethesda MD 20817}
\letterspace to .4\textwidth{TEL: 301 555 3234}
\letterspace to .4\textwidth{FAX: 301 555 1234}
\letterspace to .4\textwidth{Email: Max@erols.com}
\vspace{.1pc}\emp }
```

The PrintOut:

> M A X   L .   J O E L S
>
> 9 9   A r t h u r   R o a d
> Bethesda MD 20817
> TEL: 301 555 3234
> FAX: 301 555 1234
> Email: Max@erols.com

The MarkUp:

```
\bmp{2.5in}
\includegraphics[bb=0 0 175 200,clip]{max3.eps}\emp
\hspace*{-1in}\bmp{2.75in}\vspace{.3in}
\Large Max L. Joels\\
\normalsize\hspace*{.5in}99 Arthur Road \\
\hspace*{.75in}Bethesda MD 20817\\
\hspace*{1in}Email: Max@erols.com\emp
```

The PrintOut:

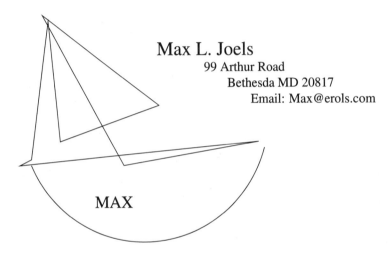

Tom Whatever

Personal Sales Rep

Netscape Communications Corporation

455 East Middlefield Road

Mountain View CA 94043

Dear Mr Whatever,

I would like to thank the people in your organization for their advice on how to download Netscape to work under Unix and Linux.

For UNIX: ftp://ftp.netscape.com/pub/cooltalk/unix

For Linux, the binaries are in: ftp://ftp.netscape.com/pub/unsupported/gnu/

Also: ftp://ftp.netscape.com/pub/navigator/3.04/ shipping/english/unix/linux12/naviga-tor_gold_complete

For the communicator: ftp://ftp.netscape.com/pub/communicator/3.04/ shipping/english-/unix/linux20/

and help notes in: http://help.netscape.com/faqs.html

Sincerely,

32.7   FAX Formats

Use the same instructions in the preamble as those in the *letters* preamble in the previous section. Adjust them for different size paper and font.

The MarkUp:

```
\documentclass{article}
\newcommand{\faxadd}[2]{
\large \parindent=0in
\textbf{#1} \\[1pc]
\normalsize  #2 \\ }

\begin{document}
\faxadd{FROM:}
{Max L. Joels \\
FAX: 301 555 1234 }

\faxadd{TO:}
{L.E. Lewis \\
FAX: 301 555 0245}

\faxadd{DATE:}
{\today}

\faxadd{NUMBER OF PAGES:}
{2 including this one}
\newpage
PAGE 2: WRITE STUFF HERE
```

The PrintOut:

FROM:

Max L. Joels
FAX: 301 555 1234

TO:

L.E. Lewis
FAX: 301 555 0245

DATE:

July 11, 1998

NUMBER OF PAGES:

2 including this one

PAGE 2: WRITE STUFF HERE

32.8 Front Covers

The different cover designs shown below have simple elements: a title, an author name and a here-be-logo.

A is an example of a half and half vertical split, shared between author and logo. Variations would center the logo and the author's name in their territories. Or push the logo flush left and the author's name flush right. It is also a 1/3 and 2/3 horizontal split, with the title 1/3 of the distance down. Simple changes in font style, font size, the addition of a background wash, an assertive graphic or a fade-into-the background picture make for profoundly different visual effects.

B use roughly a 1/3 and 2/3 vertical split, where a complicated logo is balanced by the other elements. This is a lot trickier. Weight (created by the size and volume and color of the logo) makes or breaks the visual impact.

C is a classic design. It is balanced by its nature. It would take a lot to muck it up. Like Design A, this can be subjected to much variability in font, color and background image, without losing balance. It is also fairly easy to add icons or colorful stick figures or swatches of elegant equations, without making the cover appear cluttered.

The design instructions are encased in the FrameCoverPage macro, a variant of FrameIt. (See Section 23.4) It differs in that it includes four placeholders, one for each of the complete set of minipage parameters. This lets us set minipage height as well as width.

```
\newsavebox{\FrameCoverPage}
\newenvironment{FrameCover}[4]%
{\begin{lrbox}{\FrameCoverPage}\begin{minipage}[#1][#2][#3]{#4}}%
{\end{minipage}\end{lrbox}\fbox{\usebox{\FrameCoverPage}}}
```

#1 is box alignment—where the box sits on the current baseline. The possibilities are Top, Bottom, Center.

#2 is box height. This is particularly useful if you use a vertical stretch command to apportion the empty space.

#3 is text position in the box. Like #1, the text can be pushed *t, b* or *c*. There is an additional possibility: *s*, to stretch the text through the box's vertical extent.

#4 is box width.

The grammar is straightforward. For example:

```
\begin{FrameCover}{c}{3in}{s}{2.5in}
end{FrameCover}
```

We will also make use of these two new commands:

```
\newcommand{\BFC}{\begin{FrameCover}}
\newcommand{\EFC}{\end{FrameCover}}
```

The Markup For A :   *The Printout For A:*

```
\BFC{c}{3in}{s}{2.50in}
\vspace*{\stretch{1}}
\textit{\LARGE  A TALE OF}
\vspace{4mm}

\hspace*{.85in}
\textit{\LARGE TWO CITIES}

\vspace*{\stretch{2}}
\bmp{1.2in}
\large\textsc{Charles\\Dickens}
\emp
\hspace{.1in}
\FramePix{.5in}
{Logo\\ Here\\}
\EFC
```

$$A\ TALE\ OF$$

$$TWO\ CITIES$$

CHARLES
DICKENS

Logo
Here

The Markup For B :

```
\BFC{c}{3in}{s}{2.50in}
\vspace*{\stretch{1}}
\begin{flushright}
\textit{\LARGE A TALE OF\\[5mm]
\LARGE TWO CITIES}
\rule{\linewidth}{.8mm}
\end{flushright}
\vspace*{\stretch{2}}
\FramePix[b]{.5in}
{\bfseries Logo\\ Here}
\hspace{.1in}
\bmp[b]{1.2in}
\hspace*{.4in}
\large\textsc{Charles}

\hspace*{.4in}
\large\textsc{ Dickens}
\emp
\EFC
```

The Printout For B:

A TALE OF
TWO CITIES

| Logo Here | CHARLES DICKENS |

The Markup For C :

```
\BFC{c}{3in}{s}{2.50in}
\vspace*{\stretch{1}}
\rule{\linewidth}{.8mm}
\prsc{\large A TALE OF TWO CITIES}
\rule{\linewidth}{.8mm}

\vspace*{\stretch{2}}
\bmp[b]{2.5in}
\centering
\large\textsc{Charles Dickens}
\emp
\vspace*{\stretch{1}}
\centering\FramePix[b]{.45in}
{\bfseries \small Logo Here}
\EFC
```

The Printout For C:

A   TALE   OF   TWO   CITIES

CHARLES DICKENS

| Logo Here |

32.9 Chapter Starts

Aside from the fairly stylized numbered sections of technical articles, the graphics of chapter headings is unrestricted. Here are a few picked at random and copied. The examples are boxed to keep things tidy. These box parameters are also set. Recall that *fboxrule* controls line thickness; *fboxsep* sets the distance from the frame to the text.

```
\setlength{\fboxrule}{.5pt}
\setlength{\fboxsep}{5pt}
```

For Example 1, we begin by defining yet another box environment: SaveDoc. It differs from most of the ones we've used in that it uses all the minipage options. In this way, we can force the box to a specific height.

To obtain the width, however, we need to fill the box with something; so we use some spaces. Recall that the *\rule* command writes the width *before* the height of the rulebox. If there are three arguments, the first is the height the line is raised.

And we define a light gray as a secondary color.

Example 1:

```
Complete Minipage Format: #1-3 are options. #4 is mandatory.
#1: box alignment (t is default); #2: box height.
#3: text posn in box.  #4: box width.

\newsavebox{\SaveDocPage}
\newenvironment{SaveDoc}[4][t]%
{\begin{lrbox}{\SaveDocPage}\begin{minipage}[#1][#2][#3]{#4}}%
{\end{minipage}\end{lrbox}\usebox{\SaveDocPage}}
\NC{\BSD}{\begin{SaveDoc}}
\NC{\ESD}{\end{SaveDoc}}
\definecolor{lightgrey}{gray}{.7}
```

The MarkUp:

```
\bbmp{\textwidth}                  %bbmp is AKA \begin{boxedminipage}.
\fcolorbox{lightgrey}{white}{      %This section creates a inner gray
\colorbox{lightgrey}{              %box and the frame of an outer box.
\BSD{2pt}{t}{\textwidth-.5in}      %BSD is AKA \begin{SaveDoc}
\ \ \ \
\ESD  \\[1pc] }                    %ESD is AKA end{SaveDoc}


\hspace{-\textwidth}               %This writes the text in the boxes.
\bmp{\textwidth-1.82in}            % \bmp is AKA \begin{minipage}
\textit{\Huge I\normalsize t was  the best of times,
it was the worst of times.}        % } ends the \colorbox argument.
\emp                               % \emp is AKA \end{minipage}
\hspace{1.5in}
\Huge 1 }                          % } ends the \fcolorbox argument.
\ebmp                              %ebmp is AKA \end{boxedminipage}.
```

*I*t was the best of times, it was the worst of times.   **1**

Example 2:

The MarkUp:

```
\NC{\Di}[1]{\fontsize{8}{10pt}\usefont{U}{pzd}{m}{n}\symbol{'#1}}
\NC{\Dib}{\Di{104}}

\rule{\textwidth}{2pt}\\
\rule{\textwidth}{1pt}\\[-.5pt]
\Dib\Dib\sgap\Dib\Dib\sgap\Dib\Dib\sgap\Dib\Dib\sgap\Dib\Dib\sgap
\Dib\Dib\sgap\Dib\Dib\sgap\Dib\Dib\sgap\Dib\Dib\sgap\Dib\Dib\sgap
\Dib\Dib\sgap\Dib\Dib\sgap\\[1pc]
\normalfont
\begin{center}
\LARGE Chapter 1\\[1pc]
\end{center}
\normalsize It was the best of times, it was the worst of times.
```

Example 3:

'Chapter' was done in XFig, using a large font and rotation.

It was the best of times, it was the worst of times.

Example 4:

The MarkUp:

```
\setlength{\fboxrule}{1mm}
\setlength{\fboxsep}{1pc}
\hspace*{2in}\fbox{ONE}\\[1pc]
\Large It was the best of times,\normalsize it was the worst of times.
\setlength{\fboxrule}{0.5pt}
\setlength{\fboxsep}{3pt}
```

ONE

It was the best of times, it was the worst of times.

Example 5:

The MarkUp:

```
\begin{minipage}[b]{.9in}
\rule{1.2in}{1mm}\vspace*{.5mm}
\textbf{\large Chapter 1}
\vspace*{.5mm}
\rule{1.2in}{1mm}
\end{minipage}
\hspace*{1in}
\bmp[t]{2in}
It was the best of times, it was the worst of times.
\emp
```

```
┌─────────────────────────────────────────────────────────────┐
│  ▬▬▬▬▬▬▬▬▬▬▬                                                  │
│                                                              │
│  Chapter   1                                                 │
│                           It was the best of times, it was the│
│  ▬▬▬▬▬▬▬▬▬▬▬              worst of times.                     │
│                                                              │
└─────────────────────────────────────────────────────────────┘
```

32.10   Footnotes And End Notes

Section 17.4 discussed a way to list footnotes at the end of the chapter rather than at the bottom of each page. This section demonstrates endnotes that do not necessarily interfere with the ordinary LaTeX footnotes. Depending on the journal or academic area, these notes may or may not substitute for footnotes. These endnotes combine references, acknowledgements, notes, glosses, etc; they have become a popular substitute for *in situ* footnotes in scholarly journals where the amount of note text to body text is high.

To utilize the endnote, we first create a new counter, *endnote*, and a new command, \EN. \EN will mark the endnote in the body text. Then we create an Enumerate List wherever we wish to place the List of Endnotes.

```
\newcounter{endnote}
\setcounter{endnote}{0}
\newcommand{\EN}{\addtocounter{endnote}{+1}\textit{\theendnote}}
```

Example 1: *Science*[3] **style.**

The MarkUp:

```
Computer modeling (\EN) has become an essential tool in genome (\EN)
research on environmental genes. Smith et al (\EN) pioneered the
utilization of heuristic processing. (See also \EN, \EN\ and \EN.)

\textbf{REFERENCES AND NOTES}
\be
\item Brown, A, \prit{Comp. Methods}, \prbf{20}, 23 (1989). An early
reference to decision trees.
\item The Genome Project has stimulated the systematic
determination of what genes are associated with what diseases.
\item Smith, R, Green, M. and Black, T. \prit{Science}, \prbf{179},
720 (1986).
\item
..
\ee
```

The PrintOut: Computer modeling (*1*) has become an essential tool in genome (*2*) research on environmental genes. Smith et al (*3*) pioneered the utilization of heuristic processing. (See also *4, 5* and *6*.)

(on a new page)

REFERENCES AND NOTES

1. Brown, A, *Comp. Methods*, **20**, 23 (1989). An early reference to decision trees.

2. The Genome Project has stimulated the systematic attack on determining what genes are associated with what diseases.

3. Smith, R, Green, M. and Black, T. *Science*, **179**, 720 (1986).

   ....

Example 2: *TRADITION*[4] **style.** This is an example of a journal where biblical and other standard references are parenthesized in the text. Footnotes and extensive notes are numbered as ordinary footnotes, but placed in a single place per article. We redo the *EN* command this way:

---

[3]*Science* is published by the American Association for the Advancement of Science. This is not an actual excerpt.

[4]*TRADITION* is a publication of the Rabbinical Council of America. The example is not an actual excerpt.

```
\setcounter{endnote}{0}
\renewcommand{\EN}{\addtocounter{endnote}{+1}%
{\footnotesize\raisebox{.8ex}{\theendnote}\ }}
```

separated by commas:

```
\newcommand{\ENc}{\addtocounter{endnote}{+1}%
{\footnotesize\raisebox{.8ex}{\theendnote,}}}
```

The MarkUp:

```
Another approach\EN to understanding the text\EN is to compare it with
translations of earlier versions\ENc\EN (\textit{Gen.} 24:10--14.) ...
```

```
\textbf{NOTES}
\be
\item The text never identifies the narrator. Reasoning from similar
episodes, however, we may reduce the possible candidates to three; see
\textit{infra}.
\item The usual practice is to abide by the translation in the Revised
Edition. See, however, Nehama Leibowitz, pp. 123-5, \textit{Ibid}.
\item Nahum Sarna, pp 50 ff, \textit{Ibid}.
\item Nehama Leibowitz, Chapter 4, \textit{Ibid}.
......
```

The PrintOut:

Another approach[1] to understanding the text[2] is to compare it with translations of earlier versions[3,4] (*Gen.* 24:10–14.) ...

\newpage
NOTES

1. The text never identifies the narrator. Reasoning from similar episodes, however, we may reduce the possible candidates to three; see *infra*.

2. The usual practice is to abide by the translation in the Revised Edition. See, however, Nehama Leibowitz, pp. 123-5, *Ibid*.

3. Nahum Sarna, pp 50 ff, *Ibid*.

4. Nehama Leibowitz, Chapter 4, *Ibid*. ......

APPENDIX

Appendix A

CONSTRUCTING A *root* FILE

A.1   The *root* File

As your manuscript grows, processing it through LaTeX, viewing it and returning to the markup to make modifications takes longer and longer, particularly if it includes inserted pictures and graphics. At some point, it will pay you to restructure your manuscript in such a way that you can work on one or just a few sections at a time.

LaTeX provides an way to focus systematically on segments of a document; yet all the sections or chapters can be compiled as a unit whenever you wish. It encourages the creation of what is called a *root* file—a file that acts as outline and control file for the entire document.

The practice document you opened in Part 2 will serve as illustration.

1. Begin by moving the macros and newcommands and newenvironments and abbreviations you have constructed to a separate file; call it *macros.tex*.

2. Partition sections of the text of *practice.tex* at natural breakpoints and move these sections to separate files; say, *part1.tex*, *part2.tex*, and so forth.

3. As in Figure A.1, write a **\input** command in the preamble to bring in the macros file. Write **\include** commands for each of the text sections you moved to different

files[1]. Your root file may eventually look something like Figure A.1.

4. You do markups and corrections on individual text files: *part1.tex* or *part2.tex* and so forth. Note that in naming an *include* or *input* file in the root document, you don't write the file extension if the extension is *.tex*.

   The virtual[2] assembly of the command and text files listed in the root file—call it, say, *practroot.tex*—is done by LaTeX, and is output as a binary file. In more prosaic terms, LaTeX uses the instructions in the root file as a blueprint to direct its processing of files, which, were they written in a single file in the order in which they are listed in the root file, would be your document, complete with markup instructions.

5. As you revise your paper or book, keep *practroot.tex* up to date.

Admittedly, there are disadvantages in partitioning your document.

1. If you leave a text file out of a LaTeX compile, numbering is only guaranteed to be locally accurate.

2. Each \include file is printed beginning on a separate page, so it is best to break a document along its natural fault lines; e.g., chapters would not be run together in any case. If the breakdown is in segments that should form a seamless continuation in the final printout, these segments can be merged when the document is almost ready for the printer—and the root file revised.

3. To correct errors, you need to go to the right text file. But LaTeX tells you which one it is in this way:

```
) [37] [38] [39] (part2.tex [40]
Chapter 4.
! Undefined control sequence.
```

---

[1] As a general rule, keep all the files that accumulate around one document in a single directory, separate from the components of another document. That way, the part1 file won't be overwritten by part1 of another document. Similarly, the macro file can be modified and customized for the particular document. You may, if you wish, keep macros that apply to a particular class of documents in one file and macros specific to the current document in a separate file.

[2] By *virtual*, we mean that the files are not physically combined or copied into a single file that you can read with a text editor.

```
%       THE ROOT FILE: practroot.tex

\documentclass[dvips,10pt,twoside,letterpaper]{article}

%list of packages
\usepackage{latexsym}
\usepackage{afterpage}
\usepackage{calc}

% \input brings in a file unconditionally.
\input{macros}          %Cribs, macros, aliases.
\input{hyphenation}     %Unusual hyphenations
\input{pagelo.tbk}      %This has page layout instructions.
\input{tables}          %This has templates for different tables.

%These next three instructions are mainly for articles and reports.
\title{<text>}       % Declare the title inside the braces.
\author{<text>}      % Declare the author's name inside the braces.
\date{<text>}        % Declare the date you want or use \today.

%Use next 3 if you want space between paragraphs and no indent.
\flushbottom
\parindent=0pc
\setlength{\parskip}{\baselineskip}

\includeonly{<files>}

\begin{document}    % Use this ONLY in the root file.
\maketitle          % Using \title, \author and \date.
\pagenumbering{roman}
\include{preface}
\pagenumbering{arabic}
\setcounter{page}{1}
\include{part1}     % Don't use the extension for .tex files.
\include{part2}
\include{part3}
\include{part4}
\include{appendix}
\end{document}      % Use this ONLY in the root file.
```

Figure A.1: A simple root file.

```
1.37 Or you can cut to Figure~\reff
```

```
{fig:practice}, shown below.
```

Disadvantages are more than offset by the advantages of modularity.

A.2   Controlling The Processing Of Files

Actual files are brought in for LaTeX processing as *input* files or as *include* files. *input* files can be listed anywhere in the root file, including the preamble; *include* files are listed after *\begin{document}*. *input* is imperative; *include* can be made conditional.

An **\input** command may be issued at any point in the *root* file It causes LaTeX unconditionally to examine the file(s) named in its argument, at the point in which the file is listed in the root file. For example, *pagelo.tbk* can be visualized as being written at the tail end of *hyphenation.tex*. Input files usually contain markup instructions applicable to the entire document or, at least, to a large part of it, but it can be any text file. An input file may contain other input commands that bring in other text files.

An elementary but effective way to make use of a root file such as the one shown in Figure A.1 is to delete the *\includeonly* statement in the preamble and comment out all the *include* files in the root file except the one(s) on which you are working. LaTeX will bring in an **include** file at the point where the command is issued. Assuming the root file is called *practice.tex*, to see just the currently active portions of the document, type this in an xterm: **latex practice**. View it with *xdvi*. Or print it with *dvips*. To view the entire document, remove the comment signal (%) from all the *\include* statements.

LaTeX has a more elaborate way of controlling what segments of the document are processed. None of the *\include* statements are ever commented out. But whether the program will examine this file depends on the status of the single *\includeonly* command; e.g., \includeonly{preface,part2,part4}. The argument of the **\includeonly** command lists the files you want to compile; separate the names with commas and no spaces. LaTeX will ignore the other segments of the document.

If a file is first included and then excluded, its numbering and text is 'frozen' as it was the last time it was processed through LaTeX, even though recent editing may have changed the section radically.

If you only need to view a couple of files, the \includeonly statement can be commented out and the \includeonly information stated as a **\typein** option when LATEX is run. See Section 19.2.4.

The **\includeonly** command is written in the preamble. Its argument names the files that will be processed when you call LATEX. So you can permanently write the components of a large document as a set of include files in their proper sequence, but files not named in the \includeonly statement will be ignored.

These are the different relationships between include files and the includeonly command.

1. *The include file is named in the \includeonly argument: it is processed.*

2. *The include file is not named in the \includeonly argument: it is not processed.*

3. *There is no \includeonly command: all the include files are processed.*

4. *The \includeonly command has an empty argument: no include file is processed.*

A.3 Summary

The general procedure in writing a document is to write individual chapters, or even small sections, as separate files. Use another file to store the instructions for page and paragraph layout, complete with header and footer instructions, if the default options don't suit. Start a file to store the macros you write as you go along. Write templates for the various types of tables in another file. Put style instructions that apply only to one or two of the chapters into still another file.

Section 7.2 discussed how to teach the program to hyphenate a word *in situ*. If an unusual word occurs often in the text, it is better to write a hyphenation rule for it, using the *hy-phenation* command. If there are just a few such words, they can be written in the preamble of the root file. Otherwise, create a file of hyphenation rules. A hyphenation command can list the various forms of the word. It can also be used to prevent hyphenation, as in the second rule.

\hyphenation{con-dense con-den-sa-tion con-den-sing }
\hyphenation{Cplusplus JAVA LaTeX HTML}

Set up a root file. We call it *practroot.tex* in this example. In it, write a tentative outline of the complete document.

In the preamble, you write input commands for the various files that manipulate format. Write the files that have your basic formatting instructions and abbreviations as input files; e.g., `\include{macros}`.

Global declarations (those that apply generally to the document such as *\textwidth*) are also written in the preamble—unless they are default values.

Somewhere in the preamble, write a *single* `\includeonly` command that will contain the name of the file you are currently working on.

Anywhere after the `\begin{document}` command, you will list the sections or chapters you have written, are writing and plan to write in the order they will appear in the final document. Write these individually as `include` files. You can often rearrange a whole document by rearranging the order of the include files.

In all cases, for both input files and include files, if a file has a *tex* extension, do not write the extension; otherwise, write out the full name; e.g., **\input{macros.chap1.tbk}**.

When you are want to work on a particular file, write directly in that file. Write, rewrite, and mark up the text with formatting instruction.

Create labels for figures and references and tables and equations and any other object that is numbered. Do not repeat a label name in one include file if it already occurs in another.

Create macros as you go along. Whenever you have one that you like and use frequently, add it to a file of same-type new commands. All figure styles can be put in, say, *fig-macros.tex*. Or lump all the new commands together in a file called, say, *macros.tex* and sort them later.

When you wish to screen or print a particular file or set of files, write the name(s) in `\includeonly{...}` in the root file; e.g., `\includeonly{smithacct.sec1,sect3}`.

Run LaTeX on the root file; e.g., **latex practroot** or **latex demo.ctl** or whatever the root file is called. Some errors will stop LaTeX, and need instant fixing. Others are finessed; they are still errors, but, if you insist, LaTeX can work around them and get on with the processing.

LaTeX will write out a file whose name is the name of the root file up to the dot and will add **.dvi** as extension; e.g., *practroot.dvi*. This DVI file can be screened or converted to a PostScript file that can be printed. In our example, you would screen what the hard copy will look like by typing: **xdvi practice.dvi**. Or you can turn the DVI file into a PostScript file with *dvips*; e.g., **dvips practice.dvi**.

Appendix B

CONVERTING HTML TO LATEX AND THE REVERSE

B.1 Using *typehtml* To Convert HTML To LATEX

B.1.1 The HTML Markup

The HTML markup is a recipe that was siphoned from http://www.eskimo.com/ jefffree-/recipes/- linchees.htm and titled lindy.htm. *base target* was pushed into a single word.

The MarkUp:

```
<HTML>
<HEAD><TITLE>Lindy's Cheesecake</TITLE></HEAD basetarget="home">

<BODY background="../images/tanpaper.jpg" text="#000000" link="#008080"
 vlink="#FFFF00" alink="#ff00ff">

<H2 ALIGN=CENTER><B><I>LINDY'S CHEESECAKE</I></B></H2>

<P>Graham cracker crust</P>

<P>Filling:</P>

<UL>
```

```
<LI>2 1/2 pounds cream cheese, softened
<LI>1 3/4 cups sugar
<LI>3 tablespoons flour
<LI>1 1/2 teaspoons grated orange zest
<LI>1 1/2 teaspoons grated lemon zest
<LI>1/2 teaspoon vanilla
<LI>5 eggs
<LI>2 egg yolks
<LI>1/4 cup heavy cream
</UL>

<P>Preheat  oven to 350.  Bake graham cracker crust in bottom of 9-inch
springform pan 8-10 minutes.  Cool crust and butter sides of pan.</P>

<P>Preheat oven to 500.</P>

<P>In a bowl, beat the cream cheese, sugar, flour, zests, and vanilla
until smooth.  Beat in the whole eggs and the egg yolks, one at a time,
beating lightly after each.  Stir in the cream.  Pour the filling in
the prepared pan and bake for 12 minutes.  Reduce heat to 200 and bake
the cheesecake for 1 hour more.  Let the cheesecake cool in the pan on
rack, chill overnight, and serve.</P>

<HR>

<P ALIGN=CENTER>
[ <A HREF="homepage.htm">Archives Homepage</A> ][
<A HREF="cheindex.htm">Cheesecake Index</A> ]

</BODY>
</HTML>
```

B.1.2   An example of *typehtml* usage

typehtml was written by David Carlisle [Carlisle96d]. To use it, first write a
\usepackage{typehtml} statement in the preamble.

You write the HTML code directly into the LATEX document.

You use the \dohtml command to convert the HTML code.

The HTML code MUST be bracketed by <html> statements. If you are scooping out a chunk of code from a larger unit of HTML code, add <HTML> brackets at the beginning and end of the code segment. There's not much call for it in the example shown here, but note that \typehtml is capable of converting math arrays and formulae to LATEX format.

The MarkUp:

```
\dohtml
<HTML>
<HEAD><TITLE>LINDY'S CHEESECAKE</TITLE></HEAD>
<BODY background="../images/tanpaper.jpg" link="#008080"
  vlink="#FFFF00" alink="#ff00ff">
........
<HTML>
```

B.1.3   The LATEX output

Lindy's Cheesecake

Graham cracker crust

Filling:

- 2 1/2 pounds cream cheese, softened

- 1 3/4 cups sugar

- 3 tablespoons flour

- 1 1/2 teaspoons grated orange zest

- 1 1/2 teaspoons grated lemon zest

- 1/2 teaspoon vanilla

- 5 eggs

- 2 egg yolks

- 1/4 cup heavy cream

Preheat oven to 350. Bake graham cracker crust in bottom of 9-inch springform pan 8-10 minutes. Cool crust and butter sides of pan.

Preheat oven to 500.

In a bowl, beat the cream cheese, sugar, flour, zests, and vanilla until smooth. Beat in the whole eggs and the egg yolks, one at a time, beating lightly after each. Stir in the cream. Pour the filling in the prepared pan and bake for 12 minutes. Reduce heat to 200 and bake the cheesecake for 1 hour more. Let the cheesecake cool in the pan on rack, chill overnight, and serve.

[*Archives Homepage*Cheesecake Index]

B.2   Using *LATEX2HTML* To Convert LATEX To HTML

B.2.1   Obtaining LATEX2HTML

LATEX2HTML is the way to write web pages, filled, if you wish, with complex mathematical expressions. As Web-browser support for mathematics increases, it becomes an increasingly important tool. It can be obtained from http://www-dsed.llnl.gov/files/programs/unix-/latex2html/sources. It was originally written by Nikos Drakos, at the University of Leeds. Most recently, Ross Moore, Mathematics Department at Macquarie University, Sydney, has done the documentation. A manual, *The LATEX2HTML Translator* by Nikos Drakos [Drakos97], comes as part of the tar file. So just beam over the latest tar file.

Preliminaries:

1. Make sure you have *perl*[1] on your machine. It may be in /usr/local/bin or in /usr/bin. If it isn't there, you will have to download it from the Net. Or check your Linux package. It should be there, so you can add the package directly using your package manager.

2. Make sure you have *ghostview*, *netpbm* or *pbmplus* on your machine. netpbm and pbmplus come as tar files with Netscape for Linux. They may be under /root/.netscape.

---

[1]The first time I tried, I didn't get very far because I didn't have a /bin/csh because I use Bash, not C shell. INTERESTING OBSERVATION: In the program FAQ, there's a group of reasons of what might have gone wrong, if the program doesn't work. Not having a C shell isn't among them—not surprising because the C shell is in common use by the Perl crowd. Linux uses Bash to settle in the kernel, so if you only have one shell, it's probably Bash.

Unboxing the LATEX2html program:

1. Go to http://www-dsed.llnl.gov/files/programs/unix/latex2html/sources

2. At the time I was writing this section, the latest tar file was the july 1997 version: latex2html-97.1.tar.gz

3. There's a bunch of files. About 1/3 of the way down in README, we get to Installing the program. Follow the instructions in sequence.

README suggests as a test of the program working that you convert *docs/manual.tex*, which is of course a LATEX document, to HTML. If you are in /usr/local/latex2html-97.1/, you do this by typing **latex2html docs/manual.tex** in an xterm. I did this without making any attempt to finetune the program or even to meet all the requirements for file placements. So it was not surprising that the program reported problems along the way; for example:

No implementation found for style 'dvips'
No implementation found for style 'a4paper'

The resulting HTML code was written into multiple files in the */usr/local/latex2html-97.1/manual* directory.

Afterwards, I picked one of the HTML files at random from the converted manual to reconvert to LATEX using *typehtml*. The file, called *node4.html*, turned out to be page vi of *manual.ps*. The original LATEX page that gave rise to *node4.html* is shown in Figure B.1. The start of the resulting HTML code is shown in Section B.2.2.

I then reconverted this HTML file to LATEX using the *typehtml* package (see above). The LATEX log reported problems *typehtml* had identifying some terms; for example:

Package typehtml Warning: </small>UNDEFINED on input line 136.
Package typehtml Warning: </sup>UNDEFINED on input line 136.

Nevertheless, the retranslation, although incomplete, was good—see Section B.2.3.

B.2.2 The Resulting HTML Code

```
<!DOCTYPE HTML PUBLIC "-//W3C//DTD HTML 3.2//EN">
<!--Converted with LaTeX2HTML 97.1 (release) (July 13th, 1997)
 by Nikos Drakos (nikos@cbl.leeds.ac.uk), CBLU, University of Leeds
* revised and updated by:  Marcus Hennecke, Ross Moore, Herb Swan
* with significant contributions from:
```

1st LaTeX2HTML Workshop
Darmstadt, 15 February 1997

Thanks again to Jens Lippman and members of the LiPS Design Team for organising this meeting; also to the Fachbereich Informatik at Darmstadt for use of their facilities.

This was an opportunity for many of the current LaTeX2HTML developers to actually meet for the first time; rather than communication by exchange of electronic mail messages.

- Nikos Drakos talked about the early development of LaTeX2HTML, while...

- ...Ross Moore, Jens Lippman and Marek Rouchal described recent improvements.

- Michel Goossens presented a list of difficulties encountered with earlier versions of LaTeX2HTML, and aspects requiring improvement. Almost all of these now have been addressed in the v97.1 release, so far as is possible within the bounds inherent in the HTML 3.2 standard.

- Kristoffer Rose showed how it is possible to create GIF89 animations from pictures generated by TeX or LaTeX, using the Xy-pic graphics package and extensions, developed by himself and Ross Moore.

Also present were representatives from the DANTE e.V. Praesidium and members of the LaTeX3 development team. In all it was a very pleasant and constructive meeting.

TUG'97 — Workshop on LaTeX2HTML
University of San Francisco, 28 July 1997

On the Sunday afternoon (2.00pm–5.00pm) immediately prior to the TUG meeting, there will be a workshop on LaTeX2HTML, conducted by Ross Moore[6].

Admission: $50, includes a printed copy of the latest LaTeX2HTML manual.

Figure B.1: Page vi of *manual.tex*, the LaTeX2HTML manual.

```
     Jens Lippman, Marek Rouchal, Martin Wilck and others -->
<HTML>
<HEAD>
<TITLE>1st LATEX2HTML WorkshopDarmstadt, 15 February 1997</TITLE>
<META NAME="description" CONTENT="1st LATEX2HTML WorkshopDarmstadt,
            15 February 1997">
<META NAME="keywords" CONTENT="manual">
<META NAME="resource-type" CONTENT="document">
<META NAME="distribution" CONTENT="global">
<META HTTP-EQUIV="Content-Type" CONTENT="text/html; charset=iso_8859_1">
<LINK REL="STYLESHEET" HREF="manual.css">
<LINK REL="next" HREF="node5.html">
<LINK REL="previous" HREF="node3.html">
<LINK REL="up" HREF="node3.html">
<LINK REL="next" HREF="node5.html">
</HEAD>
<BODY >
<!--Navigation Panel-->
<A NAME="tex2html72"
 HREF="node5.html">
<IMG WIDTH="37" HEIGHT="24" ALIGN="BOTTOM" BORDER="0" ALT="next"
 SRC="/usr/local/latex2html-97.1/icons.png/next_motif.png"></A>
<A NAME="tex2html68"
 HREF="node3.html">
<IMG WIDTH="26" HEIGHT="24" ALIGN="BOTTOM" BORDER="0" ALT="up"
 SRC="/usr/local/latex2html-97.1/icons.png/up_motif.png"></A>
<A NAME="tex2html62"
 HREF="node3.html">
<IMG WIDTH="63" HEIGHT="24" ALIGN="BOTTOM" BORDER="0" ALT="previous"
 SRC="/usr/local/latex2html-97.1/icons.png/previous_motif.png"></A>
<A NAME="tex2html70"
 HREF="node10.html">
<IMG WIDTH="65" HEIGHT="24" ALIGN="BOTTOM" BORDER="0" ALT="contents"
 SRC="/usr/local/latex2html-97.1/icons.png/contents_motif.png"></A>
<A NAME="tex2html71"
 HREF="node15.html">
<IMG WIDTH="43" HEIGHT="24" ALIGN="BOTTOM" BORDER="0" ALT="index"
 SRC="/usr/local/latex2html-97.1/icons.png/index_motif.png"></A>
<BR>
<B> Next:</B> <A NAME="tex2html73"
 HREF="node5.html">TUG'97   Workshop L<SUP>A</SUP>TEX2HTML</A>
<B> Up:</B> <A NAME="tex2html69"
 HREF="node3.html">Recent Developments: late 1996,</A>
<B> Previous:</B> <A NAME="tex2html63"
```

```
        HREF="node3.html">Recent Developments: late 1996,</A>
<BR>
<BR>
<!--End of Navigation Panel-->
<H2 ALIGN="center"><A NAME="SECTION00031000000000000000">&
 #160;</A><A NAME="darmstadt"> </A>
1st L<SUP><SMALL>A</SMALL></SUP>T<SMALL>E</SMALL>X2HTML Workshop
<BR>
Darmstadt,
15 February 1997
</H2>
Thanks again to <A NAME="1034"> </A><A NAME="tex2html1"
 HREF="http://www-jb.cs.uni-sb.de/~www/people/lippmann">Jens Lippman</A>
 and members of the <A NAME="1038"> </A><A NAME="tex2html1"
 HREF="http://www-jb.cs.uni-sb.de/LiPS/node2.html">LiPS Design Team</A>
 for organising this meeting;
also to the <A NAME="1041"> </A><A NAME="tex2html1"
 HREF="http://www.informatik.th-darmstadt.de/">Fachbereich Informatik</A>
 at <A NAME="1044"> </A><A NAME="tex2html1"
 HREF="http://www.th-darmstadt.de/Welcome.de.html">Darmstadt</A>
 for use of their facilities.
<P>
```

B.2.3   Reconverting HTML To LATEX With *typehtml*

Running *\dohtml* on *node4.html* resulted in:

370next 260up 630previous 650contents 430index

Next: *TUG'97 Workshop LATEX2HTML* **Up:** *Recent Developments: late 1996,* **Previous:** *Recent Developments: late 1996,*

1st LATEX2HTML Workshop
Darmstadt, 15 February 1997

Thanks again to *Jens Lippman* and members of the *LiPS Design Team* for organising this meeting; also to the *Fachbereich Informatik* at *Darmstadt* for use of their facilities.

This was an opportunity for many of the current LATEX2HTML developers to actually meet for the first time; rather than communication by exchange of electronic mail messages.

- *Nikos Drakos* talked about the early development of LATEX2HTML, while...

- ... *Ross Moore* , *Jens Lippman* and *Marek Rouchal* described recent improvements.

- *Michel Goossens* presented a list of difficulties encountered with earlier versions of LA-TEX2HTML, and aspects requiring improvement. Almost all of these now have been addressed in the V97.1 release, so far as is possible within the bounds inherent in the HTML 3.2 standard.

- *Kristoffer Rose* showed how it is possible to create GIF89 animations from pictures generated by TEX or LATEX, using the *Xy-pic* graphics package and extensions, developed by himself and *Ross Moore* .

Also present were representatives from the *DANTE e.V. Praesidium* and members of the *LATEX3* development team.

In all it was a very pleasant and constructive meeting.

370next 260up 630previous 650contents 430index
Next: *TUG'97 Workshop LATEX2HTML* **Up:** *Recent Developments: late 1996,* **Previous:** *Recent Developments: late 1996,*

root

10/18/1997

B.3   Summary

It is clearly easier to write a simple language like HTML into a more complex one. The reverse is difficult. The demonstration here was to indicate what could be done with very little (read zero) polishing. To use the LATEX2HTML program seriously requires, at the least, that you meet the basic requirements of the program. There is a user's group and a FAQ that help.

Appendix C

LIST OF REFERENCES

Using Linux.

[Hekman96] Jessica Perry Hekman, *Linux in a Nutshell*, Cambridge, MA: O'Reilly & Associates, 1996. This summarizes Linux commands and options with cogent examples.

[Husain96] Kamran Husain, Timothy Parker *et al*, *Linux Unleashed*, Indianapolis, IN: SAMS Publishing, 1996. A wide-ranging early user's manual.

[Komarinski96] Mark Komarinski, *The Linux Printing Usage HOWTO*, February, 1996. Filed as *Printing-Usage-HOWTO.gz* in `/usr/doc/faq/howto`. This presents additional material on printing in Linux.

[Taylor96] Grant Taylor, *The Linux Printing HOWTO*, March, 1996. Filed as *Printing-HOWTO.gz* in `/usr/doc/faq/howto`. This is a basic document that discusses the commands for printing and faxing in Linux.

[Welsh96] Matt Welsh and Lar Kaufman, *Running Linux*, Cambridge, MA: O'Reilly & Associates, 1996. A thorough, relatively concise, guide to the Linux system and many of its key subsystems. It's also a pleasure to read.

On T_EX, the progenitor program.

[Knuth86] Donald E. Knuth, *The T_EX Book*, Reading, Massachusetts: Addison Wesley, 1986. The basic document that spawned the multitude of collateral programs and documentation files grouped as teT_EX. Dr. Knuth contributed T_EX to the public domain.

[Snow92] Wynter Snow, *T_EX for the Beginner*, Reading, Massachusetts: Addison Wesley, 1992. An excellent introduction to T_EX.

525

These are the basic references for LaTeX.

[Lamport94a] Leslie Lamport, *LaTeX: A Document Preparation System*, Reading, Massachusetts: Addison-Wesley, 2nd Edition, 1994. This is the basic reference for LaTeX. Dr. Lamport contributed LaTeX to the public domain.

[Goossens94] Michel Goossens, Frank Mittelbach and Alexander Samarin, *The LaTeX Companion*, Reading, Massachusetts: Addison-Wesley, 1994. This is an elaboration of LaTeX, with detailed information on more recent packages that can be integrated into LaTeX.

TeX in Linux and Unix.

[Anon] Anon, *The TeX System*. Filed as *helpindex.dvi* in `~/texmf/doc`. It's invaluable; it lists all the documentation files for the TeX and LaTeX programs.

[Berry95a] Karl Berry, *Kpathsea library*, Version 2.6, January, 1995. Filed as *Kpathsea.dvi* in `~/texmf/doc/programs`. This discusses the paths used to find fonts and the hash-coded index of the files subsumed under texmf.

[Berry95b] Karl Berry, *A Directory Structure for TeX Files*, draft version 0.999, 30 November 1995. Filed as *tds.dvi* in `~/texmf/doc/help`. This is the basic standard for organizing all LaTeX-related files and directories.

[Esser96] Thomas Esser, Dirk Hillbrecht and Craig Bateman, *The teTeX Guide— Installation and Maintenance*, June 1996. Filed as *TETEXDOC.dvi* in `~/texmf-/doc/tetex`. The Linux distributions more or less use teTeX, which distributes the files for LaTeX and its friends in specific directories, utilizing Berry's Kpathsea library.

These encapsulate the classic commands or contain information on recent additions to LaTeX. They can also function as reviews of basic LaTeX.

[LaTeX3PT95] LaTeX3 Project Team, *LaTeX2ε for authors*, 8 December 1995. Filed as *usrguide.dvi* in `~/texmf/doc/latex/base`. This includes previous commands that have been refined or enhanced and new commands that almost certainly will be an integral part of LaTeX3. They are immediately usable.

[Lamport94b] Leslie Lamport et al, *LaTeX2ε*, Edition 1.6, December 1994. Filed as *LaTeX2ε* in `~/texmf/doc/latex/general`. This spells out all the LaTeX commands for the different classes.

[Oetiker96] Tobias Oetiker, Hubert Partl, Irene Hyna, and Elisabeth Schlegl, *The Not So Short Introduction to LaTeX2ε*, Version 2.2-Beta, 25 January, 1996. Filed as *lshort2e.dvi* in `~/texmf/doc/latex/general`. This is both an excellent introduction and review of LaTeX.

[Rahtz94a] Sebastian Rahtz, *A LaTeX survival guide for Unix systems*, 10 January 1994. Filed as *guide.dvi* in `~/texmf/doc/latex/general`. This is a companion to Warbrick's manual. I wish I'd known about these two manuals early on, and not after I'd decoded where the reference manuals were located on the disk. Moreover, the same text is printed in various available fonts, so you can really compare them.

[Warbrick94] Jon Warbrick (with additions by David Carlisle, Michel Goossens, Sebastian Rahtz and Adrian Clark), *Essential LaTeX++*, January, 1994. Filed as *essential.dvi* in `~/texmf/doc/latex/general`. This is a very readable introduction to LaTeX. It emphasizes mathematical typesetting; its tables list various mathematical symbols that can be printed by command name.

Packages that enhance LaTeX.

[Arseneau93] Donald Arseneau, *shapepar Instructions*, March 1993. Filed as *shapepar.sty* in `~/texmf/tex/latex/misc`. The instructions for running the program start about two-thirds down the file.

[Arseneau95] Donald Arseneau, *wrapfig Instructions*, 2 November 1995. Filed as *wrapfig.sty* in `~/texmf/tex/latex/misc`. The instructions for running the program start about half way down the file.

[Barratt95] Craig Barratt and Michael C. Grant, *The PSfrag system*, 10 March 1995. Filed as *pfgguide.dvi* in `~/texmf/doc/latex/psfrag`. psfrag lets you label graphics in a PostScript file with TeX math mode fonts.

[Barroca95] Leonor Barroca, *A style option for rotated objects in LaTeX*, 22 August, 1995. Filed as *rotating.dvi* in `~/texmf/doc/latex/rotating`. This documents the text and figure rotation package written by Barroca and Sebastian Rahtz.

[Carlisle95a] David Carlisle, *The afterpage package*, 27 October, 1995. Filed as *afterpage.dvi* in `~/texmf/doc/latex/tools`. The afterpage package fills a page with text before moving onto the next page to place a float.

[Carlisle96a] David Carlisle, *The longtable package*, 24 May, 1996. Filed as *longtable.dvi* in `~/texmf/doc/latex/tools`. This lets a tabular environment table extend over a page.

[Carlisle96b] David Carlisle, *The dcolumn package*, 28 February, 1996. Filed as *dcolumn.dvi* in `~/texmf/doc/latex/tools`. This aligns decimal numbers in a table column.

[Cornelius92] James Cornelius, Michael Frey, Dan Gruber, Fang Wang, *Xspread Reference Manual*, 12 December, 1992. Filed as *xspread.dvi* in `/usr/doc/xspread`. The xspread directory includes a tutorial and examples demonstrating how to construct and label a table.

[Cochran95] Steven Douglas Cochran, *The subfigure package*, 6 March, 1995. Filed as *subfigure.dvi* in `~/texmf/doc/latex/styles`. This lays out several figures within a larger unit.

[Dahlgren96a] Mats Dahlgren, *Welcome to the floatflt package!*, 27 February 1996. Filed as *floatflt.dvi* in `~/texmf/doc/latex/floatflt`. This places floats, figures and tables at the left or right side of running text.

[Dahlgren96b] Mats Dahlgren, *The Tale of flatflt*. Filed as *floatexm.tex* and *floatexm.dvi* in `~/texmf/doc/latex/floatflt`. An example of using floatflt.

[Drucbert94] Jean-Pierre Drucbert, *The Minitoc Package*, 1994. Filed as *minitoc.dvi* in `~/texmf/doc/latex/minitoc`. This explains the minitoc package, which lets you write multiple table of contents in different sections of the document.

[Fairbairns96] Robin Fairbairns, *The moreverb package*, 23 June, 1996. Filed as *moreverb.dvi* in `~/texmf/doc/latex/styles`. This adds line numbers to the verbatim command.

[Kneser90] Thomas Kneser, *LaTeX-Paragraphs Floating around Figures*, 20 August, 1990. Filed as *floatfge.dvi* in `~/texmf/doc/latex/floatflt`. An early program that placed floats at the left or right side of text.

[Lamport96] Leslie Lamport and Johannes Braams, *alltt.sty*, 1996. in ~/texmf/tex-/latex/base. This is the loading package for an improved verbatim.

[Lavagnino91] John Lavagnino, *endnotes.sty*, 24 September, 1991. This writes all the footnotes at the end of the document.

[Lingnau95] Anselm Lingnau, *An Improved Environment for Floats*, 29 March 1995. Filed as *float.dvi* in ~/texmf/doc/latex/styles. A way of creating different classes of floats.

[McCauley95] James Darrell McCauley and Jeff Goldberg, *The endfloat package*, 10 November, 1995. Filed as *endfloat.dvi* in ~/texmf/doc/latex/styles. This puts all floats—figures and tables—in their own section at the end of the document.

[McPherson95] Kent McPherson, *Displaying page layout variables*, 23 November, 1995. Filed as *layout.dvi* in ~/texmf/doc/latex/tools. This is an actual layout demonstrating the parameters that set up a page.

[Mittelbach96a] Frank Mittelbach, *An environment for multicolumn output*, 19 June, 1996. Filed as *multicol.dvi* in ~/texmf/doc/latex/tools. This is the documentation for a program that prints a document in up to 10 columns per page.

[Mittelbach96b] Frank Mittelbach, *Footnotes in a multi-column layout*, 19 June, 1996. Filed as *ftnright.dvi* in ~/texmf/doc/latex/tools. This moves all the footnotes that belong on a two-column page tidily to the bottom of the right column.

[Mittelbach96c] Frank Mittelbach and David Carlisle, *A new implementation of LaTeX's tabular and array environment*, 19 June, 1996. Filed as *array.dvi* in ~/texmf/doc-/latex/tools. Enhancements of the tabular and array environments.

[Mittelbach96d] Frank Mittelbach and David Carlisle, *An extension of the LaTeX theorem environment.*, 19 June, 1996. Filed as *theorem.dvi* in ~/texmf/doc/latex-/tools. This offers different styles appropriate for different journals.

[Oostrum98] Piet van Oostrum, *Page Layout in LaTeX*, 6 Sept, 1998. Filed as *fancy-headings.dvi* in ~/texmf/doc/latex/fancyhdr. This is a thorough discussion of how to modify the appearance and size of headers and footers beyond what is available in classic LaTeX.

[Page86] Stephen Page, *doublespace.sty*, 3 September, 1986. You can use this for double spacing a document.

[Rahtz94b] Sebastian Rahtz and Phil Taylor, *The textfit package for scaling up text to a desired size*, 15 April, 1994. Filed as *textfit.dvi* in ~/texmf/doc/latex/styles. This packages lets you scale up to very large sizes.

[Schrod95] Joachim Schrod, *The package footnpag*, 4 August, 1995. Filed as *footnpag-user.dvi* in ~/texmf/doc/latex/styles. This renumbers footnotes every page rather than every chapter.

[Sommerfeldt95] Harald Axel Sommerfeldt, *The caption package*, 5 April, 1995. Filed as *caption.dvi* in ~/texmf/doc/latex/styles. This adds flexibility to caption placement.

[Sowa95] Friedhelm Sowa, *Beispiele zu picinpar*, 1995. Filed as *picinpar.dvi* in ~/texmf/doc/latex/styles. This is the documentation for the picinpar package.

[Taylor94] Philip Taylor, *letterspace.sty*, 1994. This has no documentation. Indeed, if [Goossens94] didn't cite the author, we wouldn't know who wrote it.

[Thorup95] Kresten Krab Thorup and Frank Jensen, *The calc package: Infix notation arithmetic in LaTeX*, 10 April 1995. Filed as *calc.dvi* in `~/texmf/doc/latex-/styles`. This documents *calc*, a program that allows you to do ordinary arithmetic easily. It is very useful in setting lengths and counters.

[Wujastyk95] Dominik Wujastyk and Chris Rowley, *fnpara.sty*, 11 December, 1995. This lists the footnotes on the page as running text, rather than as a list. Look at the *fnpara.sty* notes if you get a overflow stack error.

[Zandt93a] Timothy Van Zandt, *fancybox.sty*, 10 February, 1993. It produces a set of shadow and oval boxes that are variations of the *fbox*.

[Zandt93b] Timothy Van Zandt, *Seminar.sty User's Guide*, 1 April, 1993. Filed as *sem-users.dvi* in `~/texmf/doc/latex/seminar`. This provides enhancements for slide production, including color and overlays.

Fonts.

[AMS95a] American Mathematical Society, *Users Guide to AMS Fonts*, Version 2.2, January, 1995. Filed as *amsfndoc.dvi* in `~/texmf/doc/ams/amsfonts`. A discussion of the different components that make up the distribution. It provides the symbol, the symbol name commands and source font for many necessary math symbol.

[AMS95b] American Mathematical Society, *AMS-LaTeX Version 1.2 User's Guide*, January, 1995. Filed as *amsldoc.dvi* in `~/texmf/doc/ams/amslatex`. This discusses AMS features and how to use them properly in equations. The error messages resulting from incorrect syntax are listed.

[Berry96] Karl Berry, *Fontname*, version 2.1, July, 1996. Filed as *fontname.dvi* in `~/texmf/doc/fonts/fontname`. This parses font filenames into Encoding type, family name, shape and size. The major fonts–some of which come with the TeX conglomerate—are listed.

[Braams96] Johannes Braams, *Babel, a multilingual package for use with LaTeX's standard document classes*, 14 August, 1996. Filed as *user.dvi* in `~/texmf/tex-/generic/babel`. The babel package consists of separate files, each designed for a different language.

[Carlisle96c] David Carlisle, *pslatex*, 24 July, 1996. Filed as *00readme.txt* in `~/texmf/doc/latex/pslatex`. 24 July, 1996. This package makes LaTeX default to standard PostScript fonts—Times, Helvetica and Courier.

[Hafner95] Jim Hafner, *The FoilTeX class package*, 14 September, 1995. Filed as *foiltex.dvi* in `~/doc/latex/foiltex`. This is a new document class with large size fonts to create slides and transparencies.

[Hoenig98] Alan Hoenig, *TeX Unbound: TeX & LaTeX Strategies For Fonts, Graphics, & More*, New York, NY: Oxford University Press, 1998. This is an elegantly typeset book that discusses METAFONT, MetaPost and PSTricks. Its systematic and well-illustrated discussion of how to create virtual fonts is a major contribution.

[Hilbrich96] Torsten Hilbrich, *A Package for using the bbm fonts in math environment*, 22 July, 1996. Filed as *bbm.dvi* in `~/texmf/doc/latex/styles`. This contains instructions for running the *bbm* package in math mode.

[Jeffrey94a] Alan Jeffrey, *Building virtual fonts with **fontinst***, 9 January, 1994. Get this from a CTAN; e.g., *ftp://ftp.cdrom.com/pub/tex/ctan/fonts//utilities/fontinst/doc/*. This is a short overview of *fontinst*.

[Jeffrey94b] Alan Jeffrey, *The package, v1.332 fontinst*, 27 June 1994. Get this from a CTAN; e.g., *ftp://ftp.cdrom.com/pub/tex/ctan/fonts/utilities/fontinst/doc/*. This discusses *fontinst*.

[Jensen95a] Frank Jensen, *The beton package*, 5 March 1995. Filed as *beton.dvi* in `~/texmf/doc/latex/styles`. The beton package is an enhanced version of Concrete.

[Jensen95b] Frank Jensen, *The euler package*, 5 March 1995. Filed as *euler.dvi* in `~/texmf/doc/latex/styles`. This is a discussion of the euler fonts, designed by Hermann Zapf for the American Mathematical Society. If you are planning to use Euler together with other fonts, this is must reading.

[Knappen96] Jörg Knappen, *The European Computer Modern Fonts Documentation*, 1 June, 1996. Filed as *dcdoc.dvi* in `~/texmf/doc/fonts/dc`. This explains the dc fonts that include the accents and ligatures needed to print European and other non-English languages. It also discusses the text companion (tc) symbols.

[Knuth90] Don Knuth, *Virtual fonts: More fun for Grand Wizards*, 08 January, 1990. Filed as *ftp://ftp.cdrom.com/pub/tex/ctan/documentation/virtual-fonts.knuth*. This lays out the implementation of virtual fonts with practical examples. Knuth credits David Fuchs with the idea of creating virtual fonts in 1983.

[LaTeX3PT96] LaTeX3 Project Team, *LaTeX2ε font selection*, 10 June, 1996. Filed as *fntguide.dvi* in `~/texmf/doc/latex/base`. This describes how to specify and select fonts.

[Mittelbach94] Frank Mittelbach, *The fonts for use with LaTeX2ε*, 27 May, 1994. Filed as *pandora.dvi* in `~/texmf/doc/latex/mfnfss`. Some notes on Pandora, including references to writeups by the designer, Nazeen N. Billawala.

[Mittelbach96e] Frank Mittelbach, *The package for use with LaTeX2ε*, 8 February, 1996. Filed as *oldgerm.dvi* in `~/texmf/doc/latex/mfnfss`. An extensive writeup of the Old German fonts designed by Yannis Haralambous.

[Rahtz95] Sebastian Rahtz, *The textcomp package for using Text Companion fonts*, 11 December, 1995. Filed as *textcomp.dvi* in `~/texmf/doc/latex/styles`. How to call up Text Companion symbols by name.

[Waldi92] Roland Waldi, *The Symbol Font wasy*, Version 2.0, September, 1992. Filed as *wasydoc.dvi and wasysym.dvi* in `~/texmf/doc/latex/wasysym`. This package provides symbols in math and physics as well as text-mode symbols.

Graphics and Picture Packages.

[Bleser92] J. Bleser and E. Land, *bar.sty*, September, 1992. Filed as *bar.sty* in `~/texmf/tex/latex/misc`. You can build bar charts from striped and solid *bar* objects.

[Bradley94] John Bradley, *XV*, Version 3.10, 1994. Filed as *xvdocs.ps* in `/usr/doc/xv`. This is the official manual for the xv program. It is shareware: commercial, government and institutional users must register. When you register, you get a printed edition of the manual.

[Carlisle95b] D.P. Carlisle, *Packages in the 'graphics' bundle*, 7 December 1995. Filed as *grfguide.dvi* in `~/texmf/doc/latex/graphics`. This is a basic document on the available graphics packages and their usage.

[Hammel97] Michael J, Hammel, *The Quick Start Guide to the GIMP*, Parts 1-4 in LINUX JOURNAL. Part 1, November, 1997: pp 14. This is a 4-part series on using GIMP.

[Hobby96] John D. Hobby, *The MetaPost System*, 25 July, 1996. Filed as *mpintro.ps* in `~/texmf/doc/metapost`. This is a thorough description of how to use MetaPost, which is a picture-drawing programming language, modeled on METAFONT, that outputs PostScript commands rather than bitmaps. See also: *mpintro.dvi* and *mpgraph.dvi*.

[Kimball97] Spencer Kimball, *Script-Fu: Graphic Art for Everyone*, Fall, 1997. Filed as *script-fu.tex* in `~/gimp-(version #)/docs`. This describes a scripting language to create Web page graphics in GIMP.

[Kylander97] Karin Kylander and Olof S Kylander, *GIMP User Manual*, Version 0.7, 1997. You can ftp it from ftp://ftp.frozenriver.ale.se/pub/Gimpmanual. This is an excellent way to learn GIMP.

[Maclaine95] Ian Maclaine-cross, *Curves in LaTeX Pictures: A Manual for CURVESST and CURVESLSST*, 22 August, 1995. Filed as *curves.tex* in `~/texmf/tex/latex/misc`. This draws curves and graphic objects accurately. Examples come from mechanical engineering.

[Podar86] Sunil Podar, *epic.sty*, 14 July, 1986. Filed as *readme* in `~/texmf/doc/latex/eepic`. The eepic directories under doc and under latex/tex/.. contain information on the program and its extensions.

[Reckdahl96] Keith Reckdahl, *Using EPS Graphics in LaTeX2ε*, version 1.8b, 19 June, 1996. Filed as *epslatex.ps* in `~/texmf/doc/latex/graphics`. This discusses how to introduce Encapsulated PostScript (EPS) files into LaTeX. Some examples use the PSFrag program to substitute LaTeX font for the Encapsulated PostScript font.

[Rose95a] Kristoffer H Rose, *Xy-pic User's Guide*, 19 September, 1995. Filed as *xyguide.dvi* in `~/doc/generic/xypic`. This summarizes the graph and diagram objects available in Xypic and how to write the layout instructions.

[Rose95b] Kristoffer H Rose, *Xy-pic Reference Manual*, 19 September, 1995. Filed as *xyref.dvi* in `~/texmf/doc/generic/xypic`. This is major documentation for this mathematical typesetting system for matrices and diagrams.

[Vanroose90] Peter Vanroose, *trees.sty*, 18 April, 1990. Filed as *trees.sty* in `~/tex/latex/misc`. This draws trees in the LaTeX picture environment.

BIBTeX-related Papers.

[Daly] Patrick W. Daly, *Natural Sciences Citations and References (Author-Year and Numerical Schemes*. Filed as *natbib.dvi* in `~/texmf/doc/latex/natbib`. This is a package for formatting bibliographic citations.

[Patashnik88a] Oren Patashnik, BIBTeXing, 8 February, 1988. Filed as *btxdoc.tex* in `~/texmf/doc/bibtex`. This and *Designing BibLaTeX Styles* are the basic documentation files for BIBTeX.

[Patashnik88b] Oren Patashnik, *Designing* BIB*T_EX Styles*, 8 February, 1988.   Filed as *btxhak.tex* in `~/texmf/doc/bibtex`. BIBT_EX is a rich and carefully-designed program. It will pay you to read the documentation for it carefully.

Conversing with Other Programs.

[Carlisle96d] David Carlisle, *The typehtml package*, 28 March 1996. Filed as *typehtml.dvi* in `~/texmf/doc/latex/styles`. This lets you install HTML code in a LAT_EX markup document.

[Drakos97] Nikos Drakos, *The LAT_EX2HTML Translator*, 19 October, 1997.   Filed as *manual.dvi* in `/usr/local/latex2html/docs`. This is required reading to run the program, which translates LAT_EX to HTML.

[Rokicki95] Tomas Rokicki, *A DVI-to-PostScript Translator*, Version 5.58f, January, 1995. Filed as *dvipsk.dvi* in `~/texmf/doc/programs`. This is the documentation for printing a device independent file on a PostScript printer.

Appendix D

INDEX AND GLOSSARY

Commands for LaTeX and ancillary packages are in bold and usually show their generic components. Declarations are also in bold. NI indicates a non-LaTeX new instruction created in this book to show usage. Many instructions indicate where examples can be found. Value arguments: *leng* is a length/width measurement value; *num* is a counter value; *docdivn* is any document division such as chapter or section; *text* is text fill-in. AKA is the command name or calling name. *same as* means an exact replacement macro. Where the number of page references is large, there are usually one or more numbers in bold to get you started.

533

D

$\dag$ (†) and $\ddag$ (‡), math symbols—168, 252-253, 264, 269, 346-347

$\dagger$ (†) and $\dagger\dagger$ (††), footnote symbols —263-264, 275-277, 279

Dahlgren, Mats—244, 527

Daly, Patrick W—532

dashes—64, 77, 196

databases—162, 260, 421, **424-427**, 431-432

$\date$, to print as part of title page—31, 41, 43

DC fonts—*see* European Computer Modern fonts

dcolumn package, to line up decimals in a table—264-265, 330, 485, 527

$\ddagger$ (‡) and $\ddagger\ddagger$ (‡‡), footnote symbols—264, 275-277

$\ddots$ (⋱), to write diagonal dots, math mode—196

declaration—11-12, 14, **88-89**, 100-101, 118-119, *see specific declarations*

    format: **\DeclarationName**

Debian, Linux distribution—xxvi

DEC10, an early interactive main frame computer—3

decimal point, in tabular tables—263-266, 485, 527

\DeclareFontShape{*encoding*}{*family*}{*series*}-{*shape*}, to list shapes available in the FD file —130, 139

\DeclareMathAlphabet{ \AKA}{*encoding*}-{*family*}{*series*}{*shape*}, to define a new math mode alphabet —316-317, 319

\DeclareMathSize{*display*}{*text*}{*script*}-{*scriptscript*} to set sizes, math mode—313-314

\DeclareMathSymbol{ \AKA}{ \math   op}-{*symbol font*}{*symbol code*}, to give a symbol a command name —175, 319-320

\DeclareSymbolFont{*AKA*}{*encoding*}{*family*}-

{*series*}{*shape*} to give a symbol font an AKA—319-320

\def, TEX command—482

\definecolor{*AKA*}{*primary color*}{*% white in color* }, to give a color shade a name—240-241, 249, 366-367, **413**, 415-416, 492, 498-499

defun, to define a function in LISP—46, 48, 51-53

demand, to force an immediate \(no)pagebreak or \(no)linebreak—65, 67-68, 226, 474

\depth, length below reference point— **148-149**, 358-359, 401

description list—48-50, 62-63, 76, 102-103, **214-219**, 352-353

Deutsch, L. Peter—xxiii

diagram and graph drawing programs—371-376, 379-380, 532

$\diamond$ (◇), math symbol—158, 181, 363-364

\diamondpar{*text*}, a shapepar design—250

dictionaries for decoding font information—155, **388**, 393, 418-419, 443, 466

\DiF, NI, to typeset dingbat symbols—172-173

dimensions—*see* measurements

\ding{*dingbat symbol code*}, pifont package, to print a dingbat symbol —173

dingautolist environment, *pifont* package, to number a list with dingbats —174

dingbats, novelty font —141, 143-144, 152, 163, **172-174**, 181, 188, 499

\dingfill{*dingbat symbol code*}, pifont package, to fill rest of line with the dingbat—173

\dingline{*dingbat symbol code*}, *pifont* package, to fill line with the dingbat—173

dinglist environment, *pifont* package, to use dingbats as bullets —174

displayed paragraph environments, ready-to-use paragraph formats —228-231

displaymath environment, math mode, for single unnumbered equations— 307, 309, 314, **326-327**, 329, 332-334

G

H

I

T

W